nifer Kyrnin

Sams **Teach Yourself**

HTML5

Mobile Application
Development

in 24 Hours

 800 East 96th Street, Indianapolis, Indiana, 46240 USA

Sams Teach Yourself HTML5 Mobile Application Development in 24 Hours

ISBN-13: 978-0-672-33440-5
ISBN-10: 0-672-33440-2

Library of Congress Cataloging-in-Publication Data:

Kyrnin, Jennifer.
  Sams teach yourself HTML5 mobile application development in 24 hours / Jennifer Kyrnin.
    p. cm.
  Includes bibliographical references and index.
  ISBN 978-0-672-33440-5 (pbk. : alk. paper)
  1. HTML (Document markup language) 2. Mobile computing—Programming. 3. Application software—Development. I. Title.
  QA76.76.H94K97 2012
  006.7'4—dc23

                            2011036380

Printed in the United States of America

First Printing: November 2011

Trademarks

All terms mentioned in this book that are known to be trademarks or service marks have been appropriately capitalized. Sams Publishing cannot attest to the accuracy of this information. Use of a term in this book should not be regarded as affecting the validity of any trademark or service mark.

Warning and Disclaimer

Every effort has been made to make this book as complete and as accurate as possible, but no warranty or fitness is implied. The information provided is on an "as is" basis. The author and the publisher shall have neither liability nor responsibility to any person or entity with respect to any loss or damages arising from the information contained in this book or programs accompanying it.

Bulk Sales

Sams Publishing offers excellent discounts on this book when ordered in quantity for bulk purchases or special sales. For more information, please contact

> **U.S. Corporate and Government Sales**
> **1-800-382-3419**
> corpsales@pearsontechgroup.com

For sales outside of the U.S., please contact

> **International Sales**
> international@pearson.com

Editor-in-Chief
Mark Taub

Acquisitions Editor
Trina MacDonald

Development Editor
Michael Thurston

Managing Editor
Kristy Hart

Project Editors
*Jovana San
Nicolas-Shirley and
Jess DeGabriele*

Copy Editor
Paula Lowell

Senior Indexer
Cheryl Lenser

Proofreader
Leslie Joseph

Technical Editors
*Evan Burchard
Pascal Rettig*

Publishing Coordinator
Olivia Basegio

Cover Designer
Gary Adair

Compositor
Nonie Ratcliff

Contents at a Glance

Table of Contents

Preface

The web is changing very quickly these days. New browser versions are being released every few months rather than every few years, and new devices are entering the marketplace all the time. For a web developer, staying up to date on the latest trends and technology is important, and the trending technology right now is HTML5.

In fact, some news outlets are claiming that HTML5 and mobile applications are two of the fastest-growing areas of job creation. According to Freelancer.com and iTWire, requests for freelancers knowing HTML5 rose by 34% in the first quarter of 2011, while general HTML jobs rose only by 7%. They also noted that Android jobs rose by 20%, and iPhone jobs rose by 9%.[1] HTML5 and mobile applications are where the jobs are, and this book can help you learn all about HTML5 and the application programming interfaces (APIs) that relate to it. After 24 hours, you will be able to build complex web applications and convert them into native mobile applications.

HTML5 Is More Than HTML

This book covers more than HTML tags and attributes. Although these things are the basis of the HTML5 specification, when people talk about HTML5 they often include many other programming interfaces that are not strictly part of the HTML5 specification, like geolocation or the History API. This book covers the basics of HTML5 and how it has changed from previous versions of HTML. It also introduces you to some of the technologies that are lumped in with HTML5, including:

- ▶ Drawing with the canvas element
- ▶ Adding streaming media with the video and audio elements
- ▶ Editing pages online and checking spelling
- ▶ Using drag-and-drop functions on web applications

---

[1] "Freelancer.com job listings show growth in HTML5, Adsense, and Android." iTWire. July 11, 2011. www.itwire.com/it-people-news/recruitment/48392-freelancercom-job-listings-show-growth-in-html5-adsense-and-android. July 25, 2011.

▶ Building more user-friendly forms

▶ Creating semantic divisions with new elements, such as `article`, `section`, and `nav`

This book covers several other specifications beyond HTML5, including:

▶ Web Open Font Format (WOFF) web fonts

▶ Microformats and Microdata

▶ WebSockets

▶ Web Workers

▶ Files API

▶ Web Storage

▶ Offline Web Applications API

▶ History API

▶ Geolocation

Web Pages Are for More Than Computers

HTML used to be used primarily in web browsers on computers, but now, with the advent of smartphones and tablet computers, more people are accessing web pages on mobile devices.

Every hour of this book provides examples of how the lesson's contents apply both to web browsers and mobile devices and shows you techniques for getting your applications to look better on mobile devices.

With this book, you will learn how to create applications that work on the most popular mobile smartphones and tablets out there: Android and iOS (iPhone, iPad, and iPod touch devices). Screenshots from both Android and iOS devices appear throughout as well as tips and warnings about how the different devices perform.

How to Use This Book

This book is divided into 24 lessons. Each lesson covers a specific topic related to HTML5 or an API that is part of the Open Web Standard. Each lesson takes about an hour to complete.

Organization of This Book

This book is divided into three sections:

▶ Part I, "Building Web Pages and Applications with the Open Web Standard," teaches you the basics of HTML, CSS, and JavaScript, and teaches you how to build a basic web application for mobile and non-mobile devices. After reading this section, you will know how to build a basic website with HTML, CSS, and JavaScript.

▶ Part II, "Learning the HTML5 Essentials," covers some of the more important new features of HTML5. You will learn more about new HTML5 elements to help you build better applications.

▶ Part III, "HTML5 for Mobile and Web Applications," describes some of the more useful APIs and tools for mobile application development and goes into detail about how to create mobile applications.

Conventions Used in This Book

Code samples are written in mono font within the text of the book, while blocks of code will be called out separately, for example:

```
This is a block
Of code
```

Some code examples that are too long to display as one line in the book use the ➡ symbol to indicate that these lines should be all on one line, like this:

```
<link rel="stylesheet" href="styles-320.css"
➡media="only screen and (max-width:320px)">
```

This book has three types of sidebars:

By the Way notes provide additional information about the topics that are discussed in the hour.

Did you Know? tips share interesting facts or tidbits about the related content.

Watch Out! warnings alert you of things that can cause problems for your applications.

You can also use the Try It Yourself sections to help you practice what you've learned in the hour.

Try It Yourself ▼

Nearly every hour will have at least one step-by-step tutorial called "Try It Yourself" to help you use what you've learned. ▲

Q&A, Quiz, and Exercises

Every hour ends with a short question-and-answer section to help with follow-up questions that occur as a result of reading the hour. You can also take a short quiz on the hour (Appendix A provides the answers) as well as do some suggested exercises to help you get more out of what you learned and apply this knowledge to your own applications.

Where to Go to Learn More

Appendix C includes more websites and books you can access to learn more about HTML5 and mobile web applications. This book also has a companion website at www. html5in24hours.com/ where you can go to see the examples, view and download the source code for each hour, view and report errata about the book, and continue to learn and ask questions about HTML5 mobile applications.

About the Author

Jennifer Kyrnin has been teaching HTML, XML, and web design online since 1997. She has built and maintained websites of all sizes from small, single-page brochure sites to large, million-page databased sites for international audiences. She lives with her husband, son, and numerous animals on a small farm in Washington state.

Dedication

To Mark and Jaryth, you helped me find time I didn't know I had. I love you.

Acknowledgments

I would like to thank all the people at Sams for the opportunity to write this book and work with you. I would particularly like to thank Trina MacDonald and Olivia Basegio for keeping me moving and the book on track as well as my two fabulous technical editors Pascal Rettig and Evan Burchard for all the great suggestions and corrections. Any technical errors you find in the book are mine alone; they probably tried to stop me.

I would also like to thank my family for putting up with me while I wrote the book, and the members of the Woodinville Writers Group, without whom I would have felt very alone as I hunkered down writing.

We Want to Hear from You!

As the reader of this book, *you* are our most important critic and commentator. We value your opinion and want to know what we're doing right, what we could do better, what areas you'd like to see us publish in, and any other words of wisdom you're willing to pass our way.

You can email or write me directly to let me know what you did or didn't like about this book—as well as what we can do to make our books stronger.

Please note that I cannot help you with technical problems related to the topic of this book, and that due to the high volume of mail I receive, I might not be able to reply to every message.

When you write, please be sure to include this book's title and author as well as your name and phone or email address. I will carefully review your comments and share them with the author and editors who worked on the book.

E-mail: webdev@samspublishing.com

Mail: Mark Taub
            Editor-in-Chief
            Pearson Education
            1330 6th Avenue
            New York, NY 10019 USA

Reader Services

Visit our website and register this book at informit.com/register for convenient access to any updates, downloads, or errata that might be available for this book.

HOUR 1

Improving Mobile Web Application Development with HTML5

What You'll Learn in This Hour:

▶ How HTML has grown and changed since it was invented

▶ Where HTML5 fits in with the other versions of HTML

▶ What the Open Web Standard is and how it relates to HTML5

▶ How a web application differs from typical web pages

▶ How to build a very simple HTML5 web page

▶ Why you want to use HTML5 for your mobile applications

HTML5 is the latest version of HTML, and although adoption on desktop browsers such as Internet Explorer is slow, mobile devices are jumping on the bandwagon in record numbers. Nearly every smartphone and tablet device sold today supports HTML5, and those numbers are growing.

In this hour you will learn how HTML5 came into being and how it has changed the landscape for web designers and developers as well as the customers viewing your pages. You'll learn to build a simple HTML5 document and why HTML5 is the language you should know if you want to design and develop mobile applications.

Understanding How We Got to HTML5

In March 1989, Sir Tim Berners-Lee wrote a proposal that suggested using hypertext to link related documents together over a network. After collaborating with others at CERN, hypertext eventually became HTML or Hypertext Markup Language.

HTML was based on a language already in use for marking up documents—SGML (Standard Generalized Markup Language). In September 1991, a discussion began across the internet about how the web and HTML should evolve.

Up until around 1993, the only browser available was a text-only browser called Lynx. Then Mosaic came out with features such as images, nested lists, and forms. Most designers these days take these things for granted, but back in the early 1990s many people browsed the web in a black-and-white (or green-and-black), text-only environment. Getting a browser to support images was very exciting.

It wasn't until 1994 that the HTML working group was set up by the IETF (Internet Engineering Task Force). In July it released a working draft of HTML 2. Later that year, the W3C, or World Wide Web Consortium, was formed at MIT to act as a standards body for HTML. HTML 3 was released as a draft in 1995, and HTML 3.2 was endorsed as a standard in 1997. HTML 4 was published as a recommendation in 1999.

XML and XHTML

After 1999 things began to change. The W3C no longer felt that HTML should remain as it was. Instead, they wanted to make it more machine-readable, more consistent, and much stricter. So, rather than working on a new version of HTML, they began turning HTML into a strict markup language called XHTML.

XHTML was created as a version of HTML 4.01 that was rewritten in XML (eXtensible Markup Language). It was developed in 1998 as a way to create markup languages that are machine readable. XHTML documents must be well formed and valid. In fact, the W3C wanted all browsers that read XHTML to stop rendering the page if the page's HTML was not valid or well-formed.

XML is still used by many companies. For example, many content management systems (CMSs) use XML on the back end to manage large websites; many books are written in DocBook, which is an XML language for publishing; and ePub books use XML to create ebooks.

> **Well-Formed Versus Valid**
>
> A document that is well-formed has the declaration statement at the top—including the specification, all attributes are surrounded by quotation marks, all elements are closed, and there is only one container element. A document that is valid is one that is checked against the specification and has no errors.

HTML5 is Born

XHTML, because it is based on XML, has the same strict requirements as XML, which makes XHTML very difficult to write. Although most web designers recognize the importance of creating HTML that is valid, at the end of the day the most important thing is that the HTML works in readers' browsers. Every beginning web designer who has ever validated a page knows that just because a page isn't valid doesn't mean browsers won't be able to display it. In fact, web browsers have no problem displaying technically invalid HTML.

Because of these difficulties, a group of web designers and developers as well as browser makers and others got together in 2004 and formed the Web Hypertext Application Technology Working Group (WHATWG). They started building the HTML5 specification to address the needs of designers, developers, and browser makers. Finally, in 2008, the W3C decided to scrap XHTML development in favor of reintegrating with the HTML5 community, and added the HTML5 specification into the W3C framework.

Learning What's Different with HTML5

HTML 4 is the last recommendation developed by the W3C alone. Most web pages right now are built in HTML 4 because it is widely supported by web browsers and editors.

XHTML was created by rewriting the HTML 4.01 specification as XML, which means that all tags must be closed, the XHTML tags must be written in all lowercase, all attributes must have quotation marks around them, and tags must be nested without overlapping.

Nesting Tags Correctly

When you nest two HTML tags, you should think of them as a stack of bowls—one inside the other. Always close the nested tag first, and then close the outer tag.

Incorrect:

```
This text is <em>italic, and this is <strong>bold and
italic</em></strong>
```

Correct:

```
This text is <em>italic, and this is <strong>bold and
italic</strong></em>
```

HTML5 goes back to a less restrictive version of HTML. End tags are no longer required for all elements, you can write in upper- or lowercase, and attributes don't need to have quotations around them all the time.

HTML5 also adds a lot of new elements, including a streamlined doctype (or DTD—the first line of your HTML document. It tells the browser that this document is an HTML5 one), sectioning elements, many new form features, and support for drag and drop and other features useful for creating web applications.

Did you
Know?

> **A New HTML5 Doctype**
>
> HTML5 has a new streamlined doctype that is very easy to remember—
> `<!doctype html>`. Nothing else is required. It doesn't even have to be written in
> all caps.

Defining Web Applications

Applications are software programs that are used on a local computer to do various tasks. The most commonly used applications are web browsers (such as Internet Explorer or Firefox), document editors (such as Word), and email clients (such as Outlook or Thunderbird). These programs are very similar to one another because they all run on the same operating system. They have features such as

▸ A similar look and feel, such as the menus at the top

▸ Functionality such as drag-and-drop, saving to the hard drive, and interactivity

Web applications are web pages that are attempting to look and act like desktop applications. They are written to run inside a web browser, rather than directly on the computer. This means that they are limited by the functions that the web browser can and cannot do:

▸ Web applications rely on the web browser for functionality that would otherwise have to be coded (such as the back button, rendering the page, and so on).

▸ Web applications are limited the same way a browser is limited. They can't save data to the hard drive, they have only limited scripting functions, and they can't interact directly with the computer operating system.

Web applications, unlike desktop applications, are not limited to one operating system. A web application runs in a browser, and so anywhere a browser will run, the web application will run.

Using the Open Web Standard

HTML5 was written primarily as a way to develop better, more efficient web applications, and it is part of the suite of APIs and specifications developed under the Open Web Standard. The Open Web Standard or Open Web Platform is a collection of royalty-free technologies that enable the web.

Many people think HTML5 includes more than it does. In fact, features such as the History API (discussed in Hour 22, "Controlling the Browser History with the History API"), local storage (Hour 21, "Web Storage in HTML5"), and geolocation (Hour 23, "Adding Location Detection with Geolocation") are all separate specifications that work with HTML5 to create a suite of tools you can use to build web pages, web applications, mobile applications, and more. These all are part of the Open Web Standard.

Some of the specifications in this standard include:

- ▶ HTML5

- ▶ CSS3

- ▶ Web Fonts

- ▶ HTML Canvas

- ▶ SVG

- ▶ Web storage

- ▶ Geolocation

By using standards-based specifications for your web applications, you will know that your pages and applications will work for a wider audience, and that your pages and applications will last longer.

Try It Yourself ▼

Building Your First HTML5 Document

HTML5 is, at its heart, HTML, which is what you use to build web pages. So before you can get started on the applications that you'll develop in later hours, you need to know how to build a web page.

You start by writing some HTML, which is very easy to write. All you need is a text editor.

Finding Your Computer's Text Editor

If you have access to a computer, you have access to a text editor for writing HTML. On Windows type in **Notepad** in the Search programs and files box in your Start menu. On Macintosh, type in **TextEdit** in the Spotlight. Use either the vi or Emacs command on a Linux computer.

Did you Know?

After you have a text editor up and running, you can begin writing your HTML, which is defined by tags that are written inside of less-than (<) and greater-than (>) signs.

1. Open your text editor and type the following:

```
<!doctype html>
<html>
    <head>
        <title>This is my first HTML5 page</title>
    </head>
    <body>
        <h1>My First HTML Document</h1>
        <p>This is my first HTML5 document.
    </body>
</html>
```

2. Save your file as **mypage.html**.

Watch Out!

> **Check That File Extension**
>
> Make sure to check the extension of your HTML file in your file system. Notepad will often convert it to a .txt file if you aren't careful. If it does, simply close Notepad and replace the .txt extension with .html.

3. Now open this page in your favorite web browser (by browsing to it in the File menu) to test that your page displays correctly. If it doesn't display correctly, you'll need to check that you opened the right file and that you wrote the HTML correctly.

As you can see from the missing closing tags, the HTML is not nearly as strict as XHTML, and the first line (the doctype or DTD) is simple to use and easy to remember.

Using HTML5 with iOS and Android Devices

Many designers are reluctant to get started using HTML5 on their web pages because Internet Explorer has relatively little support for it. In fact, only Internet Explorer 9 has decent HTML5 support. Other computer browsers, such as Firefox, Chrome, Opera, and Safari, all have good support for most HTML5 features.

> **Testing Is Critical**
>
> If you plan to create pages and applications for iOS and Android devices as well as desktop browsers, always test your documents in Internet Explorer 8. This browser (and IE 7) still has the lion's share of the browser market, and if your page or application doesn't work with it, your page or application won't work for most people browsing the web. If you don't have a Windows machine you can use an online tool such as Browsershots (http://browsershots.org/) to test in Internet Explorer and other browsers.

But what about mobile devices running on Android and iOS, such as a Xoom tablet or iPad? They all come with HTML5 support pretty much out of the box because they each run a browser (Safari on iOS and Chrome on Android) based on WebKit, which has excellent support for HTML5.

The best thing about designing web pages and applications using HTML5 for Android and iOS is that what you are creating will work on future devices. Right now operating systems exist that run on tablets and phones and to some extent televisions. But these operating systems are moving into other devices such as cars, picture frames, and even refrigerators.

Writing Mobile Websites

In some ways, writing websites for mobile devices is a lot easier than it used to be. Although a lot more devices are out there, including smartphones and not-so-smart phones, tablets, internet TV devices, and even some picture frames, the devices are converging in what HTML5 features they support, and even in their sizes and shapes (to some extent).

When you're creating a mobile website, the first thing to remember is that a mobile website is just a website. The best websites are built for every browser and operating system, or as many as possible.

However, you should still consider some basic questions when building a website that is intended for mobile devices:

- ▶ What is the screen size and resolution of the mobile device?
- ▶ What content do your mobile users need?
- ▶ Is your HTML, CSS, and JavaScript valid and compact?
- ▶ Should your site have a separate domain for mobile users?
- ▶ What testing does your mobile site need?

What is the Screen Size and Resolution of the Mobile Device

When you're working with mobile devices, obviously the screen size is going to be smaller than on a desktop. In general, with smartphones, you have to prepare for a few standard sizes:

▶ **128 x 160 pixels**—Phones such as the Fujitsu DoCoMo F504i

▶ **176 x 220 pixels**—Phones such as the HP iPAQ 510

▶ **240 x 320 pixels**—Smartphones such as Blackberry 8100 or the HTC Elf

▶ **320 x 480 pixels**—PDAs such as the Garmin-AsusA50 or the Palm Pre

Tablets add to the mix by having not only an increased screen size, but also having a variation in how they can be viewed. For example, most tablets (and some smartphones for that matter) can be viewed in portrait or landscape mode. This means that sometimes you might have a 1024-pixels-wide screen to work with, and other times 800 pixels wide or less.

However, in general, the tablets provide a lot more screen space for you to play with on mobile devices. You can assume you have around 1024–1280 pixels by 600–800 pixels for most tablet devices.

Browsing most websites in their standard format on an iPad is easy because the browser is as clear and easy to use as on a computer monitor. Plus, with the zooming capabilities on both iOs and Android, making small, harder-to-read areas bigger is easy.

What Content Do Your Mobile Users Need?

When you are designing a site for mobile devices, remember that users don't always want to access the same content as someone browsing on a desktop.

For example, mobile customers are often, well, mobile. In other words, they may be in motion or away from their home or office and have a very specific need or desire when they visit your site. For example, when visiting a restaurant website on a mobile phone, a user riding in a car might need to quickly find the location of the restaurant and the phone number. If the mobile site doesn't have the phone number and location front-and-center, the user might quickly give up on the site.

Don't Limit the Content
One thing mobile sites often get wrong is that they remove content from the mobile version of the site. Adjusting the content so that information that is most important to mobile users is easily available is essential. But if the content they need isn't on the mobile site, you must allow the user the opportunity to look for the content on the full site.

Content for mobile sites shouldn't be limited, however. In fact, the W3C recommends "...making, as far as is reasonable, the same information and services available to users irrespective of the device they are using."[1]

This doesn't mean that you can't change the format or location of your content, but getting to the same content on a mobile device as on a computer should be possible.

Is Your HTML, CSS, and JavaScript Valid and Compact?

You don't have to worry about writing well-formed XHTML for mobile devices, but sticking to correct, standards-based HTML, CSS, and JavaScript ensures that your pages are visible by the largest number of devices. Plus, by validating your HTML, you will know it is correct.

The W3C Validator

The W3C has a validator located at http://validator.w3.org/ that you can use to check HTML, XHTML, and other markup languages. But you can also validate CSS and RSS, and even find broken links on your pages from this site. Don't be afraid to check your site in the validator periodically. You may be surprised at what you find.

Beyond writing valid HTML, you should consider avoiding a few things if you are writing web pages for mobile devices:

▶ **HTML tables**—Avoiding tables as much as you can in mobile layouts is best because of the small size of the screen. Scrolling horizontally is difficult and makes the tables hard to read.

▶ **HTML tables for layout**—You shouldn't use HTML tables for layout of web pages in general, but on mobile devices they can make the pages load slower and look bad, especially if the table doesn't fit in the browser window. Plus, when you use tables for layout, you almost always use nested tables, which make the pages load slower and are much more difficult for mobile devices to render.

▶ **Pop-up windows**—Pop-up windows are often annoying in general, but on mobile devices they can make the site unusable. Some mobile browsers don't support them and others open them in unexpected ways (often by closing the current window to open a new one).

---

[1] Mobile Web Best Practices. www.w3.org/TR/mobile-bp/#OneWeb.

▶ **Graphics for layout**—Like using tables for layout, adding invisible graphics to add spaces and affect layout typically make many older mobile devices choke or display the page incorrectly. Plus, they add to the download time.

▶ **Frames and image maps**—Many mobile devices don't support these features in HTML. In fact, HTML5 no longer includes frames (other than the iframe) as a part of the specification because of the usability issues involved.

> **Fewer Limitations for iOS and Android**
> Although avoiding tables, popup windows, and image maps in mobile pages is best, if you are focusing on mobile pages for iOS or Android, you can rest easy. Both of these handle them without trouble. Frames, however, are not part of HTML5, and you should not rely on their being supported in iOS or Android.

Also remember that mobile users often have to pay a fee for their bandwidth, so your web pages should be as small (in KB) as you can make them. The fewer HTML tags and CSS properties you use and server requests you make, the better browsing will be for mobile users.

Should Your Site Have a Separate Domain for Mobile Users?

Many websites have a separate subdomain for their mobile site. This makes finding the mobile site without having to bother with the regular domain easy for mobile users. These domains are typically something like `m.example.com`.

Having a separate mobile domain offers several advantages:

▶ It makes your mobile site easier to find.

▶ You can advertise the mobile URL separately from the normal URL, giving you more reach.

▶ Having a separate mobile domain enables people on tablets or smartphones to switch to the full site just by switching domains.

▶ Detecting mobile users and sending them to a separate domain is much easier than scripting changes to your CSS for mobile users.

When trying to decide how to handle your mobile site version, consider how you are going to maintain the site. You can create the mobile domain manually with completely separate pages, or you can use a content management system. Hour 4, "Detecting Mobile Devices and HTML5 Support," covers this topic in more detail.

What Testing Does Your Mobile Site Need?

Be prepared to test your site on as many mobile devices as you possibly can. Although you can use your browser to test or emulate things such as screen size, you won't see some of the horrible things that can go wrong if you don't test on mobile devices directly, such as the following:

- ▶ Packet size limitations by mobile carriers preventing your page or images from loading

- ▶ Images loading incorrectly or not at all

- ▶ Inability to scroll horizontally (which is nearly impossible to do on some phones)

- ▶ Device-specific features not working that you were relying on

- ▶ File formats not being supported

You likely don't have an unlimited budget for buying mobile phones (and their associated cellphone plans), so what do you do? Here are some suggestions:

- ▶ **Use emulators**—Both online and offline emulators are available for many different mobile devices. Most are free to use and they give you at least a start at testing your site for mobile devices.

- ▶ **Rent time on devices**—Services exist that will allow you to rent time on multiple phones. You can justify the cost by getting a sense of how the phones handle your applications.

- ▶ **Buy some phones**—This might seem like an expensive option, but if you are planning on doing a lot of mobile web development, it could be a reasonable investment.

- ▶ **Get help from friends and co-workers**—This is one of the least expensive ways to test your site—simply ask to borrow phones or tablets from people you know. You just need to put your site on a live web server.

Ultimately, if you are going to do mobile development, you should have at least one mobile device you can test your pages on directly. The more devices you can test on, the better your sites will be.

Summary

In this hour, you have learned how HTML started and the reasons for the move from HTML to XHTML to HTML5. You know the basic differences between HTML 4,

XHTML 1, and HTML5 as well as what web applications are and how they relate to the Open Web Standard. You learned how to write a basic HTML web page and why HTML5 fits in so well with mobile devices. You also learned some powerful tips for building mobile web pages.

The most important things to remember from this hour are the best practices for building a website for mobile users:

▶ Focus first on building a website or application for every user, not just mobile ones.

▶ Determine who your mobile users are and what they are looking for, and present that content to them first, but not only that content.

▶ Build a site that uses standards-based technology so that your applications are more future proofed.

▶ Always test your sites and applications in as many web browsers and devices as you can.

Q&A

Q. *I am not familiar with HTML, and I'm worried that I will have trouble building an HTML5 application. Do I need to know HTML 4 before I learn HTML5?*

A. Although knowing HTML 4 will make moving forward easier for you, learning HTML5 is a fairly straightforward process. Although this book focuses mostly on HTML5, by copying the code samples provided and looking at the source files for the companion website (www.html5in24hours.com/), you should be able to figure it out.

Q. *I already have a website, and I want to make sure that mobile users can get the most out of it. How do I make sure that I am providing what mobile users need?*

A. The best way to do this is to ask them. Surveys asking your customers how they access your site and what parts are most useful to them are a good indicator of what they want. But you can also look at your web statistics. If you don't have analytics on your website, I recommend installing one such as Google Analytics or Piwik to track what people are looking at on your site. After you know what the popular pages are, you can ensure those pages are easy to access in your mobile version.

You can also use your web analytics to see what browsers (Firefox, IE, Chrome, etc.) are visiting your website and how your customers use the site (pages they click on, where they leave, and so on). With this method, even if you can't get direct customer feedback you can see what features they are currently using and adjust your site accordingly.

Q. *You mentioned using a content management system for maintaining a mobile site. Do you have any you can recommend?*

A. I use WordPress with the WordPress Mobile Pack to maintain a lot of sites for mobile and non-mobile users.

Workshop

The workshop contains quiz questions to help you process what you've learned in this chapter. Try to answer all the questions before you read the answers. See Appendix A, "Answers to Quizzes," for answers.

Quiz

1. Who decided to initiate HTML5 and why?

2. What is the first line in an HTML5 document?

3. Why is HTML5 so well suited to mobile application development?

Exercises

1. Create an HTML5 page. Your page should have a title, headline, and at least two or three paragraphs of text in it as well as the HTML5 doctype. Hour 3, "Styling Mobile Pages with CSS3," covers more about how to use CSS for styling the layout and look of your page.

2. Start planning your mobile website. List the content that you have that is particularly well suited to mobile users. List the content you need to create for mobile and non-mobile users. Ask yourself whether you have the resources to maintain a completely separate mobile site or whether you are going to use a content management system to maintain it.

HOUR 2

New HTML5 Tags and Attributes with Mobile Development

What You'll Learn in This Hour:

▶ How to use the many new tags and attributes in HTML5

▶ Other changes in HTML5

▶ Mobile support for HTML5

▶ Reasons to use HTML5 for mobile web applications

HTML5 has many new tags and attributes that you can use for building web pages and applications. In this hour you will learn about many of the new HTML5 features and how they work on mobile devices. The new smartphones and tablets are driving the adoption of HTML5, and this chapter tells you what you can do to be a part of the revolution.

The New HTML5 Tags

HTML5 adds a lot of new features to the HTML specification, but the easiest ones to understand are the brand-new tags. These are HTML elements that have never been a part of HTML in the past.

New Layout Tags

Most of these new tags are called "sectioning" elements and they provide semantics for the layout and sections of an HTML document. Hour 9, "Adding Meaning with HTML5 Sectioning and Semantic Elements," covers these tags in more detail.

These tags are:

▸ **\<article\>**—An independent portion of the document or site.

▸ **\<aside\>**—Content that is tangential to the main part of the page or site.

▸ **\<figcaption\>**—Caption for a figure.

▸ **\<figure\>**—A figure or quotation pulled out of the flow of text.

▸ **\<footer\>**—The footer of a document or section.

▸ **\<header\>**—The header of a document or section.

▸ **\<hgroup\>**—A group of headings.

▸ **\<nav\>**—A navigation section.

▸ **\<section\>**—A generic section that cannot be defined by one of the above types.

You use these tags to define specific areas of your HTML documents. They provide you with ways to attach CSS styles (often called hooks for CSS) and give some semantic meaning to the parts of your pages.

By the Way

> **Providing Meaning with Semantic Tags**
>
> Semantic tags tell the browser or user agent (a technical term for a tool that can parse web pages) something about the contents of the tag. In other words, rather than just defining where a block of text should appear in the page flow, a semantic tag such as \<article\> tells the browser that the contents are part of a stand-alone article.

Using these new layout tags is easy. In fact, many web pages already use \<div\> tags for the same purpose as these tags. For example, in many web designs you might see a \<div id="header"\> section of the page. Now, with HTML5, you can just write \<header\>.

▼ **Try It Yourself**

Converting to New Layout Tags

You probably have a lot of web pages that have a markup similar to this:

```
<!DOCTYPE HTML PUBLIC "-//W3C//DTD HTML 4.01 Transitional//EN"
    "http://www.w3.org/TR/html4/loose.dtd">
<html lang="en">
<head>
```

```
    <title>My HTML 4 2-Column Page</title>
    <link type="text/css" href="styles.css">
</head>
<body>
    <div id="main">
        <div id="header">
            <h1>My HTML 4 2-Column Page</h1>
        </div>
        <div id="nav">
            <ul>
                <li><a href="#">Home</a></li>
                <li><a href="#">Products</a></li>
            </ul>
        </div>
        <div id="contents">
            <p>Lorem ipsum dolor sit amet, consectetuer adipiscing elit,
nibh euismod tincidunt ut laoreet dolore magna aliquam erat volutpat. Ut
minim veniam, quis nostrud exerci tation ullamcorper suscipit lobortis nisl
ea commodo consequat. Duis autem vel eum iriure dolor in hendrerit in
esse molestie consequat, vel illum dolore eu feugiat nulla facilisis at
accumsan et iusto odio dignissim qui blandit praesent luptatum zzril
dolore te feugait nulla facilisi.</p>
        </div>
    </div>
    <div id="footer">
        <p>&copy; 2011 J Kyrnin</p>
    </div>
</body>
</html>
```

As you can see, there is a header, called <div id="header">, a footer
<div id="footer">, a navigation area <div id="nav">, and an area for the
main contents of the page <div id="contents">.

You can easily convert these <div> tags into HTML5 sectioning content tags:

```
<!doctype html>
<html lang="en">
<head>
    <title>My HTML 4 2-Column Page</title>
    <link type="text/css" href="styles.css">
</head>
<body>
    <section id="main">
        <header>
            <h1>My HTML 4 2-Column Page</h1>
        </header>
        <nav>
            <ul>
                <li><a href="#">Home</a></li>
                <li><a href="#">Products</a></li>
            </ul>
```

```
      </nav>
      <section id="contents">
          <p>Lorem ipsum dolor sit amet, consectetuer adipiscing elit,
nibh euismod tincidunt ut laoreet dolore magna aliquam erat volutpat. Ut
minim veniam, quis nostrud exerci tation ullamcorper suscipit lobortis nisl
ea commodo consequat. Duis autem vel eum iriure dolor in hendrerit in
esse molestie consequat, vel illum dolore eu feugiat nulla facilisis at
accumsan et iusto odio dignissim qui blandit praesent luptatum zzril
dolore te feugait nulla facilisi.</p>
      </section>
   </section>
   <footer>
      <p>&copy; 2011 J Kyrnin</p>
   </footer>
</body>
</html>
```

▲

By the Way

Using the `id` Attribute

One thing you should note is that the new HTML5 elements, `<header>`, `<footer>`, `<nav>` and so on, represent more than just the page's header, footer, and navigation. A page can have several of these elements, so adding an `id` attribute (for example, `<nav id="mainNav">`) is often helpful to help style the document. Hour 9 describes these elements in more detail.

Additional Semantic Elements

You can use a number of semantic elements in HTML5 to define specific items in your documents. Semantic elements let the browser or user agent know that the contents of the tag have a specific meaning beyond the meaning of the text itself. Hour 9 covers these tags in more detail. Here are the new semantic tags in HTML5:

▶ **`<details>`**—Control for adding more information.

▶ **`<figcaption>`**—Caption for a figure.

▶ **`<figure>`**—A figure or quotation pulled out of the flow of text.

▶ **`<mark>`**—Content that has been highlighted or marked.

▶ **`<meter>`**—A scalar gauge.

▶ **`<output>`**—Results from a script or form.

▶ **`<progress>`**—Progress indicator.

▶ **`<summary>`**—Summary or legend for a `details` element.

▶ `<time>`—Date or time.

▶ `<wbr>`—Optional line break.

One of the easiest new semantic elements to understand is the `<time>` element. This tag says that anything inside it is a time or a date. Calling out times and dates enables user agents to do things such as add calendar links automatically. Although no browser currently supports the `<time>` tag, Figure 2.1 shows how this tag might be used.

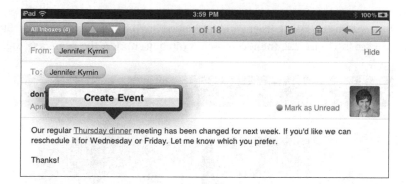

FIGURE 2.1
An example of an iPad evaluating a date element in an email message.

Semantic Tags May Not Do Anything

One of the most common complaints about semantic tags is that they don't do anything. These tags are intended to provide additional information about the contents, and user agents may choose to simply leave them alone. This does not mean that the tags are useless. They provide hooks for CSS to style your pages more efficiently and they allow for the possibility that user agents will do something with them in the future. Plus, while your browser may not do anything with the tag, another browser might be using it extensively.

Watch Out!

Don't add content just to use semantic tags. Instead, when you see a section of your document that has a semantic meaning, enclose it in that semantic tag.

New Multimedia Tags

Some of the most talked about new tags in HTML5 are the multimedia tags. The following tags let you add multimedia elements right into your HTML:

▶ `<audio>`—Embedded sound files.

▶ `<canvas>`—Embedded dynamic graphics.

▶ **<embed>**—To add other technologies that don't have a specific HTML5 element.

▶ **<source>**—The source files for embedded sound and video.

▶ **<track>**—Supplementary media tracks for embedded sound and video.

▶ **<video>**—Embedded video files.

The <canvas> tag lets you draw vector images right inside your HTML page (as well as other things). This gives you the ability to add custom fonts to your pages, create simple and very complex games, animate vector graphics, and control all these things from within the HTML itself. You don't need any plug-ins or extra XML files. As you can see in Figure 2.2, the iOS browsers already support the <canvas> tag.

FIGURE 2.2
A simple page with a <canvas> tag creating a big blue square on an Android tablet.

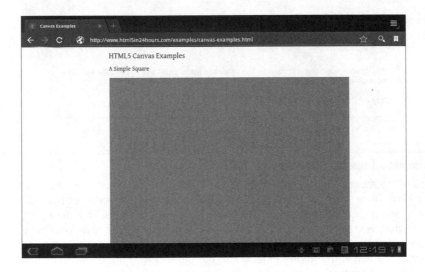

The HTML for Figure 2.2 is just one line:

```
<canvas id="simple-square" width="800" height="800"></canvas>
```

Adding some additional JavaScript in the <head> creates the square:

```
<script type="text/javascript">
    function drawSquare () {
        var canvas = document.getElementById('simple-square');
        if (canvas.getContext) {
            var context = canvas.getContext('2d');

            context.fillStyle = "rgb(13, 118, 208)";
            context.fillRect (2,2,798,798);
        } else {
```

```
        // put code for browsers that don't support canvas here
        alert("This page requires an HTML5 compliant browser to render
correctly. Other browsers may not see anything.")
    }
  }
</script>
```

Don't Forget to Load Your Script

If you use the preceding script to add a <canvas> square to your web page, don't forget to change your <body> tag to load the script to <body onload="drawSquare">. Otherwise, your <canvas> will remain blank.

Hour 10, "Drawing with the HTML5 Canvas Element," covers the <canvas> tag in more detail.

HTML5 has some other interesting additions to the language. For example, now the <embed> tag is a valid part of the specification. Up until HTML5, the <embed> tag was supported by most browsers but was not valid HTML, so you couldn't use it if you needed your pages to validate.

HTML5 also introduces the <audio> and <video> tags to embed audio and video files directly in your HTML just like you would an image with the <img> tag. You can use the <track> and <source> tags to support these new multimedia tags.

Embed Any Type of Video or Audio

The great thing about HTML5 multimedia is how flexible it is. You can use the <video> and <audio> tags to embed any type of video or audio file that you can save on a computer. Not all types will play natively in the browsers, but this flexibility means that when formats improve, your web pages won't need to change to a new tag.

Hour 12, "Audio and Video in HTML5," goes into more detail about HTML5 video and audio support.

New Form Features

HTML5 forms have a lot more functionality than HTML 4 forms did. You can now collect form field data of many different types beyond the standard text fields, drop-down menus, and other types common to HTML 4 forms.

With HTML5 you can set up form <command> tags to define a single action for multiple form elements. You can provide pre-defined data in a <datalist> tag. With the

`<keygen>` tag you can generate public-private key pairs to keep your forms secure. And best of all, the `<input>` tag now has 13 new types for collecting specific data:

▶ `<input type=color>`

▶ `<input type=date>`

▶ `<input type=datetime>`

▶ `<input type=datetime-local>`

▶ `<input type=email>`

▶ `<input type=month>`

▶ `<input type=number>`

▶ `<input type=range>`

▶ `<input type=search>`

▶ `<input type=time>`

▶ `<input type=tel>`

▶ `<input type=url>`

▶ `<input type=week>`

The new input types will work in every browser out there. Even if they don't do anything special with the tags, all browsers will display a form text field for collecting data. As you can see in Figure 2.3, browser support is still growing, but using types such as `<input type="tel">` will provide additional functionality for those browsers and user agents that can support it.

You will learn a lot more about HTML5 forms in Hour 13, "HTML5 Forms."

Improved International Support

Five new tags in HTML5 help improve the support for non-English language documents. These tags are

▶ `<bdi>`

▶ `<meta charset>`

▶ `<rp>`

▶ `<rt>`

▶ `<ruby>`

FIGURE 2.3
On the left is a form in Safari and on the right the same form (zoomed in) on an iPod touch.

The <bdi> tag lets you change the direction of text that is written in HTML. So if you have a document written in English (a left-to-right directional language) and you want to add some Hebrew (a right-to-left directional language), you can surround the Hebrew with the <bdi> tag to indicate that the direction has changed for that span of text.

The <meta charset> tag lets you define the character encoding that your web page is using. For example, to define your HTML as using the utf-8 character set, you would write:

```
<meta charset="utf-8">
```

Finally, if you write HTML with double-byte languages such as Chinese and Japanese, you may already be familiar with ruby characters. These are small glosses placed next to the characters, usually to indicate pronunciation. The <ruby> tag indicates the span of ruby characters and can include <rt> for ruby text and <rp> for parentheses around the ruby text. Here is an example using pseudo-code:

```
<ruby><rp><rt>ruby text</rt></rp></ruby>
```

The New HTML5 Attributes

Many of the new attributes in HTML5 extend the tags they are associated with. A bunch of new event attributes enable you to associate scripts to many more actions as they happen on your web page. Plus, you can use new global attributes that apply to all HTML5 elements.

An attribute is written in HTML after the tag name, separated by a space, inside the greater-than and less-than signs. If the attribute can have a value, that value is attached to the attribute by an equal sign. If spaces exist in the value, then you should surround the whole value with quotation marks. For example:

```
<elementname attributename=value>
```

Or:

```
<element name="value value">
```

Boolean attributes are also available in HTML5 that don't require a value. Instead, if they are present, the attribute is applied, and if they are absent the attribute is not applied. Following is an example:

```
<elementname attribute>
```

The most well-known Boolean attribute in HTML 4 is the `checked` attribute on checkboxes:

```
<input type=checkbox checked>
```

Event attributes indicate an event that might happen when the page is loaded. The new HTML5 event attributes include:

- **onabort**—Fires when an action is aborted.
- **onbeforeonload**, **onbeforeonunload**, and **onunload**—Fires just before an element loads or unloads and as an element unloads.
- **oncontextmenu**—Fires when the context menu is triggered.
- **ondrag**, **ondragend**, **ondragenter**, **ondragleave**, **ondragstart**, and **ondrop**—These fire when various drag-and-drop actions occur.
- **onerrror** and **onmessage**—These fire when errors or messages are triggered.
- **onscroll**—This fires when the user scrolls the browser scroll bar.
- **onresize**—Fires when an element is resized.

You can use these event attributes on nearly every element in HTML5, which gives you much flexibility in how your web applications react to events.

HTML5 also adds a bunch of new global attributes that you can apply to nearly every HTML element. The new global attributes are:

- `contenteditable`
- `contextmenu`
- `draggable`
- `dropzone`
- `hidden`
- `spellcheck`

`Contenteditable` and `spellcheck` allow you to set some elements to be editable inside the browser, and while they are edited, the browser can check the spelling. Hour 14, "Editing Content and User Interaction with HTML5," describes these elements in more detail.

`Draggable` and `dropzone` provide elements that can be dragged and places to drag them to. Hour 16, "Working with HTML5 Drag-and-Drop Functionality," covers more about using drag-and-drop within your applications.

The `contextmenu` attribute allows you to define a menu that appears only when you right-click or mouse over an element. Hour 17, "HTML5 Links," provides you more information about this attribute.

The `hidden` attribute has the same action as writing `display: hidden;` in CSS, but it also allows you to semantically describe an element that is currently not relevant to the page, such as a form element that only is required if they fill out other fields in a specific way. This feature is most useful for accessibility, because screen readers would not read out the contents of an element that is hidden, but they might if only the CSS was hiding it.

Changes to HTML 4 Tags and Attributes

A number of changes have been made to existing tags and attributes in HTML 4 to give them a wider functionality or to change their function, more clearly define their meaning and scope, or to provide a semantic definition.

For example, a number of tags that didn't have a semantic aspect to them in HTML 4 have been given semantic meanings in HTML5, including:

▶ **\<b\>**—Text that would normally be displayed as bold.

▶ **\<i\>**—Text that would normally be displayed as italics.

▶ **\<hr\>**—A paragraph-level thematic break in the text.

▶ **\<s\>**—Content that is no longer accurate or relevant.

▶ **\<small\>**—Small print such as in legal documents.

A few tags have had their meaning changed or had a new use added:

▶ You can now write the \<a\> tag with no attributes. In this situation it is considered a placeholder for a link.

▶ The \<address\> tag is now part of sectioning content (see Hour 9).

▶ The \<cite\> tag now represents the title of a work, but you cannot use it to mark up the name of a person.

▶ With the \<menu\> tag you can create toolbars and context menus.

A few elements have also had features or descriptions changed or removed:

▶ The \<dl\> tag is now a list of name=value pairs, and should not be used for displaying dialog like a script.

▶ When displaying the \<label\> element, user agents should not move the focus from the label to the control unless that is standard behavior for the platform.

▶ The \<strong\> element now indicates importance rather than strong emphasis.

▶ You can no longer include \<object\> elements inside the \<head\> element.

Most HTML 4 attributes have remained the same, but you no longer have to have the type attribute on \<script\> and \<style\> tags, unless you are using non-standard scripts (that is, not JavaScript) or style sheets (that is, not CSS).

A few attributes exist that, while allowed, HTML5 strongly recommends you find alternate solutions for, as described in the following situations:

▶ If you include the border attribute on an \<img\> tag to turn off the border, you must give it a value of "0." Using CSS, such as img {border: none;} instead is better.

▶ If you use the language attribute on a <script> tag, it must say "javascript" (case insensitive) and cannot conflict with the type attribute. Simply leaving out this attribute is better because it has no useful purpose.

▶ If you use the name attribute on an <a> tag, you should change that to use the id attribute instead because the name attribute is obsolete.

▶ If you write complex tables and want to provide a summary using the summary attribute, you still can. However, putting that summary in the surrounding text, inside a table <caption>, inside a <details> element of the caption, or inside a <figure> or <figcaption> that the table is also a part of is better because it is more accessible.

▶ If you use images with the width attribute, you can no longer use percentages for the width.

Also, you should no longer use a few elements and attributes; they are considered obsolete in HTML5. This hour won't go over all of them in detail, but if the element or attribute you are considering using is not in the HTML5 elements and attributes list in Appendix B, you should consider using another option.

The most noticeable omissions are

▶ **<frame>**, **<frameset>**, and **<noframes>**—Frames are no longer in HTML5, so you cannot use these.

▶ **<basefont>**, **<big>**, **<center>**, **<font>**, **<strike>**, **<tt>**, and **<u>**—These tags have been removed because they are purely presentational and their function is better handled by CSS.

▶ **<acronym>**—This tag was removed because it was confusing. Use <abbr> for abbreviations instead.

▶ **<applet>**—This tag has been made obsolete in favor of <object>. Similarly, the <dir> tag has been dropped in favor of <ul>. These were dropped because the replacement element is more accessible or easier to use.

Changes to HTML Syntax in HTML5

HTML5 does not offer a large number of syntax changes from HTML 4. You still surround tags with greater-than and less-than characters, you still start your documents with a doctype, and you still enclose your document contents inside the tags.

The biggest change that most people will notice is the doctype. As mentioned in Hour 1, "Improving Mobile Web Application Development with HTML5," it has been radically simplified. All you need to write is

```
<!doctype html>
```

Plus it can be in all lowercase, uppercase, or even mixed case if you like.

If you use an HTML generator that can't use the short doctype, you can add a doctype legacy string to the doctype, as follows:

```
<!DOCTYPE html SYSTEM 'about:legacy-compat'>
```

Like HTML 4 (not XHTML), you can write your tags in any case you want. The <html> tag is the same as <HTML> and <hTmL>. Most designers use lowercase because it's easier to read. You also don't have to quote attributes unless a space exists in the value. However, if you think you're ever going to convert your HTML to XHTML, consider using lowercase tag names and attributes and continue to quote all your attributes.

Mobile Support of HTML5 Tags and Attributes

Older mobile devices, such as non-smart phones and older PDAs, don't have support for HTML5 and probably never will. But the reality is that mobile devices are moving beyond those devices at a break-neck speed.

The majority of smart phones and tablets being put out today have good (if not perfect) HTML5 support. Both Android and iOS devices (as well as phones and tablets by Nokia, Palm, and Rim) use browsers based on the WebKit browser, which has good HTML5 support that gets better every day.

Interestingly, Windows mobile devices are the one holdout in this category. As recently as August 2010, Microsoft was saying it was not going to support HTML5 in its Windows 7 mobile devices. But that changed in March 2011, when Microsoft stated that an HTML5 browser was on track for release to its mobile platform.

Unfortunately, being able to design a web page or application, test it in one browser, and expect it to work in all devices is not possible. But mobile devices, especially Android and iOS, will drive HTML5 development. These devices already have extensive support for HTML5 and more is added all the time.

Benefits of HTML5 for Mobile Web Development

Remember that HTML5 is not available for every mobile device in every mobile web browser. As mentioned earlier, many older devices, non-smart phones, and tablets don't have good HTML5 support. But for those that do support it, a lot of great reasons exist for moving to HTML5 for your mobile development.

HTML5 Includes APIs That Work Well

HTML5 introduces Application Programming Interfaces, or APIs, for video, audio, web applications, editing content on the page, drag-and-drop, and exposing the browser history. These all work well with mobile because they mean that the mobile browser won't need a plug-in or add-on to get these features to work. If the browser is HTML5 compliant then it will support these APIs. This book will cover how to use several APIs in other Hours.

Plus, HTML5 and the Open Web Standard have APIs for geolocation, web storage, and offline web applications that are well suited for mobile devices. Most smart phones and tablets have a GPS or other way of determining location that can use geolocation features. Web storage helps turn a standard web page into an application with saved data that can be kept with you at all times on your mobile device. Offline applications are important when the phone isn't connected to the internet. In fact, a mobile device is more likely to need offline capabilities than most desktop computers.

HTML5

Getting into mobile development can seem daunting. For the average web developer, Objective C is virtually unintelligible. But developers already know HTML 4, CSS, and JavaScript, and with those three languages you can build robust applications using HTML5 and the Open Web Standards.

This means that if you've built any web pages before, you can be up and running with mobile applications in a short period of time (24 hours or less, in fact) because you already know the basics of the languages involved.

Customers Prefer Web Applications

In a study done in late 2010, in nearly every category examined (except for games, music, and social media) people preferred using their mobile browser rather than a separate app.[1]

Although it's true that applications are getting more and more popular, web applications offer the best of both worlds. You can create an HTML5 web application that runs in the mobile browser, so users can bookmark it and use their familiar tool, but it also contains the features and functionality of a typical application.

Also, when you build an HTML5 web application for a mobile device, that application will work on HTML5 browsers on non-mobile devices as well. Depending upon how you code your application, you might not need to create anything more than a different stylesheet for standard web browsers and mobile devices. Maintaining this is much easier than having to create a separate application for every platform that comes out.

Summary

In this hour, you learned the new HTML5 tags and attributes and the HTML 4 tags and attributes that have changed in HTML5. You also learned the changes in syntax that HTML5 added. The new tags are the bulk of the change to the HTML5 language, and you learned the basics for adding them into your documents.

This chapter also covered some of the reasons why HTML5 is well suited for mobile devices, including the APIs that have been added to the standard, how this affects development of HTML applications, and the usage patterns of customers on mobile devices (and off).

Q&A

Q. *Where can I go to learn more about the new HTML5 tags and attributes?*

A. Many of these new tags and attributes will be discussed in later hours of this book. But you can always get the most up-to-date information by going to the W3C site at www.w3.org/.

---

[1] "Mobile Users Prefer Browsers Over Apps." eMarketer. October 27, 2010. www.emarketer.com/Article.aspx?R=1008010. Referenced April 24, 2011.

Q. *I want to get started using HTML5 tags right now, how can I tell whether I'm writing them correctly if the browsers don't support them?*

A. Web browser support has long been a struggle for most web developers, and HTML5 has not changed that situation. But an experimental HTML5 conformance checker is available at the W3C (http://validator.w3.org/), and you can find another highly experimental validator at http://html5.validator.nu/. Using a validator isn't the same as testing, but it will tell you whether you're using the tags correctly.

Q. *What if a lot of my customers use Internet Explorer 8 or older? Will these new HTML5 tags work in their browsers?*

A. Internet Explorer 8 is the only modern browser that does not support HTML5 tags. If you need to support this browser, then consider using a workaround such as the HTML Shiv. To use it, you add this code snippet to the <head> of your documents:

```
<!—[if lt IE 9]>
<script src="http://html5shiv.googlecode.com/svn/trunk/html5.js"></script>
<![endif]—>
```

Workshop

The workshop contains quiz questions to help you process what you've learned in this chapter. Try to answer all the questions before you read the answers. See Appendix A, "Answers to Quizzes," for answers.

Quiz

1. What are some of the new layout tags in HTML5?

2. What makes the <section> tag semantic, or is it not semantic at all?

3. What are some new attributes that allow for drag-and-drop operations?

Exercises

1. Create an HTML page with the sectioning elements discussed in this chapter. Include at least one <section>, <header>, <nav>, and <article>.

2. Open your HTML5 page on a mobile device. The easiest way to do this is to put your page up on a web server and then browse to it on your phone or tablet. If you have access to both an Android and an iOS device, try viewing it in both to get in the habit of testing.

Styling Mobile Pages with CSS3

What You'll Learn in This Hour:

▶ How to create a CSS style sheet

▶ Great features for applications with CSS3

▶ Media queries to change styles based on device attributes

▶ How to use special meta tags for better-looking mobile pages

Cascading Style Sheets (CSS) are an important part of mobile web development. In this hour you will learn about how to write CSS and use it to style your mobile pages, including media queries to build style sheets for specific devices. You'll also learn about a few meta tags that will affect how your mobile devices display content.

Quick Introduction to CSS

You use Cascading Style Sheets (CSS) to define how your HTML documents will look. You can style HTML for print, for web pages, and even for specific mobile devices. The same HTML content can also be displayed completely differently in each of those places.

CSS has been around for more than 10 years and is widely supported by most browsers and mobile devices. Therefore, understanding how to use CSS to define how your web applications will look is very important.

Creating a CSS Style Sheet

CSS is made up of one or more selectors with style properties attached. For example, to change the text color of a paragraph you would write:

```
p {
    color: red;
}
```

The selector is p and the style property (enclosed in the curly braces) is `color: red;`.

To add a second selector, simply separate it with a comma:

```
p, .redText {
    color: red;
}
```

After you have a style, you attach it to a web page in one of three ways:

▶ Inline in the tags themselves

▶ Embedded in the head of your HTML

▶ In a separate document as an external style sheet

The easiest way is inline. Styles that are placed inline inside a tag don't need a selector because the selector is defined by the tag it's in. You add a `style` attribute to the tag, and put the styles in the attribute value (separate multiple styles by a semicolon (;). For example, to color the text of a single paragraph in your HTML red you would write:

```
<p style="color: red;">
```

The problem with inline styles is that they only style the tag they are in. So if you needed every paragraph to have red text, you would have to add that `style` attribute to every paragraph in your document. I recommend using inline styles only for testing. For more efficient and faster loading pages, use embedded or external style sheets instead.

Embedded style sheets sit in the <head> tag of your document. You use the <style> tag and write your styles as mentioned previously with a selector and styles enclosed in curly braces. For example, here is a simple page with paragraphs in red text:

```
<!DOCTYPE html>
<html>
<head>
    <title>Example of Embedded Styles</title>
    <style>
        p {
```

```
            color: red;
        }
    </style>
</head>

<body>
<p>The text in this paragraph would be red.</p>
<p>And this paragraph as well.</p>
</body>
</html>
```

The problem with embedded styles is that, similar to inline styles, they only put the styles on the page they are on. If you need these same styles in another web page, you have to copy them and paste them into the head of every page you need them on. Using embedded styles only for testing and for small style changes that are applied to only the one page is best.

The best way to add your styles to a document is with an external style sheet. To create an external style sheet:

1. Open a new document.

2. Write your styles as in the earlier embedded style sheet example, but without the <style> tag surrounding them.

3. Save that file as a style sheet with a .css extension, such as styles.css.

Here is a style sheet with some additional styles along with the red paragraphs:

```
html, body {
    margin:0;
    padding:0;
    border:0;
}
body {
    font: 1cm/1.25 Arial, Helvetica, sans-serif;
}
p {
    color: red;
}
```

Writing the style sheet document is not enough; you have to also attach it to your web page. To do this, add a <link> tag to the head of your document that points to the style sheet. For example:

```
<link href="styles.css" rel="stylesheet">
```

By the Way

> **External Style Sheets Speed Up Websites**
>
> External style sheets, especially if you put all your styles in only one, can speed up the download of your website. After a style sheet has been downloaded, it will stay in the browser cache and not be re-downloaded for other pages on the same site, and the faster your site loads, the better.

As long as your HTML file is in the same folder as your style sheet file, it will load all your styles when your page is loaded.

Changing the Fonts with CSS

One of the first things that most web designers want to adjust is the fonts used on a web page, specifically the fonts used for headlines. As you can see from Figure 3.1, <h1> headlines, while an important part of most web pages, unstyled tend to be big, bold, and ugly.

FIGURE 3.1
A sample web page with an <h1> headline displayed on an Android tablet.

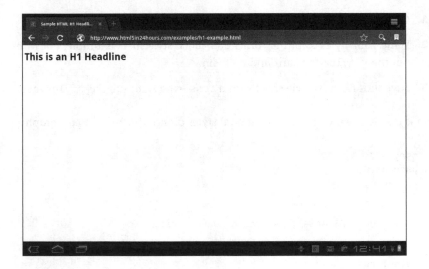

You can use several style properties to style the font and text of headlines and other text on your pages, including:

- ▶ **font-family**—The face of the font
- ▶ **font-size**—The size of the font
- ▶ **font-weight**—Make the font bold or not
- ▶ **font-style**—Make the font italic or not

▶ **font-variant**—Set small caps

▶ **font**—A shortcut style to set any or all of the preceding styles in one line

While all the preceding properties are good to know, the one that you should focus on is the `font` property. This, as mentioned, lets you style the majority of font styles all from one property.

The syntax for using the font property is:

```
font: font-style font-variant font-weight font-size/line-height font-family;
```

Most of the font styles are straightforward. If you want your text to be italic, you set the `font-style` to italic, and if you want the text to be bold or 12 pixels high, you add those with the `font-weight` (bold) or `font-size` style properties. However, many beginners have trouble with the `font-family` style property.

When you choose a font for your HTML documents, you have to rely on the font libraries on your customers' machines. In other words, if you want to use a fancy font like a free font from FontSquirrel.com, you have to hope that your customers have downloaded that font as well. Otherwise, the browser will choose the font, which could cause questionable results.

To ensure that your web page looks the way you want it to, you can use a list of font faces that you want to display, in the order you want them used. This is called a font stack. You can list as many or as few fonts in your stack as you want, but you should always finish the list with a generic font family, as follows:

▶ cursive

▶ fantasy

▶ monospace

▶ sans serif

▶ serif

Always Include Common Fonts

Some common fonts can be found on most computers. Even if you don't use these fonts as the first choice in your font stack, using at least one or two is a good idea. Some common fonts include Arial, Helvetica, Comic Sans, Courier, Georgia, and Times New Roman.

Did you Know?

Web typography involves more than just fonts, and Hour 11, "Fonts and Typography in HTML5," goes into more detail on the new HTML5 web typography features.

Using CSS for Layout

CSS is an invaluable tool for the layout of web pages, and your layout choices are mostly limited by your imagination. The two basic ways to use CSS for layout are floating and absolute positioning. *Floating* relies on the CSS property `float` to place elements with defined widths next to one another, whereas *absolute positioning* takes elements and places them in precise positions on the page.

To lay out your web pages, you must understand how web pages are built. Every element in your document has a square shape, even if you can't see it. In fact, the easiest way to see that is to put a border around your elements with the `border` style property, like this:

```
border: 1px solid black;
```

A major part of CSS layout surrounds the boxes that are created by the elements. In fact, it's so important that it's called the CSS box model. Every box on a web page has a content area, padding, a border, and a margin. In Figure 3.2, you can see how those parts fit together. With CSS you can affect the width or thickness of all of them.

FIGURE 3.2
The CSS box model.

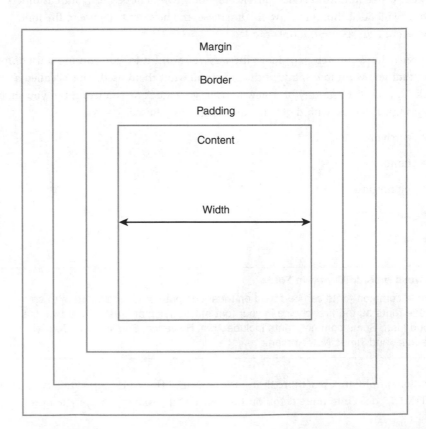

To change the box model with CSS, you can use these style properties:

- ▶ margin
- ▶ padding
- ▶ border
- ▶ height
- ▶ width

After you have defined the box model on your web page elements, you can use CSS floats to position your elements where you want them on the page.

Try It Yourself

Laying Out an HTML5 Web Page

When you build an HTML5 web page you should put your content inside the sectioning tags discussed in Hour 2, "New HTML5 Tags and Attributes with Mobile Development": navigation in a <nav> tag, article content in an <article> tag, and so on.

1. Build your HTML5 document:

```
<!DOCTYPE html>
<html>
<head>
    <title>Page Title</title>
</head>
<body>
<header>
    <h1>Page Title</h1>
</header>
<nav>
    <ul id="">
        <li><a href="#">Home</a></li>
        <li><a href="#">About Us</a></li>
        <li><a href="#">Products</a></li>
        <li><a href="#">Services</a></li>
    </ul>
</nav>
<article>
    <p>This is the text of the article.</p>
</article>
<footer>&copy; 2011</footer>
</body>
</html>
```

2. Set the width on the body element with CSS in the <head> of your document:

```
<style>
    body { width: 100%; }
</style>
```

3. Clearing the borders, margins, and paddings on the body tag is also a good idea.

```
body {
    width: 100%;
    margin:0;
    padding:0;
    border:0;
}
```

> **Get in the Habit of Resetting Styles**
>
> Most browsers set defaults on things such as margins, padding, and so on, and those defaults aren't all the same. If you want your web pages to look similar on different browsers, you need to start with a clean slate. The best way is to use a "reset" style sheet. You can find an excellent CSS reset style sheet at Eric Meyer's site: http://meyerweb.com/eric/tools/css/reset/.

4. Set the width of the header and footer to 100% as well:

```
header { width: 100% }
footer { width: 100% }
```

5. Set the width of the navigation element (<nav>) to 38% and the article to 62%:

```
nav { width: 38%; }
article { width: 62%; }
```

6. Float the navigation to the left:

```
nav { width: 38%; float: left; }
```

7. Clear the float on the footer, so that it doesn't float next to the navigation by mistake:

```
footer { width: 100%; clear: left; }
```

The full HTML and CSS looks like this:

```
<!DOCTYPE html>
<html>
<head>
    <title>Page Title</title>
    <style>
        body { width: 100%; margin:0; padding:0; border:0; }
```

```
        header { width: 100% }
        nav { width: 38%; float: left; }
        article { width: 62%; }
        footer { width: 100%; clear: left; }
    </style>
</head>
<body>
<header>
    <h1>Page Title</h1>
</header>
<nav>
    <ul id="">
        <li><a href="#">Home</a></li>
        <li><a href="#">About Us</a></li>
        <li><a href="#">Products</a></li>
        <li><a href="#">Services</a></li>
    </ul>
</nav>
<article>
    <p>This is the text of the article.</p>
</article>
<footer>&copy; 2011</footer>
</body>
</html>
```

As with all web pages, you should test this document to make sure it works. Figure 3.3 shows how it looks in Safari.

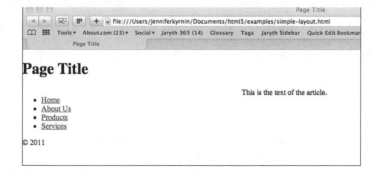

FIGURE 3.3
A simple layout displayed in Safari.

What CSS3 Adds to the Party

CSS3 is the latest version of CSS. Unlike previous versions, it is being released in modules. Modules are available for color, selectors, backgrounds and borders, and so on. These modules are at all stages of the standards process, but many web browsers provide support already.

CSS3 offers many great new features:

▶ Multi-column layout and grid layout

▶ Rounded corners

▶ Border images

▶ Text and box shadows

▶ Marquee overflow on non-browser devices

▶ Font and typography modification

▶ Animations

▶ Three-dimensional transformations

Support for CSS3 style properties isn't always as straightforward as learning a list of new properties. Most web browsers add new styles in with keywords at the front of the property to indicate that it's a browser-specific property. These keywords are

▶ `-moz`—Firefox and Mozilla

▶ `-ms`—Internet Explorer

▶ `-wap`—WAP and Opera

▶ `-o`—Opera

▶ `-webkit`—Chrome and Safari

You can use many of the new CSS3 properties right now, as long as you include the corresponding browser-specific extensions.

Rounded Corners

Rounded corners in CSS3 are achieved with a property called `border-radius`. Nearly every designer in the world has been waiting for this style to have better support because the blocky, boxy look of CSS2 web pages has gotten boring. In fact, until this style came along, designers were forced to use awkward HTML structures, images, and even tables to get rounded corners.

As with the `font` property discussed earlier, you can style all four corners with the shortcut property `border-radius` or you can set the curve on specific corners with styles for each corner:

- ▶ `border-bottom-left-radius`

- ▶ `border-bottom-right-radius`

- ▶ `border-top-left-radius`

- ▶ `border-top-right-radius`

However, you also need to include the browser extensions for Firefox and WebKit to have your styles show up in those browsers. WebKit extensions will apply to iOS and Android devices as well as Safari and Chrome. Opera uses the CSS3 properties rather than any extension. Table 3.1 shows the CSS3 properties and their browser-specific extensions. Be sure to test in the browsers you support, because the most modern versions of Chrome, Firefox, and Safari don't need the extensions.

TABLE 3.1 Border-Radius Browser Extensions

CSS3	Firefox	WebKit
`border-radius`	`-moz-border-radius`	`-webkit-border-radius`
`border-bottom-left-radius`	`-moz-border-radius-bottomleft`	`-webkit-border-bottom-left-radius`
`border-bottom-right-radius`	`-moz-border-radius-bottomright`	`-webkit-border-bottom-right-radius`
`border-top-left-radius`	`-moz-border-radius-topleft`	`-webkit-border-top-left-radius`
`border-top-right-radius`	`-moz-border-radius-topright`	`-webkit-border-top-right-radius`

To use the `border-radius` styles, you set the length of the radius for the border. You can create a rounded corner by using one length value, and an elliptical corner by using two values.

Try It Yourself ▼

Building a Box with Different Corner Styles

You can create a box with four different corner styles using the border radius styles.

1. Open an HTML5 document and add in a `<div>` with a short paragraph of text inside it:

```
<div>
    <p>Here is a short paragraph of text.</p>
</div>
```

2. Give your `<div>` tag an ID so it can be styled uniquely with the CSS:

```
<div id="all-four">
```

3. Create a new style sheet and give the `<div>` a background color, border, width, and height:

```
#all-four {
    background-color: yellow;
    border: solid black 2px;
    width: 200px;
    height: 200px;
}
```

4. Style the top-left corner with a round corner, and don't forget the browser extensions:

```
border-top-left-radius: 25px;
-moz-border-radius-topleft: 25px;
-webkit-border-top-left-radius: 25px;
```

5. Style the top-right corner with an even ellipse (which is the same as a rounded corner):

```
border-top-right-radius: 65px 65px;
-moz-border-radius-topright: 65px 65px;
-webkit-border-top-right-radius: 65px; 65px;
```

6. Give the bottom two corners uneven ellipses:

```
border-bottom-left-radius: 100px 50px;
-moz-border-radius-bottomleft: 100px 50px;
-webkit-border-bottom-left-radius: 100px 50px;
border-bottom-right-radius: 135px 25px;
-moz-border-radius-bottomright: 135px 25px;
-webkit-border-bottom-right-radius: 135px 25px;
```

Save the document and view it in a web browser. Your result should be similar to Figure 3.4.

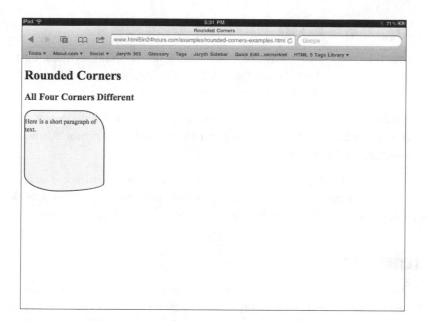

FIGURE 3.4
A `div` with different types of rounded corners, on an iPad.

Box Shadows and Text Shadows

You can add shadows to text and boxes using the CSS3 properties `text-shadow` and `box-shadow`. The format for these styles is:

```
text-shadow: horizontal-offset vertical-offset blur-radius color;
box-shadow: horizontal-offset vertical-offset blur-radius color;
```

The offsets are the amount that the shadow should be offset from the original element. The blur radius is the amount of blur to be applied; the color is the color of the shadow.

Transparent Colors

CSS can display colors as RGB with the format `rgb(r,g,b)` where the r, g, and b are numbers from 0-255 for the colors red, green, and blue. For example `rgb(0,0,0)` is the color "black." CSS3 adds support for RGBa, so you can define the opacity as well. This means you can create more interesting designs with background colors that are semi-transparent. To use RGBa, add a fourth number between 0 and 1 to the end of your RGB code. 0 is transparent and 1 is 100% opaque. For example:

```
rgba(0, 0, 0, 0.5)
```

This creates a color that is black, but 50% transparent.

Using CSS3 on Mobile Devices

CSS3 is well supported by modern smartphones and tablets that use WeKit- and Opera-based browsers. Both Android and iOS devices support many elements of CSS3, but older phones might have trouble with these styles.

Also, mobile devices using Windows operating systems may not have good CSS3 support. Internet Explorer has not had good CSS3 support until version 9, and the mobile versions of this browser are just as bad.

When you're using CSS3, be sure to always use the browser extensions as well as the CSS3 styles for the most support, and always test in as many browsers as possible when you're using a style you're not familiar with.

Summary

In this hour you learned how to write CSS styles, choose the best way to add those styles to a style sheet, and attach that style sheet to your HTML. You learned how to style the fonts and layout of your web page as well as how to use fancier CSS3 properties for creating shadows, rounded corners, and transparent colors.

Mobile devices provide good support for CSS3 properties, especially the more modern smartphones and tablets. If you are building HTML5 web applications, using CSS3 is a natural adjunct.

Q&A

Q. *I want to use special fonts for my header, but since I can't be sure that my customers have the font, should I just use an image instead?*

A. Every website is different, but using an image for fonts is generally not a good idea. They increase the time needed for your page to download and can be difficult for screen readers to process. They are also not search engine–friendly. But you shouldn't give up. Ways exist to get your fancy font onto the page. You can use image replacement techniques or embed fonts using web fonts (discussed more in Hour 11). But for now, you can put that font first in your font stack.

Q. *Are there other CSS3 properties that I can use?*

A. This book does not cover many CSS3 properties, because they aren't well supported by modern browsers. You can use some properties to help you create magazine-style layouts with columns. You can create borders with images using the border-image style. You can create transition effects with the transition property. If you're worried that the properties you want to use won't work with some browsers or devices, you can discover compatibility tables at the site "When can I use..." (http://caniuse.com/).

Q. *I've read that Internet Explorer doesn't handle the CSS box model correctly. What should I do about that?*

A. This is partially true. Internet Explorer 5, 6, and 7 all implemented the CSS box model slightly differently than other, more standards-compliant browsers. These versions of IE did things like double the padding when you float an element inside another and count the padding as part of the width of the element, rather than adding it on. You can find hacks online to fix these problems, but luckily Internet Explorer 8 and 9 both were brought into compliance with the standards, and so you may only see these issues in older browser versions.

Workshop

The workshop contains quiz questions to help you process what you've learned in this chapter. Try to answer all the questions before you read the answers. See Appendix A, "Answers to Quizzes," for answers.

Quiz

1. What are three ways you can add styles to a web page, and which is the best way to add them?

2. What is a CSS selector?

3. What is a browser extension? What are the browser extensions for the border-radius CSS3 style property?

Exercises

1. Build an external style sheet for one of the HTML documents you created in Hours 1 or 2. Give your document a two-column layout using float and setting the width of your elements.

2. Create a fancy headline using a creative font stack, colors, and text-shadow or box-shadow.

3. Be sure to visit the W3C CSS site (www.w3.org/Style/CSS/learning) to learn more about CSS and the properties that were not covered in this hour.

HOUR 4

Detecting Mobile Devices and HTML5 Support

What You'll Learn in This Hour:

▶ How to choose the browsers and features to support
▶ What browsers support HTML5
▶ How to detect support for HTML5
▶ How to create fault-tolerant web applications
▶ How CSS3 media queries enhance detection scripts

When you're working with a language that is as cutting edge as HTML5, taking one of two roads is tempting:

▶ Either you decide to support everything you possibly can, and are tempted to ignore anything that doesn't work.

▶ Or you decide to support none of the new standards until widespread support exists across the entire browser eco-system.

In this hour, you will learn how to take the third road, the middle ground. Creating cutting-edge web applications that will work in a good percentage of the browsers out there without doing huge amounts of duplicate work or leaving out vast amounts of either users or technology is possible. By making smart decisions on what to support and then handling the non-compliant situations gracefully, you will create a web application that is effective and useful to many people.

Choosing What HTML5 Elements to Use

The problem many web designers have with using HTML5 and CSS3 is that the majority of web browsers don't support them. By *majority*, I mean Internet Explorer. Internet Explorer 9 only came out in early 2011, and all versions prior to it have virtually no HTML5 support and limited CSS3 support.

Plus, there's mobile. Hundreds of mobile devices are on the market. Most cell phones have some type of web browser on them, and even the smartphones and tablets have different degrees of support for the more modern standards.

However, the question, "How do I detect HTML5 support?" is also wrong. For one thing, HTML5 (and CSS3 for that matter) isn't really one "thing." It's a giant collection of specifications, standards, and tools that are all wrapped up together under the title HTML5. So, when a browser "supports" HTML5, what it is really saying is that some of the features and functions of HTML5 work in that browser. But as of this writing, no web browser supports all the HTML5 standards. In fact, many of the standards are still being written.

When you're choosing what parts of HTML5 you want to use, think about the features that you want on your site, rather than the browsers and devices you want to support. That may sound like I'm advocating going back to the bad old days when websites had notes written to certain browser users suggesting they go download a better browser, but I'm not. Remember, some organizations and schools have rules about what browsers and versions can and can't be used, and these are often much older than most web designers would prefer.

As you'll see in this hour, choosing the technology you want to support without leaving the people and the browsers and devices they use out in the cold is possible.

Android and iOS Support for HTML5

The most current versions of iOS and Android have about 47% and 49% HTML5 support, respectively. Opera Mobile has 58% HTML5 support. This isn't very good compared to current versions of desktop browsers, as you can see in Table 4.1.

The market share numbers were only available for the top 10 web browsers, so some of the data is not available.

However, when you look at browser usage statistics, this paints a very different picture. The most recent versions of Chrome, Firefox, Opera, and Safari support more than 60% of the HTML5 features, and even IE9 supports 52% of HTML5. But the problem comes when you look at their market share. Chrome 10 through 13 have the most HTML5 support, but only 17% of the browser market. In fact, the largest market share in desktop markets still belongs to Internet Explorer 8, 7, and 6 with 29.6% in July 2011[1], and these versions only support at best 20% of the HTML5 features.

In comparison, iOS and Android have nearly 40% of the market and with Opera, the penetration is closer to two-thirds. Now, how many of those browsers are using the most recent versions of their operating systems isn't clear, but iOS and Android have had at least 25% HTML5 support going back two generations.

TABLE 4.1 HTML5 Support in Modern Browsers[2,3,4]

Browser	Market Share	HTML5 Support
Chrome 13	Not available	88%
Chrome 12	17.54%	88%
Chrome 11	Not available	83%
Chrome 10	Not available	83%
Internet Explorer 9	5.96%	52%
Internet Explorer 8	19.31%	20%
Internet Explorer 7	7.60%	16%
Firefox 5	14.96%	78%
Firefox 4	2.83%	78%
Firefox 3.6	8.16%	52%
Opera 11	1.16%	73%
Opera 10	Not available	57%
Safari 5	5.47%	76%
Safari 4	Not available	47%
Android	18.17%	2.3: 49%
iOS	19.95%	4.2–4.3: 47%
Opera Mini/Mobile	22.07%	Mini 5–6: 15%
		Mobile 11: 58%

[2] "March 2011 Web Browser Market Share." W3Counter. July 2011. www.w3counter.com/globalstats.php?year=2011&month=7. Referenced August 10, 2011.

[3] "Top 9 Mobile Browsers from Aug 10 to Jul 11." StatCounter GlobalStats. http://gs.stat-counter.com/#mobile_browser-ww-monthly-201008-201107. Referenced August 10, 2011.

[4] "Summary HTML5 Support." When Can I Use.... August 8, 2011. http://caniuse.com/#eras=now&cats=HTML5. Referenced August 10, 2011.

[1] "March 2011 Web Browser Market Share." W3Counter. July 2011. www.w3counter.com/globalstats.php?year=2011&month=7. Referenced August 10, 2011.

> **Opera Mini Is Not Great at HTML5**
>
> Opera Mini, unlike its bigger cousin, Opera Mobile, does not have good HTML5 support—only 15% in fact. But it is a very commonly used mobile browser. This browser was written for very small screen cell phones (128 pixels wide or smaller) and does not act like a smartphone browser. But it can look like Opera mobile in your web statistics. You should not assume that if someone comes to your page on a device using Opera that they are using Opera Mobile.

As you can see from Table 4.1, people don't upgrade their desktop browsers, but they do upgrade their mobile browsers. This is because when they purchase a new phone, they get a new browser, and many people purchase new cellphones almost every year. In fact, a prediction is that mobile users will overtake desktop internet users by 2014, and possibly even sooner.[5] By keeping your eye on mobile development and HTML5 applications, you are keeping your skills strong and your website future-proofed.

Detecting HTML5 Functions

Now that you know that mobile devices are an important part of what is driving HTML5 development, you're probably thinking "well, then I should start detecting those Android, iOS, and Opera Mobile browsers." But as said above, detecting browsers or devices, while tempting, can only lead to frustration. The problem is that these browsers are written with functions to hide what they are. For example:

▶ Some browsers send user agent strings that imply they are a different browser.

▶ Privacy software can cloak the user agent string.

▶ Browser features can change while the user agent stays the same.

Instead, you should try detecting the HTML5 features you want to use. When you detect for features rather than browsers, you never have to update your detection scripts.

> **HTML5 Is Many Things**
>
> The W3C includes eight separate areas within the HTML5 technology, more than 18 different specifications for standards exist within those groups. HTML5 is just the vocabulary that allows all these different standards to work together.

---

[5] "Morgan Stanley Internet Trends." Morgan Stanley. April 12, 2010. www.morganstanley.com/institutional/techresearch/pdfs/Internet_Trends_041210.pdf. Referenced April 28, 2011.

Before you scoff, think about it a moment. If you have decided you want to use geolocation (Hour 24, "Converting HTML5 Apps to Native Apps") in your web application, you can come up with a list of every browser that you know supports geolocation, and then write or buy a script to support them. Then every time a new browser version comes out you have to update your script. But if you just detect to see whether geolocation works, then any new browser that comes out with geolocation will work with your application.

The four basic ways to detect for HTML5 functions are to

- ▶ Check for the property on a global object
- ▶ Check for the property on an element you create
- ▶ Check that a method returns a correct value
- ▶ Check that an element retains a value

Checking for the Property on a Global Element

Every HTML5 document is displayed in a *global element*. This is usually called the navigator or the window.

Some HTML5 properties are created right on those global elements, and if they are there, then the browser can use them.

For example, to test for offline web applications you would write:

```
if (window.applicationCache) {
        document.write("Yes, your browser can use offline web
➥applications.");
    } else {
        document.write("No, your browser cannot use offline web
➥applications.");
    }
```

If your browser sees the applicationCache item, then it can use offline web applications.

Checking for the Property on an Element You Create

Checking for the property on an element you create is slightly trickier, because you have to create an element to test it. After you've created an element you can see whether the browser Document Object Model (DOM) recognizes it.

That Created Element Isn't Really Created

When you create an element in the DOM, you are really just creating a dummy element in your browser's memory. You can use it for detection without it ever showing up on the page.

You have to do it this way because you can add any element to the DOM. But if you add an element that the browser doesn't recognize, it will add the standard global attributes to it and then essentially ignore it. If the browser does recognize it, then it will add other properties to that element that are specific to the element.

For example, as you'll learn in Hour 10, "Drawing with the HTML5 Canvas Element," the <canvas> element always has a context. So if you create a canvas on the DOM, you can check to make sure there is a context; if there isn't, you know the browser doesn't support <canvas>:

```
if (document.createElement('canvas').getContext) {
        document.write("Yes, your browser can use the
➥<code>&lt;canvas&gt;</code> tag.");
    } else {
        document.write("No, your browser cannot use the
➥<code>&lt;canvas&gt;</code> tag.");
    }
```

Checking That a Method Returns a Correct Value

You check that a method returns a correct value to validate elements like <video> and <audio> that have codecs that are supported differently. The primary codecs are WebM and H.264.

WebM or H.264?

Although Hour 12, "Audio and Video in HTML5," will go into more detail, you should be aware of at least two video codecs when you're building HTML5 pages with the <video> tag: WebM and H.264. WebM is not supported by Safari or Internet Explorer, but you can get a plug-in for IE. H.264 is not supported by Firefox or Opera. Creating and testing for both codecs is important.

For these types of elements, you should check first that the element has the properties you expect, as mentioned in the "Checking for the Property on an Element You Create" section, and then, assuming that the element works, that support exists for the method you need.

So, to check for H.264 support in the `<video>` tag, first you would check that the video element supports the `canPlayType` method:

```
return !!document.createElement('video').canPlayType;
```

Then, assuming `<video>` is supported, you check for the H.264 codec:

```
!!video.canPlayType('video/mp4; codecs="avc1.42E01E, mp4a.40.2"')
```

Try It Yourself

Checking for H.264 Support on Your Page

If you're going to use H.264 video on your web pages, you should make sure that the browsers viewing the page support it, then you can provide fallback options if they don't.

1. Create a script in the `<head>` of your HTML5 document:

```
<script>
```

2. Write a function to check for video support:

```
function videoCheck() {
    return !!document.createElement('video').canPlayType;
}
```

3. Write a function to check for H.264 support:

```
function h264Check() {
    if (!videoCheck) {
        document.write("not");
        return;
    }
    var video = document.createElement("video");
    if (!video.canPlayType('video/mp4; codecs="avc1.42E01E,
➥mp4a.40.2"')) {
        document.write("not");
    }
    return;
}
```

4. Close the script:

```
</script>
```

5. Add a script inside your document to call the check script and write the results:

```
<script>
    document.write("Your browser does ");
```

```
        h264Check();
        document.write(" support H.264 video.");
    </script>
```

▲   Test this page on both iOS and Android devices (or Firefox and IE9) to see the results.

Checking That an Element Retains a Value

Checking that an element retains a value is the most complicated method to check for support. You have to first create a dummy element, then you have to check for a specific method, and finally you check to see that the values on that method are retained as you expect.

This is an important testing method to learn because it is used to test for many different HTML5 features. For example, the new <input> types you can use on HTML5 forms (more about this in Hour 13, "HTML5 Forms") can only be checked for with this method. For example, in Safari 5, if you use the input type range you will get a slider bar that looks like that in Figure 4.1.

FIGURE 4.1
A range type form input in Safari 5.

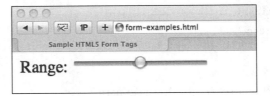

However, other browsers don't display anything but a text box. If you want to use a custom script for those browsers that don't have a built-in slider, you need to detect that support.

So, to detect a range input element, first you add a new input element:

```
var i = document.createElement("input");
```

Then add the range attribute:

```
i.setAttribute("type", "range");
```

Finally, check to see whether the browser resets that attribute to text. If it does, it doesn't support the range element:

```
if (i.type == "text") {
    document.write("not");
}
```

Here's the HTML to implement it:

```
<!doctype html>
<html>
<head>
<title>Check for Range Input</title>
<script>
    function rangeCheck() {
        var i = document.createElement("input");
        i.setAttribute("type", "range");
    if (i.type == "text") {
        document.write("not");
    }
        return;
    }
</script>
</head>
<body>
<article>
    <p>
    <script>
        document.write("Your browser does ");
        rangeCheck();
        document.write(" support the <code>&lt;input type=range&gt;</code>
➥input type.");
    </script>
    </p>
</article>
</body>
</html>
```

Handling Internet Explorer 8, 7, and 6

Internet Explorer is the only exception to the rule about not detecting browsers. Although IE 8 and lower don't support HTML5 tags automatically, there is a way to force these versions to at least recognize the HTML5 tags, so that you can style them using conditional comments and a script called html5shiv.

Conditional comments are comments that are only supported by IE. They use if statements to check for specific versions of IE. If you use them in the <head> of your document, you can load the html5shiv script only for the versions of IE that need it.

To support HTML5 in IE 8, 7, and 6, add the following to the <head> of your HTML5 document:

```
<!--[if lt IE 9]>
<script src="http://html5shiv.googlecode.com/svn/trunk/html5.js"></script>
<![endif]-->
```

Then just add any of the new HTML5 tags and apply some styles to them. When you test in older versions of Internet Explorer, the new tags will have styles.

> **HTMLShiv Only Lets IE Recognize the Tags**
>
> The HTML5shiv script tells Internet Explorer to recognize the new HTML5 tags as HTML. It does not add functionality to the tags. So, with the script, Internet Explorer 8 will recognize that it can apply styles to an <article> tag, but it won't draw a circle in a <canvas> tag. You still need to detect the support as explained in the previous sections of this hour.

Degrading Gracefully

The trick to detecting HTML5 functions is not what you do when they work, but rather what you do when they *don't* work. Seeing messages at the top of completely unusable pages that read, "This page only works in Internet Explorer. Please upgrade your browser," used to be common. Of course, most people using a browser other than Internet Explorer often already considered their browser an upgrade, and were not likely to switch to IE just to see one site. They were much more likely to laugh and never visit that site again.

Back when IE had the majority browser share, expecting people to switch to IE was almost understandable, but these days IE is just one of a number of equally good browsers, and at the rate things are changing IE probably won't even be the most popular before too long.

These days, thinking about what features you want to include and then degrading the site so that browsers with less functionality get less, but still get a usable site, is best. This practice is called *graceful degradation*, and it's a type of fault tolerance system.

The idea behind graceful degradation is that a system should continue to function even if one or more of its components fails. In web design, this means that your web page should continue to work even if the HTML5 components aren't fully supported by the browser.

A good example is the <video> tag. This tag requires support for video codecs built into the browser as well as support for the <video> tag. If either type of support is missing, your video won't play. When this happens you have a few choices:

▶ Ignore the problem and display nothing or an error message—whatever the browser decides to do.

▶ Detect the problem and tell users to upgrade their browsers.

▶ Detect the problem and provide a fallback mechanism.

The solution that works the best is to detect the problem and provide a fallback mechanism. With this solution you recognize that not all browsers or users are the same, and you try to mitigate the problem by providing an alternative.

Remember, the solution doesn't have to be perfect. For one thing, you want to make it worthwhile for people to switch to a more HTML5-compliant browser, and by creating a complete replica of your site in another language, you defeat that purpose, plus you possibly double the amount of work you need to do.

Try It Yourself ▼

Choose Degradation Choices

The secret to graceful degradation is making good choices.

1. Choose what technology your HTML5 application is going to support for the best features. This is your ultimate app—the app that only cutting-edge users will see.

2. Decide which features are absolutely critical to the app's functionality. This should not be the same as the list you came up with in step 1. Choose only those features that are absolutely critical. If you find it hard to decide, think about how you would describe the application in a Twitter post—140 characters or less. These features are your core features. They are the minimum your app needs to be functional for all readers.

3. Draw up a fallback plan for your core features. Depending upon who your users are, you may need fallbacks for your fallbacks for these features. Remember, these are the items that *must* stay running for your application to work.

4. Finally, come up with fallback options for your best features. Because it's not as critical that these work perfectly, you can be a little looser with your fallback options.

The goal is to create an application that has the core functionality on the largest number of platforms. Then, as your readers improve their tools, they will think your application is improving as well. ▲

Using CSS3 Media Queries to Detect Mobile Browsers

CSS2 introduced media-dependent style sheets to allow designers to create separate style sheets for different types of media. For example, you could create a style sheet for

- **all**—All media types

- **aural**—Speech synthesizers

- **braille**—Braille devices

- **embossed**—Paged braille printers

- **handheld**—Small, usually monochrome, devices

- **print**—Paper formats and "print preview"

- **projection**—Overhead projectors

- **screen**—Color computer screens

- **tty**—Teletype devices with a fixed-pitch character grid

- **tv**—Television devices with low resolution, color, and sound

To define the media type on a style sheet you could add it to a style sheet with the media attribute, such as:

```
<style media="screen">
```

Or in an external style sheet link:

```
<link media="screen" rel="stylesheet" href="style.css">
```

Or add the styles in an existing style sheet with an @media tag:

```
<style>
@media print {
// add styles here
}
</style>
```

CSS3 extends the media attribute to allow you to check the user agent against various conditions. If the browser or device meets those conditions, it is delivered that style sheet. For example, you might want to deliver a different style sheet to customers with very small screens:

```
<link rel="stylesheet" media="screen and (max-width: 128px)"
➥href="small-screen.css">
```

You can test your browsers against a number of media features:

- Width and height of both the screen and the device
- Orientation of the screen
- Aspect ratio of the screen and device
- Colors, including number of colors, whether monochrome or color, and the color bit depth
- Resolution
- Scanning process of TV devices
- Grid or bitmap devices

Checking the Width and Height

You can detect the width and height of the device or the width and height of the actual viewing area. In other words, the `width` keyword applies to the actual width of the viewing area and the `device-width` keyword applies to the width of the device itself. The same is true of the `height` and `device-height` keywords for height.

Testing with Media Queries Can Get Tricky

If you set your `max-device-width` to 480px to show a different style sheet to small screens, you won't be able to test it by resizing your browser. The `device-width` keyword knows that your web browser has a larger actual size, even if you've resized it to be really small. To offset this, you can use the `width` keyword as well.

Watch Out!

Although you can set your style sheet to only apply to devices with exactly the width or height you are looking for, using the `min-` and `max-` extensions is more effective.

Try It Yourself

Attaching a Style Sheet Just for Smaller Mobile Devices

An easy way to know you are probably seeing a mobile device is by how wide the screen is. Many smartphones have only 480px wide screens, so creating a style sheet just for them makes sense.

1. Write your style sheet link:

   ```
   <link rel="stylesheet" href="smartphone.css">
   ```

2. Add in the media type:

   ```
   media="screen"
   ```

3. Add the `max-width` and `max-device-width` keywords to your link:

   ```
   media="screen and (max-width: 480px), screen and (max-device-width:
   ➥480px)"
   ```

4. Include the keyword only so that your style sheet is hidden from older browsers:

   ```
   media="only screen and (max-width: 480px), only screen and
   ➥(max-device-width: 480px)"
   ```

   The completed link looks like this:

   ```
   <link rel="stylesheet" media="only screen and (max-width: 480px), only
   ➥screen and (max-device-width: 480px)" href="smartphone.css">
   ```

Checking the Screen Orientation

Tablets and some smartphones will change the width when the orientation changes. You can use the `orientation` keyword to test what orientation the device is displaying in:

```
only screen and (orientation: landscape)
only screen and (orientation: portrait)
```

Checking the Aspect Ratio

You can create styles for devices with specific, maximum, or minimum aspect ratios with the `aspect-ratio` keyword. The ratio is specified as the `device-width` divided by the `device-height` and is written with a slash between the numbers. For example, two common aspect ratios you might see are 16:9 and 4:3. These are written:

```
only screen and (aspect-ratio: 16/9)
only screen and (aspect-ratio: 4/3)
```

Checking Colors

Media queries let you test against several color options:

▶ **color**—Tests for color or the number of bits per color component, such as 8-bit or 24-bit color

▶ **color-index**—Tests for the number of colors the media can display, such as 256 color monitors

▶ **monochrome**—Tests for monochrome display or the number of bits per pixel in a monochrome display

You can use the min- and max- prefixes with all of these options for your tests.

Checking Resolution

Testing for devices with a specific resolution is easy—just use the resolution keyword to test for various dots per inch (dpi). You can also specify the min- and max- prefixes to show style sheets for low-res and high-res machines.

4G iPhone and iPod touches use a high-definition Retina display. You can use a WebKit keyword to test for that: -webkit-min-device-pixel-ratio. To display only to Retina devices you would write:

```
only screen and (-webkit-min-device-pixel-ratio: 2)
```

Checking for TV and Grid Devices

You can use the scan and grid keywords to check the scanning process of a television device or whether a tty or braille device is grid based or bitmap:

```
only tv and (scan: progressive)
only tty and (grid)
```

Testing Your Applications

Testing applications, especially mobile applications, can be difficult. But it is a critical step in creating any web page or application. However, you don't have to go out and buy every tablet on the market just for testing.

Here are the steps you should take to test your mobile applications:

▶ Test first in the browsers you have on your desktop. If you're like most developers, you have a favorite browser that you use all the time, but make a point of downloading other browsers for testing as well.

▶ Change the size of your browsers. When you are using CSS3 media queries, just the width of the browser window display area may affect how the page appears. You can adjust that by adjusting your browser window. If you use

Firefox or Chrome, you can install the free Web Developer extension (http://chrispederick.com/work/web-developer/) and add some size presets to make this step of testing fast.

▶ Because you're building a web application, you should also test other operating systems. The most efficient way is to install a virtual machine with another OS on your computer. VirtualBox (www.virtualbox.org/) is an open source virtualization product that runs on Windows, Macintosh, and Linux; it can host many flavors of guest OS.

▶ Test on a local iOS or Android device. If you don't have both an Android and an iOS device, find an emulator to test on them. Hour 8, "Converting Web Apps to Mobile," discusses more about how to use emulators.

▶ Check any fallback browsers you are concerned about. You can test these either on your local machine (or in a virtual machine) or in online tools like Browsershots (http://browsershots.org/).

Summary

In this hour, you learned that you shouldn't be asking how to detect either browsers, devices, or HTML5. Instead, you should decide what technology you need on your site and detect for support for exactly that. Then you are not relying on knowing all the features of every browser and device, and you are also not required to test for aspects of HTML5 that you never use.

To do this detection, you learned four methods of testing for HTML5 technology as well as how to target specific devices with CSS3 media queries. You also learned the importance of graceful degradation or fault tolerance and how to ensure your sites look good in the majority of user agents. Finally, you were given five steps for testing your applications to make sure that your detection scripts and queries worked correctly.

Q&A

Q. *I noticed that you didn't tell me exactly what I should support and detect for. Can you give me a clue as to the most important features of HTML5 I should detect?*

A. If you're writing HTML5 documents, you should always include the `HTML5shiv` script and conditional comments referred to in this chapter. This ensures that at the very least, IE 6, 7, and 8 will have a chance at displaying correctly. But beyond that it really depends upon your application. If you never use the

`<canvas>` tag then detecting it is pointless. But if you're using geolocation and are not detecting for it, then you're making a mistake. Hour 8 covers some specific detection scripts you can install on your site to help detect the technology you want to detect.

Q. *I really want to detect specific browsers or devices because I know my site won't support them. What can I do?*

A. You can always use a browser detection script for detecting specific browsers. But they can be more trouble than they are worth. You can find a nice one at Quirks Mode: www.quirksmode.org/js/detect.html.

Q. *What if I want to redirect my mobile users to a completely different domain? How can I do that?*

A. One way you can do this is with an `.htaccess` redirect on mobile devices. Add the following to your `.htaccess` file in the root of your Apache web server:

```
RewriteCond %{HTTP_USER_AGENT}
"android¦blackberry¦ipad¦iphone¦ipod¦iemobile¦opera
➥mobile¦palmos¦webos¦googlebot-mobile" [NC]
RewriteRule ^(.*)$ http://m.yoursitename.com/ [L,R=302]
```

This script checks for Android, Blackberry, iPad, iPhone, iPod, Windows Mobile, Opera Mobile, PalmOS, WebOS, and the Google mobile search robot, and redirects them to your mobile site at http://m.yoursitename.com/.

Workshop

The workshop contains quiz questions to help you process what you've learned in this chapter. Try to answer all the questions before you read the answers. See Appendix A, "Answers to Quizzes," for answers.

Quiz

1. What desktop browser and what mobile browser have the highest support for HTML5 devices (at the time of this writing)?

2. Why would you write a detection script to detect for a property on an element you created?

3. Why should you care about degrading gracefully?

Exercises

1. Write down your fault tolerance plan. Be sure to include both the minimum your site should support and the maximum, as well as your fallback plans for each scenario.

2. After you have fallback plans, research how to test for the technology that may need fallback options. An excellent resource is Mark Pilgrim's "Guide to Detecting Almost Anything" (http://diveintohtml5.info/everything.html).

HOUR 5

JavaScript and HTML5 Web Applications

Web design consists of three parts: content, style, and behavior. In the previous hours, you learned about HTML (the content) and CSS (the style). JavaScript is the behavior. Having all three of these layers in your designs, and keeping them separated, is important.

In this hour, you will learn what JavaScript is and how to add it into your web page. It also provides a few scripts to get you going.

This hour then introduces you to a JavaScript framework called jQuery. This framework makes adding scripts to pages easy for designers and developers. This hour includes a couple jQuery scripts, as well.

Finally, this hour gives you an introduction to a mobile framework—jQuery Mobile. This framework makes building an HTML document that looks and acts like a mobile application easy.

What is JavaScript?

JavaScript is a programming language that you can use to affect the user interface and create dynamic websites. You can use it to affect the Document Object Model (DOM) to control the elements on the page, including color, size, position, even the visibility of the elements themselves and to open new browser windows.

To add JavaScript to a web page, you use the `<script>` tag. You can place scripts in the `<head>` or in the `<body>` of your document. You also can trigger script functions in any event attribute, such as onmouseover or onload.

▼   **Try It Yourself**

Adding a Simple Script to a Page

The first program almost every programmer learns is how to write "Hello World" on the screen. You can do this with JavaScript as well.

1. Create your web page as you normally would:

```
<!DOCTYPE html>
<html>
<head>
    <title>Simple JavaScript</title>
</head>
<body>
</body>
</html>
```

2. Add a script tag to the `<head>` of the page:

```
<script>
</script>
```

3. Add the JavaScript function inside the script tags to write "Hello World" in an alert window:

```
function hello() {
    alert("Hello World");
}
```

4. Add a link to the body of your document to call the script:

```
<a href="#" onclick="hello();">Click Me</a>
```

5. Include a `<noscript>` tag below the link with alternative text:

```
<noscript>
<p>Hello World
<p>This text is not written with JavaScript.
</noscript>
```

The full HTML document looks like this:

```
<!DOCTYPE html>

<html>
```

```
<head>
    <title>Simple JavaScript</title>
    <script>
        function hello() {
            alert("Hello World");
        }
    </script>
</head>

<body>
<a href="#" onclick="hello();">Click Me</a>
<noscript>
<p>Hello World
<p>This text is not written with JavaScript.
</noscript>

</body>
</html>
```

▲

The previous hour discussed fault tolerance. This applies to JavaScript just as it does with HTML5, but unlike HTML5, JavaScript offers a built-in function for fault tolerance—the <noscript> tag.

The <noscript> tag can contain any HTML that you need to provide an alternative to your script contents. Then, when people come to your page with JavaScript turned off or with a user agent that doesn't support the script, they see the contents of the <noscript> tag.

Some of the most common web page scripts include:

- ▶ Rollovers

- ▶ Verifying form data

- ▶ Opening new windows

- ▶ Setting cookies

Creating Rollovers

Rollovers are a nice way to interact with your users. They add some interactivity to the page without causing a negative effect for users who can't see JavaScript.

The easiest way to create a rollover is with CSS on a link, not JavaScript. You simply add styles for both the standard link and then different styles for the rollover state. For example:

```
a:link { color: blue; }
a:hover { color: purple; }
```

This creates a link that is blue, and when the mouse hovers over it, the link turns purple.

Rollovers and Mobile Don't Mix

Never use rollovers for critical functionality in your applications, especially if you plan on attracting mobile customers. Mobile devices such as smartphones and tablets don't have a way to roll over a link. Instead, it is just clicked. If you have things such as pop-up help that appear on rollover, your mobile users will never see them.

Try It Yourself

Displaying Extra Content

You can add extra text to the end of a paragraph as a rollover with JavaScript and CSS.

1. Create your paragraph, and include the extra content at the end as if it were always visible:

```
<p>
This paragraph will display a popup when you mouse over it. This is
➥a popup
</p>
```

2. Add a <span> tag around the text that will appear on mouseover and give the tag an ID of "popup":

```
<span id="popup">This is a popup</span>
```

3. Style the #popup ID and be sure to include display: none;:

```
#popup {
    display: none;
    width: 100px;
    position: relative;
    background-color: #efefef;
    color: blue;
}
```

Display vs. Visibility

When you are hiding content with CSS, you can use two properties: display and visibility. At first they might seem to be the same, but knowing the difference is important. When you remove an item from your page with display: none; you are completely removing it from the DOM; it's as if it were never there. When you remove an item with visibility: hidden: you are simply hiding it from sight. It still will take up space in your design.

4. Add the JavaScript in the onmouseover and onmouseout states of the paragraph to turn on and off the pop-up text:

```
<p onmouseover='document.getElementById("popup").style.display="inline"'
   onmouseout='document.getElementById("popup").style.display="none"'>
```

Verifying Form Data

When you have a web form on your site you want to make sure that people fill it out correctly. This is called *form validation*. JavaScript enables you to validate the form data before it is sent to the web server.

The thing you should be aware of when validating form data with JavaScript is that getting around it is very easy. All someone needs to do to bypass validation is turn off JavaScript, submit the form, and turn it back on. If having correct data is critical, you should validate it on the server as well.

You can find dozens of scripts pre-built online for validating all types of form data, just search for "form validation" in your favorite search engine.

Opening a New Window

Most people are familiar with JavaScript advertisements that open in a new window. Although this JavaScript usage can be annoying, it can be useful for web applications, for things like displaying extra information and requesting data.

The simplest way to open a new window in JavaScript is with the built-in function window.open();. To open a window called "test" pointing at http://www. html5in24hours.com/, you would write:

```
window.open('http://www.html5in24hours.com/', 'test');
```

To close an open window, write:

```
window.close();
```

You can't close a window from outside the window.

Setting and Reading Cookies

Cookies are little pieces of data that are stored on the local machine. They allow the web developers to store data off the website on the local machine. Developers store everything from login credentials to game play information in cookies, anything they want available later. JavaScript makes setting, reading, and deleting cookies easy.

Cookies are saved as name=value pairs, and they have an expiration date and a path on your server that they can be read from. Following is an example of how you would write a cookie with JavaScript:

```
document.cookie = 'name=value; expires=Day, dd Mon yyyy hh:mm:ss UTC;
➥path=/';
```

To read a cookie, you need to read document.cookie as a string and parse it looking for the equal signs or the semicolons. By splitting the cookie at the semicolons, you can see the name=value pairs more easily.

To delete a cookie, you just set the value of the cookie to -1.

Here are three functions you can use to set, read, and delete cookies. This function creates or "sets" the cookie:

```
function createCookie(name,value,expireDays) {
    if (expireDays) {
        var date = new Date();
        date.setTime(date.getTime()+(expireDays*24*60*60*1000));
        var expires = "; expires="+date.toGMTString();
    }
    else var expires = "";
    document.cookie = name+"="+value+expires+"; path=/";
}
```

This function reads the cookie:

```
function readCookie(cookieName) {
    var name = cookieName + "=";
    var ca = document.cookie.split(';');
    for(var i=0;i < ca.length;i++) {
        var c = ca[i];
        while (c.charAt(0)==' ') c = c.substring(1,c.length);
        if (c.indexOf(name) == 0) return c.substring(name.length,c.length);
    }
    return null;
}
```

This function deletes the cookie:

```
function eraseCookie(cookieName) {
    createCookie(cookieName,"",-1);
}
```

What is jQuery?

All the preceding information about JavaScript is interesting, and it shows you some of the things that JavaScript can do for a web page. But what you'll probably notice is that getting a project planned, designed, and built when you're writing JavaScript from scratch takes a lot of time.

In fact, most developers tend to look for pre-written scripts that they can modify for their needs rather than writing them from scratch.

But you can use something even better than using plain JavaScript jQuery. jQuery is a JavaScript library that is built to help you create cross-platform, multifunctional JavaScript websites as quickly as possible.

No Need to Know JavaScript

The benefit to learning to write jQuery is that you don't have to learn JavaScript to be able to use it. In fact, you can probably tell what this line of jQuery does even if you don't know JavaScript:

```
$(".red").css("background-color", "#f00");
```

If you guessed that it puts a red (#f00) background on all elements with the class red you would be right.

By the Way

Try It Yourself

Getting Started with jQuery

jQuery is very easy to use and is readable even by designers who don't write any code. Follow these steps to add an alert when a link is clicked.

1. Get a copy of jQuery. You can download the most recent version of jQuery at http://docs.jquery.com/Downloading_jQuery. Save this file as a .js file and upload it to your web server. You can place it in any directory you want; just remember where you put it.

2. Write a basic web page and add a `<script>` that points to your jquery.js file:

```
<!DOCTYPE html>
<html>
<head>
    <title>Testing JQuery</title>
    <script src="jquery.min.js"></script>
</head>
<body>

</body>
</html>
```

3. Write a link in your HTML:

```
<a href="#">Click Me</a>
```

4. jQuery uses the DOM extensively, so you need to make sure that the DOM is ready to be manipulated. The following code is called the document-ready handler. Add this to a new script below your jQuery script:

```
$(document).ready(function(){
});
```

5. Now tell jQuery what to do and when to do it. In this case, you want an alert to open when you click a link. Add this to the document-ready handler:

```
$("a").click(function(event){
    alert("Hello World");
});
```

This page will have the same functionality as the first JavaScript function you wrote in the first Try It Yourself, "Adding a Simple Script to a Page." When you click the link an alert box appears. As you can see in Figure 5.1, the alert message appears in mobile browsers as well as desktop browsers.

FIGURE 5.1
A simple alert message on an Android Tablet.

The complete HTML is as follows:

```
<!DOCTYPE html>

<html>
<head>
    <title>Testing JQuery</title>
    <script src="jquery.min.js"></script>
    <script>
```

```
    $(document).ready(function(){
        $("a").click(function(event){
            alert("Hello World");
        });
    });
    </script>
</head>

<body>
<a href="#">Click Me</a>
</body>
</html>
```

▲

With jQuery, you can do all the same things you can do with JavaScript, but you can do them quicker, and without needing to know JavaScript. jQuery uses the same formatting as CSS for things such as IDs (#) and classes (.) and the element names define the elements themselves.

Making Rollovers with jQuery

Image rollovers are something that most designers want at one point or another, and they are easily written in JavaScript. But with jQuery, you will spend more time building the images than you will writing the JavaScript.

All you need are two images that have suffixes in their filenames of something like _on and _off, such as button_on.gif and button_off.gif.

You then place your image inside a link on your web page as normal, and tell jQuery to replace _on with _off and vice versa when the mouse rolls over. You don't need an onmouseover attribute at all.

> **Preload Your Rollover Images**
>
> If your rollover images are large, you should preload them or use image sprites (a single image file with multiple images positioned with CSS) so that the rollovers load more quickly. If you don't, the rollovers won't work and you risk having nothing display while they load.

Watch Out!

The full HTML reads:

```
<!DOCTYPE html>
<html>
<head>
    <title>Testing JQuery</title>
    <script src="jquery.min.js"></script>
    <script>
    $(document).ready(function(){
```

```
    $("#link1 img").hover(
      function() {
        this.src = this.src.replace("_off","_on");
      },
      function() {
        this.src = this.src.replace("_on","_off");
      }
    );
  });
  </script>
</head>
<body>
<a id="link1" href="#"><img src="images/get-scifi_off.png" alt="Get Science
Fiction!"></a>
</body>
</html>
```

You can see this example in action at www.enjoyscifi.com/rollover-test.html.

Verifying Form Data with jQuery

Although creating a form validation script in JavaScript with just a few lines is possible, with jQuery you can turn a basic check for required fields into a dynamic validator that checks the fields as the users type.

One of the great things about jQuery is how complex your scripts can get without a lot of effort. In fact, as in other aspects of jQuery, writing the scripting is faster than writing the HTML and CSS you want to modify.

▼   **Try It Yourself**

Create a Form Validated with jQuery

This HTML form will collect the name, email address, and message from the users, and the data will be validated with jQuery before being sent to the server.

   1. Write your form. Though it's not critical, getting into the habit of labeling all your input fields and giving them all IDs is a good idea:

```
<form action="#" id="contactForm">
<label for="name">Name:</label> <span id="nameInfo">What's your full
➥name?</span><br>
<input type="text" size="30" id="name"><br>
<label for="email">Email:</label> <span id="emailInfo">Please use a
➥valid email address</span><br>
<input type="email" size="30" id="email"><br>
<label for="message">Speak:</label> <span id="messageInfo"></span><br>
<textarea rows="5" cols="27" id="message"></textarea><br>
<button type="submit" name="submit">Make it So</button>
</form>
```

Notice that all three input fields have a <span> next to them. Although the name and email fields have text, the textarea does not. This is a tag that gives us a place to add error codes when needed.

2. Write your CSS to style the form fields, information labels, and an error class:

```css
#contactForm input, #contactForm textarea {
    width: 400px;
    border-radius: 1em;
    -moz-border-radius: 1em;
    -webkit-border-radius: 1em;
}
#contactForm span {
    color: #999;
}
#contactForm span.error {
    color: #C00;
}
#contactForm input.error {
    background-color: #465f82;
}
```

3. Now add your jQuery; first add the link to jQuery itself and then add the document-ready function, where you will put the rest of your script:

```html
<script src="jquery.min.js"></script>
<script>
$(document).ready(function(){

};
```

4. Add a couple variables so that the script is easier to follow:

```javascript
var form = $("#contactForm");
var name = $("#name");
var nameInfo = $("#nameInfo");
```

5. Write a function to check that the name field is filled in:

```javascript
function requiredName() {
    if (name.val().length < 1) {
        name.addClass("error");
        nameInfo.text("The name field is required");
        nameInfo.addClass("error");
        return false;
    } else {
        name.removeClass("error");
        nameInfo.text("What's your full name?");
        nameInfo.removeClass("error");
        return true;
    }
}
```

6. Call the name field validation when users leave the form field or tab out of it:

```
name.blur(requiredName);
name.keyup(requiredName);
```

7. Repeat steps 4 through 6 for the email and message fields in the form.

8. Finally, check that all the required fields are filled in when the form is submitted as well:

```
form.submit(function() {
    if (requiredName() && requiredEmail() && requiredMessage())
        return true;
    else
        return false;
});
```

When the user fills in the form but leaves one of the fields blank, an error message appears. This validation works just fine on mobile devices, too, as you can see in Figure 5.2.

FIGURE 5.2
Validating a
form with jQuery
on an iPad.

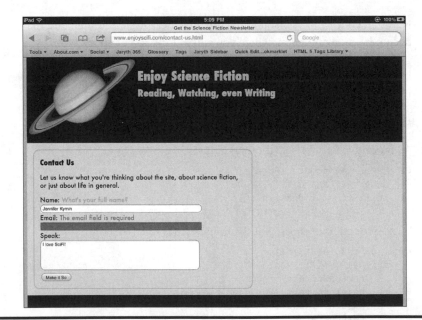

Using jQuery for Web Applications

jQuery is useful for building web applications because it is so easy to use. However, ease-of-use isn't the only consideration when building a web application, and many JavaScript libraries are available that you can use.

Learning jQuery is a good idea for web application developers for a number of reasons, including the following:

▶ **jQuery condenses the JavaScript**—Approximately five lines of jQuery is equivalent to five times that much JavaScript, but web applications, especially mobile applications, must be small and nimble.

▶ **jQuery has robust browser support**—The jQuery developers are constantly updating the library to make sure that it is supported in the widest number of browsers, so web developers don't have to know all the different implementation rules for cross-browser scripting.

▶ **jQuery uses familiar syntax**—If you are familiar with CSS selectors, then you will understand jQuery.

▶ **jQuery includes built-in animations**—Windows open and close by fading in or sliding out, text can scroll, and images can be put into a slideshow. All these add to a web application to make it look more like a traditional application.

▶ **jQuery does not impact content**—All content is written in the HTML and does not disappear, even if JavaScript is not enabled on the client. This provides a built-in fallback mechanism.

Using jQuery Mobile

Like jQuery itself, jQuery Mobile is built to work on many different platforms. In fact, jQuery Mobile supports iOS, Android, Blackberry, Palm, WebOS, Nokia/Symbian, Windows Mobile, Bada, and MeeGo, and has baseline support for all devices that understand HTML—in other words, most smartphones, tablets, and cell phones on the market today.

What's nice about jQuery Mobile is that you can build one application that works across all the mobile devices. jQuery Mobile has a graded browser support grid (http://jquerymobile.com/gbs/) that shows you what it supports. This grid is especially useful for planning your website, because you can base your site's support plan on it.

jQuery Mobile helps you create a mobile site that is similar to most mobile applications, and it does it with attributes on your HTML tags. All you need to do is add the jQuery Mobile style sheet and JavaScript file as well as the jQuery JavaScript file, and then build a web page.

Here is a sample HTML document using jQuery Mobile:

```
<!DOCTYPE html>
<html>
<head>
    <title>Page Title</title>
    <link rel="stylesheet"
➥href="http://code.jquery.com/mobile/1.0a4.1/jquery.mobile-
1.0a4.1.min.css" />
    <script type="text/javascript" src="http://code.jquery.com/jquery-
1.5.2.min.js"></script>
    <script type="text/javascript"
src="http://code.jquery.com/mobile/1.0a4.1/jquery.
➥mobile-1.0a4.1.min.js"></script>
</head>

<body>
<section id="page1" data-role="page">
    <header data-role="header">
        <h1>Enjoy Science Fiction</h1>
        <h1>Reading, Watching, even Writing</h1>
    </header>
    <section id="content1" data-role="content">
        <p>Science fiction is my passion. I've read science fiction for as
➥long as I can
remember (well, I remember reading "Pat the Bunny" and "The Boxcar
➥Children" before
SciFi, but not much before).</p>
        <p>My preference is for reading SciFi, but I also like watching TV
➥and movies,
and I even write some in my spare time (which I don't inflict on
➥people).</p>
    </section>
    <footer data-role="footer">
        <h4>&copy; Enjoy SciFi</h4>
    </footer>
</section>
</body>
</html>
```

<table>
<tr><td>By the Way</td><td>

Using Cloud Scripts Keeps Your Pages Fast

Linking to script libraries such as jQuery from an internet location (such as http://code.jquery.com/jquery-1.5.2.min.js in the HTML here) is a way of using a content delivery network (CDN). When many developers link to the same location for a script, that script is more likely to be cached by your readers and load more quickly. Also, your browser may have a limit of as few as two connections to a specific host name at once, so this sends a request to a separate domain, increasing the speed.

</td></tr>
</table>

What's nice is you can add all your pages into one document (if you want) and jQuery Mobile will display them correctly. For example, you could add a second page section with an ID id="page2" to the preceding HTML and just link to it with <a href="#page2">. Figure 5.3 shows how jQuery Mobile styles look on an iPod touch. The HTML is no different than what is written in the preceding. If you go to the URL of that page (http://m.enjoyscifi.com/basic-mobile-page.html), you can see the transitions that jQuery Mobile adds to the links.

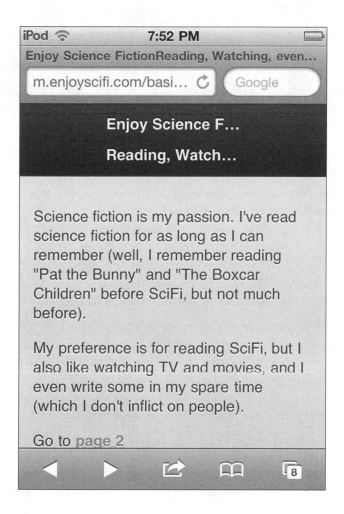

FIGURE 5.3
A standard jQuery Mobile page on an iPod touch.

You can use several other frameworks to help you build both mobile and non-mobile applications. Hour 8, "Converting Web Apps to Mobile," covers them more.

Summary

This hour provided an overview of the behavior of web pages. JavaScript controls the behaviors, and you can use it to make things happen on your web pages. Some of the common things people script on web pages include:

▶ Creating rollovers out of images and text

▶ Verifying form fields

▶ Opening new windows

▶ Setting, reading, and deleting cookies

You also learned in this hour that you can do all those things with both JavaScript and jQuery. jQuery is a framework that makes installing and using scripts for your website easy.

After you have jQuery installed, you can also use jQuery Mobile to make your web pages look more like mobile applications.

If you are interested in learning more about JavaScript, jQuery, and jQuery Mobile, see the resources listed in Appendixes B and C.

Q&A

Q. *I noticed that you never include the* `type="application/x-javascript"` *or* `type="text/css"` *attributes on your script and style tags. Why is that?*

A. HTML5 no longer requires those attributes if the script or style is the standard one that browsers expect. You can always add in another scripting language than JavaScript or another style sheet language than CSS, but then you would need to specify the type.

Q. *I heard that jQuery was just for animations—is that true?*

A. jQuery does make adding animations to your documents easy, and many people think that that is all jQuery does because it's so widespread. But jQuery is much more than that. The best way to learn all about what jQuery can do for you is to read the documentation on jquery.com (http://docs.jquery.com/Main_Page).

Q. *I don't like the styles that come with jQuery Mobile—is there any way to change the styles?*

A. Several themes are pre-built into jQuery Mobile that you can use to change the colors of your applications, or you can adjust the styles yourself. Plans are also in place for a theme roller so that you can create your own.

Workshop

The workshop contains quiz questions to help you process what you've learned in this chapter. Try to answer all the questions before you read the answers. You can find the answers in Appendix A, "Answers to Quizzes."

Quiz

1. True or false: You can place the `<script>` tag in both the `<head>` and the `<body>` of your document.

2. What style selectors can you use to create text rollovers?

3. Why would you use the property `visibility: hidden;` rather than `display: none;`?

4. What is the code you write to insert jQuery commands into your document?

Exercises

1. Build a jQuery page with rollover text. Change the color and background image of a paragraph when the mouse rolls over it.

2. Create a website with jQuery Mobile. Add at least four pages on the site and use different transitions between the pages. Find out more about jQuery Mobile at http://jquerymobile.com/.

HOUR 6

Building a Mobile Web Application

What You'll Learn in This Hour:

▶ How to create a website or web application that is mobile friendly

▶ How to plan a new mobile web application

▶ How to put your plan into practice with HTML and CSS

▶ Best practices for creating mobile web applications

This hour you will learn the best ways to create a mobile web application. You will see how to plan an application so that it works for both mobile and non-mobile devices.

You will also learn how to put together the HTML, CSS, and any jQuery you learned in previous hours to create the beginnings of a simple application.

Most importantly, you will learn some of the best practices already in use for building web applications for mobile devices. You'll find out what layouts work best as well as other tips for optimizing for mobile.

Building a Site that Works on All Devices

The key to designing excellent mobile web pages and applications is to *not* design for mobile devices—at least not specifically. The W3C calls this "designing for one web."[1] Instead of designing just for desktop browsers or just for smartphones or just for tablets, try to design applications and sites that keep all these devices in mind.

To do this you should:

▶ Make sure that the content displayed to mobile devices has the same meaning (if not the exact wording) as that displayed to non-mobile devices.

▶ Add enhancements to your pages that reflect the capabilities of the user agents.

▶ Use graceful degradation to help older and less capable browsers view your content.

▶ Test all your pages on as many devices and browsers as you can find.

> **Using Progressive Enhancement**
>
> *Progressive enhancement* is an alternative to graceful degradation. Instead of starting by building the cutting-edge features for your site and creating fallback options, you start by building the more widely supported features and then enhance the site with cutting-edge features for those browsers that can support it. Ultimately, the best solution combines a little of both—you create fallback options for your cutting-edge features and cutting-edge enhancements for your more mainstream features.

When you're planning your site, you most likely start with the desktop version and then work on the mobile sites. But what if you started the other way around?

If you are planning on building a mobile application, start your plans with the mobile browsers you want to support. After you've designed a mobile site, then you can improve it or change it for your desktop clients.

Deciding on What Type of Application You Want

Planning is key to websites as well as mobile web applications. When you sit down to start building a website or web application, you may be tempted to start writing HTML or designing the styles and scripts. However, taking some time to plan out your application gives you a much clearer idea of what you need for your site and how to implement it.

---

[1] "Design for One Web." Mobile Web Best Practices Flipcards. 2011. www.w3.org/2007/02/mwbp_flip_cards#design_for_one_web. May 2, 2011.

Try It Yourself ▼

Creating an Application Plan

Answer the following questions to come up with an application plan. Writing down your answers is best so that you can refer to your plan later.

1. What is the purpose of this web application?

   This is the overview of your application. In just a few sentences, describe what your application will do and how it will do it better than any other website or application already available.

2. What are your goals for the application?

   Consider both your personal goals and the goals of the application itself. Creating actionable goals that you can work toward is best. These are sometimes called "SMART" goals because they are Specific Measurable, Actionable, Realistic, and Time-bound. The more specific and measurable your goals are, the more likely you'll achieve them.

3. Who are the customers or users of the application?

   Be as specific as you can be about who you see as your target markets. You can have more than one, but you should include details such as gender, age, education level, job industry, hobbies, and income. A good idea is to create aggregates, even give them names and photographs, to help you visualize your customers and potential customers.

4. Who are the competitors for the application?

   Remember to think outside the application realm. Just because you are the first one to think of creating this kind of application for mobile devices doesn't mean that there aren't competitors in the offline space, in retail, or in the public sector.

   Do as much research as you can on your potential competitors. How much do they earn from their competing product, and what is their market share? What do they do well and poorly?

   The more you know about your competitors, the better you will be able to position your application to take advantage of their weaknesses and exploit your strengths.

5. What other risks could affect the success of the application?

   Competitors are not the only risk to any new venture. Do you need more money to get started? Is your application reliant on external data that you may have to pay for? What about the application market? Are your target customers willing to pay for services or do they prefer things to be free and advertising supported, and if so, is there enough money in advertising to make the applica-tion profitable?

Don't forget to take into account things such as your knowledge of program-ming or design and availability of contractors to help. Even the weather could be a risk depending upon your application.

6. What is the timeline for the application development?

Write down both what your desired timeline is as well as how much time you think it will take you to complete the various parts of the application. Remember that if you're hiring outside contractors for parts of your applica-tion, you need to be aware of their availability as well as your own. Don't forget to include time for testing, revision, and user testing and feedback.

After you have a plan for what you want your application to do, you'll want to start working on what the application should look like. I like to do simple mockups on paper or in a graphics program to get a feel for what I think the application or page will look like. Figure 6.1 shows a simple mockup of how you might want an applica-tion to look on a smartphone such as an iPhone and a tablet such as an iPad.

FIGURE 6.1
A mockup of a puzzle app for a tablet and smartphone.

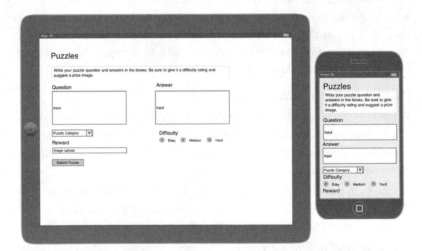

As you can see, the preliminary mockups do not have to be fancy. In fact, you don't even need to have colors or images. You just need a general sense of how you want the pages to look.

Building the Application in HTML

After you have a basic plan of the functionality and how you want it to look, you can start building the layout. I like to build the smartphone layout first because it is usually one column and straightforward HTML.

Building the HTML for a Puzzle Application

The puzzle application will let people write simple text puzzles online and save them for others to solve. To build this application you need at least four pages:

▶ A homepage

▶ A puzzle list page

▶ A puzzle creation page

▶ A puzzle solve page

Here are the steps to build a puzzle application.

1. First write the HTML for the home page:

```
<!doctype html>
<html>
<head>
    <title>Puzzles</title>
</head>
<body>
    <section id="container">
        <header id="header">
        <h1>Puzzles</h1>
        </header>
        <section id="intro">
            <p>This is the introductory text to my puzzles home
➥page.</p>
            <p>Duis aute irure dolor ut enim ad minim veniam, ut
➥aliquip ex ea commodo consequat. Sed do eiusmod tempor incididunt
➥velit esse cillum dolore in reprehenderit in voluptate. Eu fugiat
➥nulla pariatur. Duis aute irure dolor mollit anim id est laborum.
Qui officia deserunt lorem ipsum dolor sit amet, velit esse cillum
➥dolore.</p>
        </section>
        <section id="login">
            <h2>Login</h2>
            <form action="#">
                <label for="username">Username:</label><br>
                <input type="text" name="username" size="12"><br>
```

```
                <label for="password">Password:</label><br>
                <input type="password" name="password" size="12"><br>
                <input type="submit" value="Login">
            </form>
            <p><a>Lost password</a>  <a>Register</a></p>
        </section>
        <footer>
            <h3>&copy;2011 &#8211; My Puzzle Site</h3>
        </footer>
    </section>
</body>
</html>
```

All the subsequent pages will have a similar format for the HTML.

Notice that all the boxes are placed in sections to make them easier to adjust with CSS and JavaScript.

2. For the subsequent pages, create sections for the additional elements on each page, such as the puzzle entry fields and data. First, create a section that provides a list of available puzzles for the user to choose from:

```
<section id="puzzle-list">
    <h2>Puzzles List</h2>
    <table>
        <tr>
            <th>Name</th>
            <th>Author</th>
            <th>Category</th>
            <th>Difficulty</th>
            <th>Completed?</th>
        </tr>
        <tr>
            <td>Puzzle1</td>
            <td>Author1</td>
            <td>Category1</td>
            <td>Easy</td>
            <td>No <a>Try Now</a></td>
        </tr>
    </table>
</section>
```

3. Next, provide a section that allows the user to create a new puzzle:

```
<section id="create-puzzle">
    <h2>Create a New Puzzle</h2>
    <form method="post" action="#">
        <label for=pname>Puzzle Name:</label><br>
        <input type=text name=pname size=50><br>
        <label for=pquestion>Puzzle Question:</label><br>
        <textarea name=pquestion rows=5 cols=50></textarea><br>
        <label for=panswer>Puzzle Answer</label>
```

```
            ...
        </form>
    </section>
```

4. Finally, create a section where the user can complete the puzzle:

```
<section id="solve-puzzle">
    <h2>Solve a Puzzle</h2>
    <h3>Puzzle Name</h3>
    <p class="question">Q: This is the puzzle question?</p>
    <form method="post" action="#">
        <label for=panswer>Your Answer</label>
        A: <textarea name=panswer rows=5 cols=50></textarea><br>
        <input type=submit name=submit value=Submit>
    </form>
</section>
```

These four pages are pretty ugly, but you can use CSS to make them look better.

After you have the HTML, you have the beginnings of a web application. By using JavaScript and server-side scripting, you make your page interactive. Scripts turn a plain web page into an application. Hour 5, "JavaScript and HTML5 Web Applications," discusses them in detail.

Using CSS to Make the HTML Look Good

Looking at plain HTML is about as boring as you can possibly imagine. Plain HTML documents are black and white, have no images or colors, and don't even change the positions of the items in the layout. The text is displayed on the page in one long column in the same order it's placed in the HTML. By using CSS you can change the font family and color, add background colors and images, and even change how the page layout looks.

Changing the Type

Changing the type in your web application is typically a case of choosing the size and font family you want to use for your headlines and body text. Hour 11, "Fonts and Typography in HTML5," offers more information about fonts but for now, focus on the font sizes and families.

You might think that choosing a font size is just a matter of using whatever the browser decides to use. But there's more to choosing a size than the browser consideration. Most computers display fonts at a default size of 16px. However, to build a site or application that works well in mobile devices, you should not use pixels as a measurement. You should use a measurement that is relative to the browser: either ems or percentages.

An *em*, in HTML documents, is equal to the current default font size. So, minus any styling, 1 em would be 16px. But this font size is pretty big, so most designers want to scale it down. Although you can simply give your fonts a smaller em size (like 0.8 em), scaling down the default size, and then using ems, is much easier.

To reset the default font size from 16px to 10px (a number most people have no problem multiplying and dividing), add the following to your style sheet:

```
body {
    font-size: 62.5%;
}
```

Notice that you use a percentage here: 10px is 62.5% of 16px.

Perhaps you want to use 14px font for your pages. Set your paragraph tags to 1.4 ems (14px divided by 10 is 1.4):

```
p {
    font-size: 1.4em;
    line-height: 1.8em;
}
```

Specifying the line height in ems is also a good idea. For the best-looking text, having nice wide spaces between lines is a good idea. This makes the pages easier to read. I generally add 5 to 7 pixels to the font size for the line height. So with a 10px base font, that would be around 0.5 ems added to the font size. Be sure to play around with it, as you can see in the earlier code, only 0.4 ems was added to the font size for the line height.

Font families are a fun thing to play with. As mentioned in Hour 3, "Styling Mobile Pages with CSS3," you should use a font stack to make sure that at least one of the fonts is one that your users have on their machine. But beyond that, what fonts you choose are completely up to you.

Watch
Out!

Don't Go Crazy with Fonts
Most mobile devices, even modern smartphones and tablets, don't have a lot of fonts installed. Android came with three: Droid Sans, Droid Mono, and Droid Serif, but users can download more. iOS comes with more than three, but still not nearly as many as your average computer.

One thing you shouldn't worry too much about is sans serif versus serif. The feeling used to be that sans serif fonts were easier to read online because of the pixelation caused by low-resolution monitors. The serifs tended to run together in smaller font sizes. But these days most people have fairly high resolution monitors that can clearly display both serif and sans serif fonts without a lot of trouble.

You should limit your page to no more than two or three different typefaces. For body text and headlines you should limit yourself to just serif and sans serif fonts (rather than using the more specialized script, fantasy, and monospace fonts). For the puzzle application, the headlines are in serif and the body text is sans serif:

```
h1, h2, h3, h4, h5, h6 {
    font-family: "Palatino Linotype", "Book Antiqua", Palatino, serif;
}
p {
    font-family: "Trebuchet MS", Arial, Helvetica, sans-serif;
}
```

Watch
Out!

> **Paragraphs are Not the Only Text**
>
> Remember that when you set the base font size on the body tag, that is the size that all fonts that are not styled will be. Fonts that are 10 pixels in size can be very difficult to read, so be sure to add styles for other plain text elements such as <li>, <dd>, and <dt>, or make sure that all your text is enclosed in a paragraph tag.

Adding Colors and Background Images

You can choose colors for your application or website in many different ways. Some people just start with a favorite color, or you can grab the palette of a photograph. If you don't know what colors you want to use, the site ColourLovers (www. colourlovers.com/) can provide inspiration. They have a whole section just for web palettes, patterns, and colors.

For the Puzzles application, start with a blue color as the base as well as white and a few other colors in the design. Following is the complimentary scheme to use for the application:

- ▶ #3c6ac4—The blue you started with
- ▶ #3c3cc3—A darker blue for accents
- ▶ #c3963c—A tan for highlights
- ▶ #000000—Black for text
- ▶ #ffffff—White for the background

The application will also have an image for the logo area of a puzzle piece. Having several versions of the image is a good idea so you can eventually change them periodically.

You can change the color of your fonts with the `color` property, like this:

`color: #000000;`

If you want to change the color of a background, you use the `background-color` property, like this:

`background-color: #3c6ac4;`

CSS also lets you set background images on your designs with the `background-image` property. You set the image by pointing to a URL like this:

`background-image: url('background.png');`

This tiles the image in the background. To prevent the tiling, you can use the `background-repeat` property. You should then define where the image should display with the `background-position` property. You can also set the background image, color, tiling, and position with one property: `background`.

To add a background image on a white background that is not repeated and placed 1 em down and 1 em left of the upper-left corner of the container element, you would write:

`background: #fff url(background.png) no-repeat 1em 1em;`

Styling the Layout

From the mockup in Figure 6.1, you can see that, for iPad and larger screens, you're going to create a two-column layout with what is often called a *fat footer*. This is where the footer contains additional information and is often much taller than strictly necessary. This has the design benefit of weighting the bottom of the page, which draws the eye down, helping to encourage your users to read the whole page.

But the really interesting part of this layout is how it will handle the mobile and non-mobile pages. You want devices that have a viewing window of less than 480 pixels to see just one column, while larger viewing windows will display the two-column layout (and four-column footer). Then, for devices with less than 320 pixels of viewing width, you will remove the graphics as well, so that the pages display more quickly and don't take up a lot of space. Figure 6.2 shows the same page in three ways—in a less than 320-pixel-wide feature phone emulation, on an iPod touch (320 pixels wide), and in a full-screen Android tablet. The HTML remains completely the same; only the CSS changes depending on the width of the viewport.

FIGURE 6.2
The same
HTML page on
a smartphone,
an iPod touch,
and an Android
tablet.

> **Don't Repeat CSS that Remains the Same in All Devices**
>
> When you use CSS3 media queries, you can leave out styles that will remain the same across different devices. The main CSS style sheet should have a media type of all or screen, so all devices will read it. Then you use your media query style sheets only to modify the main one.

Did you Know?

Try It Yourself

Adding CSS3 Media Queries to a Web Page

Learn how to add media queries to your web applications to support feature phones, smartphones, tablets, and computer browsers. In this example, tablets and browsers use the same style sheet, but you can create a style sheet just for tablets if you want.

1. Link your main style sheet as usual in the <head> of your document.

2. Below that style sheet, add your first media query style sheet for feature phones that are less than 320 pixels wide:

   ```
   <link rel="stylesheet" href="styles-320.css"
   media="only screen and (max-width:320px)">
   ```

3. Add your media query for smart phones that are between 320 and 480 pixels wide:

   ```
   <link rel="stylesheet" href="styles-480.css"
   media="only screen and (min-width:320px) and (max-width:480px)">
   ```

   You can test what your style sheets are doing by resizing your web browser to smaller than 320 pixels wide and between 320 and 480 pixels. When you reload, the page should change.

One thing you may notice: If you test it right now in a device such as an iPhone or Nexus, you will see the full version of the site, not the smartphone version. This is because these devices have actual dots per inch (DPI) of more than 480 pixels wide. The next section shows you how you can solve that problem.

▲

Adding Mobile Meta Tags for More Effective HTML5 Pages

If you followed the earlier instructions to create a mobile version of your site, you may notice that the single column layout does not appear when you test it on modern smartphones such as the iPhone. This is because the media queries are asking the browser for the width, and the iPhone (and Android phones as well) reports the width based on its resolution. This means that instead of seeing a layout like that shown in Figure 6.2 on your iPhone or iPod touch, you see the full two-column layout, as shown in Figure 6.3.

This layout is not very friendly on a small screen. It is true that on iOS and Android you can zoom in on the layout, but that is one extra step. Instead, you can use a meta tag to tell the browser to consider the width the same as the device width, rather than the DPI width. You do this with the viewport meta tag:

```
<meta name="viewport" content="width=device-width">
```

You can use a number of meta tags to help make your web application more friendly to mobile devices:

▶ `mobileOptimized`—This meta tag was created for Pocket IE. For the content, you put a width in pixels. When this tag is present, the browser will force the layout to one column.

▶ `handheldFriendly`—AvantGo and Palm originally used this meta tag to indicate content that should not be scaled on mobile devices. The content is true for mobile pages and false for non-mobile pages.

▶ `viewport`—This meta tag controls the dimensions and scaling of the browser window in iOS, Android, webOS, Opera Mini, Opera Mobile, and Blackberry. This tag is covered in detail later in this section.

▶ `apple-mobile-web-app-capable`—If the content attribute of the meta tag is "yes" then the web application runs in full-screen mode. If "no," then it doesn't.

FIGURE 6.3
The two-column
layout on an
iPod touch.

▶ **apple-mobile-web-app-status-bar-style**—If your application is in
full-screen mode, then you can change the status bar on iOS devices to
"black" or "black-translucent."

▶ **format-detection**—This meta tag turns on or off the automatic detection
of possible phone numbers. The content value can be telephone=no. The
default is telephone=yes.

▶ **apple-touch-startup-image**—This isn't a meta tag. It is a <link> that
allows you to specify a startup image that is displayed while your web
application launches. iOS will otherwise use a screenshot of the web application the last time it was used. Set a startup image that is 320 x 460 pixels
by adding <link rel="apple-touch-startup-image"
href="/startup.png"> to your document.

▶ `apple-touch-icon` and `apple-touch-icon-precomposed`—This also isn't a meta tag. But if you add `<link rel="apple-touch-icon" href="/icon.png">` to your document, you can specify an icon that will be used to save your application to the home screen. Adding `-precomposed` to the end will help it work on Android 1.5 and 1.6 and will remove effects from the icon on iOS. Save your icons as a PNG at least 57 x 57 pixels in size.

> **Android Doesn't Always Support All the Meta Tags**
>
> Some versions of Android (1.5, 1.6, 2.1, and so on) don't support all the preceding meta tags reliably. The touch icon can be messed up by expired SSL certificates for secure (https) websites, and some HTC-manufactured phones such as the Evo display them oddly. The other `apple-*` meta tags may or may not be supported. Be sure to test on Android if these are critical to your application.

In most cases, the only meta tag you'll need to add to your application is the `viewport` meta tag. The best way to do this is to set the width of your application to the device width. This keeps your application from scaling within the browser and prevents your users from having to zoom in to view your application.

When using the `viewport` meta tag, you can adjust several properties:

▶ `width`—The width of the viewport in pixels. The default is 980. You can set this to a number between 200 and 10,000.

▶ `height`—The height of the viewport in pixels. The default is calculated based on the width and the aspect ratio of the device. You can set this to a number between 223 and 10,000.

▶ `initial-scale`—How zoomed in your application starts out at. The user can then scale in and out from that starting point.

▶ `minimum-scale`—The minimum scale value of the viewport. The default is 0.25. You can set it between 0 and 10.0.

▶ `maximum-scale`—The maximum scale value of the viewport. The default is 1.6. You can set it between 0 and 10.0.

▶ `user-scalable`—You can set whether your users can zoom in and out in your application. The default is "yes." Set it to "no" if you don't want to allow scaling.

> **Be Careful When You Disallow User Scaling**
>
> Although you can do things with the `viewport user-scalable` property such as turn off the ability of users to zoom in and out, this can affect whether your users can even see all the content. If the content is hidden, and you've turned off zooming, they will just leave, rather than tell you that they couldn't view your page.

You can also use two property values: `device-width` and `device-height`. These set the width and height to those available on the device.

You can set more than one viewport option in your meta tag by separating them with commas. For example:

```
<meta name="viewport" content="width=device-width, user-scalable=no">
```

Optimizing Your Site for Mobile

Mobile users have somewhat different needs than desktop and laptop users, both because they are on smaller screens and often have bandwidth limitations. So to make sure your site is best optimized for mobile users you should keep some of the following best practices in mind:

▶ **Keep the design simple**—The smaller the device, the simpler the design should be. The simplest layout is a single column.

▶ **Never use horizontal scrolling**—Some phones simply can't scroll horizontally, and so the content is completely unavailable to them. Even on the iPad, scroll bars don't always show up until the user tries to scroll, so horizontal scrolling can hide your content there, too.

▶ **Use big buttons**—Putting lots of tiny links together all in one place can be incredibly annoying for mobile users. Both Android and iOS handle taps well, but don't create links that expect people to have the fingers of a two-year-old. This is especially important if you have turned off their ability to scale the page.

▶ **Always offer a choice of how to view the site**—You can do your best to optimize a site so that it works well on mobile devices, but sometimes people will want to see the full site, and you should allow them to do so.

Don't Simply Redirect to Your Mobile Home Page

When a user clicks on a link from another source (such as Google), many sites simply redirect the user from the page he wanted to the mobile-friendly home page. In most cases, unless the user was intending to visit your home page, this practice is more annoying than helpful, especially if the link he wanted to visit is not visible on the home page. This is an effective way to lose mobile visitors.

▶ **Remember user preference**—After you know that users like viewing the full version of your site on their iPad or Xoom, then you should use cookies to always show them that version, with, of course, the option to switch back if they want.

▶ **Make data input as painless as possible**—Even on large tablets like the Xoom, doing data entry can be more difficult than on a computer. Having automated sign-in functions, saving data, and using the relevant <input> types to get better input fields all make filling in a form on a mobile device easier.

▶ **Keep your applications small**—Focus on bandwidth at all stages of your application, from the images and content, through the HTTP requests to the web server, and to compressed files. Remember that most smartphones have a data limit, so the smaller your pages are, the less they will impact that limit.

▶ **Add mobile-specific functions**—By using the device functionality such as built-in GPS and telephones, your application will feel more like a native application. Plus, these functions are designed for mobile devices, and so are easier to use than any non-mobile counterparts.

Using Click-to-Call

Click-to-call or click-to-talk is a way of adding links to web pages and applications that point directly to telephone numbers. This enables users of browsers that support this feature to simply tap on a linked number and either call it or send an SMS message. All you need to write is <a href="tel:14255025366"> as your phone number link. Figure 6.4 shows how this might work.

▶ **Reduce perception of wait times**—Use techniques to make wait times seem less onerous like putting your scripts at the bottom of the HTML, using spinners and progress bars to show that something is happening, and preload images and data to make use of caches.

▶ **Optimize all images**—Avoid large and high-resolution images, specify the size of images in the HTML, and always use alternative text.

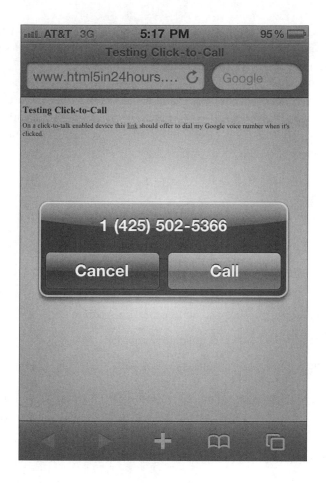

FIGURE 6.4
Click-to-talk link
on an iPhone.

▶ **Use colors that are readable**—Good contrast between the foreground and background is important to make sure that your site is readable on small screens.

▶ **Do not use pixel measurements**—Pixels and absolute measurements do not render well on small screens. Use ems or percentages instead.

▶ **Keep your content as clear as possible**—All your pages should have a page title that is short and descriptive. And the contents of your pages should be clear and use direct language.

▶ **Be careful of technology that might break on some devices**—Some modern technology is not well supported on older mobile devices. Be sure to have a fallback for things like cookies, embedded objects, tables, style sheets, fonts, and colors.

▶ **Avoid technology that is known to break on mobile devices**—This includes pop-up windows, nested tables, tables for layout, graphics for spacing and layout, frames, and image maps.

Many of the best practices for building mobile web applications are just as important for non-mobile devices as well. If you design applications that work for one web, in other words, as many devices and browsers as possible, you'll have applications that are more robust and happy customers.

Summary

In this hour you learned how to create a website and application that is mobile friendly as well as non-mobile friendly. You learned how to design for "one web."

You learned how to create a site plan, which is important for creating an application or site that meets the needs of all your users. This includes:

▶ Determining the purpose and goals of the application

▶ Identifying the customers, competitors, and risks

▶ Preparing a timeline for creating the application

You also learned how to start building a web application with HTML and CSS, as well as how to use CSS3 media queries and mobile meta tags to get your designs to show up effectively on different devices.

Finally, you learned a number of tips for optimizing a site for mobile devices.

Q&A

Q. *In Hour 4 you discussed graceful degradation, but in this hour you discussed progressive enhancements. Which should I use?*

A. Use both methods if at all possible. This way, your site will appear to improve as users get more capable browsers, and yet you can still set a minimum standard of browser that you will fully support. This makes your work slightly less onerous, because you don't have to fully support every browser and mobile device out there, but you can add in the fun, cutting-edge things to your site.

Q. *I noticed that your HTML did not have a lot of support for IE 8 and lower, but I need to support those browsers. What can I do?*

A. The best way to support IE 8 and lower is to surround your HTML5 tags with `<div>` tags with IDs on them. For example, the HTML provided in this hour had sections called `<section id="container">`. You could put a `<div>` in front and move the ID to that: `<div id="container"><section>`, and then your styles will work even in IE 8.

Q. *Where can I learn more about the mobile meta tags?*

A. The Apple iOS Developer Center (http://developer.apple.com/devcenter/ios/index.action) is a great place to start. It offers many articles, guides, and references on building applications for iOS. The Android Developers pages (http://developer.android.com/index.html) are also a great resource.

Workshop

The workshop contains quiz questions to help you process what you've learned in this chapter. Try to answer all the questions before you read the answers. See Appendix A, "Answers to Quizzes," for answers.

Quiz

1. What is a "SMART" goal?

2. How big is an em?

3. What does the `apple-touch-startup-image` meta tag do? How do you install it in your web page?

4. What are three best practices you should follow when building a mobile web application?

Exercises

1. Write a plan for a web application or website based on the information you read in this hour.

2. Check out the HTML source code for the application you started in this hour. You can see the working application, with all the features discussed in this hour at http://puzzles.kyrnin.com/.

3. Build a web page and turn off the scaling with meta tags. Upload the page to a web server and test the page in a mobile device. If you did it correctly, you should not be able to resize the page.

Upgrading a Site to HTML5

What You'll Learn in This Hour:

▶ Facts about HTML 4 and the browsers you think support it

▶ How to make the jump to HTML5—it's not as hard as you think

▶ How to evaluate the browsers that currently visit your site

▶ What HTML5 features you can use now

▶ What features you can use with minimal risk

Building a website is a challenging endeavor. One of the biggest challenges is deciding when to update an existing website to new technology. This hour will show you how to decide when moving to more modern technology is a good idea.

You'll learn more about the differences between HTML5 and HTML 4 and what features are supported by which browsers.

Browser support isn't the only reason to consider updating your website. Some features of HTML5 can take your site from good to great, even if not all browsers support them, and some features can turn a standard website into a killer mobile application.

Deciding When and How to Upgrade from HTML 4

HTML 4 or HTML 4.01 has been supported by many browsers since the 1990s. It was made a standard in 1998. The benefit to using an established standard is that browser support is nearly universal, or at least it should be.

But before you start thinking about staying with HTML 4 for the long term, you should consider a few things:

▶ HTML 4 support in web browsers isn't nearly as widespread as you might think. In fact, some of the most popular browsers in use today don't follow the standard.

▶ Many devices have browsers that don't support all of HTML 4 or only support it minimally.

▶ Many devices also have browsers that have good support for HTML5, and their use is growing.

Ultimately, if you are planning on working as a web designer for the next few years, sticking with only HTML 4 is a bad career move. HTML5 offers more features and more functionality than HTML 4, and the devices that use them are growing in popularity.

Popular Browser Support for Current Standards

At the end of April 2011, Internet Explorer 6 had 2.86% of the browser market.[1] This may not seem like a lot, but extrapolated over the entire web, that is a huge number of browsers. In fact, IE 6 is still in the top 10 most popular browsers.

The problem is that IE 6 has a large number of bugs that make it very difficult to design for. The most well-known bug is the way IE 6 handles floated margins. If you use the CSS from the standards to add a margin to a box with a floated element inside it, IE 6 will double that margin, as shown in Figure 7.1

Many other bugs similar to this one exist, where Internet Explorer 6 does not support the HTML and CSS standards correctly. Yet, it is a very popular browser.

Of course, then IE 7 came out and fixed this problem—but it didn't, exactly. You see, Microsoft was concerned that many web pages were written with hacks to support IE 6, so it added a "compatibility mode" to IE 7 and 8. This mode forces the browsers to act like the buggy IE 5 and IE 6 versions.

Many designers feel they can't move from HTML 4 to HTML5 (or CSS2 to CSS3) until the majority of browsers support HTML5 and CSS3 features. Compatibility mode means that even if people upgrade to modern versions of IE, these versions will still not support HTML5 and CSS3.

---

[1] "April 2011." W3Counter. April 30, 2011. www.w3counter.com/globalstats. php?year=2011&month=4. Referenced May 5, 2011.

Standards add 100px to the left margin

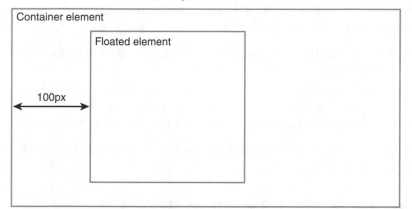

Internet Explorer Doubles that to 200px

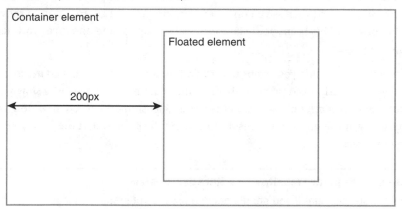

FIGURE 7.1
A representation of a well-known IE 6 bug where margins are doubled.

In many ways, Internet Explorer single-handedly held back web designs with the bad standards support in versions 5 and 6 and the implementation of "compatibility mode" in versions 7 and 8. Because of compatibility mode, web designers are forced to continue to support hacks and workarounds just to ensure that their pages are viewable by Internet Explorer, the most commonly used browser.

Even Microsoft Wants IE 6 to Die

Microsoft has a website called "The Internet Explorer 6 Countdown" (www.theie6countdown.com/default.aspx) to help people transition away from this old browser. The company is counting down to the day when Internet Explorer 6 is no longer used and is encouraging companies and individuals to move away from this browser version. Microsoft even offers a banner you can display just to IE 6 users to encourage them to upgrade (www.theie6countdown.com/join-us.aspx).

Other popular browsers include Firefox, Chrome, and Safari. Popular mobile browsers are Opera, Android, and iOS Safari. Mobile browsers are not as far along in their support of HTML5, but they have better support than IE 6, 7, or 8.

On desktop browsers, Firefox 4, Safari 5, Chrome 5, and Opera 11 all have good support of HTML5 features. These browsers support 60% or more of the features in the HTML5 specifications. Mobile browsers don't have as good support as desktop browsers with Android 3.0 and Opera mobile 11.5 supporting 60% or more of the features. iOS and Android 2.3 support a little less than 50% of HTML5 features.

So when you design pages in HTML5, in general, the only browser you need to worry about is Internet Explorer.

Making a Gradual Switch to HTML5

Instead of waiting for that distant day when all browsers support the HTML5 standard, you should use progressive enhancement and graceful degradation to move your site forward. This keeps your skills and website up to date and gives your users a reason to upgrade.

The best way to upgrade your website is to do it gradually. This is called *iterative design*. Iterative design is a process where changes are made to a website slowly and gradually and with a lot of testing. Rather than releasing an entirely new and different website, you use an iterative design to add small changes that are barely noticed by the customers.

Some Very Popular Websites Use Iterative Design

If you are still not sure if you should begin a process of gradual changes to your website to move it from HTML 4 to HTML5, then you will be relieved to know that many popular sites make changes in exactly this way. Amazon.com, a popular ecommerce site, uses iterative design to add changes to its pages gradually. In fact, many of its changes have been done so gradually that its customers don't even realize it's happening. This provides minimal disruption to customers, and so minimal disruption to the company's income.

When you're considering upgrading to HTML5, you should take into account things such as:

▶ What browsers are used to visit your site

▶ The amount of mobile use your site gets

▶ How your site could benefit from upgrading to HTML5

▶ What resources you have to commit to a major redesign

When making gradual changes, start with your least popular pages, the ones that get the fewest page views. That way, if a huge problem occurs with the changes you make, it won't affect as many people and you can more easily fix the problem.

To add HTML5 to your site gradually, you can add the HTML5 features in a *split test* (some users seeing the old version, some the new) to compare how the new features perform. This type of testing lets you discover how to best make the transition to HTML5. You can use the Google Website Optimizer (www.google.com/websiteoptimizer/b/index.html) to do split testing on your websites.

Evaluating What Browsers Are Used to Visit Your Site

The first thing you should think about when deciding to upgrade your site is what browsers support the technology you're considering. You might be tempted to go to a site like W3Counter.com, note that Internet Explorer still has the largest market share, and give up on HTML5 before you even start. As mentioned earlier, many designers do exactly that.

But W3Counter.com only shows the stats for the sites that it tracks. This is a large number of sites, but every site is different. For example, consider Apple.com. Although the likelihood exists that some people on Internet Explorer visit the Apple.com site, IE's having the browser share that it has on W3Counter.com is unlikely. Another site might get as high as 76% Firefox users. That site designer should avoid focusing on Internet Explorer.

By the Way

HTML5 Can Bring You Customers

You may be losing customers because you don't use HTML5. Many designers focus so much on the users who are currently coming to their site that they forget that current customers aren't the entire market. The possibility exists that people using Safari (which has good HTML5 support) or Chrome (which has excellent support) would spend more money or give you more revenue than the Internet Explorer users to whom you are currently catering.

Before you change your site because of the apparent lack of HTML5 browser support globally, look at your site's statistics. What are the top 10 browsers and versions that are used to visit your site? Remember that most websites don't get as many mobile visitors as they do regular browsers, so you might want to separate out the top 10 mobile browsers as well. Don't look at just one month of data. Get between three and six months data if possible. This gives you a better idea of how the browser usage is changing on your site as well as what browsers you need to think about.

After you have an idea of the 10 most popular desktop and mobile browsers that are currently used to visit your site, you can then start thinking about what HTML5 features you want to add to your site.

▼   **Try It Yourself**

Viewing Users' Browsers in Google Analytics

If you have Google Analytics on your website, you can quickly see an overview of the browsers that come to visit.

1. Log in to your Google Analytics account (www.google.com/analytics/).

2. View your report and go to the "Visitors" section.

3. Click on "Browser Capabilities" and then "Browsers."

4. Click on the name of the browser to find out the versions that are used to visit your site. Be sure to count out the page views you may have added during testing so that you don't include those.

▲

The Trending Up of Mobile Internet Browsing

After you know what browsers are used to visit your site, you might be tempted to build your site to cater to them. But browser use changes all the time. In fact, just because right now your site doesn't get a lot of mobile use, doesn't mean that it won't in the future. In December 2010, it was found that 20% of all US and UK internet users *only* browse the web over mobile devices.[2] In Africa and Asia, that number is closer to 50%. A lot more people do periodic web browsing on mobile, and with the growth in popularity of tablets like the iPad, that fact is becoming even more so. The first iPad had sales figures in the millions in just the first few weeks, and analysts estimate that between 400,000 and 800,000 iPad 2s sold in the first three days.[3] Mobile use will likely continue to grow in the future for all sites. If you are starting to write pages that support mobile, your site will be ahead of the game.

---

[2] "Mobile web growth: 1 in 5 internet users don't use a computer." GoMo News. Dec 14, 2010. www.gomonews.com/mobile-web-growth-1-in-5-internet-users-dont-use-a-computer/. May 7, 2011.

[3] "Apple's iPad 2 Chalks Up Strong Sales in Weekend Debut." *Wall Street Journal*. Mar 14, 2011. http://online.wsj.com/article/SB10001424052748704027504576198832667732862. html#ixzz1Lhyg4KkS. May 7, 2011.

HTML5 is well positioned to support mobile devices. iOS and Android devices are growing in popularity, and as they do, it's going to become more apparent that applications based on standards that work on both are more cost effective. HTML5, as a standard that is already gaining support on these platforms, is a natural progression.

HTML5 Features that Work Right Now

If you are wondering where to start with HTML5, you should start with the things that are working right now. By *right now*, either they really do work in the majority of modern browsers and devices out there or they are ignored by modern browsers, and so don't break things in browsers that don't support them.

To change an existing page from HTML 4.01 to HTML5, follow these steps:

1. Change your doctype to the new HTML5 doctype: `<!doctype html>`. This won't hurt any browsers at all. If they don't recognize the doctype they will simply ignore it. At worst, IE 8 and lower might go into compatibility mode.

    By changing your doctype to the new HTML5 doctype you are in effect announcing your intentions to move ahead with the new soon-to-be standard. The new doctype also is smaller and so helps reduce the characters your users have to download.

2. Use the new character set meta tag: `<meta charset=utf-8>`. This is already supported by all the major browsers.

Always Declare Character Encoding

Even if you never plan to use any non-English characters, you should specify your character set in the `<head>` of your HTML. If you don't your site could be vulnerable to cross-site scripting attacks.

---

3. Simplify `<script>` and `<style>` tags. You no longer need to use the `type` attribute for JavaScript (ECMAScript) or Cascading Style Sheets. Leaving this attribute off helps streamline your HTML.

4. Link entire blocks rather than just the text within them. Browsers don't have a problem if you put an `<a>` tag around a `<p>`, and linking an entire paragraph is much easier to click than one or two words within it. This includes all the elements within the paragraph block as well.

5. Use the form input types. If you are requesting a telephone number, then use the `type=tel` and use `type=email` for email addresses. Browsers that don't support them will display a text field as normal, and browsers that do

support them will give extra functionality. Hour 13, "HTML5 Forms," discusses this topic more.

6. Use the `<video>` and `<audio>` tags for video and audio and include fallback options for older browsers. Hour 12, "Audio and Video in HTML5," discusses more about how to do this.

7. Even if you don't use the HTML5 tags, you can use the sectioning elements as class names in your document.

   For example, instead of using `<header>` you could use `<div class="header">`. This is sometimes also called *POSH* or Plain Old Semantic HTML.

8. Finally, use the new semantic tags whenever appropriate. Tags such as `<mark>` and `<time>` provide additional information about the content. Browsers that don't support them simply ignore them.

Even if the preceding steps represent all the HTML5 you feel comfortable with doing right now, you will be improving your website. But if you want to move into more cutting-edge technology, look at the state of browser support and at what features you want to add and why.

The State of HTML5 Browser Support

Before you dismiss HTML5 because Internet Explorer 8 doesn't support it, you should realize that even IE 8 supports some bits of HTML5. For example:

▶ **contenteditable**—This is a new HTML5 attribute that Internet Explorer supports back to version 5.5. However, this attribute is not supported by any mobile browsers as of this writing. Hour 14, "Editing Content and User Interaction with HTML5," discusses this more.

▶ **Drag and drop**—Drag and drop is another implementation that was developed by Microsoft and has been supported by IE since version 5. It's not currently supported by Opera or iOS, however. Hour 16, "Working with HTML5 Drag-and-Drop Functionality," discusses this more.

▶ **Datasets and the data-* attributes**—This has great support on Chrome and Opera 11.1, but it has limited support on IE, Firefox, Safari, Android, iOS, and Opera Mini and Mobile. Hour 17, "HTML5 Links," covers this topic more.

HTML5 also has a number of things that, though they aren't supported by IE 8, they are supported in IE 9:

- ▶ **Canvas**—IE 9, as well as all the other browsers, can display canvas tags. In fact the only browser that doesn't support it is Opera Mini. Hour 10, "Drawing with the HTML5 Canvas Element," covers the canvas element.

- ▶ **Video**—IE 8, Safari 3.2, iOS 3.2, Opera Mini, and Opera Mobile 10 don't support the video tag. Android 2.2 and 2.1 have limited support. However, many browsers and more recent versions of Safari and iOS support it. You'll learn about the video tag in Hour 12.

- ▶ **Audio**—Audio has the same support as video. Hour 12 covers it as well.

- ▶ **Offline web applications**—This feature isn't supported by IE 9, but it does have good mobile support on iOS and Android, and good support on Firefox, Safari, Opera and Chrome. Hour 21, "Web Storage in HTML5," goes into more detail.

But that's not the sum total of features available in HTML5. Other features have support in various browsers:

- ▶ **The new semantic elements**—These new elements are supported in all the current browser versions. They aren't supported by IE 8, but a workaround is available. Hour 9, "Adding Meaning with HTML5 Sectioning and Semantic Elements," covers these elements.

- ▶ **Ruby annotations**—Although no browser has full support for ruby annotations, IE has supported them partially since version 6. Chrome has had support since version 8. Safari 5 and Android 3 have partial support as well. Learn more about ruby annotations in Hour 14, "Editing Content and User Interaction with HTML5."

- ▶ **History management**—Current versions of Chrome, Android, and Firefox all support the history API. Safari and iOS have partial support. Hour 22, "Controlling the Browser History with the History API," can teach you all about the history API.

Adding HTML5 Features as Extras on Your Site

One way you can add HTML5 to your site is to add it as extras so that if the browsers ignore them, the user won't miss anything. But if the browsers do support them, the users will get an added bonus.

Here are some HTML5 elements you can add to your pages right now:

▶ **figure** and **figcaption**—These tags allow you to define sections of your documents as self-contained content blocks.

▶ **mark** – With the mark tag you can highlight a block of text for reference purposes.

▶ **small** – This HTML 4 tag has been made more semantic in HTML5. Now it refers to fine print, not just text written in a smaller font.

▶ **time** – The time tag defines both dates and times.

Hour 9 covers these sectioning and semantic elements in more detail.

Using the preceding elements is not all you can do to improve your site with HTML5. For example, HTML5 has some syntax rules that are more relaxed and will help your pages load more quickly:

▶ You don't need to quote attributes. If your attributes don't have spaces in them, then you can leave off the quotation marks. This simplifies your HTML and reduces the characters to download.

▶ Use the new doctype: `<!doctype html>`. It's shorter, easy to remember, and doesn't affect browser performance at all.

By the Way

Using the New Doctype Is Catching

Even Google.com uses the new doctype, and Google gets some of the most page views on the internet. If Google can use the new doctype, it shouldn't hurt your site either.

▶ You don't have to worry about case. HTML5 doesn't require that you worry about the case of your tags and attributes. I recommend that you still stick with all lowercase, but it's not a requirement.

Browsers also ignore form features if they don't support them. But browsers that support them make your forms more effective. Here are some HTML5 form features to add value to your forms:

▶ **Use placeholder attributes.** Placeholder text is a great way to show how form fields should be filled out.

▶ **Define required fields.** Always validate required fields at both the server and client level. Browsers that don't support the `required` attribute ignore it.

▶ **Set autofocus.** Autofocus puts the cursor right inside the first form element. You are probably already doing this with JavaScript, so adding the `autofocus` attribute won't hurt anything.

▶ **Check out local storage options.** Local storage can improve your forms and applications by giving more space to the data.

Hour 13 covers the form elements in more detail. You can learn more about local storage in Hour 21.

Some new features aren't technically HTML5, but they can also add more sparkle to your website:

▶ **CSS3**—Cascading Style Sheets level 3 has support in many browsers, and more parts of it are supported all the time. Using it is a great way to improve your site. See Hour 3, "Styling Mobile Pages with CSS3."

▶ **SVG**—Scalable Vector Graphics is supported in the current versions of all web browsers except Android 2.3. Hour 10 discusses more about SVG.

HTML5 Features that Turn Your Site into a Killer Mobile Application

HTML5 isn't just a way to improve websites for computer browsers. Some features of HTML5 seem almost custom-made for mobile devices:

▶ **Geolocation**—Geolocation is a separate API that is often included in the HTML5 basket, and it is a perfect tool for mobile applications. Location services are very useful on mobile devices, which move around. You'll learn how to use the Geolocation API in Hour 23, "Adding Location Detection with Geolocation."

▶ **Offline applications**—Mobile devices move around, and they are not always online. Offline applications are perfect for mobile devices because they work whether there's an internet connection or not. You'll learn more about these apps in Hour 20, "Offline Web Applications."

▶ **Voice recognition**—HTML5 adds the speech attribute to form tags. Talking into a cell phone is much easier than typing into it.

▶ **The new input types**—The new form input types make forms much easier to fill in for mobile devices. Hour 13 covers all the new forms and input types.

▶ **Canvas**—The canvas tag is a great way to add animation, games, and images to mobile applications. You'll learn how to use the `<canvas>` tag in Hour 10.

▶ **Video and audio tags**—Both these tags are well supported by both Android and iOS and these tags make an easy task of putting video and audio in your web applications. You'll learn how to use them in Hour 12.

▶ **Mobile events**—Specific events such as `touchstart` and `touchmove` were created specifically for touch screen mobile devices. Hour 16 goes into more detail about these events.

Summary

You discovered this hour that HTML 4 isn't a perfect version of HTML. It requires a lot of hacks and workarounds to work in the more popular browsers. You learned to focus on modern browsers and how to discover what browsers visit your site.

This hour discussed ways you can start implementing HTML5 on your website slowly, adding new design elements iteratively and making small updates. You also learned many things you can do today with HTML5 that have no negative impact on your site.

This hour also showed you some of the HTML5 tags and tools that have good support across browsers. You may have been surprised to learn that parts of HTML5 are supported as far back as Internet Explorer 5.5.

Finally, you learned a little about the features of HTML5 that can add value to your websites and make your mobile applications stand out from the crowd.

Q&A

Q. *What is a good cut-off for deciding when to stop supporting a browser version?*

A. This is a difficult question to answer, because it is different for every website. But a good general rule is to consider how many visitors you currently get and then compare that to the percentage of users using an older browser. For a site that gets a million unique visitors a day, 1% might be too high, as that's 10,000 visitors a day getting a less-than-optimal experience. But for a site getting 1,000 visitors a day, 10% might be fine. You have to evaluate your site and your comfort level.

Q. *I hate the idea of losing any customers. Isn't there any way I can use HTML5 and not drive them away?*

A. You should never try to drive a customer away. Remember that many of the new features of HTML5 don't make your site unusable for less supporting browsers; they just don't get all the features. Also keep in mind that site owners do this all the time already. A number of sites don't provide alternatives to Flash, so iPad and iPhone users are completely shut out. Visitors might not leave if they don't have access to a video, because the rest of your content is still useful, but they may never come back if your whole site is blank.

Q. *What can I do to use more HTML5 mobile features sooner even if many of the users coming to my site are using browsers that don't support them?*

A. You can add HTML5 mobile features to your site while also supporting less compliant browsers in many ways. Using a detection script such as Modernizr, as you will learn in Hour 8, "Converting Web Apps to Mobile," is a first step. But you can go further using media queries to style your designs to fit specific devices (discussed in Hour 4, "Detecting Mobile Devices and HTML5 Support") and use polyfills as fallback options for other HTML5 APIs and features. You can find an excellent list of fallback options and polyfills on the Modernizr wiki (https://github.com/Modernizr/Modernizr/wiki/HTML5-Cross-browser-Polyfills).

Q. *If using a modern browser gives so many advantages, why don't people upgrade?*

A. People don't upgrade their browsers for many reasons:

► They don't know there is a new version that they can upgrade to.

► They are afraid that an upgrade would cause things to break.

► They use a plug-in or website that won't work in the new version of the browser.

► Their organization has specific browser version requirements, and they aren't allowed to upgrade.

Until just recently, most web browsers did not have built-in checks for new versions, and if they did, they could be easily cancelled by users who did not want to upgrade.

Workshop

The workshop contains quiz questions to help you process what you've learned in this chapter. Try to answer all the questions before you read the answers. See Appendix A, "Answers to Quizzes," for answers.

Quiz

1. How has Internet Explorer held back the development of standards-based web pages?

2. What is iterative design and why should you use it?

3. What are some features of HTML5 that work right now?

4. What features of HTML5 are supported by IE as far back as version 5.5 or 6?

Exercises

1. If you don't already have Google Analytics or another analytics package on your website, you should install one right away. After you have one installed, follow the instructions provided in this hour to find out the breakdown of browsers to your website.

2. Go to one of your existing websites, and add in the HTML5 features that can be used right now. Change the doctype and character set tag, and simplify your scripts and styles. You should also look at where you can remove quotes around attributes and simplify your HTML even more.

3. Pick a page on your website that gets fewer page views than most and start making iterative changes to it to bring it more into the HTML5 standard. Add semantic tags, and think about how you might use some of the new HTML5 features to enhance the document.

HOUR 8

Converting Web Apps to Mobile

What You'll Learn in This Hour:

- ▶ How to make mobile design as easy as possible
- ▶ What tools can help you build your mobile applications
- ▶ How to find images and designs that look mobile
- ▶ The tools available for testing without your purchasing dozens of phones
- ▶ How to make sure that less-compliant browsers still look okay

Creating HTML5 web applications takes a lot of time and effort. The most important part of designing a mobile application, as discussed in previous hours, is to create a site or application that is as universal as you can make it—that is, build for the one web. But that doesn't mean you need to reinvent the mobile wheel. You can use dozens of software tools and development skills to help you build your mobile application or convert your existing site into a mobile site.

In this hour, you'll learn about tools that help you test your existing documents for mobile support. You'll also learn the skills needed to design a mobile application using the basic elements of design. You'll then find out about some scripts you can use to help detect HTML5 support and even add some limited support for the tags in older browsers. This hour will also show you where to find tools such as emulators and online simulators to check your applications in devices you don't own. You will learn how to evaluate your existing site with an eye toward mobile users, as well as how to convert those pages to mobile-friendly designs.

Choosing a Web Editor

Your web editor is the most important tool you can use for developing mobile web applications. Although creating a web application using just a text editor such as Notepad is possible, a professional web editor or integrated development environment (IDE) can provide you with many extra features that easily justify the price.

Professional web editors and IDEs offer features such as:

▶ Code validation

▶ Browser previews

▶ Website file management

▶ Project management

▶ Script debugging

▶ Integration with other tools

Some of the best web editors for mobile applications are

▶ **Dreamweaver**—Dreamweaver CS5.5 includes integration with PhoneGap, a tool you'll learn more about later in this hour and again in Hour 24, "Converting HTML5 Apps to Native Apps." You can get a trial version of Dreamweaver from the Adobe website (www.adobe.com/products/dreamweaver.html).

▶ **Komodo IDE**—Komodo IDE supports many different programming languages, and it is a good text editor for building HTML5 applications using jQuery. You can try Komodo by downloading the free version, called Komodo Edit, from its website (www.activestate.com/komodo-ide).

▶ **TopStyle**—TopStyle (www.topstyle4.com/) is a CSS editor for Windows that also does a lot of HTML. It includes mobile device previews and scripts for mobile users that make it a good choice for editing mobile web applications.

▶ **SiteSpinner Pro**—SiteSpinner Pro (www.virtualmechanics.com/products/spinnerpro/index.html) is a WYSIWYG (What You See Is What You Get) editor for Windows that offers scripts for handling mobile devices as well as previews.

You have your choice of web editors to use to build your mobile web application or convert your existing site to mobile. If you are already using one, there is no reason to change, but if you're still building web pages with a text editor that isn't specifically for HTML (such as Notepad or TextEdit) then finding a new web page editor will make your development go faster and smoother.

Testing Your Application

The first step in testing your application is to see where your application currently stands in terms of mobile support. Take a screenshot of your design in as many mobile devices as you can—even one is better than nothing. Figure 8.1 shows the website for this book on an iPod touch. Although some adjustments have been made to the site for mobile devices, you can see right away that it's not as friendly as it could be.

Following are some problems that make this site unfriendly on a mobile device:

► The headline is a bit small.

► A mobile site should not have two levels of navigation.

► The huge "Recent Posts" headline takes up too much space.

► The colors aren't the colors originally chosen for the design.

One of the best tools you can use for testing your web pages and applications is a *validator*. Many types of validators for web applications are available, including:

► **HTML validators**—These test to make sure your HTML is correct.

► **Accessibility validators**—These test web pages to see how well they can be read by screen readers.

► **Code validators**—These check your scripts, CSS, and API calls for accuracy. Another term for these is *lint*; for example, a *JS lint* tool would check JavaScript.

► **Mobile validators**—These validators give advice on how to improve pages for mobile devices. They often act as emulators as well.

Using a validator for testing ensures that any problems you see are not caused by invalid code.

The preceding list is not all the testing you need to do. Tools are available that will evaluate your website to see how friendly it is to mobile users. One good tool is the W3C mobileOK Checker at http://validator.w3.org/mobile/. Another good one is mobiReady at http://ready.mobi/. Both the W3C mobileOK Checker and mobiReady look at pages that are live on the internet, and then give you a report of how they would perform on mobile devices.

FIGURE 8.1
Viewing a web-
site on an iPod
touch.

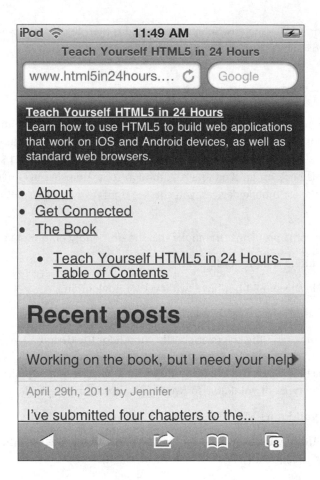

Don't Follow any Validator Blindly

The W3C mobileOK Checker is a valuable tool, but you shouldn't blindly implement all the guidelines it suggests. Many of the mobile checkers and validators
were built before HTML5 gained popularity in the smartphone market. The W3C
validator checks your site against XHTML Basic. Also, mobiReady will give you a
low score if you aren't using XHTML mobile profile, and HTML5 is more advanced
than either XHTML Basic or XHTML mobile profiles.

These tools can give you a good idea of what to be concerned about when adapting
your mobile application. Some things you should consider (and will be warned of
with these testing suites) include:

▶ **Page size**—Keep your mobile page sizes as small as possible, so that they load quickly. A good general rule is to keep mobile page sizes, including all images, scripts, and CSS, under 20KB for feature phones and 30KB–50KB for smartphones and computer browsers.

▶ **Graphic sizes**—You should offer smaller-width graphics for users on smaller devices. 200 pixels wide is about as wide as an image should get for a cell phone that can browse the web. These phones are often called *feature phones* because they offer more features than a standard phone but are not as robust as a smartphone.

▶ **Scripts and style sheets**—Many feature phones don't support scripts or CSS very well, so you should make sure that your content doesn't rely on them if you expect a lot of your site visitors to be using these phones.

▶ **Forms**—Remember that typing into form fields is difficult on a mobile phone. Using radio buttons or checkboxes where possible is a good alternative.

▶ **Access keys**—Putting access keys or keyboard shortcuts on your links will make them much easier to click for feature phone users.

Evaluating Your Content

After you know what your site looks like in a mobile device, you need to do some content evaluation. And mobile content requires different skills to create than standard website content. In Hour 4, "Detecting Mobile Devices and HTML5 Support," you learned how to use CSS3 media queries to change the look of your site depending upon the browser viewing it, but you should also change the content with those media queries.

Mobile content should be:

▶ **Short**—The smaller the device, the less content should be downloaded at once. So, a full-page article that you might deliver whole to an iPad or desktop computer should be split into pieces or have only the headline delivered to a feature phone.

▶ **Direct**—On smaller devices you have to hook your readers immediately. You should remove everything that is even slightly extraneous to the main point of the content.

▶ **Easy to use**—Pressing the Back button on a feature phone is much easier than filling in a form. You want to keep your mobile content, especially for very small devices, as easy and functional as possible.

▶ **What the customer wants**—The smaller the device, the more you should focus on providing only the minimum features that your customers want.

However, don't focus only on what content to remove. You should also be thinking about features you can add to the pages to make tasks easier for mobile customers. Some things you can add to your mobile pages include:

▶ **Back to top links**—Adding links to your navigation or to the top of the page isn't always necessary on a smartphone or computer browser, but this can make a site much easier to use on a feature phone.

▶ **Email links**—Add links to allow viewers to email sections of your page to themselves or others. This both promotes your page and helps your mobile readers use it more effectively, because reading a site on a computer is much easier than on a feature phone.

▶ **Extra services**—Links to services such as Mobilizer, Read It Later, or Instapaper let your mobile readers save your content to be read when it's convenient for them.

Changing the Visual Design for Mobile

Mobile designs have a number of things in common, but unfortunately, much of the time, the most common feature of a mobile design is how ugly it is. This is because most people read advice like that provided earlier in this hour and interpret it to mean "design for the lowest common denominator."

But that is most emphatically not what you should do.

Instead, look back at Hour 4, which talked about graceful degradation. The goal of your visual design should not be to make your site look identical in every situation. The goal should be to make it functional in a majority of devices and excellent for your target audience.

You should be designing a work of art that happens to be viewable in a feature phone—not a mediocre drawing that looks the same on an iPad and a feature phone.

Using Elements of Design to Create Great Mobile Applications

You first must learn the elements of design:

- ▶ Color

- ▶ Direction

- ▶ Lines

- ▶ Shapes

- ▶ Texture

Obviously, color refers to those colors used on a web page. Color is also present in black and white, with shades of gray.

Even Blocks of Black Text Have Color

When you look at a web page with large blocks of text, those text blocks can blend together to make the page seem brighter and whiter or darker and blacker. Graphic designers refer to this as the textual "color." You can affect the relative darkness or lightness (the "color") of your text blocks with the line-height CSS style property. The wider the space is between text lines, the brighter that text block will appear.

By the Way

You add color to your designs with the color, background-color, and border-color style properties.

Most mobile designs use color to highlight text and headlines. In fact, one of the most common styles for a mobile design is to have the headline at the top with a colored background, styled something like this:

```
<style>
h1 {
    background-color: #c16f5b;
    color: #000;
}
</style>
<h1>Mobile Site</h1>
```

This looks like the design in Figure 8.2.

Direction gives the feeling of movement in a design. It is typically defined by images on the page as well as how the entire page is laid out. Although you should consider things such as the direction people are looking in your photos and the direction elements lead the eye, for mobile design you need to also consider how the device is being held—portrait or landscape.

FIGURE 8.2
A simple head-
line style on an
iPod touch.

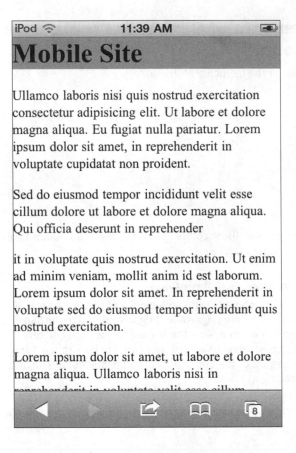

Most designers design typically in portrait mode, which for most smartphones, works great. But remember that tablets are often easier to read in landscape mode. Be sure to check how your page looks in landscape mode, so that the design isn't messed up.

Did you Know?

Android Tablets Work Best in Landscape

Although both the iPad and Android tablets can display apps in portrait or land-scape mode, most Android tablets are built at a 16:9 aspect ratio. This means that HD movies take up the full screen in landscape mode. But it also means that in portrait mode, the screen can feel very long and narrow. A reasonable assump-tion is that most Android tablet users will still browse web pages in portrait mode, but you should be prepared for more people to browse in landscape mode.

Lines are another design element that are often used extensively in mobile design. You can use the <hr> tag to add horizontal lines. You can also use lines to add borders around elements.

As you can see in Figure 8.3 lines can help break up text, but they also can cause people to stop reading because they provide a natural breaking point.

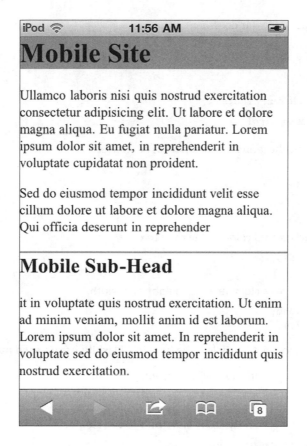

FIGURE 8.3
Adding a line above a subhead on an iPod touch.

You typically add shapes via images, but if you want to add rectangular and square shapes you can use CSS and HTML directly. The <canvas> tag lets you add more creative shapes in your pages, and with CSS3 you can even add circles to your documents.

▼   **Try It Yourself**

Turning a Square DIV into a Circle

One of the most annoying parts of web design is how boxy everything is. But CSS3 is starting to change that. You can turn a <div> that would normally be square into a circle.

1. Add a <div> to your document:

   ```
   <div>
       Click Me!
   </div>
   ```

2. Give it a class of circle:

   ```
   <div class="circle">
   ```

3. Add a style sheet and create a new circle class:

   ```
   <style>
   .circle {
   }
   </style>
   ```

4. Put a background color on the circle class:

   ```
   background-color: blue;
   ```

5. Give the circle class an equal height and width:

   ```
   height: 10em;
   width: 10em;
   ```

   It's easiest to create a circle if the height and width are an even number.

6. Set the border radius to half the height:

   ```
   border-radius: 5em;
   ```

7. Include the browser extensions, for maximum support:

   ```
   -moz-border-radius: 5em;
   -webkit-border-radius: 5em;
   ```

8. Center the text in the middle of the circle:

   ```
   text-align: center;
   line-height: 10em;
   ```

   Note that setting the line-height to the height of the box will center one line of text in the middle of the circle, but be careful if you have multiple lines of text, because they may fall outside the boundaries of the circle.

▲

Texture can be one of the most difficult design elements for a web designer to master because texture is something you feel, and web pages are seen, but not felt. Texture in a web design is the feeling of visual texture. Most texture in web design is done with color and images.

Even a simple stripe pattern can add texture to a design. Figure 8.4 shows a diagonal stripe pattern that could be used as the background to a web page. The stripe is more interesting than plain white or gray and makes the background look like it has a texture.

FIGURE 8.4
A stripe pattern that imitates texture.

Mobile Design Patterns

Mobile design takes advantage of some common patterns that you can apply to help your users use your web applications. Using these patterns makes your web applications instantly familiar to your users, and so much easier to use:

▶ **Simple designs**—When designing for feature phones especially, keep the number of images to a minimum. Provide material in a single column with enough content that the user doesn't have to click often to go to a new page.

▶ **Buttons**—Buttons at the top of the screen, often next to the headline, help mobile users navigate. The buttons can point to the next page (usually placed on the right) or previous page (on the left), more information, categories of information, or anything to add value to the current page.

▶ **Lists**—Lists are much easier to read than paragraphs on a mobile device with a small screen. However, keep them short, three to five words at most for feature phones, and five to ten words for smartphones.

▶ **Teasers**—This is a very common mobile pattern. Typically all that is displayed is a headline, possibly a short, one-line introduction and an arrow link to read the full text. This feature is great when you have many items you want to showcase in a small area.

▶ **Menus**—Menus can be as complex as you like on mobile, but the most common patterns for menus are of a single column of items (usually only one to two words long) that expands to a second level when clicked on.

▶ **Paging**—Because most sites split mobile content into multiple pages, you need to have a way to move between those pages easily. Seeing a horizontal list of numbers at the bottom of the content is most common. The current page is bold and not a link, and the numbers are flanked by "Previous" and "Next." Even if you have more than three to five pages to display, you should display only three to five page numbers in the list.

▶ **Endless pages**—Endless pages keep getting longer as the user scrolls close to the bottom of the page. This speeds up some of the download time and allows users to keep reading without having to click anything.

▶ **Tabs**—Tabs are a familiar navigation pattern that desktop designs use as much as mobile designs. They are perfect for top-level navigation as long as there aren't too many to fit on one line.

▶ **Toggle content**—By hiding content under toggle buttons you can get more content on the page without overwhelming the user. This is great for mobile devices because after the page is loaded all the content is there, even if it's not all visible immediately.

▶ **Smart loading**—Design your mobile pages so that the content loads first, before any advertising or navigation. If the content isn't essential to mobile users, such as sidebar text, consider hiding it from mobile users.

▶ **Consistency**—Having your mobile designs look identical to your computer designs is not critical, but they should be similar. The logos, colors, and copyright information should be consistent for users who visit both sites.

Literally thousands of design patterns exist that you can use. Appendix C, "HTML5 and Mobile Application Resources," has resources you can use to find more patterns for your application.

Checking for HTML5 and CSS3

One of the best tools you can utilize to build your HTML5 website or application is Modernizr (www.modernizr.com/). It is a small JavaScript library that checks for support of CSS3 and HTML5 and provides fallbacks for browsers that don't support the features you want to use.

Try It Yourself ▼

Getting Started with Modernizr

The best way to learn how to use Modernizr is to install it and try it out.

1. Download the `modernizr-x.x.min.js` script from www.modernizr.com/.

2. Move the file to your website directory.

3. Add the script to the head of your document:

   ```
   <script src="modernizr-#.#.min.js"></script>
   ```

4. Add the class of `no-js` to your HTML element:

   ```
   <html class="no-js">
   ```

   Modernizr will then automatically load and test the availability of more than 40 different CSS3 and HTML5 functions. You can even add new tests for features that Modernizr doesn't currently test for. ▲

Use Modernizr Instead of HTMLShiv

Modernizr also enables HTML5 tags such as `<section>` and `<article>` in Internet Explorer 6, 7, and 8, so you don't need to use the html5shiv script (discussed in Hour 4 if you use Modernizr.

By the Way

However, Modernizr can't detect everything. For some features you need to do standard browser sniffing, browser inference (for example, if a specific feature such as `document.all` is present, then the browser viewing the page must be a specific browser), or provide a fallback mechanism to every browser, just to be safe.

Some of the things that Modernizr can't detect include:

▶ Date and color pickers in web forms (discussed in Hour 13, "HTML5 Forms")

▶ The inability to edit things using the `contenteditable` attribute (covered in Hour 14, "Editing Content and User Interaction with HTML5") in iOS and Android mobile devices

▶ Support for the `preload` attribute in audio and video (Hour 12, "Audio and Video in HTML5" explains this attribute)

▶ Support for soft hyphens (`&shy;`) and the `<wbr>` tag (Hour 11, "Fonts and Typography in HTML5" covers hyphenation)

▶ Consistent rendering of HTML entities

▶ PNG alpha transparency

Other things that may not be detectable are listed on the Modernizr wiki: https://github.com/Modernizr/Modernizr/wiki/Undetectables.

Supporting Multiple Devices

Planning to support the one web, as the W3C would like us to do is one thing, but the reality is that if you want your application to be usable on multiple devices, you must make accommodations for the various devices and browsers out there.

The solution is to use a framework. Frameworks take complex technologies and pull them together as a group of objects that you can use. HTML frameworks typically give you a grid to lay out your pages, typography, and objects, such as navigation, forms, and links.

Several HTML5 mobile frameworks are designed to help you create HTML5 applications for mobile devices that work on both iOS and Android devices. Some HTML5 mobile frameworks you can try include the following:

▶ **Sencha Touch**—Sencha Touch (www.sencha.com/products/touch/) is a JavaScript framework that helps you build applications that look like native apps on iOS, Android, and Blackberry. It is a very extensive framework with lots of built-in support for touch events such as pinch-zoom and swiping. But Sencha Touch is built from the JavaScript, rather than from the HTML and CSS. If you are not comfortable writing JavaScript, this framework will be difficult to use.

▶ **jQuery Mobile**—jQuery Mobile (http://jquerymobile.com/) builds off of jQuery to create pages for iOS, Android, Blackberry, WebOs, and Windows phone (as well as others). jQuery Mobile, as of this writing, is still in alpha, and so it isn't as robust as it could be. However, it builds off of the HTML so it can be easier to implement.

▶ **Jo**—Jo (http://joapp.com/) is a JavaScript framework that will help you take an HTML5 application that you built on Safari or Chrome and convert it to iOS, Android, WebOS, and Symbian. It provides all the animation and native app design features that Sencha Touch and jQuery Mobile do.

▶ **PhoneGap**—PhoneGap (www.phonegap.com/) is more than a framework. It is a tool to help you create mobile applications, but it also works to convert HTML5 applications into native mobile apps. With PhoneGap, you can use any of the aforementioned frameworks and then convert them into apps you can sell on the Android and Apple app stores. If you only want to get one framework, PhoneGap is the one you should get. Hour 24 discusses how to use PhoneGap to create native applications.

Evaluating Finished Apps on Other Devices

Testing your applications is an important part of the development process, but you probably don't have unlimited funds to go out and buy one of every device on the market. So first you test, as mentioned earlier, on the devices you own, and then when you're ready to deliver you test on other devices.

Delivering an application for a device is not a good idea if you haven't tested it on that device. You can test your application on devices you don't own in three ways:

▶ Purchase or rent a device

▶ Ask someone else to test it for you

▶ Use an emulator

Purchasing the devices, as mentioned, isn't really a viable option for most designers, but some companies will rent iPhones and other smartphones and tablets. The site Rentacomputer.com has both iPads and Android tablets for rent.

You can also ask a friend or co-worker with a device for help in testing. You could also advertise for testers online. There are also companies that will do mobile application testing, such as uTest (www.utest.com/).

However, the easiest way to test your applications without the actual device is with an emulator.

Emulators Don't Catch Everything

Although an emulator is a good fallback, they don't compare to using an actual device for testing. For example, the Android phone and tablet emulator is very slow compared to the actual device. Also, testing some phone-specific features, such as multi-touch, on emulators is difficult.

Desktop Emulators

The best emulators are the ones that run right on your desktop computer. You can get emulators for

- ▶ Android (http://developer.android.com/sdk/index.html)

- ▶ iOS (https://developer.apple.com/devcenter/ios/index.action)

- ▶ WebOS (http://developer.palm.com/index.php?option=com_content&view=article&id=1788&Itemid=55)

- ▶ Blackberry (http://us.blackberry.com/developers/resources/simulators.jsp)

- ▶ Windows Phone (www.microsoft.com/downloads/en/details.aspx?FamilyID=04704acf-a63a-4f97-952c-8b51b34b00ce)

- ▶ Opera Mobile (www.opera.com/developer/tools/)

Online Emulators

Online emulators are not always as effective as desktop ones because they aren't always as powerful, but they can be faster to use. Some online emulators include

- ▶ Opera Mini Simulator (www.opera.com/mobile/demo/)

- ▶ dotMobi Emulator (http://mtld.mobi/emulator.php)

- ▶ DeviceAnywhere (www.tryphone.com/)

- ▶ BrowserCam (www.browsercam.com/)

Getting an Application to Work on Older Browsers

One of the main reasons people give for not wanting to learn HTML5 and CSS3 is that older browsers, especially Internet Explorer 8 and lower, don't support them. Disregarding the importance of improving your own skills, creating pages and applications that older browsers can use is still possible.

The problem with older versions of Internet Explorer is that they don't recognize the new HTML5 tags as HTML tags. When they see a tag they don't recognize, they simply ignore it. The web page in Figure 8.5 is displayed with the background different in compliant browsers. But as you can see in the figure, IE 8 ignores that and displays the page with a white background. You can test this yourself by visiting www.html5in24hours.com/examples/testing-in-ie.html.

FIGURE 8.5
Simple HTML5 page in Internet Explorer 8 ignoring various tags.

The HTML looks like this:

```
<!DOCTYPE HTML>
<html>
<head>
<meta charset="UTF-8">
<title>Testing HTML5 in Internet Explorer</title>
<style>
    header {
        background-color: #CCC;
    }
    section {
        background-color: #9CF;
    }
    footer {
        background-color: #CFF;
    }
</style>
</head>

<body>
<header>
    <h1>Testing HTML5 in Internet Explorer</h1>
</header>
<section>
    <article>
```

```
        <p>This is an article. If IE supported HTML5, all the text on this
page would have background color.
        <p>Ut enim ad minim veniam, in reprehenderit in voluptate
➥consectetur
adipisicing elit. Excepteur sint occaecat lorem ipsum dolor sit amet, qui
officia deserunt. Mollit anim id est laborum.
        <p>Velit esse cillum dolore duis aute irure dolor ut aliquip ex ea
commodo consequat. Eu fugiat nulla pariatur. Ut labore et dolore magna
➥aliqua.
        <p>In reprehenderit in voluptate qui officia deserunt mollit anim
➥id est
laborum. Ullamco laboris nisi consectetur adipisicing elit. Velit esse cillum
dolore lorem ipsum dolor sit amet, quis nostrud exercitation. Ut aliquip ex
ea commodo consequat.
    </article>
</section>
<footer>
    <p>And here is the footer
</footer>
</body>
</html>
```

As you can see, there is CSS that Internet Explorer ignores. To get IE to recognize these tags, you need to add them to the DOM with JavaScript. Here is a simple script you can use:

```
<script>
(function(){
    var html5elmeents =
"address,article,aside,audio,canvas,command,datalist,details,dialog,
figure,figcaption,footer,header,hgroup,keygen,mark,meter,menu,nav,progress,
ruby,section,time,video".split(',');

    for(var i = 0; i < html5elmeents.length; i++){
        document.createElement(html5elmeents[i]);
    }
}
)();
</script>
```

This script won't make Internet Explorer suddenly play videos with the <video> tag or show vector graphics in the <canvas> tag. But it will let IE display the contents and style of the elements, as you can see in Figure 8.6.

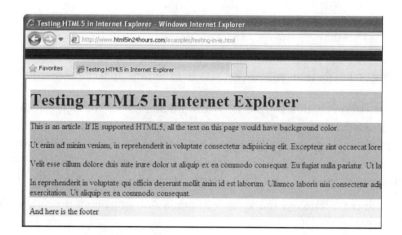

FIGURE 8.6
Simple HTML5 page with a script to help Internet Explorer 8.

You can also use scripts written expressly for this purpose. Modernizr was discussed earlier in this hour, but you can use others if that script is more than you need:

▶ **HTML5Shiv**—This JavaScript file adds new HTML5 elements to the browser. It was discussed in Hour 4. Add this script to the head of your documents inside conditional comments:

```
<!-- [if lt IE 9] -->
<script src="http://html5shiv.googlecode.com/svn/trunk/html5.js">
</script>
<!-- [endif] -->
```

▶ **IE6 Universal CSS**—Andy Clarke came up with a nearly bulletproof stylesheet for Internet Explorer 6. The important part is to hide all your other style sheets from IE6, so that it only applies the universal CSS:

```
<!-- [if ! lte IE 6] -->
<!-- style sheets for non-IE6 browsers -->
<!-- [endif] -->
<!-- [if lte IE 6] -->
<link href="http://universal-ie6-css.googlecode.com/files/ie6.1.1.css"
media="screen, projection" rel="stylesheet">
<!-- [endif] -->
```

▶ **Selectivizr**—This works with several JavaScript libraries to emulate CSS3 pseudo-classes and attribute selectors in Internet Explorer 6 through 8. You need to link to a library such as jQuery first to use it:

```
<script src="jquery.min.js"></script>
<!-- [if lt IE 9] -->
```

```
<script src="selectivizr-min.js"></script>
<!-- [endif] -->
```

It doesn't add HTML5 attributes, so you'll need a tool like Modernizr or HTML5Shiv for that. You can get Selectivizr at http://selectivizr.com/.

The key to working with HTML5 is to go forward and use it. Athough you should keep your site browser statistics in mind, your sites and applications don't have to look identical in every browser. Waiting until Internet Explorer 9 has majority market share means you'll be waiting a long time. Remember, Internet Explorer 6 is more than 10 years old, and it still has a good percentage of the market.

Using advanced technology is also more fun than worrying about the support of older browsers.

Summary

In this hour, you learned how to evaluate an existing HTML5 page to see what needs to be done to improve it for mobile use. You learned of a number of testing tools to check your pages and see what they look like in mobile devices. These tools can be online or desktop emulators or just online scripts that give you a report of how your site measures up.

This hour covered several things you should consider when converting a site to mobile or creating a mobile site from scratch, such as how to size pages and graphics, and using scripts, style sheets, forms, and access keys. You also learned how to use these in ways that are friendly even to feature phones. This hour taught you how to evaluate the design of your site so that it uses the basic elements of design in a way that works on mobile devices. This hour also covered some basic mobile design patterns that will help your applications be familiar to mobile users.

You learned that scripts like Modernizr and HTMLShiv are tools that you can use to keep your pages looking good even in browsers that don't support all the features you want to use. You also learned about some frameworks such as PhoneGap, Sencha Touch, jQuery Mobile, and Jo that can help make your mobile pages look good on both Android and iOS devices.

Q&A

Q. *You say that mobile pages should be small, with images that are also small. But what if I have an image that cannot be made any smaller?*

A. Most web designers work very hard on images and can get very attached to them. But you need to remember that an image at 400 pixels wide will look great on a computer browser, but on a smaller phone screen it might display only a fraction of the entire image. Remember that if you want your users to enjoy your images as much as you do, you need to size them appropriately for the device. By creating alternatives, cropping your image, or resizing it smaller, you can create a similar atmosphere on your mobile site without destroying how users view it.

Q. *What if I have too much content?*

A. More people are getting comfortable using small devices to browse the web, and so you can provide more content than you might think. The exception is if you think your readers are going to be viewing your site primarily on feature phones. In that scenario, using a teaser style for your articles is best, displaying just one or two lines and having users click to view the entire article. Warning users of the size of the article ahead of time is also a good idea. You can include that information in your HTML document, and then use `display: none;` styles to hide it from larger browsers.

Q. *You mentioned a bunch of different scripts and frameworks, but which one is the best?*

A. I use nearly all the scripts I mention in this hour on at least one website that I run, and I don't think there's any one that is better than another. In terms of frameworks, jQuery Mobile is probably best, but Sencha Touch is very powerful and offers a lot of device-specific features. As for the scripts, Modernizr works best, but HTML5Shiv is very easy to add and then forget about. You should try several of them and see which ones you like the best.

Workshop

The workshop contains quiz questions to help you process what you've learned in this chapter. Try to answer all the questions before you read the answers. See Appendix A, "Answers to Quizzes," for answers.

Quiz

1. Why should you test your applications?

2. How big should a mobile web page be, including all scripts, styles, and images?

3. What are the five elements of design?

4. Why would you use mobile design patterns?

5. How can you test a mobile application on a device you don't own?

Exercises

1. Download the Android emulator and browse to an HTML5 page you've written. Evaluate how the page looks and note any surprises.

2. Browse to that same page in Internet Explorer 8, 7, or 6. If you are on a Mac, you will need to get a virtual machine running Windows. If you have already upgraded to IE 9, then open that page in a tool such as Browsershots.org in an older version of IE. Evaluate how the page looks and note any surprises.

3. Add the HTML5Shiv to one of your HTML5 documents and then browse to that page in IE 6, 7, or 8 again. Did the way the page displayed change?

HOUR 9
Adding Meaning with HTML5 Sectioning and Semantic Elements

What You'll Learn in This Hour:

▶ How to define sections of HTML5 documents
▶ The four primary sectioning elements
▶ Understanding elements like `<figure>` and `<details>`
▶ Using the many semantic elements
▶ Providing meaning with semantic elements

Many of the new elements in HTML5 relate to how the content is organized on the web page. These are called sectioning and heading elements. This hour you will learn more about these elements as well as some new semantic tags that help you define your web pages more precisely.

You will learn the value of marking up your pages semantically and about some of the new and existing semantic elements that you may not be using.

What Are Sectioning Elements?

Sectioning elements were added to HTML5 to help web designers organize content. These elements create logical sections of the document, each of which would start with a heading element, and often end with a footer element.

The four sectioning elements in HTML5 are

▶ <article>

▶ <aside>

▶ <nav>

▶ <section>

Two new elements, though not explicitly sectioning elements, are sectioning roots:

▶ <details>

▶ <figure>

A few other new elements could be considered sectioning elements as well. These new elements work with the sectioning elements and sectioning roots:

▶ <header>

▶ <footer>

▶ <hgroup>

One thing to keep in mind is that sectioning and semantic elements do not, by themselves, make any visible changes to the contents of a web page. They are used to provide structure to an HTML document that a computer can read. This allows the computer to create outlines as described next or otherwise interact programmatically with the document. If you want these elements to have a visual style in your pages, you need to attach CSS styles to them.

Using the New Sectioning Elements

One thing you should keep in mind is that the sectioning elements <article>, <aside>, <nav>, and <section> each work with the header and footer elements to create a section of your document. Following each of these elements in your document with a headline tag such as <h1> should be possible. And with those headline tags, your HTML5 document will have an outline.

Creating Outlines with Sectioning Elements

HTML5 introduces a new concept into the HTML specification: outlines. HTML5 outlines look at how the document is structured, using sectioning elements and header elements to label the outline sections. These outlines are similar to ones that a word processing program might create.

The purpose of sectioning elements is to create outlines with headers and footers. Specifically, the outlines can be created with algorithms. Outlines are important because they make the pages more accessible. Accessible user agents, such as screen readers, can use the outline to determine what parts are the most important to present to the user.

An HTML5 document might look something like this:

```
<section>
    <h1>Part 1: Building Web Pages</h1>
    <section>
        <h1>Chapter 1: HTML</h1>
        <p>In this section you will learn how to write HTML
    </section>
    <section>
        <h1>Chapter 2: CSS</h1>
        <p>And this section will teach you CSS
        <section>
            <h1>CSS1</h1>
            <p>...
        </section>
    </section>
</section>
<section>
    <h1>Part 2: Publishing Web pages</h1>
    ...
</section>
```

This creates an outline that looks like this:

```
I. Part 1: Building Web Pages
    I.1 Chapter 1: HTML
    I.2 Chapter 2: CSS
        I.2.i CSS1
II. Part 2: Publishing Web pages
```

HTML 4 had no sectioning elements, and so web designers typically used the `<div>` tag to create artificial sections within their documents. Although these worked, they were inconsistent across sites, so assistive devices could never use them to help determine content priority.

Testing for the Correct Use of Sectioning Elements

One way you can test your HTML5 document to see whether you are using the sectioning elements correctly is to test your page in the HTML5 Outliner (http://gsnedders.html5.org/outliner/). This shows you how your outline looks, and you'll be able to see what headers you may be missing.

Where most web designers will find the most value in these new sectioning elements is how they provide more human-readable structure to the documents. For example, when you see the `<article>` tag, you know that the contents are an article or some other type of syndicatable content. The HTML5 outlines are a representation of that structure.

The `<article>` Element

The `<article>` element represents a section of content that can stand on its own. If you were to syndicate a web page, you would syndicate the article portions—they are the part of the page that defines the page. An article might be

- A magazine or newspaper article

- A blog post

- A forum post

- A blog comment

- Any independent item of content

You can put a `<header>` and a `<footer>` element inside an `<article>`. Most articles also have some type of headline. You can also put `<section>` tags inside articles, or you can put an article inside a section.

The easiest way to think about what type of content should be in an article is to ask yourself whether it is content that can stand alone in syndication—such as in an RSS feed.

Here is how a simple `<article>` might look (assume it has a lot more content):

```
<article>
    <h1>My Pets</h1>
    <p>I have always loved animals, and I've always had a lot of pets....
</article>
```

The `<aside>` Element

The `<aside>` element is defined as content that is tangentially or loosely related to the main content of the document. However, it can also be a sidebar on a web page, providing information that is related to the site as a whole, rather than the main content of the page.

The way you determine which type of `<aside>` you're using depends upon where that `<aside>` is found. If the `<aside>` is found inside an `<article>` tag, then it defines content that is related to the article itself, such as a glossary or list of related articles. If the <aside> is found outside of an <article> tag, then it defines content that is related to the website as a whole, but not the article(s) on the page, necessarily. Examples would be sidebar elements such as a blogroll or advertising (that is related to the page content).

Sectioning Elements Do Not Have Page Locations Defined

It is easy to think that an <aside> element will appear on the side of a web page and a <footer> element will appear at the bottom. But the placement of these elements on a web page is defined only by CSS, not by the tags. You can place <footer> content at the very top of your page, if you feel that semantically that content is information usually found in a footer, or content in an <aside> element can appear in the main column of the page. These elements are semantic only, meaning that they define what the content *is* rather than where it should display or what it should do.

By the Way

Here is an example of the two types of <aside> elements. This is an <aside> inside the <article>, which indicates that it is related specifically to the content on the page:

```
<article>
    <h1>My Pets</h1>
    <p>I have always loved animals, and I've always had a lot of pets....
    <aside>
        <h1>Photos of my Pets</h1>
        <ul>
            <li><a href="">Shasta</a></li>
            <li><a href="">Suni</a></li>
            ...
        </ul>
    </aside>
</article>
```

This <aside> is outside the <article>, so it is related to the content of the site as a whole but not to the article specifically:

```
<aside>
    <h1>My Favorite Sites</h1>
    <ul>
        <li><a href="">Dogs</a></li>
        <li><a href="">Cats</a></li>
        <li><a href="">Horses</a></li>
    </ul>
</aside>
```

What's with All the <h1> Elements?

One thing you may have noticed is that every section has a headline using the <h1> element. In HTML 4 the <h1> through <h6> tags were about the only outlining option designers had, so the recommendation was to use only one <h1> tag—for the page title. However, HTML5 added all the additional sectioning elements, and that the recommendation is now to use <h1> as the first headline for every section. This indicates that the <h1> headline is the most important headline *of that section*, leaving the <h2> through <h6> headlines as subheads there. You may find that older browsers may respond awkwardly to this convention, especially with CSS disabled, and if so, you can continue to use <h2> for second-level headlines and so on, but the W3C recommends using <h1> as the first headline in any new section.

The <nav> Element

The <nav> element defines a section of the content that links to other pages or areas of the site. You don't have to enclose every list of links you put on a page in a <nav> element. It is only for the major navigation of a page.

Most web designers are already using a form of the <nav> element when they put in a <div> or <ul> with an ID of "nav" or "navigation", such as:

```
<ul id="nav">
    <li><a href="">Home</a>
    <li><a href="">Products</a>
    <li><a href="">Services</a>
    <li><a href="">About Us</a>
</ul>
```

If you have a section on your web page like that, all you need to do is add the <nav> element around it.

```
<nav>
<h1>Navigation</h1>
<ul id="nav">
    <li><a href="">Home</a>
    <li><a href="">Products</a>
    <li><a href="">Services</a>
    <li><a href="">About Us</a>
</ul>
</nav>
```

The best way to use the <nav> element is to use it for major navigation, because that is typically the only navigation most users care about. However, what major navigation is depends on the site and the site's developers. Some sites have only one major navigation section, with other navigation elements just being links within the site. Other sites might have three or four <nav> elements. For example, my site on About.com (http://webdesign.about.com/) has several forms of navigation:

- ▶ A bread crumb trail at the top

- ▶ Four tabs below the site name

- ▶ The "Must Reads" section

- ▶ The "Browse Topic" links

- ▶ And even the "Explore Web Design / HTML" section at the bottom of the page

Most of these could be considered major navigation, but if I were to convert this page to HTML5, I would add <nav> elements around the four tabs and the "Browse Topic" links, as those provide the best navigation through the site. Until the specification is clear on this topic, either solution, marking all navigation as <nav> or just the major navigation, is okay.

Some places you might use the <nav> element, beyond the primary navigation bar on your site include:

- ▶ Table of contents

- ▶ Previous and next links

- ▶ Breadcrumb trail

You should be careful not to confuse the <nav> element with the <menu> element. The <menu> element is really a list of commands. It can be a navigation list where each item points to a different location—like a goto list. If the menu is a list of major navigation elements, then you can put it inside of a <nav> element, but it shouldn't replace the <nav> element.

The <section> Element

The <section> element is possibly the most confusing of the new sectioning elements. Most designers who use it tend to use it incorrectly. The most common way it's used is to set up page divisions for styles, which is incorrect usage. You should be using the <div> element for styling your layout.

Don't feel bad if you have been using the <section> element incorrectly. Many people have. In fact, you can find it used incorrectly on many sites teaching HTML5.

According to the W3C, "The section element is not a generic container element. When an element is needed for styling purposes or as a convenience for scripting, authors are encouraged to use the div element instead."[1]

Here are a few ways you can use to determine whether you should use a `<section>` element:

▶ Does the section have a natural headline? If it doesn't, you shouldn't use a `<section>` element.

▶ Would the section be a natural part of a page outline? If it isn't, then it shouldn't be a `<section>`.

▶ Is there more purpose to the section than just the style? If you're using the `<section>` tag just as hooks for styles, you should use the `<div>` element instead.

▶ Does the section content meet the criteria of an `<article>`, `<aside>`, or `<nav>`? If syndicating the content makes sense then you should use an `<article>`. If the content is related to the site or to the article then `<aside>` is appropriate. Of course, if it's navigation, then the `<nav>` element is best.

One place you might put a `<section>` element is in an `<aside>` for your blog. Most blogs have an `<aside>` that includes sections for a Blogroll, latest posts, categories, and so on. Each of those could be a `<section>`. For example:

```
<aside>
    <section>
        <h1>Blogroll</h1>
        <ul>
            <li><a href="http://diveintohtml5.org">Dive into HTML5</a></li>
            <li><a href="http://html5gallery.com/">HTML5 Gallery</a></li>
            <li><a href="http://dev.w3.org/html5/spec/Overview.html">HTML5
➥Specification (W3C)</a></li>
        </ul>
    </section>
    <section>
        <h1>Categories</h1>
        <ul>
            <li>...</li>
        </ul>
    </section>
</aside>
```

---

[1] "The Section Element." HTML5 Working Draft. www.w3.org/TR/html5/sections.html#the-section-element. Referenced May 12, 2011.

By the Way

When to Use <div>

The <div> element has been the standby for designs and layout for standards-based designers for several years now, but now with HTML5, that use should lessen. In fact, you should really only use the <div> element when no other appropriate element exists. For now, you may want to continue to use it in conjunction with the sectioning tags (that is, <div id="article"><article>), but you should only do that if you are having trouble getting your pages to display correctly.

Sectioning Root Elements

The sectioning root elements are elements in HTML5 that can have their own outlines, but they don't contribute to the outlines of their ancestors. These elements are:

- <blockquote>
- <body>
- <details>
- <fieldset>
- <figure>
- <td>

You should already be familiar with the <body>, <blockquote>, <fieldset>, and <td> elements. The new elements in HTML5 are <details> and <figure>.

You use the <details> element to hide and show additional information about the content. It has a related element that is also new—<summary>. The <summary> element is an optional element inside of the <details> element that represents a caption or summary of the <details> element.

Use these elements to add information to your documents that isn't critical to the content. For example, you can add information about a form field in a <details> element that people can open if they need more help:

```
<input id="phone-number" type="phone">
<details>
<summary>Format</summary>
<p>(xxx) xxx-xxxx
</details>
```

You use the <figure> element to define self-contained units of content. Most commonly a figure is an image, but it can be any type of content that can stand on its own. The related element <figcaption> provides a legend or caption for a figure.

Some common figures include:

▶ Images or groups of images

▶ Blocks of code

▶ Poetry or quotations

▶ Charts and graphs

When you are deciding whether to put content into a `<figure>` you need to determine whether the content is essential to the content of the page. If it is essential, and the exact placement in the content is not critical, then a `<figure>` element is a good choice.

You can write a simple `<figure>` like this:

```
<figure>
<img src="shasta.jpg" alt="Shasta">
<figcaption>
<p>A photo of my dog Shasta.
</figcaption>
</figure>
```

Remember that you don't use the `<figure>` element around every image on your page. Banners and advertisements are not related to the page contents and so are not figures.

Heading, Header, and Footer Elements

The heading, header, and footer elements are not technically sectioning elements because they do not contribute to the site outline, but most web designers think of them as sectioning elements because they are used to define the semantic layout of your web document.

Heading elements include `<hgroup>` and all the heading tags: `<h1>` through `<h6>`. Use the `<hgroup>` element to group a set of one or more heading elements so that they are collected as one element in the document outline. For example:

```
<h1>This is a Headline</h1>
<h2>This is a Sub-Head</h2>
<section><h1>And this is a Sub-section</h1></section>
```

This has the following outline:

```
1. This is a Headline
    1. This is a Sub-Head
    2. And this is a Sub-section
```

Suppose you group the <h1> and <h2> together in an <hgroup>:

```
<hgroup>
<h1>This is a Headline</h1>
<h2>This is a Sub-Head</h2>
</hgroup>
<section><h1>And this is a Sub-section</h1></section>
```

Then you get the following outline:

```
1. This is a Headline
      1. And this is a Sub-section
```

You can use the <header> and <footer> elements the same way you might have used <div id="header"> and <div id="footer"> in your HTML. However, don't use the <hgroup> element unless you really are grouping together more than one heading tag. Writing the following is redundant and incorrect:

```
<hgroup><h1>My Headline</h1></hgroup>
```

Also, although the <hgroup> element is valid at the time of this writing, some controversy about whether it should remain in the HTML5 specification still exists, and it may be left out of the final HTML5 specification.

The <header> can contain a section's headline as well as additional information that introduces the section, such as a table of contents, dateline, or relevant icons. What is crucial to understand is that though most of the time you will use the <header> element at the top of your document, you can also include a <header> element at the beginning of any sectioning element, such as an <article>, <aside>, or <nav>.

The <footer> element acts just like the <header> element except that it comes at the end of a section. A footer contains information about the section such as who wrote it, copyright data, or even related links. Just like the <header> element, you can include a <footer> in any sectioning element, and it does not create a new section.

Don't Get Hung Up on the Name "Footer"

Even though the most common location for a footer is at the bottom or foot of the page, you don't have to place it there in your design. For example, in a blog post, information such as the date the post was written and the author's name could be considered footer information, but you can put that footer at the top of the post if that's where you want it to appear in your design.

If you have contact information in your footer for the author of a post or the page, you should wrap it in the <address> element. You can then put the <address> in the <footer>.

There is a lot to learn when starting to build correctly sectioned HTML5 documents. But with practice you will start to understand the purpose of each of the sectioning elements so that you can build a correctly sectioned document yourself.

▼   **Try It Yourself**

Building a Blog Using HTML5 Sectioning Elements

Blogs typically have standard page elements such as posts, comments, navigation, and so on. By following these steps you can create a blog page that contains two posts, with space for comments, site navigation, a sidebar, and a site header and footer.

1. Start your HTML5 document as you normally would:

```
<!DOCTYPE HTML>
<html lang="en-us">
<head>
    <meta charset="UTF-8">
    <title>My Blog</title>
    <script src="modernizr-1.7.min"></script>
</head>
<body class="no-js">
</body>
</html>
```

2. Add a container <div> inside the <body> tag so that you have a hook for your CSS styles:

```
<body class="no-js" >
    <div id="container">
    </div>
</body>
```

3. Create a <header> element inside the <div> to contain your blog title, tagline, and navigation:

```
<div id="container">
    <header>
        <hgroup>
            <h1>My Blog</h1>
            <h2>Where I Talk About What Interests Me</h2>
        </hgroup>
        <nav>
            <h1>Navigation</h1>
            <ul>
```

```
                <li><a href="">Home</a></li>
                <li><a href="">About Me</a></li>
                <li><a href="">Photos</a></li>
            </ul>
        </nav>
    </header>
```

4. After the `<header>` add an `<article>` with a `<header>` that contains the post title:

```
</header>
<article>
    <header>
        <h1>Post #1</h1>
    </header>
</article>
```

5. Place your post contents after the article `<header>`:

```
<article>
    <header>
        <h1>Post #1</h1>
    </header>
    <p>This is my first post. It includes a photo of my dog.
    <figure>
        <img src="shasta.jpg" alt="Shasta">
        <figcaption>My Dog Shasta</figcaption>
    </figure>
</article>
```

6. Put a `<footer>` including your name and the date inside the `<article>`:

```
<footer>
    <p>By: <address><a
href="mailto:me@myurl.com">Jennifer</a></address>
    <p>Date: <time datetime="2011-05-12">May 12, 2011</time>
</footer>
</article>
```

7. Put the comments in a second `<article>` inside the post's `<article>`:

```
<article>
    <h1>Comments</h1>
    <p><a href="">Post</a> your comments or <a href="">read</a>
other comments
    </article>
</article>
```

8. Outside the post's `<article>` but still inside the `<div>` put an `<aside>` to include a site sidebar:

```
<aside>
    <h1>Learn More</h1>
    <section>
```

```
            <h1>Recent Comments</h1>
            <p>None
        </section>
        <section>
            <h1>Stay in Contact</h1>
            <p><a href="">RSS</a> or <a href="">Newsletter</a>
        </section>
    </aside>
    </div>
```

9. Finally, add a `<footer>` with your copyright information at the bottom of the document:

```
    </aside>
    <footer>
        <p>Copyright &copy; 2011 Jennifer Kyrnin
    </footer>
    </div>
```

You will want to add styles to make the page look nicer, and of course, you will want to add more content. But if you check, the HTML will outline correctly with no untitled sections.

The complete HTML is listed at www.html5in24hours.com/examples/ sectioning-example-html.html.

▲

Marking Up HTML Semantically

Marking up HTML5 documents semantically involves more than just using sectioning elements. Semantic elements describe what the content is. HTML5 has only a couple new semantic tags, but a number of HTML 4 elements have also been changed in HTML5 to be more semantic.

The benefit of using semantic HTML tags is that you provide more information to the browsers, but if the browsers don't support the tags, they just ignore them. Using them can only improve your web pages.

Mobile support by iOS and Android is really good for the sectioning and semantic elements. Android has supported them since 2.1, and iOS had partial support in 3.2 and full support in 4.0 and later.

In fact, the majority of difficulty you will have with these elements is with Internet Explorer before version 9. If you want to support these browsers, you can use the scripts mentioned in Hour 8, "Converting Web Apps to Mobile."

Semantic HTML 4 Elements

A bunch of elements that are part of the HTML 4 specification are semantic:

▶ **<abbr>** – Abbreviations

The <acronym> Element Is Obsolete

The <acronym> tag is a part of HTML 4 and defines acronyms—abbreviations that form words themselves, such as NASA, FAQ, or SCUBA. But because of the confusion between abbreviations and acronyms, and the fact that acronyms are also abbreviations, this element was made obsolete in HTML5.

By the Way

▶ **<code>**—Code samples

▶ **<del>**—Deleted text

▶ **<dfn>**—Defining instance of a term

▶ **<em>**—Emphatic stress

▶ **<ins>**—Inserted stress

▶ **<kbd>**—Keyboard input

▶ **<samp>**—Sample output

▶ **<strong>**—Strong importance

▶ **<var>**—Variable or placeholder text

Newly Semantic HTML 4 Elements

Several HTML elements were not semantic in HTML 4, but had their focus changed in HTML5 to become semantic:

▶ **<b>**—This used to mean just bold text, but now it represents text that would normally be displayed in bold, but doesn't have extra emphasis.

▶ **<hr>**—This used to represent a horizontal line, but now it represents a thematic break in the content.

▶ **<i>**—This used to mean italic text, but now it represents text that would normally be displayed in italics, but doesn't have any extra emphasis.

▶ **<s>**—This used to mean text that had a line through it (strikeout), but now represents content that is no longer accurate and has been "struck" from the document.

▶ **<small>**—This used to be text that was printed smaller than the surrounding text, but now it represents "small print" such as legalese.

▶ **<u>**—This used to be text that was underlined, but now it represents text that would normally be displayed with an underline.

Emphasis Refers to Contents Read Aloud

When referring to text that is emphasized or not to be emphasized, this generally refers to how the text might be read in a screen reader. A book title would be italicized, but when read out loud, no special distinction would be made regarding the italics, as it is just a book title. In written form, the text may seem to stand out more, but with elements like <i> and <b> they would not be called out when read aloud.

New Semantic Elements in HTML5

A few new semantic elements in HTML5 enable you to further define the meaning of your content: <mark>, <meter>, <progress>, and <time>.

You use the <mark> element to indicate text that should be highlighted or stand out for reference purposes. You see text that is marked every time you use a search engine. The words that you searched for are highlighted (usually in bold) in the results text, as you can see in Figure 9.1.

FIGURE 9.1
Searching Bing for "HTML5 mark" with the results in bold.

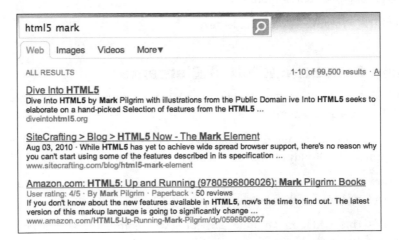

You should use the <mark> element whenever you want to draw attention to sections of the text in a document, such as with the search terms in Figure 9.1 or to otherwise highlight a portion of text, that wouldn't otherwise be highlighted. It is different from the <strong> and <em> elements because <mark> adds no extra emphasis or importance to the text, it is just highlighted.

You use the <meter> element to indicate a scalar measurement within a range, such as a star rating on a review, a letter grade on an exam, a percentage, or a fraction.

The <meter> element has six attributes:

- ▶ **value**—The measured amount shown by the meter. For example, a grade on a paper might be written <meter value="91">A-</meter>. This attribute is required, but can be what is written in the element. For example, <meter>3 out of 15</meter>. The value is "3" and the max is "15," because that is what is written in the element.

- ▶ **min**—The minimum for the range.

- ▶ **max**—The maximum for the range. For example, <meter value="91" min="0" max="100">A-</meter>.

- ▶ **low**—The point that marks the upper boundary of the "low" portion of the meter.

- ▶ **high**—The point that marks the lower boundary of the "high" portion of the meter. Along with low, high lets you divide your meter range into three parts, for example <meter value="5" low="3" high="7">1 to 10</meter>.

- ▶ **optimum**—The point that marks the optimal point on the range.

You can also use the title attribute to specify the unit, such as inches, days, or dollars.

Use the <meter> element to define ranges and provide extra information about that range. The contents of the <meter> element can be text that is then defined by the value attribute, such as:

Keep the dough <meter min="80" max="90" title="degrees">warm</meter>.

Meter Is Not for Measurements

Although putting a <meter> element around things such as weights and heights is tempting, if there is not a definitive range, you should leave the text alone. Using it on measurements is incorrect unless there is a known maximum value.

Watch Out!

The <progress> element is a form element that you use to indicate the progress of something that might take time to do, such as:

▶ Something being downloaded or uploaded

▶ A computation performing

▶ A game loading

Following is an example <progress> element:

```
I am <progress max="24" value="12" title="chapters">half way</progress>
through the book.
```

The <progress> element has limited browser support right now, working only in Opera and Chrome. However, you can use a polyfill (such as this one at http://blogupstairs.com/html5-polyfill-progress-element/) or a detection script and a jQuery plug-in for non-compliant browsers. You detect <progress> support like this:

```
return 'value' in document.createElement('progress');
```

The <time> element indicates a date or time. You use it to mark up times and dates in your document. You can add the datetime attribute to give the precise date and time, numerically. You can also add the attribute pubdate to indicate that the time is the publication date and time of the nearest ancestor <article> element or of the document as a whole.

The datetime attribute can contain a date, a time, or a date and time. It is written according to RFC3339 (http://tools.ietf.org/html/rfc3339) in the following formats:

▶ **date**—YYYY-MM-DD.

▶ **time**—HH:MM:SS. Use a 24-hour clock; seconds are optional.

▶ **time with timezone**—HH:MM:SS+Zone. Timezones range from –12:00 to +14:00.

▶ **time at UTC**—HH:MM:SSZ Z is the same as Universal Coordinated Time (UTC), or +00:00.

▶ **time and date**—YYYY-MM-DDTHH:MM:SS+Zone. The T in the middle is just a T, to separate the date from the time.

The text in your <time> elements doesn't have to display a full date or time. Here are some examples:

```
<time datetime="1940-10-04">October 4, 1940</time>
<time datetime="1940-10-04">Oct 4</time>
<time datetime="00:00:00-08:00">Midnight</time>
```

One thing to keep in mind is that the `<time>` element cannot set specific `datetime` values for pre-AD dates. You also cannot encode imprecise dates such as "March 2008." To indicate dates of this nature, you need to use microformats, which Hour 15, "Microformats and Microdata," discusses in more detail.

Summary

This hour taught you all about the new semantic elements in HTML5. You learned how to create semantic markup that can be outlined using sectioning elements as well as the semantic elements added and changed in HTML5.

Outlines may not seem important to some designers, but anyone who designs with accessibility in mind knows that outlines help screen readers use the documents more easily. Well-marked-up documents with sectioning elements create outlines that are easy to read.

Semantic elements may also not seem important, but providing extra information by indicating the semantics of text doesn't hurt either. Plus, you might be surprised at how much it does help.

Q&A

Q. *Do I have to use every sectioning element in every document I create?*

A. No, of course not. Like all other semantic elements, you should use the sectioning elements that make sense in your document. If you don't have tangential text, then you shouldn't use the `<aside>`. Likewise, if you have no sections that can't be defined by other sectioning elements, then the `<section>` element is not needed.

Q. *Why do you refer to some elements as "obsolete?" I thought the term was "deprecated."*

A. HTML 4 was a standard written primarily for browser makers. The term *deprecated* was intended to tell them that they no longer needed to support that item in the future. HTML5 was written more for web authors and so *obsolete* was considered a clearer term.

Q. *What if I used the* `<meter>` *element with a value outside the minimum or maximum?*

A. Although the possibility exists that a future browser might display some type of error message if you did this, the chances are very slim. As with all semantic elements, you should try to use the elements correctly.

Workshop

The workshop contains quiz questions to help you process what you've learned in this chapter. Try to answer all the questions before you read the answers. See Appendix A, "Answers to Quizzes," for answers.

Quiz

1. What are the four new sectioning elements in HTML5?

2. Which of the following are valid within a `<figure>`?

    a. An image

    b. A block of text

    c. Both

3. True or False. An `<aside>` should be used to mark up a site sidebar.

4. True or False. A `<section>` should be used as just a hook for styles.

5. True or False. A sectioning root contributes its contents to the entire site outline.

6. True or False. A `<footer>` is not a sectioning element.

7. What are the new, non-sectioning, semantic elements in HTML5?

Exercises

1. Write an HTML document with correct sectioning elements. Check your outline in the HTML5 Outliner (http://gsnedders.html5.org/outliner/). If you have any untitled sections, check to make sure that you need that section, and if you do, add a headline with an `<h1>` element.

2. Examine some existing web pages, either your own or online. See whether you can find places where the <mark>, <meter>, <progress>, and <time> elements would be appropriate. If you are examining your own pages, add in the elements so that your pages are more semantic.

Drawing with the HTML5 Canvas Element

What You'll Learn in This Hour:

▶ How to use the `<canvas>` element to draw on web pages

▶ How to create lines, rectangles, and circles on canvases

▶ How to use images as portions of the canvas or as patterns

▶ What mobile devices support `<canvas>`

▶ How canvas differs from Flash and SVG

The HTML5 `<canvas>` element lets you use JavaScript to draw shapes, add images, and create animations right in your web page. It is not done with a different language (such as SVG) nor does it use a plug-in (like Flash).

In this hour you will learn what the `<canvas>` element is and how you can use it to create shapes and add images and text right inside the web browser. This hour serves as a jumping-off point for how to use the `<canvas>` element—there is even more out there that you can do with it. You are limited only by your imagination.

Using the Canvas Element

In a nutshell, the HTML5 `<canvas>` element lets you draw whatever you want on your web page using JavaScript. You can use it to add images, create slideshows, display animations, and even build games.

The `<canvas>` element can be scripted. This means that you can create a canvas that changes based on user input. Although most canvas applications have focused on games, you can use it for other things, including:

▶ Dynamic graphs such as stock tickers

▶ Photo galleries

▶ Fancy fonts

▶ Online visual tools such as mind maps and image editors

Anything you can draw or animate you can do in a <canvas> element. However, like every part of HTML5, you should only use it where it's appropriate. For example, you wouldn't use a <canvas> element to insert every image on your page, nor should you use it to add your page header, but you can use it to display dynamic graphs or create online games. Instead you would use the <img> and <header> tags to define those items.

The <canvas> element is easy to add to your HTML documents:

```
<canvas></canvas>
```

This line creates a blank canvas in the browser. Because it has no width, height, or content, it doesn't display anything on the screen. Most of the time, you will also want to specify a width and height and give your canvas an ID so you can reference it in your scripts:

```
<canvas width="350" height="450" id="canvas1"></canvas>
```

Of course, if that's all you write, there will simply be a blank 350 x 450-pixel space in your HTML.

By the Way

See Your Empty Canvases

When working with the <canvas> element for the first time, setting a border around it so that you know where your canvases are is easiest. Add a line to your style sheet—canvas { border: solid thin black; }—to add a thin border around every canvas on your page. When you're done editing, you can delete the style.

The <canvas> element is supported by Chrome 3.0+, Firefox 3.0+, Opera 10.0+, and both iOS and Android 1.0 and up. Internet Explorer 9 supports it natively, and IE 7 and 8 need a plug-in such as ExplorerCanvas (http://code.google.com/p/explorercanvas/).

You should include text inside your <canvas> element to display if the element isn't supported by the browser:

```
<canvas>
This page requires an HTML5 compliant browser to render correctly.
Other browsers may not see anything.
</canvas>
```

Basic support for the <canvas> element is quite good on both iOS and Android. In fact, on mobile devices, the only one that is iffy is Opera mini.

When you compare <canvas> to Flash support, you can clearly see which you should choose for your mobile applications. Flash is not supported at all on iOS devices, and it seems likely that this will never change.

When you compare <canvas> to SVG support, the results are clear as well. Although Android 3.0 supports SVG, Android 2.3 does not, so unless you are willing to leave out the Android phone devices, <canvas> is still a better choice.

Drawing Shapes on the <Canvas> Element

To have the canvas show anything, you need to script it using JavaScript. To use JavaScript you have to attach the script to an event. An easy event to use is onclick. When a user clicks on your canvas, it will draw something. For example:

```
function drawSquare() {
    var canvas = document.getElementById("canvas1");
    var context = canvas.getContext("2d");
    context.fillStyle = "rgb(13, 118, 208)";
    context.fillRect(30, 30, 150, 150);
}
```

You Can Call Your Script When the Page Loads

Calling your script onclick is a way to make the shapes more interactive, but if you need the canvas to be drawn when the page is live, you should draw it when the body loads by calling it in the body tag: <body onload="drawSquare();">.

Did you Know?

This draws a blue square on the canvas called "canvas1." You call that function on the <canvas> element in your document:

```
<canvas id="canvas1" width="200" height="200"
➥onclick="drawSquare();"></canvas>
```

The script at the beginning of this section ("Drawing Shapes on the <Canvas> Element") does four things:

▶ **line 1**—Finds the "canvas1" element in your document

▶ **line 2**—Sets the context to two-dimensions

▶ **line 3**—Defines the fill color as blue

▶ **line 4**—Draws a rectangle with four equal sides—a square

You Must Set the Context

To draw on a <canvas> element, you must pass the string "2d" to the getContext() method. Otherwise, your <canvas> element will not display anything. This way, when other contexts become available, you will be able to take different actions on your canvas elements.

You can then clear the entire canvas by setting the width or height. You don't have to change the width or height, just set it to itself, as described in the following Try It Yourself.

▼   **Try It Yourself**

Making a Square Appear and Disappear

You can modify the preceding script to make the square appear and disappear.

1. Add the <canvas> element to your document:

   ```
   <canvas id="canvas1" width="200" height="200" style="border: solid 1px
   ➥black;"
   onclick="drawSquare();">
   </canvas>
   ```

2. Put in the JavaScript to draw the square when the <canvas> element is clicked on:

   ```
   function drawSquare() {
       var canvas = document.getElementById("canvas1");
       var context = canvas.getContext("2d");
       context.fillStyle = "rgb(13, 118, 208)";
       context.fillRect(30, 30, 140, 140);
   }
   ```

3. Create an erase function in the JavaScript:

   ```
   function eraseSquare() {
       var canvas = document.getElementById("canvas1");
       canvas.width = canvas.width;
   }
   ```

4. Call the erase function on a double-click in the <canvas> element:

   ```
   ondblclick="eraseSquare();"
   ```

▲

Drawing Rectangles

Rectangles and squares are the easiest shapes to draw with the <canvas> element because several functions are designed just for building them. The three functions for drawing rectangles are

- **fillRect**—For drawing a filled rectangle
- **strokeRect**—For drawing a rectangular outline
- **clearRect**—For making an empty, transparent rectangular shape

Figure 10.1 shows these three functions used on one canvas. The black boxes are two fillRect functions, one first filling the entire canvas and the other one last, filling the inner space. The white box is created with a clearRect function to bring the <canvas> element back to its default color (white). The thin black line is drawn with the strokeRect function.

FIGURE 10.1
A canvas with four rectangles drawn on it.

To draw a rectangle, you use any of the three functions with the values x, y, width, and height. x and y specify the position on the canvas, where 0,0 is the upper-left corner. x moves the point to the right on the horizontal plane and y moves the point down on the vertical plane. The width and height are the size of the rectangle.

If you draw two shapes on the canvas, they will layer one over the other, with the last one written in the script being on top.

The <canvas> element draws only in black and white unless you set styles. You can set the fill color and the line color with two properties:

- **fillStyle** – The fill color

- **strokeStyle** – The border color

You can use color names, hexadecimal color codes, RGB color values, and RGB with alpha transparency color values. With alpha transparency, you can adjust colors by layering one over another. For example, the following script would create a red box in the upper left of the page, and a faded blue box in the lower right, with the overlap being purple:

```
context.fillStyle = "#ff0000";
context.fillRect(10,10, 300,300);
context.fillStyle = "rgba(0,0,255,0.5)";
context.fillRect(190,190, 300,300);
```

You aren't limited to flat colors with the <canvas> element. You can also create gradients and use them to style your fills and strokes. The two types of gradients are linear and radial. In order to create a gradient you need to use three properties:

- **createLinearGradient**—This takes four arguments defining the x and y coordinates of the starting point and the x and y coordinates of the end point.

- **createRadialGradient**—This takes six arguments. The first three define a circle with x and y coordinates and a radius. The second three define a second circle with x and y coordinates and a radius.

- **addColorStop**—This takes two arguments. The first is the position of the color on the gradient between 0 and 1. 0 is the start of the gradient and 1 is the end. The second argument is the color written in CSS colors, just like the flat colors described earlier.

You can have as many stop colors in your gradient as you like. If you start your fill in the middle of the gradient, that stop color will fill the shape from the start to that stop point. Figure 10.2 shows a linear gradient on top and a radial gradient on bottom.

Here is an example of how to draw a box with a two-colored linear gradient across the diagonal:

```
var linGrad = context.createLinearGradient(0,0, 500,500);
linGrad.addColorStop(0,"red");
linGrad.addColorStop(1,"blue");

// draw gradient box
context.fillStyle = linGrad;
context.fillRect(10,10, 490,490);
```

FIGURE 10.2
Two gradients
on HTML
canvas.

Radial gradients are more complicated than linear gradients because rather than defining two points for the gradient to draw between, you are defining two imaginary circles. The gradient travels in all directions (radially) from the center point of the first circle to the outer edge of the second circle. These two circles define a cone shape that creates the gradient, as shown in Figure 10.3. Circle 1 defines the starting point of the gradient and Circle 2 defines the ending point. The radial gradient travels both along a line and a circle.

This is different than how most graphic programs create radial gradients. In those, the center point of both the first circle and the second circle is the same, so your gradient will always move smoothly out in all directions.

FIGURE 10.3
Diagram of a
how a cone-
shaped radial
gradient works.

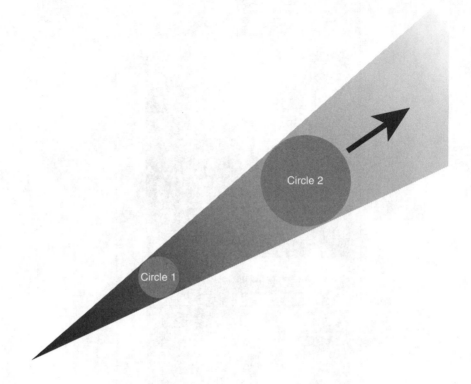

To create a radial gradient like the aforementioned one in the <canvas> element, position both circles starting at the same x and y coordinates, but make the second one larger than the first.

To define a radial gradient, you use six arguments:

```
createRadialGradient(x1,y1,r1, x2,y2,r2)
```

x1 and y1 are the coordinates of the center of the first circle, and r1 is the radius (in pixels) of that first circle. x2 and y2 are the coordinates of the second circle and r2 is the radius of the second circle.

Because radial gradients are defined as circles, you can use them to draw circles on your canvas. If you want to fill an object that is not a circle, then you need to make sure the second circle completely surrounds the object.

Here is an example of how to draw a circle with a radial gradient:

```
var radGrad = context.createRadialGradient(100,150,0, 100,150,70);
radGrad.addColorStop(0.9, "rgb(105,138,72)");
radGrad.addColorStop(0, "rgba(171,235,108,1)");
```

```
radGrad.addColorStop(1, "rgba(105,138,72,0)");
// draw gradient box
context.fillStyle = radGrad;
context.fillRect(10,10, 490,490);
```

You can see this code in action at www.html5in24hours.com/examples/
canvas-circles.html.

Drawing Polygons and Lines

To draw other shapes in the <canvas> element you use lines or paths. The five
methods used to draw and use paths are

▶ **beginPath()**—This method creates the path in the canvas.

▶ **closePath()**—This method draws a straight line from the current point to
the start. It won't do anything when paths are already closed or on paths
with only one point.

▶ **stroke()**—This draws an outline of your path.

▶ **fill()**—This fills in the shape of your path.

▶ **moveTo()**—This draws nothing, but moves the drawing position to a new
location on the canvas.

Always specify your starting position on your paths with a moveTo() command first.
The <canvas> element will treat your first construction that way regardless of what
the method actually is, and this will prevent surprising results.

After you have moved your cursor to the starting position, to draw a line you use the
lineTo() method. The lineTo() method takes two arguments: the x and y coordinates where the line should draw. To draw a line, you write:

```
context.beginPath();
context.moveTo(0,0);
context.lineTo(60,60);
context.stroke();
```

Fill Closes the Path

If you don't close the path and choose to fill the shape, the shape will close automatically with a straight line from the last point on the path to the first point. You
do not need to close the path with the closePath() method.

By the Way

To draw a triangle, you write:

```
context.beginPath();
context.moveTo(20,30);
context.lineTo(500,100);
context.lineTo(250,300);
context.fill();
```

You may need to increase the size of your canvas with the width and height attributes to allow this example to fit.

▼   **Try It Yourself**

Drawing an Octagon

In this exercise you will use lines to draw the edges of an octagon. This won't draw a perfect octagon but it will create an eight-sided figure.

1. Start your path and move your drawing point to 200,0:

   ```
   context.beginPath();
   context.moveTo(200,0);
   ```

2. Draw a line to 400,0:

   ```
   context.lineTo(400,0);
   ```

3. Draw seven more lines to 600,200; 600,400; 400,600; 200, 600; 0,400; and 0,200:

   ```
   context.lineTo(600,200);
   context.lineTo(600,400);
   context.lineTo(400,600);
   context.lineTo(200,600);
   context.lineTo(0,400);
   context.lineTo(0,200);
   ```

4. Close your path:

   ```
   context.closePath();
   ```

5. Change the fill color to red:

   ```
   context.fillStyle = "#ff0000";
   ```

6. Fill in your octagon:

   ```
   context.fill();
   ```

   If the octagon you build is too big, you may need to increase the size of your canvas to make it fit.

▲

You can also adjust the width of your path lines, the shape of the end of the lines, and how these lines are joined together using the lineWidth, lineCap, lineJoin, and miterLimit properties.

The lineWidth property changes the width from the default 1 unit (the space between grid marks—essentially a pixel) to whatever positive number you want. The width is centered on the path. To draw a line 2 units wide, you write:

```
context.lineWidth = "2";
```

The lineCap property changes how the end point of the lines is drawn. There are three values: butt, round, and square. The default is butt. Figure 10.4 shows three lines with the three different caps. The thin line shows the grid line where the path will start. As you can see the square and round styles extend past that grid line.

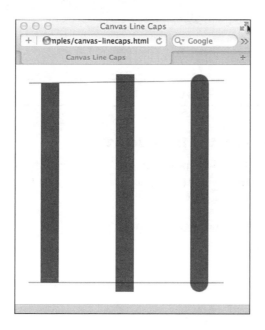

FIGURE 10.4
Three line cap styles: butt, square, and round.

Butt comes right up to the grid line where the path starts. Square adds half the width of the stroke beyond the grid line. Round adds a semicircle with a radius of half the width of the line beyond the grid line.

The lineJoin property changes how the lines in a shape are joined together. The three possible values are round, bevel, and miter. The default is miter. Figure 10.5 shows the three ways lines can join. The default, miter, makes a sharp corner, bevel cuts off the tip, and round makes it more curved.

FIGURE 10.5
Three line join
styles: miter,
bevel, and
round.

▼   **Try It Yourself**

Building a Line with the Three Join Types

You can build a line with one type of join, and then swap it with the other types to
see what they look like as well. Follow these steps to create a "W" shape and give the
corners different join shapes:

1. Set your line width and begin the path:

```
context.lineWidth = 15;
context.beginPath();
```

2. Move the starting point to slightly inside the canvas and draw a line:

```
context.moveTo(10,20);
context.lineTo(150,200);
```

3. Draw three more lines to create a "W" shape:

```
context.lineTo(290,20);
context.lineTo(430,200);
context.lineTo(570,20);
```

4. Change the line join style:

```
context.lineJoin = "round";
```

5. Stroke the path:

```
context.stroke();
```

> Look at your canvas to see the default style of `miter`. Change the line join
> style to `round` and `bevel` and look at how the corners change.

The `miterLimit` property defines how sharp or dull the miter points are on a join. The higher the miter limit, the sharper your mitered joins can be. For smaller limits, the joins are beveled when they reach that limit.

Drawing Circles

To draw a circle in the <canvas> element you use the `arc` method. To understand how to draw the circle, you have to imagine that you are physically drawing the circle with a protractor. You set the point of your protractor in the center of the circle, bend the angle so that the pen is at the radius, start drawing at a point, and lift the pen at a second point. You can draw the circle either clockwise or counterclockwise.

The <canvas> element draws a circle in the same way. You set the x and y coordinates for the center of the circle, the radius, the starting point on the circle (in radians), the ending point on the circle (in radians), and finally the direction to draw either clockwise (`true`) or counterclockwise (`false`). The method looks like this:

```
arc(x,y,radius,startAngle,endAngle,true);
```

How to Find Start and End Points for Circles and Arcs

Arcs in the <canvas> element are measured in radians, not degrees. Radians do not have the same starting point as degrees (in degrees 0° is noon, but in radians it is not). But because most people find thinking in degrees to be easier, having a conversion tool helps. In JavaScript, you can convert degrees to radians with the following expression: `var radians = (Math.PI/180)*degrees`.

By the Way

To draw a circle, write:

```
var startPoint = (Math.PI/180)*0;
var endPoint = (Math.PI/180)*360;
context.beginPath();
context.arc(200,200,100,startPoint,endPoint,true);
context.fill();
```

Try It Yourself ▼

Drawing Half Circles

Use the arc method of drawing circles, or parts of circles to build a wave pattern with half circles.

1. Decide on the diameter of your circle, and define the radius as half of that:

```
var radius = 125/2;
```

2. Define the x and y coordinates of your first circle based on the radius:

```
var y = radius+10;
var x1 = radius;
```

3. Define the coordinates of the subsequent circles as multiples of the radius:

```
var x2 = 3*radius;
var x3 = 5*radius;
var x4 = 7*radius;
```

4. Draw the first half circle using Math.PI as your end point value to get a half circle:

```
context.beginPath();
context.arc(x1,y,radius,0,Math.PI,true);
context.stroke();
```

5. Draw the second circle, only change the direction to counterclockwise:

```
context.beginPath();
context.arc(x2,y,radius,0,Math.PI,false);
context.stroke();
```

6. Repeat for as many circles as you want on your canvas:

```
context.beginPath();
context.arc(x3,y,radius,0,Math.PI,true);
context.stroke();
context.beginPath();
context.arc(x4,y,radius,0,Math.PI,false);
context.stroke();
```

Figure 10.6 shows how this might look if you added lineWidth to make a thicker line.

FIGURE 10.6
A wave pattern made with half circles.

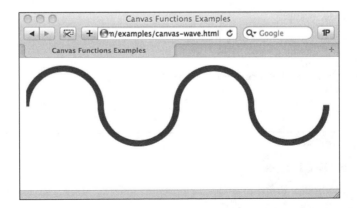

You can remove the extra `beginPath()` and `stroke()` methods (all but the first `beginPath()` and last `stroke()`) if you are filling the circles or if you want a line down the middle connecting them all.

Writing Fonts and Text on the Canvas

To draw text on the canvas, use the `fillText()` method to define what and where to draw:

```
context.fillText("Hello World", 250, 100);
```

This will put the text "Hello World" at the x and y coordinates 250,100.

Text on a canvas is drawn on rather than displayed within the CSS box model. You can't define the float, margin, padding, or word wrapping. You just set the font size, family, weight, variant, and line height, and then draw it on your canvas. You can use several attributes to draw text:

▶ **font**—This is anything that you would put in a CSS font property, such as the font family, size, weight, variation, and line height.

▶ **textAlign**—This controls the alignment of your text and is similar to the CSS `text-align` property. It uses the values `start`, `end`, `left`, `right`, and `center`.

▶ **textBaseline**—This controls where the text is drawn relative to the starting position. It takes the values `top`, `hanging`, `middle`, `alphabetic`, `ideographic`, and `bottom`.

Watch Baselines on Non-English Text

For English text, you can stick with `top`, `middle`, or `bottom` for your `textBaseline` values, but if you are going to be writing in other languages you will need to be aware of where they are anchored so that you use the correct baseline.

You can style your text in the same way you style text in CSS. If you change the font family, you should define multiple families the same way you would in CSS. Separate them with commas and put them in order of preference. You should end with a generic font type such as `serif`, `sans-serif`, or `monospace`. Remember that if your users don't have the font on their device, the `<canvas>` element is not going to provide it for them. You'll learn more about custom fonts in Hour 11, "Fonts and Typography in HTML5."

Here is an example of how to add custom text to a <canvas> element:

```
context.font = "bold 3em/3.5em 'Palatino Linotype', 'Book Antiqua',
➥Palatino, serif";
context.textAlign = "center";
context.textBaseline = "middle";
context.fillStyle = "#f93";
context.fillText("Hello World!", 250, 250);
```

As you can see, you change the color with the `fillStyle` property because you are filling with text with the `fillText` method.

> **Style Canvas Fonts with CSS**
>
> Setting the font size in CSS on the <canvas> element will affect the font size of the text. However, other CSS styles may not be applied. Be careful when you apply properties that may be inheritable, because your canvas text may end up looking differently than you expect.

You can add shadows to your drawings with four properties:

▶ **shadowOffsetX**—How far the shadow should extend on the x axis. Negative values move the shadow left.

▶ **shadowOffsetY**—How far the shadow should extend on the y axis. Negative values move the shadow up.

▶ **shadowBlur**—The size of the blurring effect. The default is 0.

▶ **shadowColor**—The color the shadow should be. The default is fully transparent black (`rgba(0,0,0,0)`).

▼   **Try It Yourself**

Adding a Shadow to Text

Use the shadow properties to add text shadows to a block of text in a canvas element.

1. Add some text to your canvas:

```
context.font = "bold 3em/3.5em 'Palatino Linotype', 'Book Antiqua',
➥Palatino, serif";
context.textAlign = "center";
context.textBaseline = "middle";
context.fillStyle = "#f93";
context.fillText("Hello World!", 250, 250);
```

2. Above the text, set the x and y offsets for the shadow:

```
context.shadowOffsetX = -2;
context.shadowOffsetY = 2;
```

3. Define the blur:

```
context.shadowBlur = 2;
```

4. Choose a shadow color:

```
context.shadowColor = "rgba(0,0,0,0.5)";
```

Having the `fillText` line last in your code is important, because otherwise the shadow and fill won't show up. You can see an example at www. html5in24hours.com/examples/canvas-text.html.

▲

Displaying Images

To display an image inside a `<canvas>` element you need to reference an image object as a source file, and then draw the image onto the canvas with the `drawImage` function.

You have two choices for the first step. You can access an existing image on the page (in an `<img>` tag), or you can create a new image in the JavaScript, as follows:

```
var img = new Image();
img.src = "images/mydogs.png";
img.onload = function() {
    context.drawImage(img, 10,10);
}
```

As you can see, first you create the image in the JavaScript, and then, after that image has finished loading, draw it on your canvas at the x and y coordinates noted in the `drawImage` method.

Scaling and Clipping Images

You can do more than just display an image with the `<canvas>` element. You can also change the size of the image that is drawn on the canvas (scaling) and the portion of the image that is displayed (clipping).

You use four parameters in the `drawImage` method to change the image size:

```
context.drawImage(x, y, width, height)
```

The x and y coordinates specify where you want the image to be placed on the canvas. The width and height parameters are the new width and height. You can make the image larger or smaller.

Clipping images is a little trickier than scaling them, but it makes sense after you've tried it. Clipping an image adds a mask around the parts of the image that should not display on the canvas, it does not edit the image or crop it. To clip an image you need to indicate the coordinates, width, and height of the area to be clipped and the coordinates, width, and height where it should go on the canvas:

```
context.drawImage(imageID, clipx, clipy, clipwidth, clipheight,
gox, goy, gowidth, goheight)
```

Following is an example of clips used in an image on the canvas:

```
var mydogs = new Image();
mydogs.src = "images/mydogs.png";
mydogs.onload = function() {
    context.drawImage(mydogs, 20,50);
    context.drawImage(mydogs, 148, 14, 92, 120, 20,370, 123,160);
    context.drawImage(mydogs, 235, 122, 65, 85, 298,370, 122,160);
}
```

As you can see in Figure 10.7, some text was added for each image, but this figure displays just one image that was drawn on the canvas in three ways, once as the full image and two other clips of the image.

FIGURE 10.7
Clips used in a
<canvas>
element.

Remember that scaling is done by the browser, and there is no quality control. Images can become blurry if scaled up too much and grainy if scaled down too much.

Adding Patterns

You can create patterns with your images with the canvas method createPattern(). You tell it which image you want to use and how you want it patterned in your canvas:

```
context.createPattern(image, repeat-x)
```

You can set a pattern to repeat-x (horizontally), repeat-y (vertically), repeat (tiled), and no-repeat.

Try It Yourself ▼

Drawing a Fancy Border on a Canvas

In this exercise you use a single image as a repeated pattern to create a border around the outside of a canvas.

1. Create a new image object for your pattern:

```
var pattern = new Image();
pattern.src = "images/leaf-icon.png";
```

2. Open a function when the image loads:

```
pattern.onload = function() {
```

3. Create a new pattern:

```
var ptn = context.createPattern(pattern,"repeat-y");
```

4. Set the fill style to the pattern:

```
context.fillStyle = ptn;
```

5. Build a rectangle and fill with the pattern:

```
context.fillRect(0,0,500,500);
```

6. Close the function:

```
}
```

Figure 10.8 shows how a border of leaves can be created using just one image and the canvas element.

FIGURE 10.8
A border pattern
on a canvas.

How Is Canvas Different from SVG or Flash?

The biggest difference between the <canvas> element and SVG or Flash is that <canvas> is an HTML element and as such is built right into the browser and the web page. This makes accessing the <canvas> element contents for scripting and dynamic web applications easy.

SVG is a completely separate language written in XML, and Flash is written in SWF. Although most modern browsers and mobile devices support SVG, Flash does not work on iOS, and Android 2.3 and Internet Explorer 8 do not support SVG. Table 10.1 shows some of the features of Canvas, SVG, and Flash

TABLE 10.1 Different Features of Canvas, SVG, and Flash

	Canvas	**SVG**	**Flash**
Vector graphics	Canvas is bitmap, but can draw vectors.	SVG is vector based, but you can load bitmaps.	Flash is vector based.
Inline HTML	Canvas is a native HTML element.	SVG is XML and must be embedded.	Flash is SWF and must be embedded with a plug-in.
Scripts required	Canvas won't display anything with JavaScript turned off.	SVG can be written completely offline and loaded.	Flash requires a plug-in, but can be written completely offline.
Program support	Few if any commercial programs exist for building canvas graphics.	Many vector graphics programs can write SVG.	Commercial applications are available to write Flash.
Speed of rendering	Canvas renders images very quickly.	SVG renders images slower than canvas.	Flash renders images slower than canvas.
Event handling	Users can only click on the entire canvas.	Users can click on individual elements in SVG.	Users can click on any element in Flash.
User adoption	Canvas is HTML5 and so requires modern browsers.	SVG requires modern browsers.	Flash has been around a long time and has wide-spread support.
Search engine optimization (SEO)	Canvas is text based and so is SEO friendly.	SVG is text based so is SEO friendly.	Flash is an embedded SWF file and is harder for search engines to read.

Summary

The <canvas> element is a powerful tool for building vector graphic images. In this hour you learned how to draw squares, polygons, lines, and circles using paths and rectangles.

You also learned how to add text and images to your canvas as well as put shadows on your drawings, add gradients to your fills, and manipulate images that are drawn on the canvas.

This hour also discussed some of the differences between the <canvas> element, Flash, and SVG. You also got a sense of what each one does well so that you can use them all effectively.

The HTML5 <canvas> element is a very complex element, and there is still a lot more you can learn about it. This hour provided a good overview, but it only touches on the surface of what you can do with the HTML5 <canvas> element. You can also:

▶ Animate your canvas

▶ Scale and transform your drawings

▶ Combine multiple drawings with clipping paths

▶ Add interactivity

▶ Build complex games

Canvas is a very fun and exciting part of HTML5. The resources listed in Appendix C, "HTML5 and Mobile Application Resources," can help you learn more about it.

Q&A

Q. *I see that you only mentioned two-dimensional canvases (2d context). Is there a three-dimensional canvas (3d context)?*

A. Right now there is no accepted standard for a three-dimensional context on the <canvas> element. It will eventually, but right now you can only create two-dimensional drawings.

An experimental context has been enabled in Chrome, Firefox 4, and Internet Explorer 9 to enable three-dimensional context: WebGL. You use "experimental-webgl" to enable this context.

Q. *When I draw a straight line, with a path, they are not as sharp as I want them to be, why is this?*

A. This is because of how the grid on the canvas works. The x and y coordinates form lines in a grid, but when these lines are drawn on the screen, they are actually drawn in the spaces *between* the grid lines. When you draw lines with an even thickness, the line is drawn down two whole pixels, but when drawn with an odd thickness, it is drawn down the line with half on one side and half on the other. Because computer monitors cannot split a pixel in half, they compensate by anti-aliasing the pixels to either side.

To fix this problem, you need to move the location of your lines to halfway between the two grid marks. So, instead of drawing a 1-pixel-wide line from 3,0 to 3,6, you should draw it from 3.5,0 to 3.5,6. This will place the line right in between the grid lines and remove the anti-aliasing.

Q. *Can you add shadows to anything other than text?*

A. Yes, you can add shadows to all the canvas shapes, but if you add a shadow to a drawing with a gradient fill applied to it, the shadow will not be displayed. This is a browser bug that has been marked as fixed, but still seems to be a problem. Adding a shadow to a gradient-filled shape works in Firefox 4 but not Chrome or Safari, as of this writing.

Workshop

The workshop contains quiz questions to help you process what you've learned in this chapter. Try to answer all the questions before you read the answers. See Appendix A, "Answers to Quizzes" for answers.

Quiz

1. When you write a `<canvas>` element in your HTML, what is displayed in the browser?

2. The `clearRect()` method does which of the following:

    a. Creates an empty, transparent rectangle

    b. Deletes the existing rectangle

    c. Removes all rectangles from the canvas

3. True or False: You cannot use transparent colors in the `strokeStyle` property.

4. Which of these is the default cap style for lines:

    a. Butt

    b. Square

    c. Round

5. True or False: Circles are drawn using radians as the start and end points, not degrees.

6. True or False: You cannot set box model styles on canvas text.

7. What two things do you need to do to draw an image file on a canvas?

8. Which of these three are vector based:

    a. Canvas

    b. Flash

    c. SVG

Exercises

1. Build a canvas item with a rainbow linear gradient of at least seven colors across the diagonal of a rectangle.

2. Put together a page that uses as many of the <canvas> element features as you can. Be sure to use images, text, shapes, fills, shadows, and gradients.

HOUR 11

Fonts and Typography in HTML5

What You'll Learn in This Hour:

- ▶ Changes to typography with HTML5
- ▶ New CSS3 properties for fonts
- ▶ How to hyphenate with CSS3
- ▶ Choosing typographical entities to use
- ▶ What the Web Open Font Format (WOFF) standard is
- ▶ How to use WOFF in your `@font-face` designations

This hour will teach you how to use typography on your web pages. Typography used to be very difficult to get precise on web pages, but as you'll see in this hour, HTML5 and CSS3 have added new tools to make it easier. You will learn CSS3 properties for improving your fonts and how to add hyphenation to web page text.

This hour will also teach you how to use WOFF (Web Open Font Format) font families to create unique designs with custom fonts. You will learn how to use the `@font-face` CSS rule to define custom fonts.

Defining the Elements of Typography

Typography is the design and use of typefaces in communication. It includes the fonts used, the way the text appears on the page, and even what entities or special characters should look like. The rules of web typography have not changed from HTML 4 to HTML5. HTML5 just gives you a few more tools to implement good typography on your web pages. Although a web designer can't always control the typography to the extent that a print designer can, many more options exist now, so you have no excuse not to learn and use them.

You should consider several elements of typography when designing your pages and applications:

▶ Typefaces

▶ Spacing

▶ Hyphenation

▶ Rag

▶ Widows and orphans

Typefaces

A *typeface* is what most people call the "font," but it is actually the "family." For example, the Arial typeface includes Arial, Arial Black, Arial Narrow, and others. Within the Arial font family you can have bold text, italic text, small caps, and so on. A typeface involves more than just the family that the type belongs to. Typefaces also include the boldness, italics, font variants, and the size.

When designing with HTML and CSS, you should get in the habit of defining all aspects of your font with the standard CSS font properties:

▶ `font-family`—A prioritized list of font family names to be used to style the text. The final name should be a generic family name, such as `serif`, `sans-serif`, `monospaced`, `cursive`, `fantasy`, and `script`; for example,

`font-family: Geneva, Arial, Helvetica, sans-serif;`

▶ `font-style`—Defines whether the font is `italic` or `normal`, as follows:

`font-style: italic;`

▶ `font-weight`—Defines the weight of the font. You can use a number (`100`, `200`, `300`, `400`, `500`, `600`, `700`, `800`, or `900`)—the smaller the number the lighter the weight, with `400` being normal weight; a relative value (`bolder` or `lighter`) that makes the font one step bolder or lighter from the parent value; or the keywords `bold` and `normal` as follows:

`font-weight: bold;`

▶ `font-variant`—Defines the text as `small-caps` or `normal`. For example,

`font-variant: small-caps;`

▶ `font-size`—Defines the size of the font. You can define the size as an absolute size determined by the browser (`xx-small`, `x-small`, `small`, `medium`, `large`, `x-large`, `xx-large`), where `medium` is the default. You can also use relative font sizes (`smaller` and `larger`), a numerical length with a measurement (in, cm, mm, pt, pc, em, ex, or px), or percentages. Here's an example:

```
font-size: 80%;
```

▶ **line-height**—Defines the distance between lines for the font. You can define this as a number to multiply by the font size, a specific length (with a unit of measure), or a percentage of the font size:

```
line-height: 110%;
```

▶ **font**—A shorthand property that describes the font style, variant, weight, size, line-height, and family in the following format: `font: font-style font-variant font-weight font-size/line-height font-family;`. For example,

```
font: italic small-caps bold 1em/1.3em Geneva, sans-serif;
```

Setting the Base Font Size

When designing for mobile devices, using a relative font size (like em or percentage) is best so that your designs scale depending upon the screen size. However, you should also set your base font size so that 1 em equals something you can measure. On most monitors the base font size (or "medium" size) is 16px, which is hard to use. Therefore, you can set your body text to be 62.5% or 10px (16 × 62.5% = 10) and then when you set a font to 1.2em you know that it will display at 12px.

Did you Know?

Several new font properties have also been added in CSS3:

▶ **font-stretch**—Lets you select a normal, condensed, or extended typeface from a font family. You can use absolute keywords such as `ultra-condensed`, `extra-condensed`, `condensed`, `semi-condensed`, `normal`, `semi-expanded`, `expanded`, `extra-expanded`, and `ultra-expanded`. You can also use the relative keywords `wider` and `narrower` to expand and condense the type one level up to the limits; for example:

```
font-stretch: wider;
```

▶ **font-size-adjust**—Lets you adjust the size of your fonts to help increase legibility if your first choice font is unavailable. To use it, you set it to the aspect value of your first choice font face. If that face is unavailable, the font face that is used will have the same aspect value as your first choice font. Some common font aspect values are listed at www.webspaceworks.com/resources/fonts-web-typography/43/. Here is an example:

```
font-size-adjust: 0.54;
```

▶ **font-effect**—Set the text to look embossed, engraved, or outlined using the keywords emboss, engrave, outline, and none:

```
font-effect: outline;
```

▶ **font-smooth**—Apply anti-aliasing to text or turn it off. By default (auto) the text will be smoothed according to the system defaults, but otherwise you can set it to none, always, or an absolute size or length. For the size and length, font smoothing would be applied to fonts that size or larger, and otherwise not:

```
font-smooth: 12px;
```

▶ **font-emphasize-style**—For some languages (such as Chinese and Japanese) you can use symbols to emphasize characters. This property lets you set the symbol to none, accent, dot, circle, or disc:

```
font-emphasize-style: accent;
```

▶ **font-emphasize-position**—This property lets you define the location of the emphasis symbol, either before or after:

```
font-emphasize-position: after;
```

▶ **font-emphasize**—This is a shorthand property for the two emphasize properties. Use font-emphasize: font-emphasize-style font-emphasize-position; for example:

```
font-emphasize: accent after;
```

Browser support for these styles is limited, so be sure to test before you rely too heavily upon them.

▼   **Try It Yourself**

Setting the Font Styles in Your Application

The base fonts of any application are in the paragraph text and headlines. In this exercise you will define your base font size to 10px using the percentages discussed in Hour 6, "Building a Mobile Web Application," and then give your headlines more style than the default browser style for those elements.

1. Open your CSS and set the base font size to 10px from the browser default of 16px by setting the size as a percentage:

```
body { font-size: 62.5%; }
```

2. Define your paragraphs with the font size, line height, and family:

```
p {
    font: 1.3em/1.8em "Trebuchet MS", Arial, Helvetica, sans-serif;
```

3. Don't forget to include a size adjustment for your fonts on your paragraph style:

```
font-size-adjust: 0.52;
}
```

4. Define your headlines with the font size, line height, family, and weight:

```
h1, h2, h3, h4, h5, h6 {
    font-family: "Palatino Linotype", "Book Antiqua", Palatino, serif;
    font-weight: bold;
    font-size-adjust: 0.46;
}
h1 {
    font-size: 2.0em;
    line-height: 2.4em;
}
h2 {
    font-size: 1.7em;
    line-height: 2.0em;
}
h3 {
    font-size: 1.5em;
    line-height: 1.8em;
}
```

5. Add other special effects to headlines:

```
h1 { font-effect: emboss; }
```

▲

Spacing

The six elements of spacing in typography are

▶ **Kerning**—The space between individual letters

▶ **Tracking**—The space between groups of letters

▶ **Leading**—The space between lines

▶ **Measure**—The length of lines

▶ **Alignment**—The placement of text on a line

▶ **Ligatures**—The joining of two letters to create a new glyph

These items can all be affected to some degree with CSS in your HTML documents.

Kerning is done with the CSS property letter-spacing. Figure 11.1 shows how this property looks.

FIGURE 11.1
Three kerning
examples:
tight, normal,
and loose.

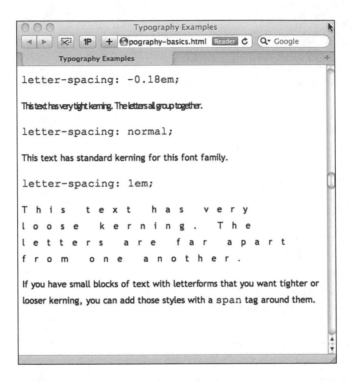

The letter-spacing property is not exactly the same as kerning. Although putting a span around every character in your document is theoretically possible, to get true, letter-perfect kerning, the reality is that that would take up too much time and make your HTML huge. In important documents, where letter-perfect kerning is important, you can set spans around specific letter groups to get the spacing you want.

For example, in many font faces, especially at larger sizes, the letter *W* followed by an *a* or *e* can give the appearance of a lot of space between the two letters. To fix that, subtract some letter spacing from the *W* with a span tag and CSS:

```
.W-tight { letter-spacing: 0.15em; }
...
<span class="W-tight">W</span>o...
```

Relative Font Measures Are Not a Fixed Size

Keep in mind that em is a relative font size. This means that the size of the text on the screen will be based on the base font size (in most cases this is 16px). So if you haven't set your body text to an absolute size or that absolute size is fairly large, 0.15 em may add space rather than decrease it. Always setting your base font size and always testing is a good idea.

If you want to affect tracking with CSS, you can use the word-spacing property. This property adds space around words similar to how letter-spacing adds or removes space around letters.

Leading is affected with the line-height property. A good general rule for setting the leading or line height is to add 20% to the size of your type. This gives the type some room to breathe. Text with smaller leading often looks cramped whereas larger leading can be hard to read because people can't track to the next line as easily.

You affect the measure of your text by changing the width of the elements containing the text. This is usually done in the layout itself. Text becomes more difficult to read if it is too wide or too narrow, but you can help improve that by changing the leading. In text with a wide measure, make the leading larger so that the text is more legible, and make it smaller for text with a narrow measure.

Alignment is done with the CSS2 property text-align. You can set the alignments to left (the default), right, center, and justify.

Ligatures are the hardest spacing to affect with CSS. If you can, getting a font face with the ligatures included is better, but web typography hasn't gotten to the point where they are automatically added. Instead, you either need to use special characters such as æ to write æ or use letter-spacing to fake a ligature by moving two letters right up next to one another.

You can also find some JavaScript libraries such as Lettering.js (http://letteringjs.com/) to help with leading, kerning, and other typography concerns on the web.

Hyphenation

HTML has two types of hyphens: a plain hyphen and a soft hyphen. The plain hyphen is just a character, and browsers render it (-) when they see it, regardless of where it appears on the line. The soft hyphen is written ­ or ­ and is supposed to only be written when at the end of a line. Figure 11.2 shows you soft hyphens in a block of text that is fully justified.

What Is a Soft Hyphen?

Some people refer to the soft hyphen in HTML as a discretionary hyphen because it appears in the text only at the user agent's discretion. In HTML 3.2 it was defined differently: as a hyphen that could have a line break after it, rather than a hard hyphen (-) that would never have a line break after it. This is why some very old browsers would display the ­ character when it's written in text.

FIGURE 11.2
Soft hyphens in
justified text.

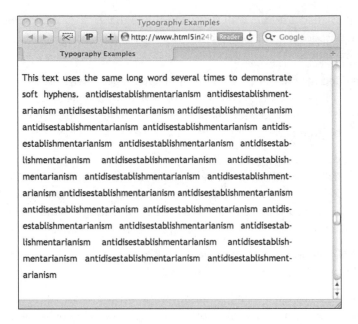

Although adding a soft hyphen inside every multi-syllable word in your document is possible, unless you have an automatic hyphening system, this isn't feasible for long documents or large sites. Instead you should use it in two places:

▶ When the width of the text block is less than four to five words, adding soft hyphens to longer words helps the text blocks look less choppy.

▶ When you have a word that is more than four or five syllables long, adding soft hyphens at the syllables ensures that it doesn't create a huge space at the end of the line.

Many designers avoid the ­ character because of the strange results it would give in various older browsers. However, that is no longer the case. All modern browsers support this character, including Internet Explorer, and mobile browsers on iOS and Android.

When working with hyphenation, you should also consider when you don't want a word to break. For example, if you wrote "X-Windows," you would never want "X-" at the end of a line, but because of the hyphen character in that word, browsers might put a line break there. To prevent this, you should use the CSS rule white-space: nowrap;, and put the word to be kept together in a span tag with that class:

```
.nobreak { white-space: nowrap; }
...
<span class="nobreak">X-Windows</span>
```

CSS3 also offers several new hyphenation style properties:

▶ **hyphens**—This property controls whether hyphenation is allowed in a block of text. The default is `manual`, but you can change it to `none`, `auto`, or `all`:

```
hyphens: auto;
```

▶ **hyphenate-character**—The character string to show between parts of hyphenated words:

```
hyphenate-character: "\2010";
```

▶ **hyphenate-limit-zone**—This is a percentage or length that specifies the maximum amount of unfilled space that may be left in the line before hyphenation occurs:

```
hyphenate-limit-zone: 3%;
```

▶ **hyphenate-limit-chars**—The number of characters in a hyphenated word and (optionally) the required minimum before and after the hyphen:

```
hyphenate-limit-chars: auto 3;
```

▶ **hyphenate-limit-lines**—The maximum number of consecutive hyphenated lines in an element. Specify `no-limit` for no limit on the number of consecutive hyphenated lines:

```
hyphenate-limit-lines: 5;
```

▶ **hyphenate-limit-last**—Defines how the hyphenation should occur at the end of elements. Values can be `none`, `always`, `column`, `page`, or `spread`. If the value is `column`, `page`, or `spread` then hyphenation should not occur at the end of those elements.

```
hyphenation-limit-last: all;
```

▶ **@hyphenate-resource** and **hyphenate-resource**—These specify a list of external dictionary resources to help determine hyphenation points.

```
hyphenate-resource: url("hyph_da_DK.dic");
```

Be Sure to Test Hyphenation Properties

The hyphens property has some browser support, but the other properties are not as well supported and may even be removed from the CSS3 specification.

Watch Out!

Rag

Rag is the uneven edge of the non-aligned side of your text. In English the rag is on the right side. You should pay attention to the shapes that are created by the rag. Large gaps on the end of lines can make your text more difficult to read.

Although there aren't any specific tags or properties you can use to define the rag of your text, you can use hyphenation, font size, and even the width of your text blocks to change how the rag looks. You can even edit the text itself to use a word that fills up the space better.

Widows and Orphans

Widows and orphans are words that are left hanging at the end or beginning of columns of text. These words sitting all alone make the text hard to read and can even change the meaning. Consider the headline:

"I Walked Across an Ocean

Liner"

Like rag, no specific tags or properties exist for dealing with widows and orphans, but you can use the text width or font size to try to get rid of them. Sometimes, the easiest thing to do is remove or add text to the content.

> **Don't Confuse the CSS Properties with Web Typography**
>
> CSS has two properties, widows and orphans, that are often confused with the typographical terms *widows* and *orphans*. The CSS properties apply only to paged media, such as printouts, and not to web applications or web pages. They define the number of lines that should be displayed at the top (widows) or bottom (orphans) of a printed page.

Using Proper Typographical Entities

Typography isn't just about the elements of typography, it's also about the characters and glyphs that you use. The most common typographic mistake that web designers make is to not pay attention to these entities. However, by taking the time to use the appropriate entities at the appropriate times, you will show a level of care that is lacking from most websites and applications.

Quotation Marks

The most common quotation marks you will see on web pages are the straight quotes (" and '). These quotation marks are called straight quotes because they are just that—straight up and down. Instead, good typography dictates that you use quotation marks that curl in towards that being quoted. These are often called curly quotes, or smart quotes.

But you can't just copy and paste these quotation marks from your Word document; those quotation marks won't display correctly and could leave your document with strange characters displaying or small black boxes. Instead, you should use character entities. You can use several entities for quotation marks, listed in Table 11.1.

TABLE 11.1 Quotation Mark Type HTML Entities

Character	Display	Human-Readable Code	Numeric Code	Replaces
Double Quotes	"	&ldquo;	&#8220;	Straight double quotes or "
	"	&rdquo;	&#8221;	
Single Quotes	'	&lsquo;	&#8216;	Straight single quotes or '
	'	&rsquo;	&#8217;	
Guillemets	<<	&laquo;	&#171;	Quotation marks inside quotations
	>>	&raquo;	&#187;	

Business Marks

Most web designers will use several kinds of business marks at some point. Seeing them rendered in a form of shorthand, such as (c) for copyright rather than using the correct symbol is common. Table 11.2 shows the correct codes for these entities.

TABLE 11.2 HTML Entities for Business Characters

Character	Display	Human-Readable Code	Numeric Code	Replaces
Copyright	©	&copy;	&#169;	(c)
Trademark	™	&trade;	&#0482;	(tm)
Registered Trademark	®	&reg;	&#174;	(R)

Advanced Punctuation

Many other typographic entities are available that you should use—too many to mention in this book. But if you are paying attention to your typography, watch out for a few other punctuation entities that are used incorrectly all the time on web pages. Learn to write the entities in Table 11.3 correctly and your documents will have much better typography.

TABLE 11.3   Punctuation HTML Entities

Character	Display	Human-Readable Code	Numeric Code	Replaces
En dash	–	`&ndash;`	`&#8211;`	A hyphen (-) in ranges such as 1–6
Em dash	—	`&mdash;`	`&#8212;`	Double hyphens --
Ellipsis	...	`&hellip;`	`&#8230;`	Three dots ... or . . .

Taking the time to use the correct character entities rather than the easier-to-use alternatives may seem like a small thing to do, but by doing so you make your text clearer and easier to read.

Understanding Web Open Font Format (WOFF)

The Web Open Font Format (WOFF) is a draft standard to compress font data for use with `@font-face` in CSS. It is an alternative to other font options such as EOT, TTF, OTF, and SVG fonts.

Before the widespread adoption of `@font-face` and web fonts, designers were forced to do workarounds to get the custom fonts into their web pages. Many techniques are available, including:

▶ Using images instead of text

▶ Replacing text with images with complex image replacement techniques

▶ Using only "web safe" fonts

"Web Safe" Is a Misnomer When It Comes to Fonts

The term *web safe fonts* came from the term *web safe colors*. Web safe colors were a subset of 216 colors that were the same on both Macintosh and Windows monitors with only 256-color displays. A web safe font was one that was believed to be found on the majority of computers on the internet. However, unlike with the color depth of their monitors, customers can change, add, and delete the fonts on their computers. So web safe fonts are more of an approximation than a reality.

The advantages to using WOFF fonts are

- ▶ WOFF fonts are compressed, which means that they download more quickly compared to raw TrueType or OpenType formats.

- ▶ WOFF contains information to tell you where the font came from without Digital Rights Management (DRM) or specific domain labeling.

Of course, WOFF fonts have some disadvantages, too, primarily around browser support:

- ▶ Internet Explorer only started supporting WOFF in version 9. All versions prior to 9 don't support it and you have to use EOT instead.

- ▶ Safari 5 does not support WOFF, although it is expected to be supported in Safari 6.

- ▶ The only mobile platform to support it currently is Opera Mobile. Neither iOS nor Android support WOFF.

Because of these drawbacks, many designers are hesitant to use WOFF, but the support for this technology is growing, and alternatives are covered in the following sections that you can use as fallback options until WOFF is fully supported.

Using WOFF with @font-face

The CSS @font-face feature has been in CSS since version 2 and has been supported by browsers for a long time. Internet Explorer added it in version 5, Firefox in 3.5, Safari in 3.2, Chrome since at least version 8, and Opera since version 10. Mobile browsers also support @font-face. iOS 3.2 through 4.1 have limited support, and 4.2 and 4.3 fully support it. Android has limited support in 3.0 and 2, and Opera Mobile fully supports it.

But even with all this support, very few designers use @font-face to add custom fonts to their web designs. However, using @font-face for custom fonts is very easy to do.

To add a custom font face to your style sheets, you need:

- ▶ A font that is licensed for web font use and saved in a web font format (EOT, OTF, SVG, TTF, or WOFF)

- ▶ A style sheet

Fonts Are Copyrighted

Thousands of fonts are out there, but most are not free. Before you upload a TTF file to your web server, you should find out what the license is for that font. Make sure that you have permission to use the font on a web page. Making sure that the font is legal for commercial use is also a good idea—some companies even consider ads on a website to be commercial.

The syntax of the @font-face property is

```
@font-face {
    font-family: FontName;
    src: url(URL);
}
```

The FontName can be anything you want it to be, and it's what you will reference in your CSS font rules. After you have a font defined, you use it exactly like you would any other font, and it should appear first in your font stack. Make sure you test your design using your fallback font, so that you know your design will still work if the embedded font doesn't.

▼   **Try It Yourself**

Adding a Custom Font to Your Web Page

Using the @font-face property to add custom fonts to your web pages is easy. Follow the steps in this exercise to add the font LemonChickenRegular as your h1 headline.

Before you start, find a font that you like that you have the rights to use on a website. Many free fonts are available, and one of the best sites for free web fonts is Font Squirrel (www.fontsquirrel.com/), which is where LemonChickenRegular came from.

1. Upload your font file to a directory on your web server. If you think you'll have a lot of fonts, create a /fonts directory; otherwise, you can upload the file to the same directory as your CSS files.

2. Edit your style sheet and add a @font-face rule:

   ```
   @font-face {
   ```

3. Define the name of your new font as the font-family:

   ```
   font-family: 'LemonChickenRegular';
   ```

4. Point to the font file as the source of your font:

   ```
   src: url('fonts/LEMONCHI-webfont.woff') format('woff');
   ```

5. Include the font weight and style for clarity and close the @font-face:

```
font-weight: normal;
font-style: normal;
}
```

6. Create a style using that font family as you would any other font family:

```
h1 {
    font: 3em LemonChickenRegular, Verdana, Geneva, sans-serif;
}
```

7. Reference the style in your HTML:

```
<h1>This Headline is Written in LemonChickenRegular</h1>
```

Be sure to test the page in a browser that supports the web font type you used.

▲

Using Alternatives to WOFF

The problem with WOFF is that not all browsers support it. So if you want your special font to show up, you need to define several source files and upload your font file in multiple versions:

- ▶ **EOT**—Internet Explorer 8

- ▶ **OTF and TTF**—Chrome, Firefox, IE 9, Opera, Safari, iOS 4.2, Android 2.2

- ▶ **SVG fonts**—Chrome, Opera, Safari 3.2, iOS, Android 3.0.

- ▶ **WOFF**—Chrome, Firefox, IE 9, Opera

To make sure your fonts show in every device possible, you should upload your font in each format. If you don't have the font in each format, you should talk to your font foundry to get the other formats. You can then define the source for each of those formats in the @font-face rule:

```
src: url('font.eot');
src: url('font.eot?#iefix') format('embedded-opentype'),
    url('font.woff') format('woff'),
    url('font.ttf') format('truetype'),
    url('font.svg#font') format('svg');
```

That Question Mark Is Important

One of the problems with using multiple source files is that Internet Explorer will download all the files it recognizes. This increases the download time for the page. A solution was created by Paul Irish called the "Bulletproof Syntax" by using a command `local()` in front of the URL. This forced IE to load the EOT file and not the others, and other browsers loaded what they needed—except Android.

By the Way

Then Fontspring came up with the Fontspring @Font-Face Syntax. By adding a question mark in the first `src` URL (for example, `font.eot?#iefix`), IE then thinks the rest of the string is a URL query string and ignores it, loading just the EOT file.

As you can see, you have to upload four versions of your font file, but this technique will get your fonts to display on Android 2.2, Chrome 8, Firefox 3.6, IE 6, iOS 3.2, Opera 10.5, and Safari 3.2 and all later versions.

If all this is still too confusing, you can use the Font Squirrel @Font-Face Generator (www.fontsquirrel.com/fontface/generator) to convert your fonts into a kit that you simply upload to your website.

Summary

This hour took you through some of the newest CSS3 font properties, such as:

- ▶ `font-stretch`
- ▶ `font-size-adjust`
- ▶ `font-effect`
- ▶ `font-smooth`
- ▶ `font-emphasize`

You also learned how to control other elements of typography including spacing, hyphenation, rag, widows, and orphans. You learned how to use correct typographical entities so that your pages don't look sloppy.

This hour also took you through the steps to use the new HTML5 web fonts format WOFF with your `@font-face` rules. With these tools you should never have to use boring "web safe" fonts again.

Q&A

Q. *Why should I care about typography?*

A. Typography is, more and more, becoming the way that the good sites are separating themselves from the bad. When you take the time to manage the typography on your web pages, you are taking the time to make sure that they are readable and useful to your customers. Your average customer might not notice the difference between a straight quote and a curly quote, but they will notice that your site is easier to read, even if only subconsciously.

Besides, typography is fun!

Q. *You list a lot of typographic entities in this hour, but you don't list all of them. Is there somewhere I can go to find out other typographic entities?*

A. I have a list of HTML entities on my About.com website: http://webdesign. about.com/library/bl_htmlcodes.htm. You can also search for "HTML entities" in any search engine to find more.

Q. *Is there a limit to the number of custom fonts I can embed in a web application?*

A. No, there is no physical limit. But you should keep in mind that every embedded font is another file your site visitors must download. To reduce the number of HTTP requests, you can use `data:` URLs (URLs pointing to data blocks and referenced with `data:` instead of `http:`) and embed your fonts that way.

From a design perspective, avoiding the use of more than three or four font faces on any one web page, including text in advertising and images, is a good general rule. The more typefaces you have on the page, the busier it looks and the harder it is to use.

Workshop

The workshop contains quiz questions to help you process what you've learned in this chapter. Try to answer all the questions before you read the answers. See Appendix A, "Answers to Quizzes," for answers.

Quiz

1. What are the six generic font families?

2. Name at least three spacing elements in typography.

3. True or False. It is okay to use (c) for copyright notices within the text of your documents.

4. Name four of the five font formats for web fonts.

5. What is the syntax for embedding a font?

Exercises

1. Go through an existing web page (either your own or one on the web) and find the typographic mistakes. Look for things such as bad entities, poor spacing, too many fonts, and so on. Decide how you would correct these problems, and if you're working on your own page, make the corrections.

2. Find a font on Font Squirrel (www.fontsquirrel.com) that you like and add it to a web page.

HOUR 12

Audio and Video in HTML5

What You'll Learn in This Hour:

▶ Why the `<video>` and `<audio>` tags are important

▶ What support is available for the new multimedia elements

▶ How to add video and audio into your HTML that works

▶ How to force older browsers to display your multimedia

▶ How to create custom controls for your video and audio files

One of the most well-known of the new HTML5 features is the `<video>` element, but there is a new `<audio>` element as well.

In this hour you will learn how to use both elements to place video and audio in your web pages in a similar way to how you put images in. You will also start to understand the reason for these tags and how they relate to the other ways already available for embedding audio and video in web pages.

You will also learn how to add video and audio that is backward compatible for browsers that don't support HTML5, how to improve your multimedia playback, and create custom controls.

Why Use HTML5 for Audio and Video vs. Flash

The HTML5 standard created the `<audio>` and `<video>` elements to allow web designers a standardized way to place video and audio files directly in their web pages. One way to think of it is as though audio and video files are the same as image files. You can embed an image in your HTML with the `<img>` element, and now you can embed sound and video with the `<audio>` and `<video>` elements. In previous versions of HTML, you had to embed your video and audio files and hope that the browsers could open them correctly, but these HTML5 elements make embedding video and audio much easier.

A lot of discussion is going on about whether HTML5 video will "beat" Flash, and people are offering many reasons why it should (or should not). Some of the pros of using HTML5 (instead of Flash) for media elements include:

▶ Adding media with these tags is more semantic. A user agent knows immediately that an `<audio>` file is sound. It has to do more analysis to determine what a sound file inside an `<embed>` or `<object>` element is.

▶ You are not limited to one vendor to play your movies and sound.

▶ Your users do not have to have a plug-in to play your movies and sound.

▶ Because these elements are part of the DOM, you have more control over them through scripts and CSS.

▶ iOS devices do not have Flash.

▶ Adding sound and video to your web pages is a lot easier.

But using HTML5 also has some drawbacks, mostly around browser support:

▶ As with most other HTML5 features, Internet Explorer 8 and lower do not support the HTML5 `<video>` and `<audio>` elements.

▶ You have to encode video in at least two or three different formats.

Many people who already do all their video in Flash see no point in switching, but Flash has some serious drawbacks of its own, not least of which is that it causes the majority of crashes on Linux and Macintosh machines.

The problem with HTML5 video isn't really HTML5 at all; it's the codecs—the way videos are encoded for viewing. User agents currently support three formats:

▶ MP4 or H.264

▶ ogg/Theora

▶ WebM

Chrome and Android support all three. Firefox and Opera support ogg/Theora and WebM. IE 9 supports MP4 and WebM with an add-on. Safari and iOS support MP4.

Still, if you are serious about creating web applications with video and audio for mobile devices, then you can't use Flash only. Flash is fine as a fallback option for desktop users, but for mobile you should encode in H.264 and WebM, at a minimum.

Choosing Video Formats for the Best Compatibility

As mentioned in the previous section, you should use the three primary video codecs (plus Flash for fallback purposes): MP4 or H.264, ogg/Theora, and WebM. Table 12.1 shows the current state of browser support for the video codecs.

TABLE 12.1   Browser Support for Video Codecs

Browser	MP4/H.264	ogg/Theora	WebM
Android	version 3.0	version 2.3	version 2.3
Chrome	version 9 (Windows) version 7 (Macintosh)	version 9 (Windows) version 7 (Macintosh)	version 9 (Windows) version 7 (Macintosh)
Firefox		version 3.6	version 3.6
Internet Explorer	version 9		version 9 (with components)
iOS	version 3		
Opera		version 10.63	version 10.63
Safari	version 5		

Watch Out!

Check Your Server MIME Types

If you are having a problem getting your web server to display videos, the MIME types might not be set up correctly. If you have access to the Apache httpd.conf file, add the following three lines and then reboot your server:

```
AddType video/mp4 .mp4
AddType video/ogg .ogv
AddType video/webm .webm
```

Contact your hosting provider if you can't add those lines yourself.

MP4 or H.264

H.264 is the codec that is supported primarily by Microsoft and Apple. H.264 files have the .mp4 extension. With it, you can create good quality videos that are small in size. Plus a lot of programs are available that will encode H.264 video. In fact, Flash uses H.264 video.

The problem is that the H.264 codec is not free. It is a licensed product owned by MPEG LA. They have stated that they won't charge royalties for internet video that uses their codec, as long as that video is free to end users. But the Mozilla group (makers of Firefox) have stated that Firefox will never support H.264 video because of patent issues and their focus on open source software.

However, if you want your videos to play on iPhones and iPads, you need to use this format, because iOS doesn't support any other format.

The benefits (beyond iOS support) to this format are that it creates small, high-quality videos, and a lot of programs are available that will create videos in this format.

ogg/Theora

Ogg/Theora is an open standard for video encoding that Firefox does support. Ogg/Theora files use the .ogg file extension. It generates high-quality videos, but they are often much larger than the same video in H.264 format. ogg/Theora videos can be 40%–50% larger than the same video in H.264.

In addition to large file sizes, the other problem with ogg/Theora is that finding a good program to encode in this format can be very difficult. Professional-level video programs such as Premiere and Final Cut Pro don't support it without a plug-in.

The benefit to ogg/Theora is that it is open source and free to use.

WebM

WebM uses the VP8 codec owned by Google. WebM files use the .webm extension. It has very good compression and creates high-quality videos. Google claims that the quality is better than H.264, but independent tests have shown it to be about the same or only slightly better (according to Streaming Media magazine www.streamingmedia.com/Articles/Editorial/Featured-Articles/WebM-vs.-H.264-A-Closer-Look-68594.aspx).

Like ogg/Theora, WebM can be hard to encode because programs such as Premiere and Final Cut Pro don't support it without a plug-in.

However, also like ogg/Theora, WebM is open source and free to use.

Choosing Audio Codecs for the Widest Support

As with video, you can use several codecs for creating audio for web pages: MP3, Vorbis, and WAV. Table 12.2 shows the current state of browser support for these audio codecs.

TABLE 12.2   Browser Support for Audio Codecs

Browsers	MP3	Vorbis	WAV
Android	version 2.3	version 2.3	
Chrome	version 6	version 6	
Firefox		version 3.6	version 3.6
Internet Explorer	version 9		version 9
iOS	version 3		
Opera		version 10.5	version 10.5
Safari	version 5		version 5

MP3

MP3 is a popular sound format because of the high compression rates and high quality. These files have the .mp3 extension. A lot of encoders are also available to create this format for your audio files.

However, because patents are associated with this format, it will not be supported by Mozilla browsers such as Firefox until the patents run out in 2017 or later.

Vorbis

Vorbis, also known as Ogg Vorbis, is an open source audio codec. These files have the .ogg extension. It generates high-quality sound files with much smaller size than other audio codecs.

Finding commercial programs to convert files to Vorbis can be difficult, but many online converters are available that will do it for you.

WAV

WAV is a codec that was designed by Microsoft and IBM. WAV files have the .wav extension. It is widely supported, and often users with a browser that won't play a WAV file inline can play it if they download it to their computer.

WAV files can be compressed, but typically are not, and so tend to be a lot larger (many times the size) than the MP3 and Vorbis files of the same audio. It does, however, create high-quality recordings. Most developers only use WAV files for sound effects.

The New HTML5 Media Elements

HTML5 has several new elements you can use to add audio and video to your web pages:

▶ **`<video>`**—Use this for a video stream.

▶ **`<audio>`**—Use this for an audio stream.

▶ **`<source>`**—This is the media source(s) for `<audio>` and `<video>` elements.

▶ **`<track>`**—Use this to create supplementary media tracks, such as subtitles and captions for `<audio>` and `<video>` elements.

Here is how to add an audio stream to your HTML:

```
<audio>
    <source src="sound.mp3">
</audio>
```

You add a video stream in the same way:

```
<video>
    <source src="movie.webm">
</video>
```

The nice thing about the `<audio>` and `<video>` elements is that you are not limited to one `<source>`. So, even though Firefox doesn't support MP3 and iOS doesn't support WebM, you can write your HTML so that it doesn't matter, by adding a second `<source>` tag to your media referencing a different source file in another format. You can add as many `<source>` elements as you have media files to reference:

```
<video>
    <source src="movie.mp4">
    <source src="movie.ogv">
    <source src="movie.webm">
</video>
```

> **iOS Issues with HTML5 Video**
>
> iOS 3.2 won't recognize video if you use a `poster` attribute. The `poster` attribute points to a URL of an image that represents the video when it isn't playing. If you have a lot of iOS 3.2 users, you should avoid this attribute. iPads running iOS 3.2 won't notice anything but the first video source listed, so if you don't list MP4 first, the video won't play. These bugs were fixed in version 4.0, but anyone who hasn't upgraded will have these problems.

You can then include the `<track>` element if you have captions or subtitles for your media:

```
<audio>
    <source src="sound.mp3">
    <source src="sound.ogg">
    <source src="sound.wav">
    <track kind="captions" src="captions.srt" srclang="en">
</audio>
```

There Is No Standard for Timed Track Formats

Captions, subtitles, and video descriptions are all information that can be stored in the <track> element. But as of this writing, no standard format for time-based data exists. Some of the formats under consideration are SRT, WebVTT, and many others. Until this format is finalized (possibly by browser implementation), adding captions or other timed track media to your media files will be difficult.

Finally, you can include fallback text and links for browsers that don't support the media element. Here is an example of using fallback content for browsers that don't support the <video> element:

```
<video>
    <source src="movie.mp4">
    <source src="movie.ogv">
    <source src="movie.webm">
    <track kind="subtitles" src="subtitles.srt"></track>
    <p>If your browser doesn't support video playback, download the video: <a
href="movie.mp4">MP4</a>, <a href="movie.ogv">ogg/Theora</a>, <a
href="movie.webm">WebM</a>
</video>
```

One attribute you should consider using every time you use a media tag is controls. This attribute provides your users with controls that they can use to start, stop, fast-forward, and rewind through your video and audio files, as well as turn off the volume:

```
<audio controls>
```

Android Issues with HTML5 Video

Versions of Android before 2.3 don't like seeing a type attribute on the <source> element. To solve this issue, always make sure your H.264 videos end with a .mp4 extension. Also, versions 2.2 and lower of Android do not support the controls attribute. You need to include your own interface controls if you have a lot of users who use 2.2 and lower. These bugs have been fixed in 2.3.

▼   **Try It Yourself**

Adding a Music File to Your HTML

Adding music to your web pages is easy with the <audio> element. In this exercise you will save your music as MP3, WAV, and Vorbis files so that it has good browser support.

1. Record your audio file and save it as an MP3 file.

2. Convert it to WAV and Vorbis.

3. Upload all three audio files to your web server.

4. Add an <audio> element to your HTML:

    ```
    <audio controls>
    ```

5. Include three <audio> elements pointing to each file:

    ```
    <source src="Slap Happy.mp3">
    <source src="Slap Happy.ogg">
    <source src="Slap Happy.wav">
    ```

6. Add fallback text for browsers that don't support <audio>:

    ```
    <p>Your browser does not support audio playback, download the file:
    <a href="Slap Happy.mp3">MP3</a>,
    <a href="Slap Happy.ogg">Vorbis</a>,
    <a href="Slap Happy.wav">WAV</a>
    ```

7. Add a Modernizr script to only show that text to non-compliant browsers:

    ```
    <script>
    if (!Modernizr.audio) {
        document.write('<p>Your browser does not support audio playback,
    download the file <a href="Slap Happy.mp3">MP3</a>,
    <a href="Slap Happy.ogg">Vorbis</a>,
    <a href="Slap Happy.wav">WAV</a>');
    }
    </script>
    ```

8. Close the <audio> element:

    ```
    </audio>
    ```

▲   Don't forget to test in as many browsers as you can.

Useful Attributes to Extend Your Media

So far, the only attributes you've used are the controls attribute on both <video> and <audio> and the src attribute on the <source> element. However, you can use a number of other attributes to control even more about your videos.

Audio and Video Attributes

Several attributes can be used on both <audio> and <video> elements:

▶ **autoplay**—This tells the browser to start playing the song or video as soon as it has streamed enough to play without stopping. This is an attribute without any values, but if you're writing XHTML, you would write autoplay="autoplay".

Autoplay Will Drive Away Your Users

One of the fastest ways to get your users to leave your page without reading or buying anything is to have music or video automatically start when they come to your page. Remember that they may have music already on or they may be in a workplace environment where sounds are inappropriate. Use the autoplay attribute with extreme caution.

Watch Out!

▶ **preload**—The preload attribute lets you give the user agent hints as to what type of preloading it should attempt to do. Values are none, metadata, and auto. The none attribute tells the browser that it shouldn't attempt to preload; metadata tells it to get the duration, track list, dimensions, and other meta information; and auto suggests that it should try to preload the whole stream. Leaving off the value is the same as writing preload=auto.

▶ **controls**—Provides a user interface for controlling the stream. This attribute has no values.

▶ **loop**—The loop attribute tells the browser to restart the stream when it gets to the end. This attribute has no values.

▶ **mediagroup**—This tells the user agent to link several streams (audio or video or both) together. For example, a video might have a separate audio track and a sign-language interpretation. These could all be linked by giving them the same mediagroup identifier.

▶ **src**—This is an alternative to the <source> element if your stream has only one source.

Video

The <video> element also has a few other attributes that you can use to improve your videos:

▶ **poster**—This is a URL of an image to be shown while no video is available. This option is a great way to provide a preview of your videos to entice people to watch them. Otherwise, they will see just a blank or black screen.

▶ **height** and **width**—Set the height and width of the video in CSS pixels. You can resize your videos using these controls, but you won't be able to change the aspect ratio.

▶ **muted**—This allows you to set the audio to mute as the default state. This attribute was only recently added to the specification, and many browsers don't support it.

Source Attributes

The `<source>` element has three attributes: `src`, `media`, and `type`. The `src` attribute is self-explanatory—it is a URL pointing to a source file. The `media` and `type` attributes are a little trickier.

The `media` attribute takes a media query list and uses it to help the user agent determine whether the media will be useful to the user. You use media queries (discussed in Hour 4, "Detecting Mobile Devices and HTML5 Support") to define a comma-separated list of media that the video can play on. For example:

```
media="screen, 3d-glasses, resolution > 900dpi"
```

This tells the user agent that this video is viewable on "screen," with "3d-glasses," and on devices with a "resolution greater than 900dpi." (Note that 3d-glasses is not a supported type, yet. If you use this, most user agents will ignore it.) Just like with CSS media queries, you can set up complex scenarios for when the source file should be used, such as:

```
media="screen and (aspect-ratio: 16/9) and (scan: progressive)"
```

Did you Know?

> **A Specific Media Query for Retina Display**
>
> If you want to send a higher quality source file to iPhones with Retina display (the higher resolution display found on newer model iPhones), you can use a special -webkit media query: -webkit-min-device-pixel-ratio: 2.

As usual, be sure to test your media queries as much as possible, because they are not widely supported in this context.

The `type` attribute provides the browser more information about the type of the video and is the trickiest for the `<video>` element. Although it's not required, using it is a good idea especially if you are using video types other than MP4, ogg/Theora, or WebM. But even for these, you should consider using the `type` attribute on your source files. If the browser doesn't think it can load a video file based on the type you list, it won't download the file, which will make your whole page faster.

The `type` attribute has the following format:

```
type='MIME type; codecs="video codec, audio codec"'
```

The MIME types for MP4, Ogg, and WebM are

- **H.264 or MP4**—`video/mp4`

- **ogg/Theora**—`application/ogg`, `video/ogg`

- **WebM**—`video/webm`

Here is how to write the `<source>` elements for a video in three formats:

```
<source src="video.mp4" type='video/mp4; codecs="vc1.42E01E, mp4a.40.2"'>
<source src="video.ogv" type='video/ogg; codecs="theora, vorbis"'>
<source src="video.webm" type='video/webm; codecs="vp8, vorbis"'>
```

Writing the MP4 HTML is the most challenging, because you need to know the correct video codec and the AVC level. For more information, check out the Video type parameters page on the WHATWG Wiki (http://wiki.whatwg.org/wiki/Video_type_parameters).

Track Attributes

The `<track>` element uses attributes to determine the source of the track file, the type of track file it is, and more:

- **src**—The URL to the timed track file.

- **srclang**—The language of the timed track.

- **label**—A user-readable title for the track.

- **default**—An attribute that defines this track as the one that should be enabled, if user preferences do not specify a different one. This attribute has no values.

- **kind**—The five different types of timed track are as follow: `subtitles`, which provide a translation of the dialog; `captions`, which provide a transcription of the video sounds and dialog, including sound effects and musical cues; `descriptions`, which are a textual description of the visual components of a video; `chapters` for chapter titles; and `metadata` for meta content used at scripted points in the video.

Creating Fallback Options for Internet Explorer

The number one reason most developers are resistant to using the new <video> and <audio> elements is because IE 8 and lower don't support these elements. To get your sound and movies to play in these browsers you have to create some type of fallback.

By including an <object> element inside your <video> or <audio> element, you provide a fallback for browsers that don't support these elements, because they ignore the elements they don't recognize and instead just play the object files. Browsers that support the <video> and <audio> elements will find a source they can play, and ignore the <object>. If you still have problems, you can wrap the <object> in a Modernizr script to check for HTML5 support.

For video, you can use any Flash video player you like. Flowplayer (http://flow-player.org/) is a good option because it is easy to use and only requires three additional files. For audio, you can use the WAV file you already created; just embed it in an <object> element like this (change FILE.wav to your filename):

```
<object>
    <param name="autostart" value="false">
    <param name="src" value="FILE.wav">
    <param name="autoplay" value="false">
    <param name="controller" value="true">
    <embed src="FILE.wav" controller="true" autoplay="false"
        autostart="false" type="audio/wav">
</object>
```

▼   **Try It Yourself**

Adding a Video File with Flash Fallback

Adding video to your web pages is easy, and in this Try It Yourself, you will learn how to include a Flash fallback option for browsers that don't support HTML5 video.

1. Create your video and convert it to four formats: MP4, ogg/Theora, WebM, and FLV.

2. Save them to your web directory and upload them all to your web server.

3. Add the HTML5 video to your page:

   ```
   <video controls height="600" width="800">
   ```

4. Add source files for the MP4, Ogg, and WebM—make sure that MP4 is first:

```
<source src="Shasta.mp4">
<source src="Shasta.theora.ogv">
<source src="Shasta.webm">
```

5. Install Flowplayer on your website (go to http://flowplayer.org/download/index.html to download).

6. Point your Flowplayer text to the FLV file you created:

```
<!— fallback to Flowplayer: —>
<a
    href="Shasta.flv"
    style="display:block;width:800px;height:600px"
    id="player">
</a>
<script>
    flowplayer("player", "flowplayer/flowplayer-3.2.7.swf");
</script>
```

7. Don't forget to add the Flowplayer script to the head of your document:

```
<script src="flowplayer/flowplayer-3.2.6.min.js"></script>
```

8. Add text links to your video so that even older browsers can still download the file:

```
<script>
if (!Modernizr.video) {
    document.write('<p>Your browser does not support video playback,
download the video:
<a href="Shasta.mp4">MP4</a>,
➥<a href="Shasta.theora.ogv">ogg/Theora</a>,
➥<a href="Shasta.webm">WebM</a>');
}
</script>
```

9. Close the video element:

```
</video>
```

You can see this video in action at www.html5in24hours.com/examples/media-examples.html.

Creating Custom Controls with API Methods

After you start testing your videos you will notice that the default controls look different on every browser and device. Figure 12.1 shows you the controls for the same video in four different browsers. As you can see, the controls look different in each and can be jarring if you are trying for a uniform look across browsers.

FIGURE 12.1
Controls for the same video in Chrome, Safari, Firefox, and IE 9 (top to bottom).

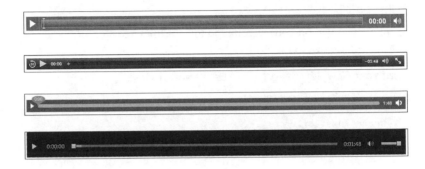

But with the DOM API for video, you can write and style your own video controls. Some controls you can use are

▶ `play()`—To play the media

▶ `pause()`—To pause the media

These are very easy to use; all you need to do is leave off the `controls` attribute on your media element, and then use some buttons and JavaScript to get your media to play:

```
<video height="600" width="800">
    <source src="Shasta.mp4">
    <source src="Shasta.theora.ogv">
    <source src="Shasta.webm">
</video>
<script>
var video = document.getElementsByTagName('video')[0];
</script>
<p>
<button value="Play" class="play" onclick="video.play()">
<img src="images/Play.png" width="32" height="32" alt="Play"></button>
<button value="Pause" class="pause" onclick="video.pause()">
<img src="images/Pause.png" width="32" height="32" alt="Pause"></button>
```

Then, to use just one button to play and pause, you need to listen for the `play()` and `pause()` events. Remember that the user can play or pause by right-clicking on the video, so you shouldn't just have it alternate on click:

```
<script>
var video = document.getElementsByTagName('video')[0];
video.onpause = video.onplay = function(e) {
```

```
    playPause.value = video.paused ? 'Play' : 'Pause';
  }
  function playPause() {
    if (video.paused ¦¦ video.ended) {
      video.play();
    } else {
      video.pause();
    }
  }
</script>
<button value="Play/Pause" id="playPause" onclick="playPause()">
<img src="images/PlayPause.png" width="26" height="28"
➥alt="Play/Pause"></button>
```

You can do a lot more with the video functions. You can add volume and mute buttons, fast forward, scanning, and so on. However, the easiest way to get a custom video player on your web pages is to use a pre-made video player. Many free ones are available to choose from. Philip Bräunlich has a list of players (http://praegnanz.de/html5video/index.php) that gives you details such as the license, what JavaScript library it uses, if it has a Flash fallback, if it supports iOS and full screen, and more. He also helpfully evaluates how easy each tool is to integrate and theme.

Summary

This hour took you through the basics of adding HTML5 video and audio to your web pages. This topic is challenging, with many pitfalls, but you should have a good sense of what you need to do to add these multimedia elements to your pages and applications.

You learned the benefits and drawbacks of HTML5 video and audio as well as why you should consider moving to HTML5 for your video and using Flash as the fallback. You also learned that it's not HTML5 itself that causes the difficulties, but the codecs and lack of across-the-board browser support for them.

You learned the three best codecs for both video and audio and which browsers support which codecs. Plus, you learned some of the pitfalls that can happen with Android and iOS browsers and how to avoid them.

You also learned how to build a fully functional page with video and audio that works in IE8 and other older browsers as well as all the modern HTML5 browsers.

Q&A

Q. *How is the* `<track>` *element intended to be used?*

A. This element is added to the `<video>` and `<audio>` elements to define information that is synchronized to the media. It can be a sign-language translation video, a text description, or captions and subtitles, which people are already familiar with.

Q. *Can I use other codecs than the ones mentioned in this hour?*

A. If you know the MIME type for the codec, you can include it as a source file for your media. You should be aware, though, that there is no guarantee that a browser or user agent will know what to do with it.

Q. *Is it really necessary to save my video in so many formats?*

A. This is one of the most common objections to using the `<video>` and `<audio>` elements in HTML5. But the reality is that if you want your video to be seen as professional, you have to create multiple versions. For example, when you go to the Apple movie trailers site, each trailer is offered in several different sizes. Site visitors choose the one they want to view. But with HTML5 and media queries, you can help users get the best quality video for their browser without them doing anything other than clicking "Play." They don't have to guess; you can just deliver the right one to them. But you can't do that if you only have one option.

Workshop

The workshop contains quiz questions to help you process what you've learned in this chapter. Try to answer all the questions before you read the answers. Refer to Appendix A, "Answers to Quizzes," for answers.

Quiz

1. What are the three commonly used audio codecs?

2. What video codecs does Internet Explorer 9 support? What about Android?

3. Name two ways you can include the source of a video in your HTML.

4. True or False. The `loop` attribute is only valid on the `<video>` element.

5. What is the format for the `type` attribute on the `<source>` element?

6. How does the fallback option work on an `<audio>` element?

Exercises

1. Add an audio file to a web page. Make sure that it plays in as many browsers as possible.

2. Choose a video player (perhaps from http://praegnanz.de/html5video/index. php) and add some HTML5 video to your application. Test to make sure that it plays on both iOS and Android.

HTML5 Forms

What You'll Learn in This Hour:

- ▶ How to include hint text in your form fields
- ▶ How to add simple attributes to make your forms easier to use
- ▶ How to create lists of content for form fields
- ▶ How to work with the new input types
- ▶ Options for browsers that don't support HTML5 forms
- ▶ How to get the browser to validate forms
- ▶ How to build, style, and manage an HTML5 form

HTML forms are an important part of any website, and in web applications they are often the part that makes the app interactive. However, HTML forms can be hard to build and hard to use. HTML5 tries to fix that.

In this hour, you'll learn about some of the new features of HTML5 forms that make them more usable. You'll learn more about the input types that you can use right now to improve your forms. Plus, you'll learn about the HTML5 attributes that help you make sure the data that's delivered is valid and in the correct format.

In the last section of this hour, you'll go through the steps to create, design, and manage an HTML5 form.

New Usability Features in HTML5 Forms

One of the best things about HTML5 is how much it takes into account the difficulty that forms pose for both designers and users. A lot of the features of HTML5 forms are things that you can already do with scripts, but now they are built into the HTML, which reduces the page load time and makes build forms easier.

Two new features that make the forms easier for users are *placeholder text* and *autofocus*. Using *autocomplete* combined with *datalists* helps make the data the forms deliver more consistent and accurate.

Placeholder Text

Placeholder text is a very useful feature in forms. It provides information about the form fields or how the data should be formatted but doesn't get in the way of what is written in the form field. Figure 13.1 shows three form fields with placeholder text. The text is light gray, and when the field has focus, the text disappears.

FIGURE 13.1
Placeholder text in a form on an iPad.

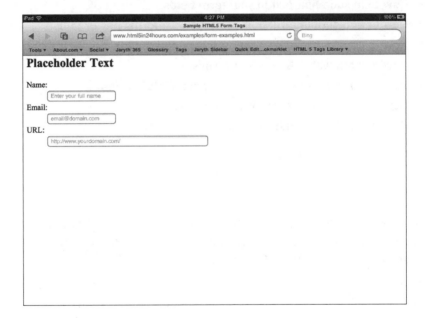

By the Way

Use Placeholder Text Instead of Field Labels

One way you can use placeholder text is as form field labels. You just put the name of each field in the placeholder text. You can see an example of this at www.html5in24hours.com/examples/form-placeholder-labels.html.

To add placeholder text to a form field, add the `placeholder` attribute to the element, with the text you want as the placeholder as the value:

```
<input type="text" id="name" placeholder="Fill in your full name">
```

For browsers that don't support the `placeholder` attribute, you can use JavaScript and CSS to fake it. The easiest way is to write the placeholder text in the value of your input field, and then use JavaScript to hide it when the field has focus:

```
<input type="text" value="Short comment field (140 char)" maxlength="140"
size="50" onfocus="if (this.value == 'Short comment field (140 char)') {
this.value = '';}"
onblur="if (this.value == '') {this.value = 'Short comment field
➥(140 char)';}">
```

If you use this method, then your placeholder text will be black, rather than gray. To fix that you need to add two classes to your style sheet:

```
.ph {
    color: #999;
}
.no-ph {
    color: #000;
}
```

You then add those styles to the form field in the script as well as the `<input>` element:

```
<input type="text" value="Short comment field (140 char)" maxlength="140"
size="50" onfocus="if (this.value == 'Short comment field (140 char)') {
this.value = ''; this.className = 'no-ph';}"
onblur="if (this.value == '') {this.value = 'Short comment field (140
➥char)';
this.className='ph';}" class="ph">
```

For best results, you should only use this JavaScript on browsers that don't support the `placeholder` attribute. You can use Modernizr:

```
if (!Modernizr.input.placeholder) { ... }
```

You can also style the `placeholder` attribute in Android, Chrome, Firefox, iOS, and Safari with two CSS browser extensions:

▶ `::-webkit-input-placeholder`

▶ `:-moz-placeholder`

The colons are required because the extensions are pseudo-classes. You also should keep these styles in separate rules, because user agents ignore rules with selectors they don't recognize. To change your placeholder text to "aliceblue," on a gray background, you would write:

```
::-webkit-input-placeholder {
    color: aliceblue;
    background-color: #ccc;
}
```

```
:-moz-placeholder {
    color: aliceblue;
    background-color: #ccc;
}
```

You can use the placeholder attribute on <input> and <textarea> elements. It works in Chrome 4, Firefox 3.7, iOS 4, Opera 11, and Safari 4. It does not work in Android or Internet Explorer.

Autofocus

The autofocus attribute is another attribute that many web developers have been forcing with JavaScript for a long time. When a form field has the autofocus attribute on it, that field will have a blinking cursor after the page has loaded.

To set the focus on an element in your form, just add the autofocus attribute to one form field element:

```
<textarea id="comments" autofocus></textarea>
```

Using scripts to force the autofocus has some problems. For one thing, if you press the spacebar expecting the page to scroll, nothing will happen because the space is placed in the form field instead. Also, if you choose a different field and start typing before the page is fully loaded, the script might move the cursor to the autofocused field, causing errors in filling out the form.

Watch Out!

> **Don't Autofocus Every Form**
>
> The autofocus attribute can be tempting to put on every form you place on your site, but you risk annoying your readers without adding value. The only forms you should use autofocus on are the ones that are the primary focus of the page—such as contact pages. Don't add it to forms that are on every page of your site such as newsletter signups or search boxes.

After you have a field for your autofocus, ensuring that it receives focus even in browsers that don't support this attribute is easy:

```
<input type="text" id="name" autofocus>
...
<script>
if (!Modernizr.input.autofocus) {
    document.getElementById('name').focus();
}
</script>
```

The autofocus attribute is valid in <button>, <input>, <keygen>, and <select>. It works in Chrome 3, Firefox 4, Opera 10, and Safari 4.

Autocomplete and Datalists

The autocomplete attribute and the <datalist> element are useful for both users
and web developers. Users can fill in form fields more easily when they have a pick
list to start from, and developers get data that is more consistent because the pick list
helps limit the options. Plus, these types of form fields take the place of two in HTML
4 forms: a drop-down list (<select> element) with the final choice of "other, please
explain" and a text input field to collect the other value. With a <datalist> of
options, if the choice the user wants isn't there, he can simply type it in the field.
Figure 13.2 shows how a datalist looks on a text field.

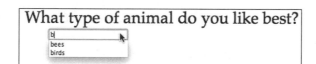

FIGURE 13.2
A simple text
field with a
datalist.

The autocomplete attribute is a toggle. If it's set on a field, either as just autocomplete
or autocomplete=yes, then the field options will complete as the user types. If you set
it to autocomplete=no, then the field will not complete as the user types.

There are three parts to a datalist with autocomplete:

▶ The input field with list and autocomplete attributes

▶ The <datalist> element

▶ <option> elements inside the <datalist>

Here is an example of a datalist that will autocomplete when the users type:

```
<input type="text" id="animal" list="animals" autocomplete>
<datalist id="animals">
    <option value="bees">
    <option value="birds">
    <option value="cats">
    <option value="cows">
    <option value="dogs">
    <option value="fish">
    <option value="horses">
    <option value="snakes">
</datalist>
```

The problem with autocomplete and <datalist> for most developers is that they
only work in Opera. But with jQuery UI (http://jqueryui.com/) you can create a fallback option for browsers that don't support it.

▼ **Try It Yourself**

Using jQuery UI as a Fallback for Autocomplete Datalists

jQuery UI has a lot of features that you can use as fallback options for HTML5 forms, so it's an important tool to know how to use. To use it follow these steps:

1. Build your jQuery UI and download it from http://jqueryui.com/download.

2. Add the script and CSS to your HTML:

```
<link rel="stylesheet" href="jquery-ui-1.8.13.custom.css">
<script type="text/javascript" src="jquery-ui-1.8.13.custom.min.js">
</script>
```

3. Write the autocomplete jQuery script and place it at the bottom of your HTML:

```
<script>
$(document).ready(function(){
if (!Modernizr.input.autocomplete) {
    var data = ["bees", "birds", "cats", "cows", "dogs", "fish",
➥"horses", "snakes" ];
    $("#animal").autocomplete({
        source: data
    });
}
});
</script>
```

Notice that the autocomplete function is surrounded with a Modernizr check. Therefore, this script will only activate if the browser doesn't support the autocomplete attribute.

You can use the autocomplete attribute on <form> and <input>. If it is on the ▲ <form> element, then all applicable fields in that form will autocomplete (or not).

HTML5 Input Types

HTML5 adds 13 new types for the <input> element. The great thing about these types is that, even without a fallback option, they will work in every browser that supports forms. If the browser doesn't recognize the type, it displays a text input field instead, so you have nothing to lose by using these form elements.

Number Types

Now, if you need to collect a number from a user, you have three ways to do so:

▶ <input type=number>

▶ `<input type=range>`

▶ `<input type=tel>`

The number type is exactly what you would think it is. However, asking for a number in a web form is trickier than you think. For example, 17, –6, 4 1/8, and π; are all numbers, but what if you want someone to pick a number between 0 and 100 that is a multiple of 3? With a standard text input box they could enter any of the numbers listed previously, and you would have to validate it with JavaScript or server-side code to make sure they submitted what you want.

With the `<input type=number>` field, you can specify the minimum value, maximum value, and the step between values:

```
<input type=number id="multi3" min=0 max=100 step=3 value=33>
```

As you can see in Figure 13.3, mobile devices do not display number types with the min, max, and step attributes like desktop browsers do, but filling in the numbers is much easier on the mobile device because the browser defaults to the number pad in number fields.

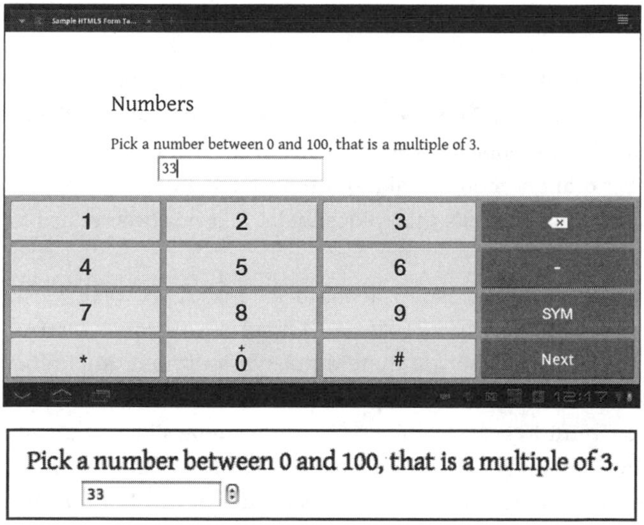

FIGURE 13.3
A number field on an Android Galaxy Tab 10.1 (top) and in Safari (bottom).

Watch
Out!

> **Don't Skip Validation**
>
> When you use the new input types, remember that in most cases, a user's putting in an incorrect value is still possible. If you need the values to always be consistent, you will need to validate the form data before it is submitted. You should think of these input fields as hints to help your users submit correct values, rather than rules that are rigidly enforced. This will help you deal with browsers that display text fields instead of the new features, as well.

What if you need a number, but it doesn't have to be precise? Rather than using the number type, you can use the `range` type. This puts a slider bar on the screen for your readers to choose a number, but without a precise scale. Figure 13.4 shows a range input field that is written like this:

FIGURE 13.4
A range field in Safari.

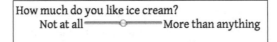

```
How much do you like ice cream?<br/>
Not at all<input type=range id=icecream min=0 max=10 value=5>More than
➥anything
```

The last number input field type is the `tel` type, which enables you to collect telephone numbers. In desktop browsers, this type won't change how the field looks, but it comes in handy on mobile devices. As you can see in Figure 13.5 the `tel` type opens a number dial on phones making it that much easier to enter a phone number. Write a telephone field like this (placeholder text has been added to make the example look nicer):

```
<input type=tel id=phonenumber placeholder="(xxx) xxx-xxxx">
```

As mentioned earlier, you can use these input types without any fallback option, and they will show up as text boxes just fine in all non-compliant browsers. However, if you want to get a number spinner or range slider, you will need to use a script. For the telephone numbers, you should validate that the number given is in a telephone format, which will be discussed later in this hour in the section "Form Validation." Nettuts+ has a great tutorial on how to build cross-browser forms with fallbacks for both range sliders and number spinners (http://net.tutsplus.com/tutorials/html-css-techniques/how-to-build-cross-browser-html5-forms/).

FIGURE 13.5
A telephone field on an iPod touch.

Date and Time Types

Dates and times are common fields on web forms, and HTML5 provides six specific input types to collect this information:

- ▶ `<input type=datetime>`
- ▶ `<input type=datetime-local>`
- ▶ `<input type=date>`
- ▶ `<input type=month>`
- ▶ `<input type=week>`
- ▶ `<input type=time>`

The date, month, week, and time types should be fairly self-explanatory. Dates are stored in the format:

YYYY-MM-DD

Months are the same, just without the day:

YYYY-MM

Weeks are sent as the year, followed by the number of the week:

YYYY-W##

Time is sent as:

`HH:MM`

The `datetime` and `datetime-local` types provide more specific dates, including both the date and the time. The only difference between the two is that the `datetime` includes time zone information and the `datetime-local` assumes the local time zone and so does not include that information. The formats for the data for these types are

▶ `datetime (YYYY-MM-DDTHH:MMZ+00:00)`

▶ `datetime-local (YYYY-MM-DDTHH:MM)`

The most frustrating aspect of these input types is that right now, although Safari 5 will create a picker that puts the dates in these formats, the only browser that provides a real date picker is Opera 9. Figure 13.6 shows what the Opera date picker looks like.

However, you have a great alternative with jQuery UI. After you've added jQuery UI to your page as detailed in the "Autocomplete and Datalists" section, just add the following script to the bottom of your HTML:

```
<script>
if (!Modernizr.inputtypes.date) {
    $(function() {
        $( "#d" ).datepicker({ dateFormat: 'yy-mm-dd' });
    });
}
</script>
```

Change the #d to the ID of your date input field. You can find out more about the jQuery UI date picker at http://jqueryui.com/demos/datepicker/.

Email, URLs, Colors, and Search Box Types

The four remaining types cover other standard form fields:

▶ `<input type=email>`

▶ `<input type=url>`

▶ `<input type=color>`

▶ `<input type=search>`

The `email` and `url` fields don't look too different from an ordinary text field, except when you view it on a mobile device. Mobile browsers change the input keyboard to reflect the type of input requested. Figure 13.7 shows a URL input field on a mobile device. For email input, the @ character and period are more prominent. For URL input iOS adds a button for typing ".com" plus the slash, which is typically two levels deep, up in front.

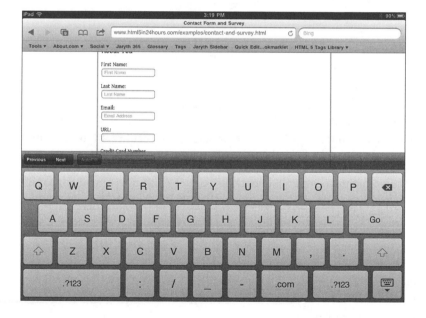

FIGURE 13.7
A URL field on an iPad.

The URL and email fields are extremely useful on mobile devices. Browsers that don't recognize them just display a text field, which looks no different than the URL and email fields on compliant browsers. But the compliant browsers do things like validate that the text is an email address or URL and mobile devices change the keyboard to make it easier to add email addresses and URLs. If you are converting an HTML 4 form to HTML5, adding in the URL and email fields should be your top priority.

The color type adds a color picker to browsers that support it. At this time, that is only Opera 11. The form delivers a six-digit hexadecimal RGB color number. Figure 13.8 shows a standard color picker on Opera.

FIGURE 13.8
A color picker in Opera.

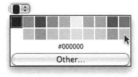

The search type changes the field to look more like a typical search box with rounded corners, inset border, padding, and so on. Figure 13.9 shows a search type input field.

FIGURE 13.9
A search field in Safari with results (indicated by the magnifying glass) and autosave.

Did you Know?

Display Search Results

An undocumented feature of WebKit browsers is the `results` attribute on the `<input type=search>` field. When you use this, Chrome, Safari, Android, and iOS browsers will show a little magnifying glass with a drop-down showing previous searches. Limit the number of results displayed by adding the number as the results value: `results=5`. You use the `autosave` attribute to save the values across page loads.

WebKit and Search Field Styles

When you create an `<input type=search>` field, WebKit browsers have a number of styles that are automatically added to your search field, such as

- ► Rounded corners

- ► Inset border

- ► Typographic control

- ► Cancel button

In fact, WebKit is so strict that you cannot change some styles even with `!important` rules. You can't easily change

- ▶ Padding

- ▶ Font family

- ▶ Font size

- ▶ Border

- ▶ Background color

If you change these styles, your search box will look radically different in non-WebKit browsers (including iOS browsers such as Safari on the iPad). Therefore, leaving those styles alone is a good idea.

If you want to turn off the search appearance, you can use some WebKit-specific styles:

```
input[type=search] {
    -webkit-appearance: none;
}
input[type="search"]::-webkit-search-decoration,
input[type="search"]::-webkit-search-cancel-button {
    display: none;
}
```

Other New Form Elements

HTML5 offers several other new form elements, including `<meter>`, `<progress>`, `<keygen>`, `<output>`, `<menu>`, and `<command>`. The `<meter>` and `<progress>` elements are considered form-associated elements. Hour 9, "Adding Meaning with HTML5 Sectioning and Semantic Elements," discusses `<meter>` and `<progress>` because they also provide additional meaning to the contents as semantic elements.

Key Generation Form Field

The `<keygen>` field is not an `<input>` type, but it is a new form field that you can use to generate a public-private key pair and for submitting the public key from that pair. When a browser submits a form with a `<keygen>` element, the private key is stored in the local keystore, and the public key is packaged and sent to the server.

You can test it with this simple form:

```
<form>
    <keygen name="pubkey" challenge="random-characters">
    <input type="submit" name="createcertificate" value="Generate">
</form>
```

This element is supported in all major browsers, except IE. It is quite possible that Microsoft never will implement <keygen> support. However, if you need to work with secure public-private key pairs, and you don't need to support IE, this element is useful.

Form Output Element

The <output> element provides the result of a calculation. Although this can be a literal calculation, it is most effectively used as a way to display dynamic JavaScript results within the page.

For example, a common dynamic form field shows the number of characters that have been typed into a text box. Before HTML5, those characters would be placed in a <div> or a <span> or sometimes another <input> field. However, you can do it with the <output> element like this:

```
<form>
<textarea id=ta></textarea>
<output id=chars onforminput="characterCount('ta','chars');"></output>
</form>
<script>
function characterCount(inputFieldId, infoBlockId) {
    var characters = document.getElementById(inputFieldId).value.length;
    document.getElementById(infoBlockId).innerHTML = characters;
}
</script>
```

Unfortunately, this element only works in Chrome 11 and Opera 11. If you want it to work in other browsers you will need to fall back to solutions such as using <span> or <input>.

Menu List of Commands

In HTML 4 the <menu> element was used to create a list, but it was used just like the <ul> element, so it was deprecated. But it was brought back in HTML5 for creating a list of commands in context menus, toolbars, and for form controls. A simple menu looks like this:

```
<form>
<menu label="my tools" type="context">
    <li><input type=checkbox value=1>1
    <li><input type=checkbox value=2>2
    <li><input type=checkbox value=3>3
</menu>
</form>
```

You can create three types of <menu>: list (the default), context, and toolbar. Inside your list, you can have either <li> or <command> elements.

The <command> element represents commands. The three types of <command> elements are

- <command type=command> or <command>
- <command type=checkbox>
- <command type=radio>

The type command represents a command with an associated action. The type checkbox provides an option that can be toggled on and off. radio allows for the selection of one item from a group of items.

The <command> element is not supported by any browser at the moment. The <menu> element still acts just like a <ul> list.

Form Validation

One of the most useful features of HTML5 forms is the validation. Now you can set up rules for required fields, and even check for valid formats (numbers in number fields, email addresses that are valid, and so on).

Of course, checking things such as email addresses with a script is almost an exercise in futility and frustration. Getting a regular expression that matches every possible form of email address while not matching things that are not email addresses is difficult. In fact, the official standard regular expression (RFC 2822) is 426 characters long.[1]

Instead, with HTML5 you can just have the browser do it for you, and while you're at it, have the browser validate URLs and numbers as well.

In Opera 9, Firefox 4, and Chrome 10, just by your adding an email or URL field these browsers will validate the email address and URL without your having to do anything else.

But on some forms, you don't want to validate, either because you're testing or some other reason. This is where the novalidate attribute comes in handy. Just add it to your <form> element and the form won't be validated:

```
<form novalidate>
```

---

[1] "How to Find or Validate an Email Address." Regular-Expressions.info. Dec 2, 2010. www.regular-expressions.info/email.html. Referenced May 25, 2011.

The most common type of validation of forms is with required fields. To mark a field required in HTML5 you add the `required` attribute:

```
<input type=text id=name required>
```

Always Validate on the Server as Well

Local validation inside the web browser is a good idea, but users can avoid it in many ways and send invalid or even malicious data. Doing validation on the web server before you add any data to your database or trust it in any way is best.

Figure 13.10 shows a Chrome alert box that appears automatically when a required field is left blank upon submission.

FIGURE 13.10
Required field in Chrome.

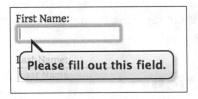

However, the required field is only supported in Chrome 10, Firefox 4, and Opera 9, so you will still need to do some validation with JavaScript as well. Using Modernizr you can check for support for `required` before you run your validation script:

```
if (!Modernizr.input.required){ ... }
```

But validation doesn't stop there with HTML5—you can now also validate the contents of a field using the `pattern` attribute on your input fields. You place a regular expression that details the pattern that the field should use.

For example, suppose you wanted to validate a credit card number. Although you could use the `<input type=number>` field, that doesn't add a lot of value. Instead, let the user type the number in a standard text field, but require that it be exactly 16 characters long and only numbers with a pattern:

```
<input id=ccnum placeholder="Please use only numbers" pattern="[0-9]{16}">
```

Figure 13.11 shows how Firefox validates a credit card field. Describing the format somewhere on the page is a good idea, because the validation message is very generic, as you can see.

The `pattern` attribute is supported by Chrome 10, Firefox 4, and Opera 9.

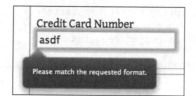

FIGURE 13.11
Validating a
pattern in
Firefox.

Try It Yourself ▼

Creating an HTML5 Form

Putting all of these features together into a coherent and good-looking HTML5 form
can be challenging. Just because you're using the new HTML5 features doesn't mean
you should neglect standard form features such as <fieldset>, <label>, and
<legend> to help improve and style your forms. As with all forms, you must have
some type of script to make them work. To create an HTML5 form, follow these steps:

1. Decide what data you want to collect.

2. Build the form using standard HTML:

```
<form>
<p>Name:<br>
<input type=text id=name>
<p>Email:<br>
<input type=text id=email>
<p>Phone:<br>
<input type=text id=phone>
<p>URL:<br>
<input type=text id=URL>
<p>Job Description:<br>
<textarea id=description></textarea>
<p>Need response by:<br>
<input type=text id=replyBy>
<p>How much can you spend?<br>
$<input type=text id=budget>
<p>
<input type=submit value="Submit Request">
</form>
```

3. Convert the text fields to specific field types:

```
<input type=email id=email>
<input type=url id=URL>
<input type=date id=replyBy>
<input type=number id=budget>
```

4. Mark the required fields:

```
<input type=text id=name required>
<input type=email id=email required>
```

```
<textarea id=description required></textarea>
<input type=date id=replyBy required>
<input type=number id=budget required>
```

5. Add any patterns, maximums, or minimums you want to validate against:

```
<input type=text id=phone pattern="\([0-9]{3}\) [0-9]{3}-[0-9]{4}"
placeholder="(###) ###-####">
<input type=number id=budget required min=300 max=5000 step=100>
```

6. Add an action to the form:

```
<form action="mailto:your-email-address" method=get>
```

Now you have a form that will work, and in Chrome, Firefox, and Opera, there is some validation of the fields. However, you should add some CSS to make the form look good, as follows:

1. Add `<fieldset>` elements around the two sections.

2. Give the sections titles with the `<legend>` element:

```
<fieldset>
<legend>About You</legend>
<p>Name:<br>
<input type=text id=name required>
<p>Email:<br>
<input type=email id=email required>
<p>Phone:<br>
<input type=text id=phone pattern="\([0-9]{3}\) [0-9]{3}-[0-9]{4}"
placeholder="(###) ###-####">
<p>URL:<br>
<input type=url id=URL>
</fieldset>
```

3. Add labels to the form field names:

```
<label for=name>Name:</label>
```

4. Give your `<input>` and `<textarea>` elements some style:

```
input, textarea {
    background: #f4f4f4;
    border: solid 1px #a3a3a3;
    padding: 0.5em 0.75em;
    -webkit-box-shadow: inset 0 0.2em 0.3em rgba(0,0,250,.1);
    -moz-box-shadow: inset 0 0.2em 0.3em rgba(0,0,250,.1);
    box-shadow: inset 0 0.2em 0.3em rgba(0,0,250,.1);
}
```

5. When a field has focus, change the style slightly:

```
input[type=text]:focus, textarea:focus {
    background: #fff;
    border-color: #333;
```

```
        outline: none;
        -webkit-box-shadow: inset 0 0.2em 0.3em rgba(0,0,0,.1);
        -moz-box-shadow: inset 0 0.2em 0.3em rgba(0,0,0,.1);
        box-shadow: inset 0 0.2em 0.3em rgba(0,0,0,.1);
    }
```

6. Set widths on your fields:

```
input {
    width: 20em;
}
input[type=submit] {
    width: 10em;
    -webkit-border-radius: 0.5em;
    -moz-border-radius: 0.5em;
    border-radius: 0.5em;
}
textarea {
    width: 35em;
    height: 20em;
}
```

7. Style the fieldsets and legends:

```
fieldset {
    border: rgba(0,0,250,.2) double 0.4em;
    background-color: #fff;
    -webkit-border-radius: 1em;
    -moz-border-radius: 1em;
    border-radius: 1em;
}
legend {
    font: 1.8em "Palatino Linotype", "Book Antiqua", Palatino, serif;
}
```

8. Finally, add scripts to validate, and add fallback options for things such as the placeholder text and date picker.

You can see a sample of this form at www.html5in24hours.com/examples/job-pro-posal.html.

Summary

This hour covered a lot of information about HTML5 forms, including new attributes, input types, and elements you can use in your forms. You now should understand how to make your forms more usable with autofocus, autocomplete, and placeholder attributes.

You learned about the 13 new input types such as `email`, `number`, and `date`. You also learned about four new elements that will give your forms more utility after these elements are better supported.

You also learned how to use the new HTML5 attributes to validate both required fields on your forms and against patterns so that the data is useful.

Q&A

Q. *Where should I put* `<datalist>` *elements in my HTML?*

A. You can put them wherever you want. The `id` attribute allows you to reference it anywhere in the document. The best place to put it is at the bottom of your HTML, so that it doesn't affect the load time of other page elements. If a non-compliant user agent then does display it or allocate space for it, it's not going to affect the design of the page.

Q. *You described a few elements such as* `<menu>`, `<output>` *and* `<command>` *that are not widely supported. Should I be using these elements anyway?*

A. I recommend not worrying too much about the `<menu>` and `<command>` elements right now. They are not widely supported and don't add any value to mobile applications. However, the `<output>` element will gain browser support, and it does add value by creating both a semantic area for your calculations and a consistent tool for dynamic applications.

Q. *I noticed you used a mailto form in your example, but when I tried it, it didn't work. Are there other options?*

A. HTML5 forms are just like previous HTML forms in that they require an action to really do anything. For contact forms, you can use a form-to-email script in PHP, ASP, or any server-side language you're comfortable working with. For web applications, many forms will be activated with JavaScript.

Workshop

The workshop contains quiz questions to help you process what you've learned in this chapter. Try to answer all the questions before you read the answers. See Appendix A, "Answers to Quizzes," for answers.

Quiz

1. What four new HTML5 features help with form usability?

2. What are the new date and time input types?

3. Name some of the styles that are difficult to change in WebKit browsers on the `<input type=search>` field.

4. What is the `<output>` element used for?

5. What attributes can you use to validate forms in HTML5?

Exercises

1. Find an existing form, either your own or on a website, and add usability features to it to improve how it works.

2. Create a survey form that collects data of at least four different types. Be sure to include `email`, `url`, and a date or time type.

HOUR 14

Editing Content and User Interaction with HTML5

What You'll Learn in This Hour:

▶ How to edit content online with `contenteditable`
▶ How to make a rich text editor with `execCommand`
▶ How to check spelling in forms
▶ How to use new features of the HTML5 UI

Web pages no longer need to be edited just by the designers who built them. HTML5 brings in a new feature to allow them to be edited by anyone who can open them in a browser.

In fact, the `contenteditable` attribute was designed for web designers to be able to embed rich text editors right in their web pages. In this hour, you will learn how to use this HTML5 feature that has been supported in browsers since Internet Explorer 5.5. and Firefox 3 (2007).

You will also learn about another attribute for editing—`spellcheck`. So, after this hour you will be able to provide your readers with the ability to edit parts of your web pages with a rich text editor and verify the spelling in form elements and the sections they edit.

You will also learn how the user interaction features of HTML have changed and improved in HTML5. Clicking on nearly anything is now possible.

The New `contenteditable` Attribute

The `contenteditable` attribute is a global element that you can use on every element in HTML5 to make sections of the page editable online. The `contenteditable` attribute really isn't new. It's been supported in every major desktop browser, including Chrome, Firefox 3, Internet Explorer 5.5, Opera 9, and Safari 3, for a long time.

To use this attribute, simply add it to an element you want to be able to edit in the browser:

```
<div id=edit contenteditable=true></div>
```

You can write the contenteditable attribute with either a true or false value. You can also leave it empty, which means the same as contenteditable=true:

```
<div id=edit contenteditable></div>
```

Design Mode and HTML5

The designmode attribute is not part of the HTML5 standard; it was created by Microsoft for Internet Explorer. It works somewhat differently from contenteditable, because when you turn on design mode the entire document is then editable whereas contenteditable turns on editing only for the one element.

To create a rich text editor, you then need to enable designmode by adding that to your element:

```
<div id=edit contenteditable=true designmode=on></div>
```

Try It Yourself

Creating a Simple WYSIWYG Editor

"What you see is what you get" or WYSIWYG editors are easy for most people to use because they display the styles directly rather than the HTML elements. In this Try It Yourself, you will turn a <div> into a WYSIWYG editor.

1. Add a <div> element to your HTML, and set contenteditable and designmode on it:

   ```
   <div id=edit contenteditable=true designmode=on></div>
   ```

2. Set styles on the <div> so that there is room to edit HTML inside it:

   ```
   <style>
   #edit {
       width: 30em;
       height: 20em;
       border: solid 0.1em #000;
       overflow: auto;
   }
   </style>
   ```

3. Add some buttons for your editor:

```
<input type=button id=bold value=B>
<input type=button id=italic value=i>
<input type=button id=underline value=U>
<input type=button id=createlink value=a>
```

4. Add jQuery to your document:

```
<script src="jquery.min.js"></script>
```

5. At the bottom of your page, add the scripts to activate your buttons:

```
<script>
$(document).ready(function(){
    function doExec(fx, extra) {
        document.execCommand(fx, false, extra);
    }
    $("#bold").click( function() {
        doExec("bold", "");
    });
    $("#italic").click( function() {
        doExec("italic", "");
    });
    $("#underline").click( function() {
        doExec("underline", "");
    });
    $("#createlink").click( function() {
        var xtra = prompt("Enter a URL:", "http://");
        doExec("createlink", xtra);
    });
});
</script>
```

False Turns Off the User Interface

You may be wondering what the "false" is for in the execCommand() method. This tells the user agent to not display a user interface. Because most of the commands used in execCommand() do not support any user interface, you should always write "false" as the second argument.

By the Way

You can see an example of this form at www.html5in24hours.com/examples/contenteditable-examples.html.

▲

The execCommand **Method**

The execCommand() method inside your script is what drives the editor. You can use dozens of commands. Table 14.1 lists the commands, their values, and what they do.

TABLE 14.1   Commands Supported by `execCommand`

Command	Value	Description
`backcolor`	Color value	Changes the document background color. In IE this changes the text background color.
`bold`		Toggles bold on and off.
`createlink`	URL	Creates an `<a href="">` link from the selection.
`delete`		Deletes the current selection.
`fontname`	Font name	Changes the font name for the selection or at the insertion point.
`fontsize`	HTML font size (1–7)	Changes the font size for the selection or at the insertion point.
`forecolor`	Color value	Changes the font color for the selection or at the insertion point.
`formatblock`	Block tag name	Adds an HTML block-level element (`<p>`, `<dl>`, `<h1>`, and so on) around the current selection, replacing the block that is there.
`indent`		Indents the block of text at the insertion point.
`inserthorizontalrule`		Adds a horizontal rule (`<hr>`) at the insertion point.
`inserthtml`	Valid HTML	Inserts a block of HTML at the insertion point or to replace the selection
`insertimage`	URL to an image	Inserts an image at the insertion point.
`insertorderedlist`		Inserts an ordered list. When you press Enter, it adds a new list item.
`insertunorderedlist`		Inserts an unordered list. When you press Enter, it adds a new list item.
`italic`		Toggles italics on and off.
`justifycenter`		Centers text with `text-align: center;`.
`justifyfull`		Sets justification to full with `text-align: full;`.

TABLE 14.1 Commands Supported by execCommand

Command	Value	Description
justifyleft		Sets text alignment to left with text-align: left;.
justifyright		Sets text alignment to right with text-align: right;.
outdent		Removes indents created by the indent command. This command removes any <blockquote> elements.
redo		Redoes the previous undo action. It must be used immediately after using undo.
removeformat		Removes formatting tags such as <b> and <i>. May not remove colors applied to the background.
selectall		Selects everything in the editable element.
strikethrough		Toggles strikethrough on and off.
subscript		Toggles subscript on and off.
superscript		Toggles superscript on and off.
underline		Toggles underline on and off.
undo		Undoes the previous action.
unlink		Removes the link (<a>) from the selection.

To use these commands, place them in the execCommand function as the first value. The second value should be false. Include any required attributes in the third value.

For example, following is a command without any values:

```
document.execCommand("bold", false, "");
```

The following command has a value:

```
document.execCommand("formatblock", false, "<p>");
```

Watch
Out!

Browsers Interpret the Editor Differently

The browsers that support the `contenteditable` attribute and the `execCommand` function do so in slightly different ways. For example, Internet Explorer applies all the fields to selected text. If there is no text or nothing is selected, it won't apply anything. Also, Firefox won't display `<blockquote>` or `<div>` elements in a `formatblock`. Be sure to test any pages that use `contenteditable` and `execCommand` before you launch.

You can also use a few other commands to work with the editable content:

▶ **`document.queryCommandEnabled()`**—Indicates whether the command can be executed on the document

▶ **`document.queryCommandState()`**—Indicates whether the command has been executed on an object

▶ **`document.queryCommandIndeterm()`**—Indicates whether the command is in the indeterminate state

▶ **`document.queryCommandSupported()`**—Indicates whether the current command is supported

▶ **`document.queryCommandValue()`**—Returns the current value of the document or selection for the given command

These methods allow you to get more information about the items in your edited content.

Try It Yourself

Building a Simple To-Do List

In this Try It Yourself, you will create a to-do list using an unordered list, `contenteditable`, and local storage (local storage is discussed in detail in Hour 21, "Web Storage in HTML5").

1. Add a `<ul>` element to your document:

```
<ul id=myToDoList>
    <li>
</ul>
```

2. Add the `contenteditable` attribute to the `<ul>`:

```
<ul id=myToDoList contenteditable=true>
```

Of course, this to-do list isn't very useful, because as soon as you leave the page, it disappears. Therefore, add a jQuery script to save it to local storage (also covered in Hour 21), and restore it when the page reloads.

3. Add jQuery to the head of your document:

```
<script src="jquery.min.js"></script>
```

4. Start the document ready function:

```
<Script>
$(document).ready(function(){
});
</script>
```

5. Save the to-do list to local storage inside the document ready function:

```
$(document).ready(function(){
    $("#myToDoList").blur(function() {
        localStorage.setItem('myToDoData', this.innerHTML);
    });
});
```

6. Load the to-do list from local storage when the page loads. Put this in the document ready function as well:

```
if ( localStorage.getItem('myToDoData') ) {
    $("#myToDoList").html(localStorage.getItem('myToDoData'));
}
```

You can see this script in action at www.html5in24hours.com/examples/to-do-list-1.html.

Adding Spellcheck to Web Pages

HTML5 provides the global attribute spellcheck, which indicates that the element's contents are subject to spell checking and grammar checking. This global attribute can be placed on any element, but browser support is best on form elements and contenteditable elements. Like the contenteditable attribute, all you need to do is add spellcheck=true to your form element, like this:

```
<textarea spellcheck=true></textarea>
```

You can write this attribute with a true or false value, or you can write it as an empty element, which means the same as spellcheck=true:

```
<textarea spellcheck></textarea>
```

The challenge with the spellcheck attribute is browser support. Internet Explorer, Safari, iOS, and Android don't support the spellcheck attribute. However, except for IE, they all offer alternatives that are built into the browser. Chrome, Opera 10, and Firefox 2 support the attribute, but even their support is different:

▶ Opera applies spellcheck to the exact form elements it is written in; applying it to the <form> element affects all child form elements. It checks contenteditable fields as you type, but not existing content.

▶ Chrome returns positive when testing for spellcheck, but only checks spelling as you type, not in existing values of forms. It checks contenteditable fields as you type, but not existing content.

▶ Firefox always checks <textarea> elements unless you explicitly turn off spell checking for them. It only checks <input> elements when the parent <form> element has spell check turned on or when the spellcheck attribute is applied right to the <input> element. It checks contenteditable fields as you type as well as the existing content.

Like the new input types, adding the spellcheck attribute to your elements is not going to hurt anything. In fact, other than Internet Explorer, most browsers provide spellcheck automatically even if you don't use the attribute. However, as they start supporting it, you can control which fields are checked and which are not.

Hiding Elements

Another global attribute that HTML5 adds is the hidden attribute. This attribute indicates that the element is not relevant to the document and so should be hidden from view. To hide an element, write:

```
<p hidden=true>
```

This is another attribute with either a true or false value. Writing it as an empty attribute is the same as writing hidden=true:

```
<p hidden>
```

You should not use the hidden element to just hide content temporarily such as with tabbed interface or content that overflows the space available. This attribute hides content from all presentations and user agents.

Additional UI Components of HTML5

Several aspects of user interaction are carried forward from HTML 4 to HTML5, but the one thing that makes HTML5 unique is that now these features can be applied to any element.

These UI features include:

▶ Activation when an element is clicked

▶ Setting the focus on an element

▶ Blurring the focus on an element

▶ Navigating through focusable elements with `tabindex`

These features are not new, but there is a bit more support in browsers for adding more event handlers to every object in your document. Plus HTML5 adds a number of new event handlers for even more functions:

▶ **onabort**—The element loading was aborted by the user.

▶ **oncanplay**—The user agent can play the current media object, but there may need to be more buffering.

▶ **oncanplaythrough**—The user agent can play the current media object all the way through without buffering.

▶ **oncontextmenu**—A context menu appears (typically on right-click by the user) for the element.

▶ **ondrag**—As the element is being dragged.

▶ **ondragend**—The dragging stops.

▶ **ondragenter**—A dragged element enters the current element.

▶ **ondragleave**—A dragged element leaves the current element.

▶ **ondragover**—The dragged element continues over the current element.

▶ **ondragstart**—The dragging starts.

▶ **ondrop**—The drop action happens.

▶ **ondurationchange**—The duration attribute of the DOM on the `video` or `audio` element changes.

▶ **onemptied**—The video or audio element returns to the uninitialized state.

▶ **onended**—The end of the video or audio element is reached.

▶ **onerror**—The element failed to load properly.

▶ **oninvalid**—The element, usually a form field, did not meet validity constraints.

▶ **onloadeddata**—The user agent can render the video or audio element for the first time.

▶ **onloadedmetadata**—The user agent has determined the duration and dimensions of the video or audio element.

▶ **onloadstart**—The user agent starts to look for media data for the video or audio element.

▶ **onpause**—The user has paused playback on the video or audio element.

▶ **onplay**—The user agent has started playing the video or audio element.

▶ **onplaying**—The playback of the video or audio element has started.

▶ **onprogress**—The user agent is fetching media data for the video or audio element.

▶ **onratechange**—The DOM attribute defaultPlaybackRate or the DOM attribute playbackRate on the video or audio element has been updated.

▶ **onreadystatechange**—The element and all of its subelements has loaded.

▶ **onseeked**—A seek operation on the video or audio element has ended.

▶ **onseeking**—A seek operation is taking long enough to fire a seeking event on the video or audio element.

▶ **onshow**—The user requested the element be shown as a context menu.

▶ **onstalled**—The user agent is attempting to fetch media data for a video or audio element but it's not happening.

▶ **onsuspend**—The user agent is not currently fetching media data, but does not have the full sound or video downloaded.

▶ **ontimeupdate**—The current playback position of the video or audio element has changed.

▶ **onvolumechange**—The DOM attribute `volume` or the DOM attribute `muted` has changed on the `video` or `audio` element.

▶ **onwaiting**—Playback of the `video` or `audio` element has stopped because the next frame is not yet available.

The most useful change is the addition of `tabindex` as a global attribute. This makes your pages much easier to navigate because you can set the tab index number on your headings or even on individual paragraphs. Figure 14.1 shows a paragraph with a tabindex of 1 tabbed to in Safari. The browser both highlights the tabbed element and brings the focus to it, and you can see that by the outline around the text and the fact that the scrollbar is all the way at the bottom. You can see this example online at www.html5in24hours.com/examples/ui-examples.html.

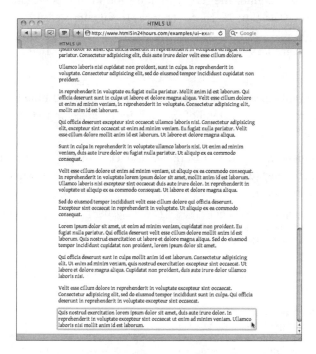

FIGURE 14.1
Tabbing to a paragraph in Safari.

Browser Support of UI and Editing Features

One of the great things about the `contenteditable` attribute is how widely it is supported. IE has had support since version 5.5, and all the other desktop browsers have followed along with fairly standard implementations.

Internet Explorer Leads the Way

Microsoft and IE were the trailblazers when it came to WYSIWYG editors right in the browser window. These days, dozens, if not hundreds of rich text editors, are built on that foundation. Tools such as TinyMCE (http://tinymce.moxiecode.com/index.php) and the YUI Rich Text Editor (http://developer.yahoo.com/yui/editor/) both build on what IE started.

However, editing content in a mobile application is impossible. The contenteditable attribute is not supported in any mobile browser at this time. Instead, you need to use a <textarea> element and provide a plain HTML (not rich text) alternative.

As usual, doing detection for the HTML5 feature you want is better than detecting for a specific browser. Detecting for contenteditable support is easy:

```
if ('isContentEditable' in document.createElement('p') == false) {
    alert('browser does not support contenteditable attribute');
}
```

This checks the DOM to see whether the contenteditable attribute is available on a newly created <p> element. Instead of the alert in the preceding if statement, you should put your alternative <textarea> and form.

Of course, this method still doesn't work because iOS and Android report that they have the attribute, they just don't support it. This is one situation where you have to check the browser version:

```
var iOS = !!navigator.userAgent.match('iPhone OS') ||
!!navigator.userAgent.match('iPad');
var Android = !!navigator.userAgent.match('Android');
```

You then add those variables to create an if statement that detects those browsers (iOS and Android):

```
var iOS = !!navigator.userAgent.match('iPhone OS') ||
!!navigator.userAgent.match('iPad');
var Android = !!navigator.userAgent.match('Android');
if ( !('isContentEditable' in document.createElement('p')) ||
➡(iOS || Android)) {
    alert('browser does not support contenteditable attribute');
}
```

> **Be Careful with "False"**
>
> All of these attributes (`contenteditable`, `spellcheck`, and `hidden`) are boolean attributes. As such, they imply the values true and false—true when the attribute is present and false when it is not. But many web browsers treat the presence of the attribute as meaning "true" regardless of the value, so you can end up with incorrect results if you write `contenteditable=false`.

You can check for spellcheck support the same way:

```
if ('spellcheck' in document.createElement('textarea') == false) {
    alert('browser does not support spellcheck attribute');
}
```

As mentioned earlier, using this attribute doesn't hurt anything, so you don't need to worry about detecting for it.

If you want to check for the `hidden` attribute, you can use the same method:

```
if ('hidden' in document.createElement('p') == false) {
```

You can then use a jQuery function to hide that content:

```
if ('hidden' in document.createElement('p') == false) {
    $("[hidden]").hide();
}
```

The UI features have good browser support because they have been in the HTML specification for a while. However, some exceptions are

▶ Mobile browsers don't generally have a way to tab between elements, so setting the `tabindex` has no effect on iOS or Android browsers.

▶ Tablets and smartphones use touch and multi-touch interface in place of clicking. In most situations the `onclick` method works as intended, but actions such as click and drag and double-clicking can be less effective.

Summary

HTML5 makes interacting with your users a lot easier. It offers a bunch of new event handlers as well as new functionality within the interface. Plus, HTML5 formalizes a feature that has been available in browsers for a long time—`contenteditable`.

This hour you learned how to make simple rich text editors right inside your browser window and then add spellcheck functionality to those editable regions.

You also learned about the new UI attribute `hidden`, which can be placed on any element to hide it from view.

Q&A

Q. *If* `contenteditable` *has been around so long, why have I only just now heard of it?*

A. This attribute was created by a browser manufacturer (Microsoft), and although many of these types of features are eventually added to the specification, one of the criteria is usage. If a feature is not widely adopted it might not be added. Until recently it was a feature that was IE-only.

Q. *What if I want to check the spelling of a different language. Is there a way to specify the dictionary that is used for checking spelling?*

A. This is typically a browser feature that only your users can control. But you can provide links to custom dictionaries that they can download and install.

Q. *You say I shouldn't use the* `hidden` *attribute for tabs and content, but why would they add it to the specification if I shouldn't use it?*

A. It's not that you should never use this attribute, but rather you should think about the reason you're using it. If you are hiding content to display later through a navigation choice such as tabs, then using CSS `display: none;` would be more appropriate. CSS is for making changes to presentation. If you are hiding the content because it is irrelevant to the whole document, and you want that information applied semantically, then the `hidden` attribute is appropriate.

Workshop

The workshop contains quiz questions to help you process what you've learned in this chapter. Try to answer all the questions before you read the answers. See Appendix A, "Answers to Quizzes," for answers.

Quiz

1. What browsers support `contenteditable`?

2. What elements can use the `contenteditable` attribute?

3. What attribute do you need to create a rich text editor in your browser?

4. There is a "gotcha" in detecting for `contenteditable`—what is it?

Exercises

1. Build a to-do list that includes rich text editing of the items. Be sure to include bold and colors so that you can highlight the most important items.

2. Add spellcheck to your forms with `textarea` elements to help your readers submit forms with correct spelling. A good place to start is in any comment fields you have.

Microformats and Microdata

What You'll Learn in This Hour:

▶ How to mark up HTML semantically with more than just HTML elements

▶ Why semantic markup is important

▶ The differences between RDFa, microdata, and microformats

▶ How to choose between microformats and microdata

This hour you will learn more about two technologies that aren't specifically part of HTML5, but that aid in the creation of more semantic documents—microformats and microdata.

Microformats and microdata are two competing standards that attempt to make human-readable web pages more readable by computers as well without affecting the visible content on the pages. In this hour you will learn how to make your HTML more semantic by using microformats. You will also learn about microdata and the most popular microdata vocabulary: RDFa.

Using Microformats

Microformats are a set of simple, human-readable formats that are added to HTML to add more meaning to that HTML. When you use microformats you add markup to your documents that defines recognizable data items.

Microformats are both the vocabulary you use to add meaning to your HTML and the method of adding that information. For example, hCard is a microformat vocabulary you can add to your pages to define contact information (name, address, phone number, and so on). You can then include the hCard information in your page using class attributes on your HTML elements—this is the Microformats method (defined by Microformats.org) of inserting this information.

Some things you can mark up with microformats include:

▶ Events using hCalendar—With hCalendar you can indicate the start date and time, end date and time, and location of an event.

▶ Contact information using hCard—The hCard microformat lets you add vcard (a file format for contact information) markup to your pages to define names, addresses, and contact information for people.

▶ Recipes using hRecipe—Recipes are already being stored by Google using the hRecipe microformat to indicate ingredients, directions, and even ratings of recipes.

▶ Reviews using hReview—The hReview format is also being used by Google to display reviews of products and services, including the star rating, pros and cons, and review text.

▶ Geography using geo—The geo format identifies longitude and latitude in documents so that they can be used by devices such as GPS or for geolocation.

▶ Anything that has a standard and recognizable format—You can learn about many other microformats at the microformats website (http://microformats.org/wiki/Main_Page).

Microformats are intended to take existing data, such as that found in HTML documents, and add human-readable attributes to provide more information about the data.

In HTML, most microformats are added with <span> tags and class attributes on those <span> tags to define the different sections of data. For example, you can mark up a name with the hCard format like this:

```
<span class="fn">Jennifer Kyrnin</span>
```

The class="fn" indicates that "Jennifer Kyrnin" is a full name.

Because you are using standard HTML elements (such as <span>) and attributes, you can take a block of HTML and mark it up with microformats without affecting how the HTML displays at all, unless you want to.

For example, here is a simple book review written in HTML without microformats:

```
<article>
<h3><a href="...">Dopplegangster</a> by Laura Resnick</h3>
<h4>A Fun, Quick Read</h4>
<p>Rating: 3 out of 5 stars
<p>Review Date: <time datetime="2010-12-15">December 15, 2011</time>
<article>
```

```
<h1>Jennifer Kyrnin&#8217;s review:</h1>
...
</article>
</article>
```

When you read the review, you know which parts are the book title, author, and rating, but a computer would have no idea. There would be no reasonable way to get this review information into a database of multiple reviews so that the information is consistent.

> **What Microformats Are Not**
>
> Microformats are not a specification, per se, but rather a set of instructions for marking up different types of data. Microformats are not separate languages, and to use microformats you don't have to throw away what is already working. However, they are also not the solution to every problem.

You can use the hReview microformat to mark up the entire review so that it can be read by a computer and added to a collection of reviews:

```
<article class="hreview">
<h3><span class="item"><a href="..."
➥class="fn url">Dopplegangster</a></span>
by Laura Resnick</h3>
<h4 class="summary">A Fun, Quick Read</h4>
<p>Rating: <span class="rating" title="3">3</span> out of 5 stars
<p>Review Date:
<time datetime="2010-12-15" class="dtreviewed">December 15,
➥2010</time></span>
<article class="description">
<h3><span class="reviewer vcard"><span class="fn">Jennifer
Kyrnin</span></span>&#8217;s Review:</h3>
...
</article>
</article>
```

You can see the entire example at http://html5in24hours.com/examples/microformats-examples.html.

Microformats combined with semantic HTML can help you create documents that can be more widely used.

The Benefits of Microformats

Microformats add data that is useful to both humans and computers into HTML documents. Although having an HTML document marked up with microformats might not seem that useful, the more that gets marked up with microformats, the more useful the documents will become.

For example, on Goodreads you can find 150 reviews of the book *Dopplegangster*. You can find 18 reviews on Amazon.com and 40 reviews in Google books, with average ratings of 3.59, 4.33, and 3.5 (approximately), respectively.

If all these reviews were marked up with the hReview microformat, you could combine all the reviews into one collection to see what the average is for all those sites. Any review that has been marked up with the hReview markup could be shared and reused effectively on many different sites.

Microformats also make taking data that is delivered via a web page and putting it into an application possible. For example, a vcard can be saved in the hCard microformat to allow people to easily save your contact information to an address book. An event stored in the hCalendar format can be added to Outlook, Google calendar, iCal, or any other calendaring program.

> **The hCard Format Is Widely Supported**
>
> One of the best reasons to use microformats with the hCard format is because it already has a lot of support. Apple and Windows will add text marked up with hCard to your contacts, as will iOS and Android.

Principles for Using Microformats

You should keep in mind a few principles when using microformats:

- ▶ Start by solving specific problems.
- ▶ Keep your solutions as simple as possible.
- ▶ Focus on keeping the tags human readable.
- ▶ Use HTML.

When adding microformats, avoid adding new elements to your HTML unless they are absolutely critical, and then when you do add elements, add elements such as <span> that don't affect how the document displays.

Some Microformats Already in Use

Many microformats are already in use around the web including:

- ▶ **hCalendar**—For marking up events to add them to calendars
- ▶ **hCard**—For creating vcard documents for address books
- ▶ **hRecipe**—To describe instructions for making food

- **hReview**—For writing reviews of products, businesses, events, and so on

- **rel-nofollow**—To tell search engines not to afford additional weight to the link

- **XHTML Friends Network (XFN)**—Represents human relationships inside links

hCard and hCalendar are both widely supported in operating systems and allow your users to add addresses and events to their address book and calendar quickly and easily. As you can see in Figure 15.1, Windows supports the hCard microformat and will add it to your Windows contacts.

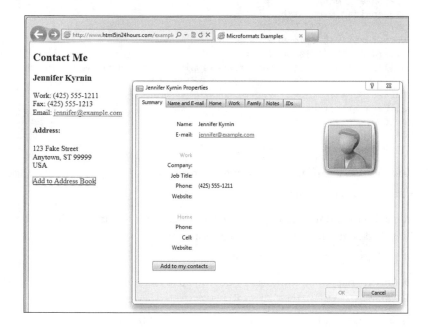

FIGURE 15.1
Windows importing a vcard from a website.

hRecipe is used by Google's recipe search to provide "rich snippets" in the search results. This makes your recipe more enticing so readers would want to click on it. Google also uses hReview in the same way to provide better results in a search for reviews.

The elemental microformat rel-nofollow is widely used by web designers who want to slow down spam on their blogs. It is called an elemental microformat because it is a format that only has one attribute or element—in this case rel=nofollow. The microformat XFN or XHTML Friends Network can be incorporated into many blogs that use WordPress.

▼   **Try It Yourself**

Adding hCard to Your Site

The easiest place to start with microformats is by adding hCard microformats to your website. An hCard lets people add your contact information to their address book. Follow these steps to add an hCard:

1. Open your contact page on your website.

2. If the contact area is not fully enclosed in a block-level element such as `<address>`, you will need to add one:

```
<address id="address">
<h2>Contact Me</h2>
<h3>Jennifer Kyrnin</h3>
<p>
Work: (425) 555-1211<br>
Fax: (425) 555-1213<br>
Email: <a href="mailto:jennifer@example.com">jennifer@example.com</a>
<p>
Address:<br>
123 Fake Street<br>
Anytown, ST 99999<br>
USA
</address>
```

3. Add the vcard class to the container element:

```
<address class="vcard">
```

4. Surround the name (either your name or the company name) with the fn class. This field is mandatory in the hCard format:

```
<h3 class="fn">Jennifer Kyrnin</h3>
```

5. Define the telephone numbers by adding span elements around the type and number:

```
<span class="tel"><span class="type">Work</span>:
<span class="value">(425) 555-1211</span></span><br>
<span class="tel"><span class="type">Fax</span>:
<span class="value">(425) 555-1213</span></span>
```

> **Set the Phone Number Type Correctly**
>
> When you define the type of your phone number, you need to use one of the types listed in the hCard instructions: home, work, pref, fax, cell, voice, video, pager, car, msg, modem, bbs, isdn, or pcs. These types are not case sensitive, so *Home* is the same as *home*.

6. Define the email address with an `email` class:

```
<a href="mailto:jennifer@example.com"
➥class="email">jennifer@example.com</a>
```

7. Add elements to the address so that you can add hCard classes:

```
<h4>Address:</h4>
<p class="adr">
<span class="street-address">123 Fake Street</span><br>
<span class="locality">Anytown</span>,
<span class="region">ST</span> <span class="postal-
code">99999</span><br>
<span class="country-name">USA</span>
```

8. Add an Add to Address Book link:

```
<p>
<a href="http://h2vx.com/vcf/Your URL">Add to Address Book</a>
```

Change the text *Your URL* to the full URL of the page where your address hCard was posted.

▲

Using Microdata

Microdata is an HTML5 extension that provides another way to embed computer-readable data into your documents. Several attributes are included in the microdata specification that extend HTML5:

▶ **itemprop**—Used instead of `class` to define the field names

▶ **itemscope**—A boolean attribute that defines a group with microdata

▶ **itemref**—A list of IDs that are associated, even if they aren't in the same `itemscope`

▶ **itemtype**—A URL that gives the context of the microdata

▶ **itemid**—A global identifier, such as an ISBN for a book

Microdata is used in a similar fashion to microformats, only instead of using the `class` attribute from HTML, microdata uses the new attributes listed in the preceding list. You can then use a microformats vocabulary, such as hReview, to mark up your HTML. Following is the review example from earlier in the hour marked up in microdata:

```
<article itemscope itemtype="http://microformats.org/profile/hreview">
<h3><span itemprop="item"><a href="..." itemprop="fn url">
Dopplegangster</a></span> by Laura Resnick</h3>
<h4 itemprop="summary">A Fun, Quick Read</h4>
<p>Rating: <span itemprop="rating" title="3">3</span> out of 5 stars
```

```
<p>Review Date:
<time datetime="2010-12-15" itemprop="dtreviewed" pubdate>December 15,
2010</time></span>
<article itemprop="description">
<h3><span itemprop="reviewer vcard fn" id="reviewer">Jennifer
Kyrnin</span>&#8217;s review:</h3>
<p>
...
</article>
</article>
```

As you can see, microdata is similar to microformats, but with more structure.

▼ **Try It Yourself**

Converting the `hCard` to Microdata

If you would rather use microdata than microformats for marking up your HTML, converting from one to the other is easy; just follow these steps:

1. Open the `hCard` you wrote in the preceding Try It Yourself:

```
<address class="vcard">
<h2>Contact Me</h2>
<h3 class="fn">Jennifer Kyrnin</h3>
<p>
<span class="tel"><span class="type">Work</span>:
<span class="value">(425) 555-1211</span></span><br>
<span class="tel"><span class="type">Fax</span>:
<span class="value">(425) 555-1213</span></span><br>
Email: <a href="mailto:jennifer@example.com"
class="email">jennifer@example.com</a>
<h4>Address:</h4>
<p>
<span class="adr">
<span class="street-address">123 Fake Street</span><br>
<span class="locality">Anytown</span>,
<span class="region">ST</span>
➥<span class="postal-code">99999</span><br>
<span class="country-name">USA</span>
</span>
<p>
<a href="http://h2vx.com/vcf/YOUR URL">
Add to Address Book
</a>
</address>
```

2. Add `itemscope` to the container element:

```
<address itemscope class="vcard">
```

3. Set the itemtype to hCard:

```
<address itemscope itemtype="http://microformats.org/profile/hcard"
class="vcard">
```

4. Remove the class from the container element, because it is defined by the itemtype:

```
<address itemscope itemtype="http://microformats.org/profile/hcard">
```

5. Change all the class attributes to itemprop:

```
<address itemscope itemtype="http://microformats.org/profile/hcard">
<h2>Contact Me</h2>
<h3 itemprop="fn">Jennifer Kyrnin</h3>
<p>
<span itemprop="tel"><span itemprop="type">Work</span>:
<span itemprop="value">(425) 555-1211</span></span><br>
<span itemprop="tel"><span itemprop="type">Fax</span>:
<span itemprop="value">(425) 555-1213</span></span><br>
Email: <a href="mailto:jennifer@example.com"
itemprop="email">jennifer@example.com</a>
<h4>Address:</h4>
<p>
<span itemprop="adr">
<span itemprop="street-address">123 Fake Street</span><br>
<span itemprop="locality">Anytown</span>,
<span itemprop="region">ST</span>
<span itemprop="postal-code">99999</span><br>
<span itemprop="country-name">USA</span>
</span>
<p>
<a href="http://h2vx.com/vcf/www.html5in24hours.com/examples/
➡vcard-example.html">
Add to Address Book
</a>
</address>
```

As you can see, other than changing the class attributes to the microdata attributes, the hCard markup is the same.

Using RDFa

RDFa (Resource Description Framework in attributes) is another language that helps bridge the gap between human-readable and machine-readable content.

The main attributes you use in RDFa are

▶ **about** or **src**—The resource the metadata is about

▶ **rel**—A relationship with another resource

▶ **rev**—A reverse relationship with another resource

▶ **href** or **resource**—The URL of the resource

▶ **property**—A characteristic of the element's content

To mark up an address in RDFa, you need to use the VCARD-RDF specification. You also need to add the namespace to your <html> tag:

```
<html xmlns:contact="http://www.w3.org/2001/vcard-rdf/3.0#">
```

Then you add meta tags around the elements and use the namespace you defined:

```
<div property="contactinfo" about="#me">
<h2>Contact Me</h2>
<h3><meta property="contact:fn">Jennifer Kyrnin</meta></h3>
<p>
<meta property="contact:tel"><meta property="contact:type">Work</meta>:
<meta property="contact:value">(425) 555-1211</meta></meta><br>
<meta property="contact:tel"><meta property="contact:type">Fax</meta>:
<meta property="contact:value">(425) 555-1213</meta></meta><br>
Email: <a href="mailto:jennifer@example.com"
property="contact:email">jennifer@example.com</a>
</p>
<h4>Address:</h4>
<p>
<meta property="contact:adr">
<meta property="contact:street-address">123 Fake Street</meta><br>
<meta property="contact:locality">Anytown</meta>,
<meta property="contact:region">ST</meta>
<meta property="contact:postal-code">99999</meta><br>
<meta property="contact:country-name">USA</meta>
</meta>
</p>
<p>
<a href="http://h2vx.com/vcf/YOUR URL">
Add to Address Book
</a>
</p>
</div>
```

Deciding Which Format to Use

Microformats, microdata, or RDFa will work for marking up your pages more semantically. However, each format has pros and cons.

Microformats are easy to use, and use existing HTML attributes such as class so your HTML will continue to validate. However, if you already use classes that are part of the microformat specification, your page design could be affected. Microformats are already implemented in a lot of places.

RDFa is based on RDF and can be complicated to learn. However, many tools are available for adding RDF and RDFa to your documents. RDFa works best with XHTML, rather than the less strict HTML and is very popular in academia.

Microdata is the newest tool. It is more extensible than microformats, and doesn't affect the design of HTML documents at all because it adds new attributes. It is easier to learn than RDFa, but more complicated than microformats. Microdata is a W3C specification, which might give it more clout in the business community over the long term. Plus, search engine providers such as Bing, Google, and Yahoo! are already using microdata in their search results.

At the end of the day, which one you use doesn't really matter, just as long as you use one of them.

Mobile and Microformats

Android and iOS have limited support for any of these systems in their built-in browsers. This is interesting when you consider that other, possibly less-sophisticated feature phones such as the Treo, Sony Ericsson W810i, and the Nokia S60 can handle vcards, and the Treo can handle hCalendar data as well.

A Useful Tool for Detecting Microformats

The Microformat website (www.microform.at/) will detect microformats on websites and then transform them into downloadable links. It will even turn them into QR codes, which your mobile users can then scan.

By the Way

Why Bother with Microformats or Microdata?

If modern smartphones don't support microformats or microdata, you may be thinking that there is no point to your using them. However, by marking up your content with this information, you are prepared for when they do start to support them. Plus, as mentioned earlier they are supported by feature phones such as the Sony Ericsson W810i, so they will likely be supported by smartphones fairly soon.

The number one benefit that microformats and microdata will bring to mobile devices is usability. Clicking one link to populate an address book is much easier than laboriously typing in the name, address, and phone number of a contact.

Many smartphones have things such as GPS that can connect GPS coordinates to a map. With those coordinates marked with microformats, the phone could generate turn-by-turn directions from the user's current location. Yes, the phone could do that without microformats, but with them, the user doesn't have to do anything.

The phone would simply know that that data (with the microformat codes) was a coordinate to map.

Two Less Formalized Microformats

Mobile devices are also starting to regularly use two other microformats: nanoformats and picoformats. These are microformats that use very few characters to provide semantic information. They are designed to be used in text messages over a mobile phone.

Nanoformats came from Twitter and provide additional information in just a few characters. In fact, two types of nanoformats have garnered common usage outside web pages:

▶ `@username`—This is used to mention another Twitter user, but it has become common to see it used in web pages and email as well to indicate who the author is talking to or about.

▶ hashtags (`#category`)—Hashtags are a way to provide more relevance for searches for specific topics.

Picoformats are even shorter than nanoformats. They use single symbols to provide information over SMS or chat. For example, someone might send an SMS message to a server with just @ in the message. The server then knows that the person sending that message is at the location sent automatically by the phone. One way this could be used is with 911 service. By texting 911 operators with a nanoformat like @ you don't have to know your exact location, and that can get emergency responders to you more quickly. Nothing like this has been enabled yet, but nanoformats would make it easier for the possibly injured person to communicate where they are.

These formats are still evolving but they do provide additional data about the surrounding text and so are considered microformats.

Summary

Microformats add useful information to your web pages and help make elements more semantic. You can mark up things such as events, recipes, and resumes. What's really nice about microformats is that they fit right into your existing HTML5 documents.

Deciding between using microformats, microdata, and RDFa might be tricky, but it boils down to this:

▶ Microformats are the easiest to use.

▶ RDFa has a lot of support.

▶ Microdata is a W3C standard.

The smallest microformats—nanoformats and picoformats—let you mark up text with very few characters and still provide more information.

Q&A

Q. Why is it important to have human-readable or machine-readable content?

A. By making your documents as semantic as possible, you create an application that is useful both to the humans reading your documents and the computers parsing them. This means that your application will be seen and understood more widely.

Q. It seems like using microdata would add a lot of extra characters to my HTML—won't that slow down the page rendering?

A. Adding microdata to your markup can seem to add a lot of extra stuff to download, but you have to remember that that content is useful. A vcard with your company's address can be added to your user's address book quickly and easily. Events marked up with hCalendar can be added to users' calendars, so they don't forget to attend. Just because the content isn't immediately visible to the user doesn't mean it's not useful.

Q. My iPod touch seems to support vCards, but you said that iOS doesn't support it.

A. This is one of the ironies of the iPhone market. The iPod and iPad support microformats better than the iPhone, but this may change. All three devices recognize addresses and contact information to some extent, without the need for microformat markup.

Q. *Microdata and microformats seem complicated—how can I make sure I've added them correctly?*

A. You can use validators to check your microformats and microdata. The W3C has an RDF validator (www.w3.org/RDF/Validator/), and Google has a tool to test your microdata (www.google.com/webmasters/tools/richsnippets).

Workshop

The workshop contains quiz questions to help you process what you've learned in this chapter. Try to answer all the questions before you read the answers. See Appendix A, "Answers to Quizzes," for answers.

Quiz

1. What are three things that you can mark up with microformats?

2. What is the `itemprop` attribute used for in microdata?

3. What does RDFa stand for?

Exercises

1. Look up the specification for `hResume`, and then write or edit your online resume to include these attributes. You can use either microformats or microdata.

2. Create a calendar of events for either yourself or your business, and use `hCalendar` to mark it up. You can use the `hCalendar` creator (http://microformats.org/code/hcalendar/creator) for help.

HOUR 16
Working with HTML5 Drag-and-Drop Functionality

What You'll Learn in This Hour:

▶ Why drag and drop is important for web applications

▶ How to use drag and drop in most modern browsers

▶ How to use the new events and attributes for drag and drop

▶ The six steps to creating a drag-and-drop interface

HTML5 drag and drop provides you with a standardized method of creating drag-and-drop functionality in your web applications. This makes your applications function even more like a native desktop application.

In this hour you will learn the HTML5 events and attributes that were added to allow drag and drop to function. You'll also learn the steps for how to implement drag and drop using HTML5.

If you have implemented drag and drop on your web pages in the past, you know how tricky it can be. But HTML5 makes the process easier, and with the better browser support, you can create applications that work in most devices and browsers.

Implementing Drag and Drop

One of the most fundamental aspects of native applications as opposed to web pages is the ability to move objects around—to drag them and drop them. HTML5 brings that functionality to web applications through an API and several new attributes.

On computer browsers, drag and drop is implemented with a mouse. The user clicks and holds on an object and then moves the mouse, dragging the object with the mouse. When the user releases the mouse button, the object is dropped in that new location. On Android devices, the drag and drop occurs when the user taps and holds an object and then slides to a new location and lets go.

The two ways to implement drag and drop are generally referred to as "old school" and "new school." New school is HTML5 drag and drop, and old school uses DHTML (Dynamic HTML). Many implementations that use DHTML only work in one specific browser or only with specific external frameworks.

Using HTML5 drag and drop provides some tangible benefits:

▶ You are not tied in to any specific browser or framework, because the HTML5 API is widely supported.

▶ HTML5 drag and drop works across browser windows, frames, and even non-web applications.

Most of the major browsers provide support for drag and drop, including Android 2.1, Chrome 3, Firefox 3.5, Internet Explorer 5, and Safari 3. It is not supported in iOS or Opera. Even though drag and drop is not supported by Opera and iOS now, they will eventually because drag and drop is part of HTML5, which both browser manufacturers support.

> **Browser Quirks**
>
> The browser support does have a few issues. Internet Explorer will only implement drag and drop on `<a>` (with `href` attribute set) and `<img>` elements. IE will drag non-image and link elements, but it also selects the text around it, and may force the user to drag an item twice before it will drop it. Firefox must have the `draggable` attribute explicitly set to `true`, rather than just be present in the element. Chrome appears to ignore the `dropzone` attribute. Only desktop Safari implements both `draggable` and `dropzone` attributes.

Drag-and-Drop Events

Several new events have been added to the HTML5 specification to monitor the drag-and-drop operation:

▶ **dragstart**—Kicks off when the drag-and-drop operation starts

▶ **drag**—Continues to fire as long as the element is being dragged

▶ **dragenter**—Kicks off when the dragged element enters the drop zone

▶ **dragleave**—Kicks off when the dragged element leaves the drop zone

▶ **dragover**—Kicks off when the dragged element is over the drop zone

▶ **dragend**—Kicks off when the drag stops

▶ **drop**—Kicks off when the element is dropped

The challenge is that browsers handle these events differently. You can see an example of this in how the browsers handle displaying the drag operation. Figure 16.1

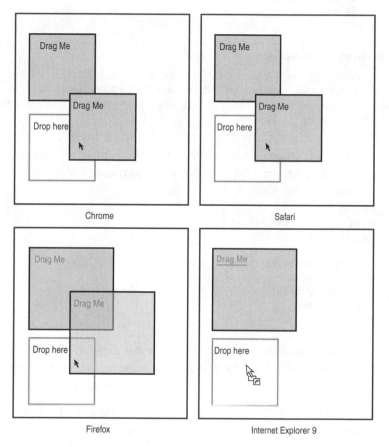

FIGURE 16.1
Drag operation in Chrome, Safari, Firefox, and IE 9.

shows you the same drag-and-drop operation in Chrome, Safari, Firefox, and Internet Explorer 9. As you can see, Safari and Chrome look fairly similar, with a repeated copy of the dragged object displayed. Firefox shows a copy of the object, but reduces the opacity so that it appears faded. Internet Explorer doesn't include a copy of the dragged element at all; it just changes the cursor.

Three of the events, dragstart, drag, and dragend, are applied to the object that can be dragged. You attach these events like you would any other JavaScript event. In jQuery you would use the bind[] method. In this example, the dragstart and dragend elements are attached to every element with a class draggableObject:

```
$('.dragableObject')
    .bind('dragstart', function(ev) {
        var dt = ev.originalEvent.dataTransfer;
        dt.setData("Text", "Dropped in zone!");
        return true;
    })
    .bind('dragend', function(ev) {
    return false;
    });
```

Use the Drag Event Sparingly

The drag event fires the entire time that an item is dragged. So if you were to set an alert() when an item is dragged, you could fire that alert hundreds of times just in a drag of a couple millimeters. Almost any action you run on a drag event can result in crashing the browser.

The other four events, dragenter, dragleave, dragover, and drop, are applied to the object that is the drop zone. For example, the dragover and drop events are attached to every element with the class dropzone:

```
$('.dropzone')
    .bind('dragover', function(ev) {
        return false;
    })
    .bind('drop', function(ev) {
        var dt = ev.originalEvent.dataTransfer;
        alert(dt.getData('Text'));
        return false;
    });
```

You may notice an element called dataTransfer inside some of the events. This element takes the information from the dragged object and transfers it to the drop zone object. You can put several objects on the dataTransfer element:

▶ **dataTransfer.setData(format, data)**—Sets the data and the format of that data.

▶ **dataTransfer.getData(format)**—Gets the data that was set. If there is no data set in that format, it will return an empty string.

▶ **dataTransfer.clearData([format])**—Removes the data from the specified formats or all data if no argument is applied.

▶ **dataTransfer.effectAllowed [= value]**—The types of operations that are allowed on the transfer. Possible values are none, copy, copyLink, copyMove, link, linkMove, move, all, and uninitialized.

▶ **dataTransfer.dropEffect [= value]**—The types of drop operations that are allowed. Possible values are none, copy, link, and move.

▶ **dataTransfer.setDragImage(element, x, y)**—Uses the specified image element instead of the browser default and places it at x, y coordinates offset from the cursor.

▶ **dataTransfer.addElement(element)**—Adds the specified image element to the list of elements used to render drag feedback.

▶ **dataTransfer.types**—Returns a list of formats that were set at the start of the drag operation.

▶ **dataTransfer.items**—Returns an array of the items transferred, with the drag data.

▶ **dataTransfer.files**—Returns a list of files being dragged, if any.

The most important objects are the setData and getData objects. These pass the information between the object being dragged and the object being dropped into.

Drag-and-Drop Attributes

Every one of the events listed earlier has a related event attribute you can use to kick off scripts:

▶ ondragstart

▶ ondrag

▶ ondragenter

▶ ondragleave

▶ ondragover

▶ ondrop

▶ ondragend

The other new attributes in HTML5 for drag and drop are the draggable attribute and the dropzone attribute. These are designed to tell the browser which items on your page are part of the drag-and-drop interface.

The draggable and dropzone Attributes Are Tricky

You should get into the habit of using the draggable and dropzone attributes to define your draggable objects and your drop zones, but keep in mind that they may have very little effect on your designs. Chrome will drag an object with the draggable attribute, but won't drop into an element with the dropzone attribute.

> Firefox needs the `draggable` attribute on any element other that an `<img>` or `<a>`. Otherwise, it treats the drag as a selection. Internet Explorer doesn't need either attribute. Safari will drag a `draggable` element, and will display drop zones with the `dropzone` attribute (but without scripts won't do anything). Without the `draggable` attribute, all the browsers treat the drag as a selection—although IE will perform the drag, if a script is attached to the element.

These attributes are not fully supported in every browser, and as you see in the Watch Out, they each perform slightly differently. But getting into the habit of using them is a good idea, so that your apps are ready when these attributes get full browser support.

Helpful CSS Extensions

Along with the new attributes, some browser extensions to CSS can also help your drag-and-drop operations look smoother:

▶ **-webkit-user-drag**—This attribute identifies elements that can be dragged in Safari and Chrome. This can also be written `-khtml-user-drag`. It is mostly supplanted by the `draggable` attribute of HTML5.

▶ **user-select**—This indicates whether the item, when dragged, should select the contents it is dragged over. This attribute has browser extensions for Firefox, WebKit, and Opera: `-moz-user-select`, `-webkit-user-select` (and `-khtml-user-select`), and `-o-user-select`.

Set these extensions on items that are draggable in your document by writing:

```
[draggable=true] {
    -khtml-user-drag: element;
    -webkit-user-drag: element;
    -webkit-user-select: none;
    -khtml-user-select: none;
    -moz-user-select: none;
    -o-user-select: none;
    user-select: none;
}
```

Building a Drag-and-Drop Interface

The six steps to build an HTML5 drag-and-drop interface are as follows:

1. Define a draggable object.

2. Set events on that object.

3. Define a drop zone.

4. Set events on the drop zone.

5. Pass information between the object and the drop zone.

6. Define the effects for the drag-and-drop operation.

The following sections discuss these steps in detail.

Defining a Draggable Object

To define a draggable object, you add the `draggable="true"` attribute to the item. For best results in Internet Explorer, you should only make images or links draggable. Other elements may cause unexpected results. Here is how to make an image draggable:

```
<img src="images/item1.png" draggable=true>
```

Setting Drag Events on the Draggable Object

Most drag events are set to fire right when the drag starts. Use the `ondragstart` attribute to set these events:

```
<img src="images/item1.png" draggable=true ondragstart="drag(this,
➥event);">
```

The drag script tells the browser what to do when the object is dragged. You attach events to the element the way you would attach any other JavaScript event. You can use the jQuery `bind()` method or just attach a function to the `ondragstart` attribute, as in the preceding example.

The `drag()` function needs to do one thing: set the drag data on the `dataTransfer` object using the `setData()` method. This method takes two values: the format of the data and the data string itself. The two format types you can use reliably are `text` and URL.

You can also use the `text/html` format type as well, but it may not work in all versions of Internet Explorer.

The drag function looks like this:

```
function drag(draggableitem, e) {
    e.dataTransfer.setData("Text", draggableitem.id);
}
```

You can run scripts as the item is dragged with `ondrag` and when the drag stops with `ondragend`, but these are less commonly used.

Defining a Drop Zone

The drop zone is where the dragged item should be dropped. Define the drop zone with the `dropzone` attribute:

```
<div id="dropZone" dropzone="copy">
<p>Drop Items Here
</div>
```

> **Use CSS to Highlight Drop Zones**
>
> Firefox introduced a new pseudo-class: `-moz-drag-over`. This property allows you to make your drop zones stand out more by changing when an object is dragged over it. This property is not supported in any browser but Firefox.

Setting Events on the Drop Zone

The drop zone has four events you can apply to it:

- ► `ondrop`
- ► `ondragover`
- ► `ondragenter`
- ► `ondragleave`

Watch Out!

> **Don't Forget to Set the `dragover` Event**
>
> Remembering the `drop` event is easy, because this is a drag-and-drop operation. However, the `dragover` event needs to be set as well. The default behavior of the `dragover` event handler is to continue dragging. To allow your object to be dropped, you must cancel this behavior. If you don't, your script won't work correctly.

Although you only need to set the `ondrop` and `ondragover` events, setting the other two as well is a good idea, so that the browser doesn't do anything unexpected:

```
<div id="dropZone"
    ondrop="drop(this, event);"
    ondragenter="return false;"
    ondragover="return false;"
    ondragleave="return false;">
```

The `drop()` function has two jobs: first to collect the data from the dragged element in the `dataTransfer` object, and second to turn off the default browser behavior when something is dropped:

```
function drop(target, e) {
    var id = e.dataTransfer.getData('Text');
    target.appendChild(document.getElementById(id));
    e.preventDefault();
}
```

Preventing the default action with the `e.preventDefault();` line is especially important in Firefox. If you leave this line off, the browser will interpret the dragged item how it would normally interpret it, so for an image it will open the dragged element in a new window.

Passing Information Between the Objects

The `dataTransfer` object is what passes the information between the dragged element and the drop zone. You set the data when the drag is started and get the data when the drop initiates.

Defining Effects for the Operation

The two methods on the `dataTransfer` object that you use to define effects are

▶ `dataTransfer.effectAllowed`

▶ `dataTransfer.dropEffect`

Don't Set the Effects to "Move"

Older versions of Chrome and Safari on Windows will not work at all if either the `effectAllowed` or the `dropEffect` is set to "move." This bug has been fixed, but may affect users with versions earlier than Safari 5 or Chrome 10.

Watch Out!

These methods must match on both the start of the drag and the drop. If they do not match, then the element cannot be dropped into that drop zone. For example, if you had the following drag-and-drop functions, the dragged element would not be able to drop into the drop zone:

```
function drag(target, e) {
    e.dataTransfer.effectAllowed = "copy";
    e.dataTransfer.setData("Text", target.id);
}
function drop(target, e) {
    e.dataTransfer.dropEffect = "move";
    var id = e.dataTransfer.getData('Text');
    target.appendChild(document.getElementById(id));
    e.preventDefault();
}
```

In the code above, the `dataTransfer.effectAllowed` is copy, while the
`dataTransfer.dropEffect` is move. Because these aren't both copy or both move,
the drag-and-drop function won't work.

Most of the time you can leave the effects alone. They default to allow all effects,
and this is usually all you need.

▼   **Try It Yourself**

Building a Puzzle Drag-and-Drop Application

Drag and drop is a great way to build simple games for your users. For example,
you can build a puzzle that your users can drag and drop the pieces to build a picture; just follow these steps:

1. Take an image that is 600 x 800 pixels and cut it into 12 equal-sized squares
   (200 x 200).

2. Build an HTML page to display the puzzle pieces and the drop zones for the
   pieces:

```
<!DOCTYPE HTML>
<html>
<head>
<meta charset="UTF-8">
<title>Drag-and-Drop Puzzle</title>
<link rel="stylesheet" href="basic-styles.css">
<script src="jquery.min.js"></script>
</head>
<body>
<h1>Drag-and-Drop Puzzle</h1>
<p>
Drag the puzzle pieces into the puzzle frame</p>
<div id="pieces">
    <h2>Pieces</h2>
</div>
<div id="frameHolder">
    <h2>Frame</h2>
    <div id="puzzle-frame">
        <div id="place1"></div>
        <div id="place2"></div>
        <div id="place3"></div>
        <div id="place4"></div>
        <div id="place5"></div>
        <div id="place6"></div>
        <div id="place7"></div>
        <div id="place8"></div>
        <div id="place9"></div>
        <div id="place10"></div>
        <div id="place11"></div>
        <div id="place12"></div>
```

```
      </div>
    </div>
  </body>
</html>
```

3. Add the drop, dragenter, and dragover events to the drop zones:

```
<div id="place1" ondrop="drop(this, event);"
ondragenter="return false;" ondragover="return false;"></div>
<div id="place2" ondrop="drop(this, event);"
ondragenter="return false;" ondragover="return false;"></div>
<div id="place3" ondrop="drop(this, event);"
ondragenter="return false;" ondragover="return false;"></div>
<div id="place4" ondrop="drop(this, event);"
ondragenter="return false;" ondragover="return false;"></div>
<div id="place5" ondrop="drop(this, event);"
ondragenter="return false;" ondragover="return false;"></div>
<div id="place6" ondrop="drop(this, event);"
ondragenter="return false;" ondragover="return false;"></div>
<div id="place7" ondrop="drop(this, event);"
ondragenter="return false;" ondragover="return false;"></div>
<div id="place8" ondrop="drop(this, event);"
ondragenter="return false;" ondragover="return false;"></div>
<div id="place9" ondrop="drop(this, event);"
ondragenter="return false;" ondragover="return false;"></div>
<div id="place10" ondrop="drop(this, event);"
ondragenter="return false;" ondragover="return false;"></div>
<div id="place11" ondrop="drop(this, event);"
ondragenter="return false;" ondragover="return false;"></div>
<div id="place12" ondrop="drop(this, event);"
ondragenter="return false;" ondragover="return false;"></div>
```

4. Add a script to the bottom of your page, just above the <body> element:

```
<script src="drag-and-drop-puzzle.js"></script>
```

5. Open the script file and add a check for the iOS operating system, because you will need a separate function to get it to work there:

```
var iOS = !!navigator.userAgent.match('iPhone OS') ||
!!navigator.userAgent.match('iPad');
```

6. Set some variables, and then create an array of your puzzle pieces:

```
var images = [];
var piece = "";
var place = "";
for (i=0; i<12; i++) {
    j = i+1;
    images[i] = "puzzle-piece" + j + ".png";
}
```

7. Randomize the pieces:

```
images.sort(function() {return 0.5 - Math.random()});
```

8. Loop through the images, and display them on the page:

```
for (i=0; i<12; i++) {
    $('#pieces').append("<img
➥src=\"/examples/images/puzzle/"+images[i]+"\"
➥id=\"piece"+i+"\" draggable=true ondragstart=\"drag(this,
➥event);\">");
```

9. Build the iOS draggable objects and drop zones:

```
if (iOS) {
    piece = "piece"+i;
    place = "place"+i;
    $("#piece"+i).css('float','left');
    new webkit_draggable(piece, {revert : false, scroll : true} );
    webkit_drop.add(place, {onDrop : function() {
        $("#place"+i).append(piece);
        }
    });
}
```

10. Close the for loop:

```
}
```

11. Add the drag function:

```
function drag(draggableitem, e) {
    e.dataTransfer.setData("Text", draggableitem.id);
}
```

12. Add the drop function:

```
function drop(target, e) {
    var id = e.dataTransfer.getData('Text');
    target.appendChild(document.getElementById(id));
    e.preventDefault();
}
```

13. Add styles to the document:

```
body { width: 85em; }
[draggable=true] {
    -khtml-user-drag: element;
    -webkit-user-drag: element;
    -webkit-user-select: none;
    -khtml-user-select: none;
    -moz-user-select: none;
    -o-user-select: none;
    user-select: none;
}
#frameHolder {
    width: 61em;
    float: left;
}
#puzzle-frame {
```

```
    border: solid black 0.3em;
    width: 60em;
    height: 80em;
}
#puzzle-frame > div {
    width: 20em;
    height: 20em;
    float: left;
}
#pieces {
    width: 20em;
    float: left;
    margin-right: 0.5em;
}
```

You can see this puzzle in action at www.html5in24hours.com/examples/ drag-and-drop-puzzle.html.

One thing to note is that on mobile devices the pieces won't snap into position like they do on desktop computers.

Using Drag and Drop on iOS

HTML5 drag and drop is not supported on iOS, even though the `draggable` function shows up as valid. Instead you have to bind the `touchStart`, `touchMove`, and `touchEnd` events to your elements. The iOS device then uses the current position of the draggable element as well as the drop zone to determine whether an element has been dropped in a correct location.

A library you can use is at GotProject (www.gotproject.com/blog/post2.html). This is an open source library for building drag-and-drop interfaces for iOS devices.

This library offers three new APIs:

- ▶ `webkit_draggable()`—Makes elements draggable

- ▶ `webkit_drop.add()` and `webkit_drop.remove()`—Adds and removes drop zones

- ▶ `webkit_click()`—Adds click events to a draggable element

Making an Element Draggable in iOS

The first thing you do to implement drag and drop in iOS is make an element draggable by adding it to the `webkit_draggable()` method:

```
var draggableItem = new webkit_draggable('id of draggable item',
➥{ options } );
```

9. Close your HTML.

```
</body>
</html>
```

You can see an example of this drag-and-drop operation at www.html5in24hours.com/examples/drag-and-drop-examples-ios.html.

▲

Summary

Drag and drop in HTML5 is complex. There are a lot of things to remember. In this hour, you learned about events, attributes, and the dataTransfer object. You also learned how to create a drag-and-drop operation in both desktop browsers and iOS, even though iOS doesn't support the HTML5 drag-and-drop technology.

Q&A

Q. *For my application, I need to know where in the drop zone the dragged element was dropped, similar to how you can get the coordinates of the click in an image map. Is this possible?*

A. You can use event.clientX and event.clientY to report the coordinates. For example:

```
<div id="dropZone" dropzone="copy" ondrop="getCoords(event);"
ondragenter="return false;" ondragover="return false;"></div>
<script>
function getCoords(e){
    alert(
        "clientX value: " + e.clientX + "\n"
        + "clientY value: " + e.clientY + "\n"
    );
}
</script>
```

Q. *Is it true that you can drag and drop files using HTML5?*

A. Yes, this is true. With HTML5 you can drag and drop files from outside the web browser, or objects from within other web page frames (as long as they are draggable) onto your drop zones. Hour 19, "WebSockets, Web Workers, and Files," covers this topic in more detail.

Workshop

The workshop contains quiz questions to help you process what you've learned in this chapter. Try to answer all the questions before you read the answers. See Appendix A, "Answers to Quizzes," for answers.

Quiz

1. What are the two best elements to make draggable and why?

2. Why must you always include the `preventDefault()` method on your drop operations?

3. What are the six steps to create a drag-and-drop application?

4. What happens if you have allowed only "copy" drag effects, and one of your drop zones allows only "move" effects?

Exercises

1. Create a drag-and-drop puzzle game with your own image. Add a highlight effect when a piece is held over a drop zone to make the puzzle easier to fill out.

2. Come up with a tool that drag and drop would make easier on your website. Some common examples include user entitlements, file upload, matching games, and reordering lists or page elements. Think about how you can combine drag and drop with what you've learned in previous hours to create more robust applications.

HTML5 Links

What You'll Learn in This Hour:

▶ How to make changes to hyperlinks using the `<a>` and `<area>` elements

▶ How to link elements on your pages

▶ How to add empty links

▶ New relationships with new link types

Links are found on every web page. They are useful for creating clickable areas in your documents. HTML5 has made some changes that make them work even better. This hour you will learn about the changes to `<a>` and `<area>` elements that HTML5 introduces.

HTML5 also adds a few new link type relations using the `rel` attribute. With Google's recent announcements about supporting authorship markup (http://googlewebmastercentral.blogspot.com/2011/06/authorship-markup-and-web-search.html), these link relations are going to be even more important as time goes by. In this hour you will also learn how to use the `<link>` element to assign relationships with the `rel` attribute, and how these relationships are used on the web.

How Links Have Changed in HTML5

At first glance, it might seem like links have not changed all that much in HTML5. After all, there are still only three elements that link documents together: `<a>`, `<area>`, and `<link>`, and none of them have gotten extensive changes. However, the changes that have been added are very useful:

▶ `<a>` and `<area>` are now much more similar. They have the same attributes (`<area>` has a few more to deal with image maps) and link to documents in similar ways.

▶ All three linking elements have a bunch of new relationships that you can apply using the rel attribute.

Hyperlinks and External Resources

Links in an HTML document represent a connection between two documents—the current document and the one referenced in the link. The two kinds of links in HTML are hyperlinks (<a> and <area>) and external resources (<link>).

These link types are not a change in HTML5, but understanding the difference is important. The two kinds of links are created with three elements:

▶ **<a>**—Links to other documents as a text or image hyperlink. It is clickable and when the link is clicked, the browser opens a new document.

▶ **<area>**—Links to other documents as an image map. It defines an area of an image that is clickable and when that area is clicked, the browser opens a new document.

▶ **<link>**—Links to other documents to be used or referenced by the current document. This element is most often used to reference style sheets, as in <link rel="stylesheet" href="styles.css">.

In most situations, the <link> element is used either programmatically (such as how the browser loads the style sheet when it sees a style sheet link) or informatively (such as when a link provides an alternative document).

Changes to <a> Attributes

HTML5 has made a few changes to the attributes of the <a> element:

▶ The name attribute is now obsolete. You can still use it if you like but using the id attribute to name a specific anchor or hyperlink is better.

▶ The target attribute is no longer deprecated. Although frames are no longer part of the HTML5 specification, iframes still are, and you can reference specific iframes or windows with the target attribute.

▶ HTML5 also adds a media attribute to indicate with media queries the devices or media that the linked document is for.

If you want to create a table of contents on a web page in previous versions of HTML, you would write a placeholder link with a name where you wanted to point to in your document:

```
<a name="block"></a>
```

You would then link to that location with a link with a hash tag:

```
<a href="#block">Linking Block-level Elements</a>
```

But modern web browsers recognize the id attribute as a unique identifier, and so you can point to them directly without using the <a name> element at all:

```
<a href="#block">Linking Block-level Elements</a>
<h2 id="block">Linking Block-level Elements</h2>
```

Watch Out!

IDs Should Be Unique in a Document

One place many novice web developers make an error is when using the id attribute. This attribute value should be unique within the current document. If it is not, and you link to a non-unique ID, the browser may not take your users where you expect. Most browsers will take the user to the first instance of the repeated ID.

To understand the target attribute, you need to understand the term *browsing context*. This refers to the window or frame that the content is in. It can include an iframe, a new window opened through a script, or a standard browser window. The target attribute is useful for linking to both iframes with an id and other browser windows. You can use four special keywords to point to different windows:

▶ **_blank**—Opens the linked document in a brand-new window (or tab)

▶ **_self**—Opens the linked document in the current window

▶ **_parent**—Opens the linked document in the parent browsing context

▶ **_top**—Opens the linked document at the top of the browsing context

In most cases _parent, _self, and _top are going to be the same window, but adding additional browsing contexts with JavaScript or iframes is possible. For example, you can give an iframe an ID and then change what is inside it with targeted links:

```
<iframe src="simple-frame.html" id="simple"></iframe>
<p>This <a href="simple-frame.html#new" target="simple">link</a> points
to a location in the iframe document.
```

Link to Any Document in a Named Frame or Window

You are not limited to the current document when you link to something using a target. When the target refers to an ID that doesn't exist, a new window will open.

Linking Block-Level Elements

The first place where HTML5 has changed links is in what you can surround with an <a> element. In HTML 4, you were not allowed to surround block-level elements (things like headlines, paragraphs, or divs) with a link. If you needed to link an entire paragraph or headline and surrounding text, you needed to add the link multiple times.

For example, to link a headline, image, and block of text to the same place in HTML 4 you had to write:

```
<h3><a href="garden.html">Come See our New Garden</a></h3>
<a href="garden.html"><img src="our-garden.jpg" alt="our new garden"></a>
<p>
<a href="garden.html">Our new garden is beautiful, lots of flowers and
➥plants. Come see photos.</a>
</p>
```

HTML5 changes that. Now you can link just about anything by surrounding it with an <a> element. So to write that headline, image, and paragraph in HTML5 you would write:

```
<a href="garden.html">
<h3>Come See our New Garden</h3>
<img src="our-garden.jpg" alt="our new garden">
<p>
Our new garden is beautiful, lots of flowers and plants. Come see photos.
</p>
</a>
```

Did you
Know?

> **There Was a Proposal to Make Everything Linkable**
>
> One proposal to HTML5 was to add the href attribute as a global (or nearly global) attribute. The idea was that every element that displays on a page can be a link, and adding the href attribute would make it a link. This idea was eventually rejected because it would make pages less backward compatible. However, it is something that still comes up periodically, and it might get added to the specification someday.

This change reflects how browsers were already implementing links. Browsers already support linking this way. The only effect this change has is in validating your HTML. Previously, if you validated a page written like that it would return as invalid, but now it is correct.

Placeholder Links

As mentioned in Hour 2, "New HTML5 Tags and Attributes with Mobile Development," another change to HTML5 links was the creation of placeholder links. These <a> elements don't have the href attribute. They are typically used as placeholders for links that don't have pages to point to yet, such as in a design mockup.

> **Link Pseudo-Classes Don't Always Work on Placeholder Links**
>
> The :link and :visited pseudo-classes won't work when you're styling place-holder links. This makes sense, because both of those classes require there to be a URL to link to or visit before they are enacted.

Prior to HTML5, the href attribute was required on <a> elements, so to make a placeholder link, most web developers would use an empty href or point it to the same page with <a href="#">. However, an empty href is not valid, it can make links do odd things, and pointing to the hash-sign can confuse users when the page reloads.

Placeholder links are not clickable, but they can be styled to look the same as other links on your web page by styling the <a> element specifically (without any pseudo-classes).

Image Maps in HTML5

HTML5 still has image maps via the use of the <map> and <area> elements. The <map> element has not changed significantly, but the <area> element has been updated to make it more like the <a> element.

In previous versions of HTML, the <area> element was somewhat crippled as a hyper-link because it didn't have all the same attributes as the <a> element. However, HTML5 adds the following attributes to the <area> element:

- ▶ **rel**—This attribute indicates the relationship of the linked document to the current document.

- ▶ **media**—Just like the <a> element, this attribute adds media queries to indi-cate what media the linked document is for.

- ▶ **hreflang**—This attribute was added to let you declare the language of the linked document.

New Global Attributes in HTML5

HTML5 adds some new global attributes that are especially useful for links:

- ▶ **hidden**—Indicates that the element is not yet or no longer relevant.

- ▶ **contextmenu**—Adds a context menu (usually accessed with an alternate-click or right-click style action) to the element.

The `hidden` and `contextmenu` attributes add some additional features that are especially useful for links.

You can use the `hidden` attribute to hide links inside pages where they are not relevant. This can be useful when maintaining a large link library where not every link is relevant on every page. You can generate the library, and then use scripts to hide irrelevant links. Figure 17.1 shows an example of how the following HTML is rendered in Chrome:

```
<ul>
    <li><a href="/">Home</a>
    <li><a href="/category/examples/">Examples</a>
    <li><a href="/examples/" hidden>More Examples</a>
</ul>
```

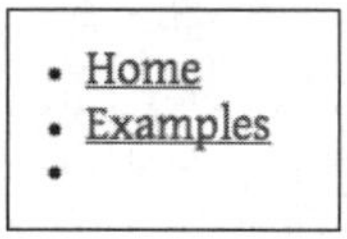

FIGURE 17.1
A list with one hidden link in Chrome.

Be careful with this attribute, because it isn't supported in Safari or Firefox without your adding the style `display:none;` to elements with this attribute. For example:

```
[hidden] { display: none; }
```

The `contextmenu` attribute adds a drop-down menu to `<a>` elements that can appear when users right-click on the link. This enables web applications to act more like desktop applications. This attribute uses the `<menu>` and `<command>` elements to create a menu that is hidden until the context menu is activated, usually with a right-click or option-click:

```
<p><a href="#attribs" contextmenu="test-menu">This link has a context
menu</a>
<menu id="test-menu">
    <command label="Home" onclick="window.location = '/'">
    <command label="Examples" onclick="window.location =
➥'/category/examples/'">
</menu>
```

The problem with this attribute is that it isn't supported by any web browsers or user agents, and that doesn't seem to be changing in any of the beta releases, either.

Link Types and Relationships

HTML5 links involve more than just hyperlinks. Although the `<link>` element hasn't changed a lot directly, one aspect of these links has changed a fair amount: link relationships.

You define link relationships (on both hyperlinks and external document links) with the `rel` attribute. You should be aware that the `rev` attribute is obsolete in HTML5 partially because most web developers who used it were using it incorrectly, and the rest of us weren't using it at all. Instead, you should use the `rel` attribute with the opposite type; for example, `prev` and `next` are opposite types.

The different link types are

- **alternate**—Alternate representations of the current document

- **author**—A link to the current document's author

- **bookmark**—The permalink to the nearest ancestor

- **external**—Points to a link that is not part of the same site

- **help**—A link to context-sensitive help

- **icon**—A link to an icon or favicon

- **license**—A link to the copyright license for the document

- **next**—A link to the next document in a series

- **nofollow**—Indicates that the link is not endorsed by the current document's author

- **noreferrer**—Tells the user agent to not send an HTTP Referer (sic) header when a user follows the link

- **pingback**—The address of the pingback server for the current document

- **prefetch**—Indicates a document that should be downloaded ahead of time

- **prev**—A link to the previous document in a series

- **search**—A link to search through the current document and related pages

- **sidebar**—A link to a document that is intended to be shown in the browser's sidebar

- **stylesheet**—A link to a style sheet to be imported

- **tag**—A link to the address of a tag that applies to the current document

Table 17.1 shows the relationship of the different types to the <a>, <area>, and <link> elements.

TABLE 17.1   Link Types and Their Effect on Link Elements

	Effect on...	
Link Type	`<a>` and `<area>`	`<link>`
alternate	Hyperlink	Hyperlink
author	Hyperlink	Hyperlink
bookmark	Hyperlink	Not allowed
external	Hyperlink	Not allowed
help	Hyperlink	Hyperlink
icon	Not allowed	External resource
license	Hyperlink	Hyperlink
next	Hyperlink	Hyperlink
nofollow	Annotation	Not allowed
noreferrer	Annotation	Not allowed
pingback	Not allowed	External resource
prefetch	External resource	External resource
prev	Hyperlink	Hyperlink
search	Hyperlink	Hyperlink
sidebar	Hyperlink	Hyperlink
stylesheet	Not allowed	External resource
tag	Hyperlink	Hyperlink

Using the New Link Types

Many web developers never use the rel attribute to define relationships between documents because they don't see the point. Although not all the link types are widely supported, some of them provide good information that is used more than you may realize.

The Alternate Link Type

The alternate link type is a good way to indicate translations of pages on your website. When used in combination with the hreflang attribute, you can give your users and search engines information about the site structure. For example, you link to the Spanish version of a page by writing:

```
<a href="http://es.html5in24hours.com/" rel="alternate" hreflang="es">
```

Google Also Supports the `canonical` Type

Though not part of the HTML5 specification, you can also define a document as being the original version of the page by setting its relationship to `canonical` when you link to it. For example, linking back to the English language site from the Spanish site, you would write: `<a href="http://www.html5in24hours.com/" rel="canonical" hreflang="en">`.

Indicating alternate pages is important, because many search engines penalize sites with duplicate content. When you indicate that duplicated content is intended as an alternative, the search engines are more forgiving.

You can have as many `<link rel="alternate">` links as you need in a document, for different languages and different formats (print, audible, and so on). But remember that the more links you have, the more your users have to download.

The Author Link Type

You should place the author link type on any article byline. If you don't have links to a biography or the author's email address, you can include the `<link>` in the `<head>` of your document.

Including email addresses in your author links is not a good idea, because it can result in the author's receiving spam. However, Google and other search engines are beginning to support authorship markup to connect users with the authors of great content. To add authorship information to your pages, you need to have a page about the author that describes and identifies the author. You then use the author type to identify that link:

```
<a href="/bio/Jennifer-Kyrnin-5105.htm" rel="author">Jennifer Kyrnin</a>
```

The Bookmark and External Link Types

The bookmark and external link types identify links about the page or site itself. Most blogs use the bookmark type to identify the permalink for a post or page. The external type indicates that the link is a link on a site other than the current one.

Most browsers don't do anything special for these link types. However, identifying external links for your customers can be useful. You can also use this attribute to open external links in a new window with a script. In jQuery, just append the target=_blank attribute to the links:

```
$("[rel=external]").attr("target","_blank");
```

The Help, License, Tag, and Search Link Types

The help, license, tag, and search link types offer more information about the page. These types are not used explicitly by any browsers, but web designers can use them to provide more information on the page. You would use these in the same way as the other link types—by adding the type attribute to links that are of the specific type. For example, here is a link to a search page:

```
<a href="/search.htm" rel="search">Search This Site</a>
```

Be Careful with Licenses

With the license type, remembering that you are identifying a link to the license, rather than describing the license for the page itself, is important. Most browsers interpret this type as identifying a license for the entire page, not just specific parts of the page. So if you have other page elements, such as images, that are presented under a different license, this information will be lost when a machine sees this link type. Keeping the most restrictive license in place with the rel=license attribute is a best practice.

The Icon Link Type

The icon link type is used by many web designers to add a favorites icon or favicon to their web pages. The favorites icon is then used in browser tabs, in bookmarks, and other places where the browser displays the page information.

You link to the icon using the <link> element:

```
<link rel="icon" href="/favicon.ico">
```

Be Careful with the Shortcuts Keyword

Internet Explorer 8 and lower requires that you include the keyword shortcuts in your favorites icon link: <link rel="shortcuts icon" href="/favicon.ico">. This is technically incorrect, because it creates a link called "shortcuts" and links to the icon. IE9 will work when you add the type "image/x-icon" to the <link rel="shortcuts icon" href="/favicon.ico" type="image/x-icon"> link. Most browsers look for a file called favicon.ico in the root of the web server, whether you have a link in your file or not.

The Nofollow and Noreferrer Types

The nofollow type tells search engine robots not to follow the link, or if they do follow it, not to pass along any page rank. However, just because you've put this attribute on a link doesn't mean that that page won't be found by search engines. You should add this attribute to some specific types of links:

- ▶ Content you don't vouch for—Although not including links to sites you don't vouch for is probably a better idea, if a reason exists for why you have to allow these links, such as in comments or guestbook entries, adding rel=nofollow to them indicates that they are not links you recommend.

- ▶ Paid links—Ads should always have the rel=nofollow attribute applied to them because most ad providers have rules about automated clicks on advertising.

- ▶ Pages search engines can't use—Search engines can't sign in or register for your site, so putting rel=nofollow on links to these pages helps the robot crawl your site more effectively.

The noreferrer type indicates that no referrer information should be passed along when the link is clicked on. This feature can be useful if you want to hide the links you're sending to certain sites, such as if you don't want your referrer information sent to an advertising site. This type works on Chrome, Opera, and Safari.

You should use the noreferrer type when leaking private information through the referrer information is possible—for example, if you run a dating site or other confidential site. Also, if you're linking to a site that displays referrer data, you might want to consider blocking the referrer data.

You can add multiple types to one link by separating them with a space in the rel attribute, for example:

```
<a href="http://spam.com" rel="nofollow noreferrer">
```

The Pingback Type

The pingback type provides a link to the pingback server for the page. Pingback servers have software that accepts XML-RPC connections. Pingbacks are used to tell one website that another website has linked to it.

You can only apply this type to the <link> element:

```
<link rel="pingback" href="pingback server">
```

The Prefetch Type

The prefetch link type tells the user agent that it should download the linked document ahead of time because the user might need it in the future. The prefetched document is downloaded during idle time. Prefetching is best used for large images or documents that are on pages that typically are visited after the page the reader is currently on.

You can only apply the prefetch type to <link> elements:

```
<link rel="prefetch" href="big-image.jpg">
```

Keep in mind that prefetching can be annoying to some users either because their browser doesn't handle it correctly or because they have bandwidth costs. Remember that most mobile users have limits on their service plan and prefetching something that they never use can eat up that bandwidth.

Previous and Next Link Types

The prev and next link types define a sequence of documents, such as in a table of contents. Most browsers don't do anything when you use these relationships, but they can help you add styles to your documents. Simply style the links with the specific relationship attribute, like this:

```
[rel=prev] { ... }
```

HTML 4 included a few other relationships in a sequence such as start, index, and contents. These are not specifically in the HTML5 specification, but if you have coding that expects them or uses them, they are okay to use.

The Sidebar Link Type

The sidebar link type is currently only supported by Firefox and Opera. When a Firefox user clicks a link with the rel=sidebar attribute, it opens in a sidebar window in the browser. Figure 17.2 shows a Firefox page with a sidebar open.

Browsers other than Firefox open sidebar links as standard Web pages.

FIGURE 17.2
A web page with a sidebar open in Firefox.

The Stylesheet Type

The most commonly used link type is the rel=stylesheet type. This links to a style sheet for the browser to apply to the web page. Linking to an external style sheet is easy:

```
<link rel=stylesheet href=styles.css>
```

Summary

HTML5 made some changes to the <a> element that make it easier to use and that makes it conform to how browsers are already displaying. In this hour you learned that you can now link block-level elements and create placeholder links with empty <a> elements.

The <area> element is no longer a second-class citizen when in regard to links. You learned how to create an image map that has the same attributes as a standard <a> element.

You also learned that the <link> element, though not getting any major changes, now has a lot of new relationships that you can apply to it and the other link elements. These relationships make your pages more semantic, and are getting more support from search engines and browsers.

Q&A

Q. *You did not include a lot of other link relationships in your list, such as copyright, glossary, section, appendix and so on. Where do these fit in web development?*

A. The relationships I listed are the ones that are included in the HTML5 specification. HTML 4 includes a different set of link relationships:

- alternate
- appendix
- bookmark
- chapter
- contents
- copyright
- glossary
- help

- index
- next
- prev
- section
- start
- stylesheet
- subsection

Many of these relationships are now defined using semantic HTML, as covered in Hour 9, "Adding Meaning with HTML5 Sectioning and Semantic Elements." Also, most of them were not widely supported by web browsers.

Using these relationships if they are appropriate is perfectly acceptable, but a strict validator might mark your document invalid.

Q. *You mentioned that the* name *attribute is obsolete, but what does that mean?*

A. In HTML5, an obsolete feature is one that can be used but that will trigger a warning in a validator. In general, it means that the feature is being transitioned out of HTML and the W3C recommends against its usage.

Many developers have gotten into the habit of using the <a name=> element to define jump zones to link to, but this is no longer necessary. All major browsers recognize the id attribute as a jump zone. So this attribute being obsolete shouldn't affect your page designs at all.

Q. *When I click on a link that is marked as a sidebar with the* rel=sidebar *attribute, it asks me to add it to my bookmarks in Firefox and Opera. Why is that?*

A. That is how Firefox and Opera support the sidebar relationship. You add a bookmark that has the sidebar option checked, and then when you click on that bookmark, it opens in a sidebar, rather than in the main browser window. You can make any bookmark a sidebar bookmark if you like.

Workshop

The workshop contains quiz questions to help you process what you've learned in this chapter. Try to answer all the questions before you read the answers. See Appendix A, "Answers to Quizzes," for answers.

Quiz

1. What is a new attribute added to the <a> element and what is it for?

2. What do you write to get a link inside an iframe to open in the container document?

3. How have image maps become more like standard <a> links?

4. When should you use the rel=nofollow attribute?

Exercises

1. Build a page for a specific media type, such as a tablet or smart phone, then create a link to that page using the `media` attribute and media queries, like you learned in Hour 4, "Detecting Mobile Devices and HTML5 Support."

2. Build an author page for all the authors on your website, and then add author links to them. You can check how Google sees your author relationships with the Rich Snippets Testing Tool: www.google.com/webmasters/tools/richsnippets.

HOUR 18

Web Application APIs and Datasets

What You'll Learn in This Hour:

▶ What a web application and an API are

▶ How web applications are changing the web

▶ The APIs that make up HTML5 web applications

▶ How to access custom data in web apps using `data-*` attributes

Scripts and programming are what turn a web page into a web application. HTML5 has some specific APIs to help you create more interactive applications. This hour you will learn more about these APIs and how to use them in your HTML5 applications.

HTML5 also introduces a new way to include custom data in your HTML—datasets. This hour will cover how to use datasets and the `data-*` attributes to create applications that use custom data.

Creating Web Applications

Web applications run inside a web browser. They use HTML, CSS, and JavaScript just like any other web page. However, they have certain features that make them more like desktop applications and less like web pages, including:

▶ Web applications use scripts to interact with the users.

▶ Functionality stays in the same window or screen rather than reloading to new screens.

▶ Interface controls change parts of the screen when the user interacts with it.

▶ User interaction is a crucial part—applications offer users more than just being able to read a document.

Web Application APIs

An API, or application programming interface, is a list of instructions for how to write different programs. Web application APIs are the JavaScript methods and functions that support a given API.

Modern web applications use the Open Web Standard, which includes HTML5, to create robust applications that are as powerful as their desktop counterparts.

The Open Web Standard includes many web application APIs that can be used, including:

▶ **Scripting**—These mechanisms cause code to run in the context of the document.

▶ **Timers**—You use the `setTimeout()` and `setInterval()` methods to schedule timer-based callbacks.

▶ **User prompts**—These are dialog boxes and printing methods that allow the application to communicate with the user.

▶ **System information**—This is information about the client that can be used by the application, such as the browser name and version.

Scripting

Scripting is an important part of web applications, because it is the way that web applications interact with the users. A script can be fired in several ways, including:

▶ Processing `<script>` elements

▶ Inline `javascript:()` URLs

▶ Event handlers

▶ Using technology such as SVG that has its own scripting features

A lot of event handlers are available that you can use in your web applications.

Following are event handlers that can be placed on all HTML elements:

▶ onabort

▶ oncanplay

▶ oncanplaythrough

▶ onchange

▶ onclick

▶ oncontextmenu

- ▶ ondblclick
- ▶ ondrag
- ▶ ondragend
- ▶ ondragenter
- ▶ ondragleave
- ▶ ondragover
- ▶ ondragstart
- ▶ ondrop
- ▶ ondurationchange
- ▶ onemptied
- ▶ onended
- ▶ onformchange
- ▶ onforminput
- ▶ oninput
- ▶ oninvalid
- ▶ onkeydown
- ▶ onkeypress
- ▶ onkeyup
- ▶ onloadeddata
- ▶ onloadedmetadata
- ▶ onloadstart
- ▶ onmousedown
- ▶ onmousemove
- ▶ onmouseout
- ▶ onmouseover
- ▶ onmouseup
- ▶ onmousewheel
- ▶ onpause
- ▶ onplay
- ▶ onplaying
- ▶ onprogress
- ▶ onratechange
- ▶ onreadystatechange
- ▶ onscroll
- ▶ onseeked
- ▶ onseeking
- ▶ onselect
- ▶ onshow
- ▶ onstalled
- ▶ onsubmit
- ▶ onsuspend
- ▶ ontimeupdate
- ▶ onvolumechange
- ▶ onwaiting

Following are event handlers that can be placed on all HTML elements except
<body>:

- ▶ onblur
- ▶ onerror

- ▶ onfocus
- ▶ onload

Following are event handlers that can be placed on Window objects such as <body> and <frameset>:

▶ onafterprint

▶ onbeforeprint

▶ onbeforeunload

▶ onblur

▶ onerror

▶ onfocus

▶ onhashchange

▶ onload

▶ onmessage

▶ onoffline

▶ ononline

▶ onpagehide

▶ onpageshow

▶ onpopstate

▶ onredo

▶ onresize

▶ onstorage

▶ onundo

▶ onunload

In HTML you use the event handlers by placing them in the HTML element that might have the event and defining the script that will run when that event fires. For example:

```
<body onload="alert(this);">
```

This pops a window that reads "[object DOMWindow]" after the page has loaded.

You can use the jQuery bind() method for attaching scripts to events. For example, in jQuery you could pop a window that reads "[object DOMWindow]" with this line:

```
$("body").bind("onload", alert(this));
```

Many of these event handlers should be familiar, but HTML5 adds many more to use.

Events are available for handling video and audio, such as oncanplay, oncanplaythrough, ondurationchange, onemptied, onended, onloadeddata, onloadedmetadata, onloadstart, onpause, onplay, onplaying, onprogress, onratechange, onseeked, onseeking, onstalled, onsuspend, ontimeupdate, onvolumechange, and onwaiting.

Other new event handlers respond to actions by the user, such as onabort, oncontextmenu, and onshow.

As you learned in Hour 16, "Working with HTML5 Drag-and-Drop Functionality," HTML5 offers several new drag-and-drop events: ondrag, ondragend, ondragenter, ondragleave, ondragover, ondragstart, and ondrop.

There is also an error event: onerror, as well as an event when the form submission does not meet validity constraints: oninvalid.

Click Events on iOS Work Differently

If you're creating an application that uses the scripting API onclick events to trigger actions in your applications, you are going to need to modify your scripts slightly to handle iOS devices. This is because iOS does not immediately register click events—a delay exists. It registers touch events immediately, instead.

To fix this, you can use a framework such as jQTouch (www.jqtouch.com/) or you can add touch handlers to your script. Here is a jQuery function you can use to turn clicks into taps on iOS devices:

```
function iosClicks() {
    var iOS = !!navigator.userAgent.match('iPhone OS') ||
!!navigator.userAgent.match('iPad');
    if (iOS) {
        $('[onclick]').each(function() {
        var onclick = $(this).attr('onclick');
        $(this).removeAttr('onclick'); // Remove the onclick attribute
        $(this).bind("click", function(e) {
            e.preventDefault;
            }); // prevent the click default action
        $(this).bind('tap', onclick); // Turn taps into click
        });
    }
}
```

Timers

Timers are used all the time in applications to set timeout functions and run functions periodically. A few methods are available that you can use:

▶ **setTimeout()**—This method sets the time (in milliseconds) after which a JavaScript expression will run.

▶ **setInterval()**—Like setTimeOut this method sets the time (in milliseconds) after which a JavaScript expression will run. The difference is that setInterval then starts the timer again to run the expression over and over.

▶ **clearTimeout()**—This method cancels the timeout expression before the time runs out.

▶ **clearInterval()**—This method cancels the setInterval method.

Try It Yourself

Building a Script that Rotates the Background Color

This script will use both the `onclick` event handler that you are probably already familiar with and the `setInterval()` method to change the background color of a div.

1. Open an HTML document in your editor and add a div to the body:

    ```
    <div id="changeColorBox">
    <p>The background of this box will change every 2 seconds
    after you click &#8220;Start&#8221;</p>
    </div>
    ```

2. In the head of your document, give the div some styles:

    ```
    #changeColorBox {
        width: 20em;
        height: 20em;
        padding: 0.25em;
        border: solid black 0.1em;
    }
    ```

3. Add a start and stop button below the div:

    ```
    <button onclick="changeColor();">Start</button>
    <button onclick="stopColorChange();">Stop</button>
    ```

    Both buttons have an `onclick` event handler pointing to two script functions.

4. At the bottom of your HTML, add your `<script>` element:

    ```
    <script>
    </script>
    ```

5. Inside the script element, add a variable to hold your interval timer:

    ```
    var intervalTimer;
    ```

6. Write the `changeColor()` function:

    ```
    function changeColor() {
        intervalTimer = setInterval(bgColorChange, 2000);
    }
    ```

    This sets the interval to run the function `bgColorChange` every 2,000 milliseconds.

7. Write the `stopColorChange()` function:

    ```
    function stopColorChange() {
        clearInterval(intervalTimer);
    }
    ```

    This turns off the color swapping, when the Stop button is clicked.

8. Write the bgColorChange() function:

```
function bgColorChange() {
    var box = document.getElementById("changeColorBox");
    if (box.style.backgroundColor == 'red') {
        box.style.backgroundColor = 'orange';
        box.style.color = 'black';
    } else {
        box.style.backgroundColor = 'red';
        box.style.color = 'white';
    }
}
```

You can see an example of this script at www.html5in24hours.com/
examples/timer-example.html.

User Prompts

User prompts are a way to communicate with the users of your application. You
have three ways to do user prompts in web pages:

▶ Simple prompts

▶ Printing

▶ Modal dialog boxes

Simple prompts are generated by the user agent itself, and can provide simple information (true/false or an answer to one question). The three simple prompts are

▶ **window.alert(message)**—This prompt simply displays a message to the
user and waits for him to dismiss it.

▶ **result = window.confirm(message)**—This prompt asks the user to con-
firm or cancel the given message. It returns true if the user clicks OK and
false if he clicks Cancel.

▶ **result = window.prompt(message [, default])**—This prompt shows a
message with a text box for the user to type in a reply. If the user cancels
the prompt, it returns null. If a default message is included, then that
value is used as the default answer (in the box for the reply), and the user
can accept it or change it.

Figure 18.1 shows these three types of prompts as displayed on an iPad.

Printing is a user prompt that many web application developers forget about, but it
is a possibility, even on tablet and smartphone devices. Calling the window.print()
method runs the steps to print the current page.

FIGURE 18.1
Three simple
prompts on an
iPad.

The most interesting type of user prompt is the modal dialog. This box opens a separate page in a new window. This makes web applications act even more like desktop applications.

> **Modal Dialogs Are Not Good on Mobile**
>
> The support for modal dialogs is limited on mobile devices. If you are going to use modal dialogs, you will need to display the information in them in some other fashion on Opera and on mobile devices.

▼   **Try It Yourself**

Building a Modal Dialog

Most modal dialogs are built as separate web pages. You then call the dialog with a script, as this Try It Yourself shows.

1. Build your first web page, which will load the modal dialog:

```
<!DOCTYPE HTML>
<html>
<head>
<meta charset="utf-8">
<title>Proposal Estimate</title>
</head>
<body>
<h1>Proposal Estimate</h1>
<p>Hours to complete: <input id=hours readonly>
<button onclick="return calcHours();">Calculate</button>
</body>
</html>
```

2. Add the script to call the modal dialog:

```
<script>
function calcHours() {
    returnValue = window.showModalDialog('modal-hours.html');
    var hours = document.getElementById('hours');
    hours.value = returnValue;
}
</script>
```

3. Build a second page for your modal dialog:

```html
<!DOCTYPE HTML>
<html>
<head>
<meta charset="UTF-8">
<title>Modal</title>
<script>
function hours() {
    var text = document.getElementById("text");
    window.returnValue=text.value;
    window.close();
}
</script>
</head>
<body>
Estimate Hours: <input type=text id=text><br>
<input type=button value="close" onclick="return hours();">
</body>
</html>
```

You can see the modal dialog in action at www.html5in24hours.com/
examples/modaldialog-examples.html.

System Information

The last aspect of web application APIs this hour will cover is the system information. You can collect information about the browser with four methods:

▶ **window.navigator.appName**—Returns the name of the browser

▶ **window.navigator.appVersion**—Returns the version of the browser

▶ **window.navigator.platform**—Returns the name of the platform

▶ **window.navigator.userAgent**—Returns the complete user agent handler

You can display the system information directly in your HTML like this:

```html
<h1>Collecting System Information</h1>
<p>
You are using:
</p>
<p id="browser">
<strong>Browser:</strong>
</p>
<p id="version">
<strong>Version:</strong>
</p>
<p id="platform">
<strong>Platform:</strong>
</p>
```

```
<p id="uaHandler">
<strong>Full User Agent Handler:</strong><br/>
</p>
<script>
$(document).ready(function(){
    var browser = window.navigator.appName;
    var version = window.navigator.appVersion;
    var platform = window.navigator.platform;
    var uahandler = window.navigator.userAgent;
    $("#browser").append(browser);
    $("#version").append(version);
    $("#platform").append(platform);
    $("#uaHandler").append(uahandler);
});
</script>
```

You can see this script in action at www.html5in24hours.com/examples/system-information-examples.html.

> **"Browser Sniffing" Is Still Not a Good Idea**
>
> An old-fashioned way of testing for compatibility is to use some of the system information methods to display different functions to different browsers. However, testing to see whether the current browser supports the technology you're using makes your site much easier to maintain. Browser sniffing requires that you remain 100 percent up to date on the capabilities of every browser. Instead, use the system information for non-critical elements of your application design, or use a tool such as Modernizr.js, as mentioned in Hour 4, "Detecting Mobile Devices and HTML5 Support."

Datasets and `data-*` Attributes

Custom data attributes are a new feature of HTML5 that can really help your web applications.

Any attribute that starts with `data-` is treated as a storage area for data that the user can't see. This data doesn't affect the layout or presentation of the page, but the browser can use it.

You can use anything after the `data-` to represent your data (that's what the `*` means). The advantage of this attribute is that it is completely customizable to your website. The only rule is that the attribute must be named with letters and numbers, so `data-jennifer` is okay, but `data-jennifer!` is not.

> **Why Datasets Are Important**
>
> Datasets solve a problem that has been plaguing JavaScript developers for a long time—where to store data. This has resulted in some workarounds that range

> from difficult to just crazy. Some developers use HTML with a custom DTD to cover the extra data fields. Others use the class attribute to hold data as well as style information. Still others use XHTML with namespaces to define the extra fields. Datasets allow you to include data in your HTML without making it invalid or risk your styles getting confusing.

When you store data in your HTML with datasets, you can create richer applications, without requiring a call to a database or even reloading the existing web page.

For example, in a list of new HTML5 elements, you might want to include a description of the elements in a data-* field, for example:

```
<li data-desc="Article section">&lt;article&gt;</li>
```

This data does not show up on the web page, but you can access it in your scripts, so you could create a script that provided more information about that element and pull the data-desc information for the details:

```
<script>
$(document).ready(function(){
    $("li").hover(function() {
        var data = $(this).attr('data-desc').valueOf();
        $(this).addClass("highlight");
        $("#details").html("<p>"+data);
    })
        .mouseout(function() {
        $(this).removeClass("highlight");
    });
});
</script>
```

See this in action at www.html5in24hours.com/examples/datasets-examples.html.

Also, as of jQuery 1.4.3, you can use $(this).attr('desc') instead of $(this).attr('data-desc').

All Browsers Support the data-* **Attribute**

The best part of data-* attributes is that you can use them in any browser. Some browsers, such as IE 10, Firefox 5, Opera 11, iOS 4.3, and Android 3.0, don't support the dataset property, but you can still get the data inside the data-* attribute by using getAttribute().

Did you Know?

The earlier example is an easy way to start using data-* attributes, and it works in all modern browsers. But it's not how these attributes were intended to be used. Instead, you should use the element's dataset property, which will return an object that includes all the selected element's data-* attributes. You can then refer to the custom data by the exact name you gave it—leaving off the data- prefix.

Table 18.1 shows the standard JavaScript methods and the dataset alternatives.

TABLE 18.1   JavaScript and Datasets

JavaScript Methods	Dataset Methods
`getAttribute("data-dataName")`	`dataset.dataName`
`setAttribute("data-dataName", "new value")`	`dataset.dataName = "new value"`
`removeAttribute("data-dataName")`	`dataset.dataName = null`

Summary

This hour you learned about web applications and how they are built differently from web pages. Web applications are web pages that have some type of scripting on them to make them interactive. You learned about how the HTML5 web application APIs can help you create your applications. You also learned about the many different event handlers you can use to set off interaction events in your applications. For example, some of the new ones include:

▶ Events for playing media, such as `oncanplay` and `onpause`

▶ Events spawned by the user, such as `onabort` and `oncontextmenu`

▶ Events used in drag and drop, such as `ondrag` and `ondrop`

▶ Events for detecting error states, such as `oninvalid` and `onerror`

You learned how to use user prompts to make your pages act much more like applications by asking for additional information in message windows and in dialog boxes. Plus you even learned how to spawn printing processes from within your web applications.

Finally, you learned about a valuable tool for web applications: datasets. These allow you to add custom data to your web pages so that you don't have to connect to databases or run complicated scripts just to get static information.

Q&A

Q. *How do I use some of the new event handlers such as* `ononline` *or* `onstorage`?

A. The event handlers `ononline` and `onoffline` both relate to the offline web applications API that are discussed in more detail in Hour 20, "Offline Web

Applications." The onstorage event handler refers to using web storage to store data, which is covered in Hour 21, "Web Storage in HTML5."

Q. *I read that I can add things such as date stamps or other information to printed pages using an event handler. How does that work?*

A. HTML5 adds the event handlers onbeforeprint and onafterprint to allow you to trigger events before and after a print job has run. These events are not widely supported by browsers, so use them with care.

Q. *Can I put anything I want inside the* data-* *attributes?*

A. Technically, you can put anything you like inside a data-* attribute, but you should avoid using these for data that has specific attributes in HTML already, such as the height or width of images.

Q. *What if a plug-in or library I use has the same* data-* *names as I do in my HTML? Will this cause problems?*

A. Yes, it can. The best way to prevent that is to use a custom string inside your data-* attributes that identifies the attributes as yours. For example, you might write data-jk-desc rather than just data-desc. This would differentiate it from any plug-in that you might use that uses desc as a data attribute.

You should also try to avoid using really generic names for your datasets. For example, height and width are very general and can refer to almost anything, but furnitureHeight and furnitureWidth makes it clear what that data is referencing.

Workshop

The workshop contains quiz questions to help you process what you've learned in this chapter. Try to answer all the questions before you read the answers. See Appendix A, "Answers to Quizzes," for answers.

Quiz

1. What are two things that differentiate a web application from a web page?

2. Name the four ways a script can be fired in a web application.

3. Which is better to use to get data from a dataset—the JavaScript `getAttribute` method or the `dataset` method?

Exercises

1. Build a simple web application using a script to change the background color on a web page to a color that the user chooses.

2. Create a web page with extra information stored in the dataset, and then write a script that accesses that data and displays it when the user requests it.

HOUR 19

WebSockets, Web Workers, and Files

What You'll Learn in This Hour:

▶ How to use WebSockets to speed up web communication
▶ Why WebSockets aren't fully supported
▶ How to thread JavaScript with Web Workers
▶ How to use the File API to connect web pages to user files
▶ How to build a drag-and-drop file upload tool

The WebSockets, Web Workers, and File APIs are useful additions to HTML5 because they give you resources such as asynchronous connections, as well as enable you to run scripts in the background and work with files in your web applications. These three APIs offer a lot of back-end functionality that most applications use.

This hour you'll learn about what these three APIs do for web applications, some explanations of how to use them, and the benefits and drawbacks to using them.

Two-Way Communication with WebSockets

WebSockets enable two-way communication between a web page and a remote host. The WebSockets API is being standardized by the W3C as a way to communicate with WebSocket servers through a web browser.

WebSockets is implemented in Firefox 4, Chrome 4, Opera 11, and Safari 5, as well as iOS 4.2. It is not available in Internet Explorer or Android. Firefox and Opera have disabled support in their browsers because of security concerns. Firefox and Opera users can re-enable it if they really want it, but it won't be available there until the security concerns are dealt with.

WebSocket Security Concerns

The problem that Firefox and Opera browser manufacturers have with WebSockets is a security concern that is not browser specific. The problem is that the handshake that sets up WebSockets connections can be exploited to run malicious code through cache poisoning.

> **Even with Security Concerns, Learning the API Is Smart**
>
> The difficulty that many web developers have with understanding the security issues surrounding WebSockets is that it's not the API that is the problem—it's the intermediate tools the sockets pass through. In other words, the methods used to connect to a WebSockets server are not the security problem; it's the server itself that is insecure. So, even if you don't plan to implement WebSockets until it's supported in Firefox and IE, you can still learn the API, so that you're ready after it is supported.

Firefox and Opera decided to disable support for WebSockets until the handshake vulnerability is dealt with, but browsers such as Safari and Chrome still support it, and users could be attacked. Although, Safari may disable WebSockets as well in the future.[1] The problem with the WebSockets protocol is not in WebSockets at all, but in implementations of some types of proxies. However, it came to people's attention when Firefox and Opera disabled support. In fact, the exploit on the handshake was discovered in raw sockets in Flash and Java first, and then were found in the same situations in WebSockets.

Ultimately, WebSockets is still in the early stages of development, so by learning this API you can put your website on the cutting edge. Most web developers will skip using it until it is supported by Firefox and Internet Explorer.

Benefits of WebSockets

When a web browser typically visits a page, it sends an HTTP request to the web server. The host server acknowledges the request and sends back a response. This means that if the server has something new to tell the browser, it cannot share it until the browser makes a request for new data. WebSockets lets the server tell the browser immediately whenever new data arrives.

Two ways that some Ajax applications attempted to solve this problem was by polling and long-polling. *Polling* is where the browser sends an HTTP request to the

---

[1] "Moving to a CONNECT-based handshake." IETF Mail Archive. Nov. 30, 2010. www.ietf.org/mail-archive/web/hybi/current/msg04782.html. Referenced June 12, 2011.

server at regular intervals, and the server responds. *Long-polling* is where the browser sends a request to the server and the server keeps the request open for a set period of time. If a response comes in during that time, the server sends it immediately to the browser.

The problem is that these methods still rely on a request-response function. In polling, unless the server always has new data every set period of time, some requests will yield nothing—resulting in unnecessary requests. In long-polling you run the risk of having out-of-control loops if the message volume is too high. Also, because the polling and long-polling methods still rely on HTTP, they must include that information in every request and response.

WebSockets establishes a connection between the browser and the server, and then data can flow in either direction at any time. This speeds up the communication, because the server can send information to the client any time it gets new information without waiting for the client to ask for it.

WebSockets lets you display real-time information on your website without extra HTTP traffic or latency. Some ways you can use WebSockets include:

▶ Stock and news tickers, including Twitter feeds

▶ Multiplayer games

▶ Chat and instant messaging

Establishing a WebSocket

The first thing you need when working with WebSockets is a server. You have several options for setting up a WebSocket server:

▶ Alchemy WebSockets (www.olivinelabs.com/index.php/projects/ 71-alchemy-websockets)

▶ jWebSocket (http://jwebsocket.org/)

▶ Kaazing HTML5 WebSocket Gateway (www.kaazing.com/products/ html5-edition.html)

▶ phpwebsocket (http://code.google.com/p/phpwebsocket/)

▶ pywebsocket (http://code.google.com/p/pywebsocket/)

After you have a server set up, you connect to it through a web application called a client. In this case a client is simply a web page with some scripts to help connect to the WebSockets server.

> **Pay Attention to Protocol Versions**
>
> One of the challenges to implementing WebSockets right now is that your sockets server must be constantly updated. Chrome 6.4 stopped supporting version 75 of the protocol (and lower) and Google continues to make changes to Chrome to support only the most current and most secure version.

You need to know four events to work with WebSockets:

- ▶ **onopen**—This fires when the socket has opened.

- ▶ **onclose**—This fires when the socket has closed.

- ▶ **onmessage**—This fires when a message has been received.

- ▶ **onerror**—This fires when an error happens.

WebSockets is a new API, and the functionality is still buggy and difficult to set up. However, if you need real-time data and interaction with a web server, WebSockets is an important new feature of HTML5.

Until WebSockets is widely supported, you can use a tool such as Socket.IO (http://socket.io/). This JavaScript tool and server-side component chooses the best socket mechanism available from WebSockets, Flash, Ajax, and others to open a real-time connection to the server.

Running Scripts in the Background with Web Workers

Web Workers is another useful API added to HTML5. It is an API for running scripts in the background and independent of the user interface. This is important because JavaScript, on its own, only runs in one thread. This means that every single thing that JavaScript does has to happen all by itself. If a script needs to handle UI input, submit server queries, and manipulate the DOM, each one of those actions happens separately, one at a time. Web Workers fixes that by adding background threads to web applications.

> **Workers Can't Manipulate the DOM**
>
> Workers work in the background, and no background threads can manipulate the DOM of a web page. So if you need to make changes to the DOM because of a Web Worker, you need to pass a message from the Worker to the creator to get it done. Workers also do not have access to the `window` object, the `document` object, or the `parent` object.

To add a new Worker to your script, you write:

```
worker = Worker("worker.js");
```

You can then communicate with your Worker by watching for a message from it:

```
worker.onmessage = function(e){
    e.data
};
```

and sending messages to it:

```
worker.postmessage("message");
```

The Worker then reads the message and sends back the results:

```
worker.onmessage = function(e){
    if ( e.data === "start" ) {
        done()
    }
};
function done(){
    postMessage("done");
}
```

Workers Fail Invisibly

Because your Web Workers are stored in separate JS files, a possibility exists that the files won't be found (404 errors). If this happens, the server won't provide any feedback; the Worker just won't perform its action. If you are having trouble with a Worker, the first thing you should check is that the file is on your server and that you are pointing to the correct location.

Watch Out!

To turn off the Worker, you can use either `worker.terminate()` in the main page or `self.close();` inside the Worker script itself.

Unfortunately, Web Workers only works on Opera Mobile 11 in the mobile world. Internet Explorer also does not support it. Web Workers is well supported in other desktop browsers.

Try It Yourself ▼

Building a Simple Calculator with Web Workers

This script will do simple math calculations in the background using Web Workers.

1. Open a new JavaScript file and call it `worker.js`.

2. Add a listener to the file to listen for events calling the Worker:

```
// event listener
this.onmessage = function (event) {
    var data = event.data;

    switch(data.func) {
        case 'add':
        postMessage(addNumbers(data.one, data.two));
        break;
        case 'subtract':
        postMessage(subtractNumbers(data.one, data.two));
        break;
        case 'multiply':
        postMessage(multiplyNumbers(data.one, data.two));
        break;
        case 'divide':
        postMessage(divideNumbers(data.one, data.two));
        break;
        default:
        postMessage("Error: Unknown operation");
    }
};
```

3. Add in the math operations the calculator supports (add, subtract, multiply, and divide) and then save the file and upload it to your web server:

```
function addNumbers(one, two) {
    return one + two;
}

function subtractNumbers(one, two) {
    return one-two;
}

function multiplyNumbers(one, two) {
    return one*two;
}

function divideNumbers(one, two) {
    if (two == 0) {
        return "no divide by zero";
    } else {
        return one / two;
    }
}
```

4. Open a new HTML document, and include the jQuery script in the head:

```
<!DOCTYPE HTML>
<html>
<head>
<meta charset="UTF-8">
```

```
<title>Web Workers Example</title>
<script src="jquery.min.js"></script>
</head>
<body>
```

5. Build your calculator:

```
<h1>A Calculator</h1>
<p>
<button id=one class=number>1</button>
<button id=two class=number>2</button>
<button id=three class=number>3</button>
<button id=divide class=fx>/</button>
<p>
<button id=one class=number>4</button>
<button id=two class=number>5</button>
<button id=three class=number>6</button>
<button id=multiply class=fx>*</button>
<p>
<button id=one class=number>7</button>
<button id=two class=number>8</button>
<button id=three class=number>9</button>
<button id=subtract class=fx>-</button>
<p>
<button id=zero class="number">0</button>
<button id=period class=number>.</button>
<button id=add class=fx>+</button>
<p>
<button id=clear>C</button>
<button id=submit>=</button>
```

Notice that the numbers all have the class number and the operators all have the class fx. This could have been done with dataset values, but with classes you can style the numbers to look different from the operators.

6. Add three text fields for the numbers to calculate:

```
<p>
First Number
<p>
<input id=first readonly class=numbers>
<p>
Second Number
<p>
<input id=second readonly class=numbers>
<p>
Result
<p>
<input id=result readonly class=numbers>
```

Notice that all three text fields are read-only. This is because you don't want users filling in their own values—only the values from the calculator buttons.

7. Initialize your Web Worker inside a script that checks whether the browser supports Workers:

```
<script>
if (supportsWorkers() ) {
    worker = new Worker("worker.js");
    // Watch for messages from the worker
    worker.onmessage = function(e){
        $("#result").val(e.data);
    };
} else {
    alert("this calculator will not work in your browser, sorry");
}
function supportsWorkers() {
    return !!window.Worker;
}
```

8. Inside the jQuery document ready function, initialize variables and set the actions when the number buttons are clicked on:

```
$(document).ready(function(){
    var next, cur, func, one, two, message;
    $(".number").click(function() {
        if (!next) {
            cur = $("#first").val();
            num = $(this).html();
            num = cur + num;
            // input first number
            $("#first").val(num);
        } else {
            cur = $("#second").val();
            num = $(this).html();
            num = cur + num;
            $("#second").val(num);
        }
    });
```

This function appends the number to the first field unless the next variable is activated.

9. Write the function for when the operator buttons are clicked:

```
$(".fx").click(function() {
    next = 1;
    func = $(this).attr("id");
    one = parseFloat($("#first").val());
});
```

This sets the next variable and assigns the operator to the func variable.

10. Write the function for the clear button:

```
$("#clear").click(function() {
    $("input").attr('value','');
```

```
    next = 0;
});
```

This resets the next variable and empties the three fields.

11. Write the function for when the equal sign is clicked:

```
$("#submit").click(function() {
    two = parseFloat($("#second").val());
    message = {
        'func' : func,
        'one'  : one,
        'two'  : two
    };
    worker.postMessage(message);
});
```

This is where the Worker is passed the information to calculate.

12. Close the document ready function, the script, and the HTML:

```
});
</script>
</body>
</html>
```

Figure 19.1 shows this page running in Firefox. You can see an example of this calculator at www.html5in24hours.com/examples/web-workers-examples.html.

▲

Handling Client-Side Files with the File API

The File API is a set of methods that you can use to handle files on the client side. Most commonly this means uploading files with progress bars and uploading multiple files without using Flash.

File API Is Still User Driven

The File API does not suddenly give web developers access to their users' hard drives. You can't simply access a local file. However, you can attach the File API to your `<input type=file>` elements to give better functionality to your file uploaders, but the user still picks the file that the web page will have access to.

By the Way

FIGURE 19.1
A calculator
application in
Firefox.

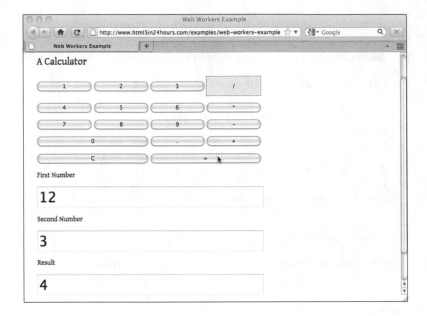

The File API includes several interfaces, including:

> ▶ **FileList**—An array of individual files selected from the underlying file system

> ▶ **File**—Read-only information about the file, including the filename and last modified date

> ▶ **Blob**—Represents immutable raw binary data

> ▶ **FileReader**—Methods to read File and Blob data

> ▶ **FileError** and **FileException**—Defines error conditions

> ▶ **URI scheme**—References binary data within web applications

The HTML5 File API allows your web applications to read the contents of a file directly from the computer, rather than their needing to upload it to a server and then open it.

By the Way

What Is a BLOB?

The term *blob* comes from the database acronym *BLOB* meaning binary large object. It refers to a large file such as an image or sound file that must be handled in some special way. The file handler doesn't need to know what the file is to handle it; it just needs to be able to manipulate it.

The File API is supported in Android 3.0, Chrome 6, Firefox 3.6, Opera 11.1, and Safari 5.1. So for IE and iOS, you need to detect it and use standard file uploading for those browsers. Here is a simple detection script:

```
if (!fileAPI()) {
    alert("This page requires File API. Sorry");
} else {
    // file uploader script

}
function fileAPI() {
    return typeof FileReader != 'undefined';
}
```

You need to take several steps, which are covered in the following sections, to use the File API.

Building an Input Field

To use the File API you must set up a file input box using the `<input type=file>` element. For example:

```
<input type=file id=imageFile onchange="getImages(this.files);">
```

iOS Doesn't Support File Upload

As mentioned earlier, iOS doesn't support the File API, but iOS devices don't support file upload input types either. This is because iOS doesn't have a file system that is visible to the end user—there is no way for the user to pick a file to upload. The only options you have for this are to point your users to an app to upload images or to use a tool such as PhoneGap to convert your HTML5 application to a native iPhone app. One application you can use is the iphone-photo-picker (http://code.google.com/p/iphone-photo-picker/).

If you want to allow people to select more than one file, you add the `multiple` attribute:

```
<input type=file id=imageFile multiple=true
➥onchange="getImages(this.files);">
```

If you want to limit the type of files that users can upload (which is a good idea), you should use the accept attribute with the MIME types that you will accept, separated by a comma.

To limit your field to only images write:

```
<input type=file id=imageFile multiple=true
accept="image/*" onchange="getImages(this.files);">
```

Getting the File Information

The files are sent to the application as an array of files in the `FileList`. You can then iterate across this array to get the name, size, and MIME type of each file.

In this example, the `getImages()` function reads the file list and displays the name, size, and type in a div called images:

```
function getImages(files) {
   var i, file;
   $("#images").html("<p>Number of files: "+files.length);
   for (i=0; i<files.length; i++) {
      file = files[i];
      $('<li/>', {
         text: "name: "+file.name+" size: "+file.size+" type: "+file.type
      }).appendTo("#images");
   }
}
```

Reading the File Information

Reading the file information is where the File API really shines. You can read the files right on the users' hard drive, without uploading them. This means that you can create previews of image files without using any server resources.

If you just use the `file.name` call to display the images, at best you will just get a broken image displaying. Instead you have to tell the user agent to read the file. You can then convert that file into a data URL and display the image dynamically.

You open a new `FileReader`:

```
var reader = new FileReader();
```

You then run a function when the reader is loaded:

```
reader.onload = (function(theFile) { ... }
```

Finally, you get the file data URL:

```
reader.readAsDataURL(file);
```

The full `getImages()` function creates a thumbnail of the image and adds it to the preview area:

```
function getImages(files) {
   var i, file;
   $("#images").html("<p>Number of files: "+files.length);
   for (i=0; i<files.length; i++) {
      file = files[i];
      // make sure they are only image types
```

```
        if (!file.type.match('image.*')) {
            continue;
        }
        var reader = new FileReader();
        reader.onload = (function(theFile) {
        return function(e) {
            var span = document.createElement('span');
            $('<span/>')
                .addClass("preview")
                .html("<img src="+e.target.result+" class=preview>")
                .appendTo("#preview");
        };
        })(file);
        reader.readAsDataURL(file);
    }
```

After you have the file you can do whatever you want with it. Upload it with
`XMLHttpRequest()`, animate it, or set the data URL in a cookie to use as an avatar
in your applications.

Try It Yourself ▼

Building a Drag-and-Drop File Uploader

One of the best ways to use the File API is to create a file uploader. With this script
you will create a drag-and-drop file uploader that is much easier to use than other
web file upload scripts.

1. Open a new HTML file and link to jQuery and jQuery UI:

```
<!DOCTYPE HTML>
<html>
<head>
<meta charset="UTF-8">
<title>Drag and Drop File Uploader</title>
<script src="jquery.min.js"></script>
<link rel="stylesheet" href="jquery-ui-1.8.13.custom.css">
<script type="text/javascript" src="jquery-ui-1.8.13.custom.min.js">
</script>
</head>
<body>

</body>
</html>
```

2. Add two boxes for your drop zone and the file preview area:

```
<div id="dropBox" dropzone="copy">
    <p>Drop Image Files Here</p>
</div>
<div id="preview"></div>
```

3. Add a progress bar box:

```
<div id="progress"></div>
```

4. Style these boxes how you like.

5. Put your `<script>` element at the bottom of the document, just above the
`</body>`:

```
<script>
</script>
```

6. In the jQuery document ready function, initialize the event handlers for your
drop zone and initialize the progress bar:

```
$(document).ready(function() {
    var dropbox = document.getElementById("dropBox")

    // init event handlers
    dropbox.addEventListener("dragenter", dragEnter, false);
    dropbox.addEventListener("dragexit", dragExit, false);
    dropbox.addEventListener("dragover", dragOver, false);
    dropbox.addEventListener("drop", drop, false);

    // initialize progressbar
    $("#progress").progressbar();
});
```

7. Prevent the default action on dragenter, dragexit, and dragover:

```
function dragEnter(e) {
    e.preventDefault();
}
function dragExit(e) {
    e.preventDefault();
}
function dragOver(e) {
    e.preventDefault();
}
```

8. On the drop event, set the `DataTransfer` to transfer the files that were
dropped:

```
function drop(e) {
    e.stopPropagation();
    e.preventDefault();

    var files = e.dataTransfer.files;
    var count = files.length;
    // only do the upload function if there are files dropped
    if (count > 0) {
        uploadFiles(files);
    }
}
```

9. Run the uploadFiles function. Be sure to check that the files are types and sizes you want:

```
function uploadFiles(files) {
    var i, file;
    for (i=0; i<files.length; i++) {
        file = files[i];
        // make sure they are only image types
        if (!file.type.match('image.*')) {
            continue;
        }
        // make sure they are not too big
        if (file.size > 30000) {
            alert(file.name+" file size too large");
            continue;
        }
        var reader = new FileReader();
        // progress bar
        reader.onprogress = handleReaderProgress;
        // load done
        reader.onloadend = handleReaderLoadEnd;
        // begin the read operation
        reader.readAsDataURL(file);
    }
    $("#dropBox p").html("Complete. Upload more?");
}
function handleReaderProgress(e) {
    if (e.lengthComputable) {
        var loaded = (e.loaded / e.total);
        $("#progress").progressbar({ value: loaded * 100 });
    }
}
function handleReaderLoadEnd(e) {
    $("#progress").progressbar({ value: 100 });
    $("#preview")
        .append("<img class=preview src="+e.target.result+">");
}
```

You can see an example of this application at www.html5in24hours.com/examples/drag-and-drop-file-example.html.

Summary

This hour you learned about three APIs that are part of HTML5 but that don't have as wide of support as some of the other APIs covered in this book. These are good tools to know, but if you are focusing on mobile applications, you will have to wait a while before widespread support is available in the mobile arena.

You learned about creating bidirectional connections to web applications with the WebSockets API. This API allows you to connect with WebSockets servers and provide close to real-time data to your customers.

This hour also covered Web Workers. Web Workers allows scripts to run in the background so that JavaScript can run multithreaded, which speeds up applications and provides more functionality.

Finally, you learned about the File API. With the File API you have more control over the `<input type=file>` element than just using the element without the API and so can create more robust file transfer applications. When combined with drag and drop, the File API makes almost any application that uses uploaded files feel more like a desktop application.

Q&A

Q. *You mentioned a number of WebSockets servers—are there any that you particularly recommend?*

A. The Kaazing server is the easiest to set up and get running, but not a lot of documentation exists on how to interact with the server. The other servers can be harder to get working, but when they do they are more responsive to the standard WebSockets API calls than Kaazing is.

Q. *The calculator created in this hour could have just as easily been done with inline JavaScript. Why should I use a Web Worker for this function?*

A. Web Workers take the work of the JavaScript outside the loading and working of the page. If you imagine a calculator of the same sort on a more dynamic page, where other things are going on at the same time, moving the scripting to a separate Worker makes sense. Web Workers help speed up pages, and they are most effective when they are on applications with a lot of JavaScript.

Q. *Your File Upload script doesn't actually upload any files—how should I do that?*

A. To start an upload you want to send the file information to the server with `XMLHttpRequest()`. The following code is a file upload function you can use in place of the `uploadFiles()` function to upload your files instead of putting them in the document:

```
function FileUpload(files) {
    for (var i=0; i<files.length; i++) {
        var file = files[i];
        // make sure they are only image types
        if (!file.type.match('image.*')) {
            continue;
        }
        // build file list
        var reader = new FileReader();
        var xhr = new XMLHttpRequest();
        this.xhr = xhr;

        xhr.upload.addEventListener("load", function(e){
            self.ctrl.update(100);
            var canvas = self.ctrl.ctx.canvas;
            canvas.parentNode.removeChild(canvas);
        }, false);
        xhr.open("POST", "upload.php");
        xhr.overrideMimeType('text/plain; charset=x-user-defined-binary');
        reader.onload = function(evt) {
            xhr.sendAsBinary(evt.target.result);
        };
        reader.readAsBinaryString(file);
    }
}
```

You also need to write a file on the server to accept the uploaded files, which in the preceding example, is upload.php.

Workshop

The workshop contains quiz questions to help you process what you've learned in this chapter. Try to answer all the questions before you read the answers. See Appendix A, "Answers to Quizzes," for answers.

Quiz

1. Why did Firefox and Opera disable support for WebSockets?

2. How do you add a new Web Worker and how do you send and receive messages from the Worker within your script?

3. How can you set up a file upload for more than one file at once and limit those files to only text files?

An offline web application takes a list of files for your web application and downloads them to an offline cache in the browser. Then when the web browser is offline it uses the cached copies of those files to build your application.

> **You Must Store User Data Locally**
>
> The offline web applications specification does not provide any access to data that is collected by the application. If your application saves state or stores any data collected from users, you need to use web storage to store that data locally while the users are offline and then synchronize it with the server when they come back online. You'll learn about web storage in Hour 21, "Web Storage in HTML5."

Several new features can help you build offline web applications:

- `window.navigator.onLine`—This is a flag in the Document Object Model (DOM) that indicates whether the user agent is online. Values are `true` or `false`.

- `checking`—This event fires when the user agent is checking for an update.

- `noupdate`—This event fires if the manifest hasn't changed.

- `downloading`—This event fires when the user agent is downloading an updated manifest or the resources listed in the manifest for the first time.

- `progress`—This is a progress event that fires when the user agent is downloading events listed by the manifest.

- `cached`—This event fires when all the files for the application have been downloaded.

- `updateready`—This event fires when the files have been redownloaded and the script can then use the `swapCache()` method to switch to a new cache.

- `obsolete`—This event fires when the manifest comes up 404 or 410, so the application cache is deleted.

- `error`—This event fires when the manifest is 404 or 410, when the page referencing the manifest failed to download, a fatal error occurred when the files were being fetched, or the manifest changed while the update was being run.

Offline web applications are supported in nearly every browser except Internet Explorer 9 and Opera Mini 5 and 6. It is fully supported in Android 2.1+, iOS 3.2+, Opera, Chrome, Safari 4+, and Firefox.

You need to do just a couple of things to convert your application into an offline application:

1. Create a cache manifest that includes every file (including images, CSS, and JavaScript) that your application uses.

2. Add the cache manifest to every HTML file with `<html manifest=offline.manifest>`.

After you have done those two things, your application is an offline application. The rest of this hour will teach you exactly how to do these two steps.

The Cache Manifest

The cache manifest is the file that drives your offline web application. This is a list of all the files and resources your application needs to access while it's disconnected from the network.

Make Sure Your Manifest Has the Right MIME Type

The cache manifest must be served with the content type `text/cache-manifest` or it will not work. You can set this on an Apache server with an `.htaccess` file in the root of your web directory that has this line: `AddType text/cache-manifest .manifest`. You then need to make sure that all your manifest files end with `.manifest`.

By the Way

The three sections of a cache manifest are

▶ **Explicit**—This defines the files to be cached.

▶ **Online whitelist**—This defines the items that should never be cached.

▶ **Fallback**—This defines substitutions for online resources that couldn't be cached.

Using a Cache Manifest File

To use a cache manifest, you add a `manifest` attribute to your `<html>` element. For example:

```
<html manifest="offline.manifest">
```

You point to the cache manifest in any file that you want to be stored offline. When the user agent comes to that page, the user agent will add that page to the cache.

Some user agents do this automatically, and others ask the users whether they want to cache the application, as shown in Figure 20.1.

FIGURE 20.1
Firefox asking
to cache an
application.

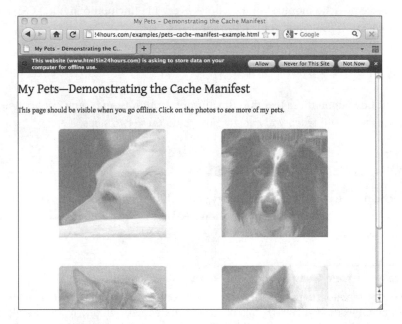

Writing a Cache Manifest

The simplest cache manifest has just the explicit section that details the files that should be cached. Here is an example of a valid cache manifest that caches three pages:

```
CACHE MANIFEST
pets.html
pets-auto.html
pets-mckinley.html
```

The first line is *always* CACHE MANIFEST. If you don't have that as the very first line of your file, the manifest will not work.

The next three lines are the explicit section—the three files that are being cached: `pets.html`, `pets-auto.html`, and `pets-mckinley.html`. You can also indicate that this is the explicit section by adding the word CACHE: above these three files. For example:

```
CACHE MANIFEST
CACHE:
pets.html
pets-auto.html
pets-mckinley.html
```

The files are listed relative to the location of the cache manifest file. Because there is no directory information, you know that these files are in the same directory as the cache manifest. But you can also use full URLs, like this:

```
http://www.html5in24hours.com/examples/pets-cache-manifest-example.html
```

Or you can use URLs in other directories, like this:

```
images/pets/mckinley1.jpg
```

The only caveat is that the URL must resolve to a valid file.

Watch Out!

Caching Secure Pages

If you have pages that are served over an encrypted connection (such as SSL or https) and you want them available for caching, you need to serve both the manifest and all files from the same secure domain. You cannot include files from another domain in a secure manifest.

The online whitelist section defines the areas of the site that should not be cached. You define the area of the online whitelist with the word NETWORK:. For example:

```
CACHE MANIFEST
pets.html
pets-auto.html
pets-mckinley.html
NETWORK:
online-only-page.html
```

This tells the user agent that the `online-only-page.html` file should not be cached and should only be available while the user is online. This is good to use for files that really do need to be online, such as tracking scripts, multi-player games, and so on.

The default online whitelist is *, which means that every file on the site should be available online. You can whitelist every page on your site like this:

```
NETWORK:
*
```

By the Way

Why Explicitly Whitelist Your Entire Site?

When you use the * to whitelist your entire site, you help your site behave more normally when the user is online. This is because the cache takes precedence in an offline-enabled application. Without the wildcard flag, if you add an image or video from another domain, such as a CDN, it won't load even if the user is online.

The fallback section gives you a way to specify what the user agent should do if a page is not available offline. The fallback section looks like this:

```
FALLBACK:
/ /offline.html
```

The first part of that line is a pattern that describes what files should have the fallback applied to them. In the preceding example, the slash (/) means that every file on the server (from the root) should be served the file /offline.html if it's not available offline.

You can specify multiple options for your offline fallbacks. So if you want one section of your site to receive one fallback page and the rest to receive another, you would write:

```
FALLBACK:
/ /main-offline.html
/examples/ /examples/example-offline.html
```

This manifest tells the user agent to set the fallback for the entire site to /main-offline.html and then to set the fallback for the /examples/ directory to /example-offline.html.

▼   **Try It Yourself**

Setting Up a Lazy Offline Application

If you have a large application with a lot of HTML pages, creating a manifest can be difficult because you have to list every file explicitly in the CACHE: section to have it cached automatically. But you can also build a cache that stores every file it sees—this is called a *lazy* cache.

You can set up your application to cache any page that the reader comes to for offline use, as follows.

1. Create your cache manifest file and save it as offline.manifest in the root directory:

   ```
   CACHE MANIFEST
   ```

2. Write a fallback web page for when a page has not been cached and call it fallback.html. Save it in the root directory.

3. Add a fallback section to your cache manifest to send uncached pages to that fallback page:

   ```
   FALLBACK:
   / /fallback.html
   ```

4. Set the online whitelist wildcard flag in the cache manifest:

```
NETWORK:
*
```

5. On every page that you want to be available offline, add the cache manifest to the <html> element:

```
<html manifest="/cache.manifest">
```

Then, whenever a user hits a page that should be stored offline, it will be cached because it references the manifest, but links to pages that have not been visited will show the fallback.html page instead.

▲

Using DOM Events and Properties for Offline Apps

When working with offline web applications, the browser handles the caching in a certain order. You can use DOM events to follow along:

1. When the browser sees a manifest attribute on the <html> element, the checking event fires. This event happens every time.

2. If the cache manifest is new, the downloading event fires and the browser starts downloading the manifest. During the download, the progress event fires periodically indicating how many files have been downloaded and how many are still left. After everything is downloaded, the cached event fires, saying that the application is fully cached and ready to go offline.

3. If the browser has seen this manifest before, either on this page or another page, it will check to see whether the manifest has changed.

   If the manifest has not changed, the noupdate event fires and the process ends.

   If the manifest *has* changed it will start downloading every resource in the manifest, firing the downloading and progress events just like in step 2. However, instead of the cached event firing, the updateready event fires.

---

updateready Means the Version Isn't in Use Yet

The updateready event means that the new version has been downloaded, but it is *not yet in use*. The new version will only go into use if the user reloads the page or you manually call the window.applicationCache.swapCache() method.

By the Way

Another useful tool is the `navigator.onLine` property. This property reports back the current online or offline state of the user. This is important to know so that you don't attempt to access online resources when a browser is offline. For example, when the user is online, you can save data to an online database, but when the user is offline, that data needs to be stored locally and saved to the database when he comes back online.

▼ **Try It Yourself**

Building an App to Listen for Changes to the Cache

This application will load a manifest of every file in the current directory that is dynamically generated with PHP. As it loads the files, you can watch the messages reported back from the application cache. Just follow these steps:

1. Build the `manifest.php` file to read the current directory and list all the PHP and HTML files (except for the manifest itself):

```php
<?php
    header('Content-Type: text/cache-manifest');
    echo "CACHE MANIFEST\n";
    echo "#revision 6\n";
    if ($handle = opendir('.')) {
        while (false !== ($file = readdir($handle))) {
            if (
                !preg_match("/examples-list\.php/i", $file) &&
                !preg_match("/manifest\.php/i", $file) &&
                (
                preg_match("/\.html/i", $file) ||
                preg_match("/\.php/i", $file)
                )
            ) {
                echo "$file\n";
            }
        }
    }
?>
```

2. Build an HTML file with jQuery:

```html
<!DOCTYPE HTML>
<html>
<head>
<meta charset="UTF-8">
<title>Listening for Cache Events</title>
<meta name="viewport" content="width=device-width"/>
<script src="jquery.min.js"></script>
</head>
<body>
</body>
</html>
```

3. Add the HTML elements including a button to recheck the cache and an area to display the events:

```
<h1>Offline Web Apps&#8212;Listening for Cache Events</h1>
<h2><span id="status">Online</span> &#8211; <span
➥id="time"></span></h2>
<p>
<button id="checkCache">Check for Cache Update</button>

<h2>Application Cache Events</h2>
<div id="events"></div>
```

4. Put a script element at the bottom of the page, just above the </body> tag:

```
<script>
</script>
```

5. Inside the script add the document ready function and set the online status and the current time:

```
<script>
$(document).ready(function(e) {

    $(window).bind("online offline", function(e) {
        $("#status").text(navigator.onLine ? "Online" : "Offline");
    });

    $("#time").text(getTime());
});
```

6. Inside the document ready function, set a variable for the applicationCache property and then bind all the events to it:

```
var appCache = window.applicationCache;
$(appCache)
    .bind("checking", function(e) {
        writeEvent("Checking if manifest is available");
    })
    .bind("noupdate", function(e) {
        writeEvent("No updates to cache");
    })
    .bind("downloading",function(e) {
        writeEvent("Downloading to cache");
    })
    .bind("progress", function(e) {
        writeEvent("File downloaded");
    })
    .bind("cached", function(e) {
        writeEvent("All files downloaded&#8212;Offline Use Ready");
    })
    .bind("updateready", function(e) {
        writeEvent("New cache available");
        $(this).swapCache();
```

```
})
.bind("obsolete", function(e) {
    writeEvent("Manifest not found");
})
.bind("error", function(e) {
    writeEvent("An error occurred");
});
```

7. The last thing that you should do is bind the click action when the check cache button is clicked. Add this to the document ready function:

```
$("#checkCache").click(function(e) {
    e.preventDefault();
    appCache.update();
});
```

8. Outside the document ready function add the getTime() function to get the current time in a friendly format:

```
function getTime() {
    var time;
    var currentTime = new Date();
    var hours = currentTime.getHours();
    var minutes = currentTime.getMinutes();
    if (minutes < 10){
        minutes = "0" + minutes
    }
    time = hours + ":" + minutes + " ";
    if(hours > 11){
        time += "PM";
    } else {
        time += "AM";
    }
    return time;
}
```

9. The last thing you need in the script is the function that adds the event message to the events area:

```
function writeEvent(msg) {
    $("#events").prepend("<p>" + msg + " at " + getTime());
}
```

10. When you have the whole application finished, add the manifest to the `<html>` tag:

```
<html manifest=manifest.php>
```

You can see an example of this application at www.html5in24hours.com/examples/offline-web-apps-listening.html.

Debugging the Application Cache

The challenge of using the application cache is that most errors will cause the caching to completely fail, with no indication of what the problem was. The error event will fire and the caching will stop.

Your Web Server Cache Will Affect Your App Cache

Web servers tell browsers to cache various parts of the site so that they download more quickly the second time a browser accesses it. However, when you are testing your application cache, this can get in the way, because the browser won't download the cache manifest until the server cache time out is reached. This can take several hours, during which you won't be able to figure out why your app isn't working offline correctly.

The first thing you should do when debugging your offline application is to make sure that the server cache isn't blocking your manifest from changing. To do this on an Apache web server, add the following to your site root .htaccess file:

```
<Files ~ "\.(manifest)$">
ExpiresActive On
ExpiresDefault "access"
</Files>
```

This tells the server to disable caching for any file called .manifest. As long as you always name your manifest files with that extension, they will not be cached.

You then need to make sure that the cache manifest has actually changed. One big challenge of working with offline files is that after a file is listed in a cache manifest, the browser considers this file a cached file and reads it from the offline cache first, because this is faster than requesting it from the server.

This means that any time you make a change to a file in your offline application, you need to change the cache manifest so the file is downloaded again. Luckily, doing this is as simple as adding a revision comment line anywhere in your cache manifest:

```
#revision 15
```

Then, when you change a file in your application, simply change the revision number, and the browser will redownload all the files:

```
#revision 16
```

You're not done yet. As mentioned earlier, not all browsers will load the new version of the app automatically. You need to swap in the new version with the window.applicationCache.swapCache() method.

To swap in the new cache with jQuery, write:

```
var appCache = window.applicationCache;
$(appCache).bind("updateready", function(e){
    appCache.swapCache();
});
```

Summary

This hour you learned how to convert an online application to an offline one. You learned the two steps required to do this:

▶ Build a cache manifest.

▶ Add the cache manifest to the application files with `<html manifest=offline.manifest>`.

You also learned the problems that can happen and how difficult debugging an offline application can be. When debugging, you learned to find answers to the following:

▶ Is the cache manifest in the correct format and served with the correct MIME type?

▶ Is the manifest being cached by the server or browser?

▶ Did the manifest file change?

▶ Did you swap in the new revision of the cache?

▶ Did you listen for events that could affect caching?

Using offline web application caching is a great way to speed up your site for your users and provide them access to it even when they are offline.

Q&A

Q. *Do I need to list the home page in the cache manifest? Isn't it already cached?*

A. You should list every page of your application in the cache manifest, and reference that manifest in the `<html>` element of every page. Although including the current page in the manifest is not required, if you leave it out and someone gets to your application from an internal page, he will not have the home page cached.

Q. *Is there a way to use wildcards to create my explicit section in the cache manifest?*

A. Although the possibility exists that some browsers support wildcards to define the cached files, the fact is that this isn't part of the specification, and most browsers don't support them. If you need to put a lot of files into your manifest, the best thing you can do is create a dynamic manifest file that reads the files in your directories.

Q. *Is there a limit to how many files you can include in a manifest?*

A. Different limits exist for your manifest files depending upon what browser is downloading the content. Firefox has a default limit of 500MB and users can change this to more or less if they like. Chrome and Safari (both desktop and iOS) have a limit of 5MB that is not easily changed.

If you want to change the offline cache size in Firefox, go to `about:config` and search for `browser.cache.offline.capacity`. The default is 512000 (500MB); change that to a larger or smaller size to change your offline cache size.

Q. *What if I'm trying to cache dynamic content? How do I do that?*

A. Dynamic content is meant to change based on information received over the network. Because of this, dynamic content should not be cached. Instead, you should place these pages of your application in the `NETWORK:` section of your cache manifest.

Workshop

The workshop contains quiz questions to help you process what you've learned in this chapter. Try to answer all the questions before you read the answers. See Appendix A, "Answers to Quizzes," for answers.

Quiz

1. What are three of the events that can fire when an application is being cached for offline use?

2. What are the keywords that identify the explicit, online whitelist, and fall-back sections of the cache manifest?

3. What is the first line of the cache manifest and what MIME type must it be served as?

4. What are the fallback and whitelist sections used for?

Exercises

1. Build a cache manifest for a site that has a lot of pages. The pages should all be added to the cache when a user visits them, but not explicitly listed in the cache manifest. Don't forget to include a fallback page.

2. Convert an application from online only to offline. Be sure to listen for events and alert the application user when the application is ready to be used offline.

Web Storage in HTML5

What You'll Learn in This Hour:

▶ How to use local storage

▶ How to detect local storage support

▶ When to use local storage versus cookies

▶ How to add local databases using Web SQL and Indexed DB

▶ How to build an application that uses local storage

Before HTML5 the only way you could store information was either by adding it to the DOM (Document Object Model) or using cookies. But both have drawbacks.

Storing data in the HTML is fairly easy to do but it requires JavaScript, and it can only store data as long as the browser is open and on the application. As soon as the user's session ends, that data is lost. Plus, data that is stored in the HTML is visible to anyone.

Cookies are limited to around 4KB of data, which is not a lot of space to store information. Plus, cookies are sent with every HTTP request, which can slow down your application. Cookies are unencrypted, so data stored that way can be sniffed unless your entire application is served on an SSL (Secure Sockets Layer) connection. SSL slows pages down, too.

This hour you will learn about web storage and how you can use space on your users' hard drives to store information about preferences, runtime state, and more. HTML5 local storage provides you with more space that is associated with the user agent and is only transferred to and from the server when the application asks for it.

However, web storage involves more than just local storage. You also have two ways to create local databases and store information in them: Web SQL and Indexed Database or Indexed DB. This hour will show you more about these two specifications and how you can use them.

What Is Web Storage?

Web storage is a separate API that was originally part of the HTML5 specification, but now is a separate document within the aegis of HTML5. It is sometimes called *Local Storage* or *DOM Storage* depending upon the browser manufacturer.

> **Several Plug-ins Are Available to Create Persistent Storage**
>
> Browser manufacturers and plug-in writers have made many attempts to create a form of persistent storage. Microsoft created `userData` (http://msdn.microsoft.com/en-us/library/ms531424(VS.85).aspx). Adobe created Local Shared Objects in Flash (www.adobe.com/products/flashplayer/articles/lso/). The Dojo Toolkit has dojox.storage integrated into it (http://dojotoolkit.org/api/1.6/dojox/storage/manager). Google Gears, Adobe AIR, and others also provide forms of local persistent storage, but all of these require either a specific browser or a plug-in for people to use.

Web storage allows web developers to store data from web applications as key/value pairs on the user's local machine. This data persists even if the user leaves the application, closes the browser, or turns off the machine. When the user comes back to the web application, that web storage data is available to the application.

Storing data is useful for many web applications. The simplest applications use web storage to store user data so that users can pick up right where they left off when they return to the site. Another way to use web storage is to store data locally when a user is offline that would normally be stored on a server (see Hour 20, "Offline Web Applications").

How Web Storage Is Different from Cookies

Many people make the mistake of thinking that web storage is the same thing as a cookie, only bigger. Although it's true that web storage provides a lot more space than cookies, other differences exist as well:

▶ Web storage is only delivered to the web page when the client requests it, whereas cookies are sent with every HTTP request.

▶ Web storage can only be accessed by the client (JavaScript), whereas cookies can be accessed by server scripts such as PHP as well as JavaScript.

▶ Cookies are specific to the browser and domain, but don't make a distinction between windows in the same browser, whereas web storage (specifically, session storage) distinguishes between windows as well as browser and domain.

Remember that web storage is not just a better cookie. Cookies serve a purpose and you should continue to use them. For example, cookies have two flags, `HttpOnly` and `secure`, that help make cookies safer. The `HttpOnly` flag tells the browser that this cookie should not be available to client-side scripts. The `secure` flag requires that the cookie only be served over a secure (SSL) connection.

You should only store session data in cookies that have been secured with at least `HttpOnly` and preferably the `secure` flag, as well. Hackers can use session information to get information about your customers.

Thinking of web storage as a place to store application preferences, non-sensitive user information, and things such as saved games and saved content is best. Also, web storage isn't as widely supported as cookies are. Cookies have been supported in browsers since 1995. Web storage is supported by all modern browsers, but only specific versions:

- ▶ Android 2.0
- ▶ Chrome 4
- ▶ Firefox 3.5
- ▶ Internet Explorer 8.0
- ▶ iOS 2.0
- ▶ Opera 10.5
- ▶ Safari 4.0

Session Storage and Local Storage

The two different types of web storage in the Web Storage specification are local storage and session storage.

Local storage is name/value pairs that are stored on the local disk. Every site has a separate storage area. The data stored in this area persists even if the user leaves the site or closes the web browser. The data is only available to the domain that added it, and that data is only sent when a client on that domain requests it.

Web Storage Stores All Data as Strings

When you store data in web storage, it will be stored as a string. This means that if you have structured data (such as database information) or numbers (integers and floating point), you need to convert them to strings so that they can be stored in web storage. Don't forget to use the `parseInt()` and `parseFloat()` methods to convert your integers and floats back when you retrieve the data.

Local storage is best for storing non-sensitive data that takes up a lot of space. It is for data that needs to be saved across sessions so that users have access to it when they return to the site.

Session storage is name/value pairs that are stored on the local disk for the length of the page session. Session storage will deliver stored data to user agents on the same domain and in the same window as when the data was stored. After that window closes (except in certain cases), the stored data is removed. If a new tab or window is opened to the same site, a new instance of session storage is created.

> **Session Storage Can Survive Reloads**
>
> If a browser has support for resuming sessions after a reload, then the session storage can be saved as well. For example, in Firefox, if the browser crashes, Firefox will restart and offer to restore your previous session. Chrome, Opera, and Safari have similar features, and plug-ins are available to add this feature to IE. In these browsers, data stored in session storage will be restored as well.

Session storage was created to solve a problem that cookies have. If you go to a website that uses cookies to store data, and then open that site in a second window, the cookie data from the first window can be accessed and contaminate the cookie data in the second window.

Session storage is most useful for temporary data that should be saved and restored if the browser session is accidentally refreshed. Like local storage, you should not store sensitive data in session storage.

Using Web Storage

As with all new HTML5 features, you should check to make sure that the browser supports web storage. To do this you can use Modernizr as mentioned in Hour 4, "Detecting Mobile Devices and HTML5 Support," or you can use this function:

```
function supportsWebStorage() {
    try {
        return 'localStorage' in window && window['localStorage'] !== null;
    } catch (e) {
        return false;
    }
}
```

When using web storage, the first thing you do is define a storage object. This tells the user agent whether you're using local storage or session storage. These objects are

- `window.localStorage`

- `window.sessionStorage`

As with other objects, the `window` portion is assumed.

Try It Yourself ▼

Saving Gift Status in an E-commerce Store

In online stores, a user can easily accidentally click away or close the browser window and lose his or her choices. This Try It Yourself shows how to use the `sessionStorage` object to save the gift status of a purchase in case of accidental browser refresh.

1. Add a checkbox, a div to hold the status, and a button to the page:

```
<p>
<label>
<input type=checkbox id=gift>This is a gift
</label>
<p>
<button id=checkGift>Check Gift Status</button>
<p><div id="isItaGift"></div>
```

2. In a `<script>` element at the bottom of the document, put a script to check for web storage support:

```
<script>
function supportsWebStorage() {
    try {
        return 'localStorage' in window && window['localStorage']
!== null;
    } catch (e) {
        return false;
    }
}
</script>
```

3. Inside the jQuery document ready function, add the check for support `if` statement:

```
$(document).ready(function(e) {
    if (supportsWebStorage()) {
        // web storage functions
    } else {
        // fallback functions
    }
});
```

4. In the web storage functions area, add the `sessionStorage` object for when the user clicks the checkbox:

```
$("#gift").click(function() {
    if ($(this).attr('checked')) {
        sessionStorage.setItem("gift", "yes");
    } else {
        sessionStorage.setItem("gift", "no");
    }
});
```

5. Add a function to check the web storage when the user clicks the button:

```
$("#checkGift").click(function() {
    var giftStatus = sessionStorage.getItem("gift");
    if (giftStatus == "yes") {
        $("#isItaGift").html("<p>This item is a gift.");
        $("#gift").attr("checked", "checked");
    } else {
        $("#isItaGift").html("<p>This item is not a gift.");
        $("#gift").removeAttr("checked");
    }
});
```

To check that this code is working, click the checkbox and then refresh the page. The browser should clear the checkbox, but if you click the button, it will update the page with the correct status. You can view this session storage example online at www.html5in24hours.com/examples/web-storage-example.html.

The previous Try It Yourself section shows you how to use two of the four methods on the web storage interface. These methods are

▶ **getItem(*key*)**—This method gets the value of the item identified by the key from storage.

▶ **setItem(*key, value*)**—This method creates the item identified by the key and sets the value to value in storage.

▶ **removeItem(*key*)**—This method removes the item identified by the key from storage.

▶ **clear()**—This method completely empties all items from storage for the current object.

▶ **key(*n*)**—This method iterates through all the currently stored keys and gets the total number of values in the storage area. You can also use this to call a key by index value (n).

The storage object also has a `length` attribute that, when called, returns the number of key/value pairs associated with the object.

> **Web Storage Can Be Hacked**
>
> As with cookies, web storage can be hacked if your site is not secured against cross site scripting (XSS). The name of any items you store in local storage is written in clear text inside your JavaScript, so a hacker can easily use XSS to collect that data.[1] To protect your readers, you should always use a `<meta charset>` element at the top of your pages before any text. Don't use web storage for session IDs; use session storage rather than local storage, and *do not* store sensitive data in local storage.

If you call the `setItem()` method with a key that already exists, the data will be overwritten with the new value. If you call the `getItem()` method and no key is stored the browser will return `null`.

The Web Storage API also provides an event to keep track of when the storage area changes: `storage`. This event creates a `StorageEvent` object that has the following properties:

- **key**—The named key that was added, removed, or modified
- **oldValue**—The previous value (including `null`) of the item
- **newValue**—The new value (including `null` if the item was removed) of the item
- **url**—The page that called a method that triggered the change

The last thing you should know about the `storage` event is that it cannot be cancelled. This is just an event to tell you what happened in the browser.

Web SQL and Indexed DB

One drawback to web storage is that it provides only storage for key/value pairs. You cannot save structured data. However, two APIs are in use now that allow you to store complex relational data and query that data using SQL: Web SQL and Indexed DB.

Web SQL Database

Web SQL Database is a specification that allows you to make SQL calls on the client side and store SQL databases. It is based on SQLite. Web SQL is supported by Android 2.1, Chrome 4, iOS 3.2, Opera 10.5, and Safari 3.2.

---

[1] "HTML5, Local Storage, and XSS." Application Security. July 12, 2010. http://michael-coates.blogspot.com/2010/07/html5-local-storage-and-xss.html. Referenced June 21, 2011.

> **Web SQL Has Been Discontinued**
>
> On November 18, 2010, the W3C decided to discontinue development of the Web SQL specification. It is still supported by some browsers, and it could be revisited in the future, but right now it is not being worked on and there are no plans to work on it.

First you should detect whether the browser supports Web SQL DB:

```
function hasWebSql() {
    return !!window.openDatabase;
}
```

You can then open a database. To create a Web SQL database use the openDatabase() method. If the database doesn't exist, Web SQL DB will create it. This method takes five attributes:

▶ The name of the database

▶ The version number of the database

▶ A text description

▶ An estimated size for the database in bytes

▶ The creation callback script

You open a database like this:

```
var db = openDatabase("addressBook", "0.1", "an online address book",
➥2000000);
```

Remember that the version number (0.1 in the above example) is required, and to open an existing database, you must use the same version number. Plus, although a changeVersion() method exist, it is not widely supported.

The creation callback is an optional script that runs when the database is created. Most of the time, you don't need this option, and in the preceding example it is not included.

The beauty of Web SQL DB is that it is a fairly simple API. After you have an open database, you use the transaction() method on that database to execute SQL commands with the executeSql() method. The executeSql() method takes SQL commands. If you don't know SQL, you should start by reviewing the documentation on SQLite at its website (http://sqlite.org/). To add a table and two entries, you write:

```
db.transaction(function(tx) {
    tx.executeSql('CREATE TABLE IF NOT EXISTS names (id unique text)');
    tx.executeSql('INSERT INTO names (id, text) VALUES (1, "Joe")');
```

```
    tx.executeSql('INSERT INTO names (id, text) VALUES (2, "Sarah")');
});
```

SQLite Ignores Data Types

When you are inserting data into a database with Web SQL, you are inserting it into an SQLite database, and SQLite ignores data types. It just uses simple strings. So you should always do data verification to ensure that the data you are inserting is the type of data you want to insert—such as dates, integers, floating point numbers, and so on.

If you wanted to add external data, such as from a form, you would want to check it for malicious code (such as SQL injection) first and then pass the executeSQL method a variable. You enter dynamic values like this:

```
tx.executeSql('INSERT INTO names (id, text) VALUES (?,?)'
➥[uniqueId, username]);
```

The uniqueId and username are variables that are mapped to the query.

Then, if you want to get data from the database, you use the SQL SELECT function:

```
db.transaction(function(tx) {
    tx.executeSql('SELECT * FROM addr', [], function(tx, names) {
        var len = names.row.length, i;
        alert(len + " names found");
    });
});
```

Indexed Database API

The Indexed Database API (or IndexedDB or IDB) exposes the object store. This can have databases with records and fields that you use just like a database, but rather than accessing them through SQL calls, you use methods on the object store. IndexedDB is supported by Firefox 4 and Chrome 11.

As usual, first you detect for IndexedDB support:

```
function hasIndexedDb() {
    return !!window.indexedDB;
}
```

You then open a database with the open() method:

```
var req = window.indexedDB.open("addressBook", "an online address book");
```

IndexedDB Requires Browser Prefixes

Although the specification lists `window.indexedDB.open()` as the method to open indexedDB databases, you need to use browser-specific prefixes to get it to work reliably. Firefox version 3 and lower uses `moz_` (with an underscore), and Firefox 4 and up uses `moz` (without). Safari and Chrome use the `webkit` prefix. So, when you work with IDB it helps to initialize the object itself:

```
window.indexedDB = window.indexedDB || window.mozIndexedDB ||
window.webkitIndexedDB;
window.IDBKeyRange = window.IDBKeyRange ||
window.webkitIDBKeyRange;
window.IDBTransaction = window.IDBTransaction ||
window.webkitIDBTransaction;
```

You have to set up the database for a first-time user:

```
req.onsuccess = function(e) {
var db = e.result;
if (db.version != "1") {
    //first visit, initialize database
    var createdObjectStoreCount = 0;
    var objectStores = [
        { name: "fnames", keypath: "id", autoIncrement: true },
        { name: "lnames", keypath: "id", autoIncrement: true },
        { name: "emails", keypath: "id", autoIncrement: true }
    ];
    function objectStoreCreated(e) {
        if (++createdObjectStoreCount == objectStores.length) {
            db.setVersion("1").onsuccess = function(e) {
                loadData(db);
            };
        }
    }
    for (var i=0; i< objectStores.length; i++) {
        var params = objectStores[i];
        req = db.createObjectStore(params.name, params.keyPath,
➥params.autoIncrement);
        req.onsuccess = objectStoreCreated;
    }
} else {
    //returning user, no initialization
    loadData(db);
}
};
```

Then to add an item to the database, you use the `add()` method:

```
req.onsuccess = function(e) {
    var objectStore = e.result.objectStore("fnames");
    objectStore.add("Jennifer").onsuccess = function(e) {
```

```
        alert("'Jennifer' added to database with id " + e.result);
    };
};
```

To list all the items in a table you would use the openCursor() method, and enumerate through it until it returned null:

```
req.onsuccess = function(e) {
    req = e.result.objectStore("fnames").openCursor();
    req.onsuccess = function(e) {
        var cursor = e.result;
        if (!cursor) {
            return
        }
        var element = $("#fnameList").append("<p>"+cursor.value.name);
        cursor.continue();
    };
};
```

Try It Yourself ▼

Building a Birthday Application for iOS and Android

This application lets iOS and Android users store and retrieve birthdays of friends and family in a local Web SQL database. Note that this application won't work in Firefox because the application uses only Web SQL, and Firefox only supports IndexedDB. It also doesn't work in Internet Explorer because IE doesn't support any web databases.

1. In your HTML5 document, write a form to enter the birthday data and display the month's birthdays:

```
<article>
<hgroup>
<h1>Birthday List</h1>
</hgroup>
<p>Store and retrieve birthdays of friends and family.
<h3>
<button id="prev">&amp;lt; Previous</button>
Birthdays in <span id=thisMonth>this Month</span>
<button id="next">Next &amp;gt;</button>
</h3>
<table id="birthdays"></table>
</article>
<section id="input">
<h3>Store a Birthday</h3>
<p>Name: <input id="fullname" placeholder="full name" required
➥pattern="[A-Z,a-z, ]+">
(only letters and spaces allowed)
```

```
<p>Birthday:
<select id="birthdayMonth" required>
    <option value="0">January
    <option value="1">February
    <option value="2">March
    <option value="3">April
    <option value="4">May
    <option value="5">June
    <option value="6">July
    <option value="7">August
    <option value="8">September
    <option value="9">October
    <option value="10">November
    <option value="11">December
</select>
<input type="number" id="birthdayDay" min="1" max="31"
size="4" step="1" required>
<p><button id="addBirthday">Store Birthday</button>
</section>
<section id="output">
<table id="submitted"></table>
</section>
```

2. Add links to script files for general functions and the Web SQL–specific functions:

```
<script src="birthday-list-websql.js"></script>
<script src="birthday-list.js"></script>
```

3. In the birthday-list.js file, check for Web SQL support and add code to display a message if the device doesn't support it:

```
if (hasWebSql()) {
    //Open or create the web SQL database
    var db = openWebSqlDb();
    //Initialize the database
    initWebSqlDb(db);
} else {
    // use plain web storage
    $("hgroup").append("<h2 id=warning>This Application Requires Web
➥SQL.</h2>");
}
// begin general functions
function hasWebSql() {
    return !!window.openDatabase;
}
```

4. In the birthday-list-websql.js file, write the openWebSqlDb and initWebSqlDb functions:

```
function openWebSqlDb() {
    var db=openDatabase('MyBirthdayDb','1.0','my birthdays app',
➥2 * 1024 * 1024);
    return db;
}
```

```
function initWebSqlDb(db) {
    db.transaction(function(tx) {
        tx.executeSql('CREATE TABLE IF NOT EXISTS birthdays(
➥id integer primary key autoincrement, fullname, birthdayMonth,
➥birthdayDay)');
    });
    // load current month's birthdays
    var thisMonth = new Date().getMonth();
    window.onload = listBirthdaysWebS(thisMonth);
}
```

5. Upon loading, the script will load any birthdays stored in the database, so add
the listBirthdaysWebS function to the birthday-list-websql.js file:

```
function listBirthdaysWebS(month) {
    db.transaction(function(tx) {
        tx.executeSql('SELECT * FROM birthdays', [], function(tx,
➥results) {
            var len=results.rows.length, i;
            for(i=0; i<len; i++) {
                if(results.rows.item(i).birthdayMonth == month) {
                    var prettyMonth =
➥getMonthName(parseInt(results.rows.item(i).birthdayMonth));
                    createTableRow(results.rows.item(i).id,
➥results.rows.item(i).fullname,prettyMonth,
➥results.rows.item(i).birthdayDay,"birthdays");
                }
            }
        });
    });
}
```

6. You will also need functions to write the table rows and display month names
in the birthday-list.js file:

```
function createTableRow
➥(insertId,inputFullName,inputBirthdayMonth,inputBirthdayDay,tableId) {
    var birthdayRow = $("<tr id=b"+insertId+"></tr>");
    var id = $("<td><p>"+insertId+"</td>");
    var fullname = $("<td><p>"+inputFullName+"</td>");
    var birthdayMonth = $("<td><p>"+inputBirthdayMonth+"</td>");
    var birthdayDay = $("<td><p>"+inputBirthdayDay+"</td>");
    // if you add an indexeddb section,
    // you will need to create a separate remove button for that db
    var removeButton = $('<td><p><button onclick="removeBirthdayWebS('
➥+ insertId + ')">Delete</button></td>');
    birthdayRow.append(fullname)
               .append(birthdayMonth)
               .append(birthdayDay)
               .append(removeButton);
    $("#"+tableId).append(birthdayRow);

}
```

```
function getMonthName(month) {
    month = parseInt(month);
    switch(month) {
        case 0:
            month = "January";
            break;
        case 1:
            month = "February";
            break;
        case 2:
            month = "March";
            break;
        case 3:
            month = "April";
            break;
        case 4:
            month = "May";
            break;
        case 5:
            month = "June";
            break;
        case 6:
            month = "July";
            break;
        case 7:
            month = "August";
            break;
        case 8:
            month = "September";
            break;
        case 9:
            month = "October";
            break;
        case 10:
            month = "November";
            break;
        case 11:
            month = "December";
            break;
    }
    return month;
}
```

7. The last thing to go in the `birthday-list.js` file is the document ready function. In it add jQuery to change the text "this Month" to the current month name:

```
$(document).ready(function(){
    var monthNum = new Date().getMonth();
    var thisMonthIs = getMonthName(monthNum);
    $("#prev").attr("class", monthNum);
```

```
$("#next").attr("class", monthNum);
$("#thisMonth").html(thisMonthIs);
});
```

8. Add the "next" and "previous" button support into the document ready function:

```
$("#prev").click( function(e) {
    var curMonth = $(this).attr("class");
    var newMonth = parseInt(curMonth) -1;
    if (curMonth == "0") {
        newMonth = "11";
    }
    $("#prev").attr("class", newMonth);
    $("#next").attr("class", newMonth);
    $("#birthdays tr").remove();
    $("#thisMonth").html(getMonthName(newMonth));
    listBirthdaysWebS(newMonth);
}); // end previous month

$("#next").click( function(e) {
    var curMonth = $(this).attr("class");
    var newMonth = parseInt(curMonth) +1;
    if (curMonth == "11") {
        newMonth = "0";
    }
    $("#next").attr("class", newMonth);
    $("#prev").attr("class", newMonth);
    $("#birthdays tr").remove();
    $("#thisMonth").html(getMonthName(newMonth));
    listBirthdaysWebS(newMonth);
}); // end next month
```

9. Add the functions to add and delete birthdays to your `birthday-list-web-sql.js` file:

```
function addBirthdayWebS(db,inputFullName,inputBirthdayMonth,
➥inputBirthdayDay) {
    var prettyMonth = getMonthName(parseInt(inputBirthdayMonth));
    var ourMonth - $("#next").attr("class");
    db.transaction(function(tx) {
        tx.executeSql('INSERT INTO birthdays(
➥fullname,birthdayMonth,birthdayDay) VALUES (?,?,?)',
➥[inputFullName,inputBirthdayMonth,inputBirthdayDay],
➥function(tx, results) {
            createTableRow(results.insertId,inputFullName,
➥prettyMonth,inputBirthdayDay,"submitted");
            if (!$('#stored').length) {
                $("#submitted").before("<h3 id=stored>Stored</h3>");
            }
            // add current month additions to current birthday list
            if (inputBirthdayMonth == curMonth) {
```

```
                     createTableRow(results.insertId,inputFullName,
   ➥prettyMonth,inputBirthdayDay,"birthdays");
             }
       });
   });
}

function removeBirthdayWebS(id) {
    db.transaction(function(tx) {
        tx.executeSql('DELETE FROM birthdays WHERE id=?', [id],
   ➥function() {
            //Dynamically remove the birthday from the list
            $("#b"+id).remove();
        });
    });
}
```

10. Finally, call the `addBirthday` function when a user clicks on the Store Birthday button in the document ready function:

```
$("#addBirthday").click( function(e) {
    var inputFullName=$("#fullname").val();
    var inputBirthdayMonth=$("#birthdayMonth").val();
    var inputBirthdayDay=$("#birthdayDay").val();
    addBirthdayWebS(db,inputFullName,inputBirthdayMonth,
➥inputBirthdayDay);
}); // end addBirthday
```

You can see an example of this application at www.html5in24hours.com/examples/birthday-list.html.

▲

Summary

This hour you learned about web storage and how you can store more data on the client side than you can with cookies. Web storage consists of local storage and session storage.

Local storage allows you to store a lot of data in name=value pairs that are stored locally on the hard drive. Items stored in this area are kept even if the browser is shut down or the computer is turned off.

Session storage allows you to store data in name=value pairs for the duration of a session. Session storage is specific to the window that it is opened in, so a user opening two windows to your website opens two different session storage instances.

This hour also covered two ways to store more structured data. These are Web SQL, which stores data using SQLite, and IndexedDB, which uses a JavaScript API to store data.

Q&A

Q. *If web storage is supported by all major browsers, shouldn't I just use it instead of cookies?*

A. As mentioned in this hour, cookies still have a valid purpose. They can be more secure, and so using them for session IDs is important. Plus, cookies are more familiar to most developers and so easier to implement. Also, users can delete local storage (just like they can cookies) and may be more likely to if it takes up too much space.

Q. *Do I have to know SQL to use Web SQL and IndexedDB?*

A. Because Web SQL uses SQLite to select and query the database, you need to write SQL calls to create and query the database. IndexedDB is easier to use because it doesn't require that you learn SQL.

Q. *If Web SQL Database was discontinued in 2010, why should I use it now? Won't it just be obsolete?*

A. Several browsers support Web SQL Database and not all of them currently support other client-side database options. Plus, it is a good way to familiarize yourself with the idea of client-side databases.

You should also keep in mind that Web SQL is the only database currently supported on mobile devices. If your application needs to work on mobile, then you should use it instead of IndexedDB. Ultimately, you should use the technology that best fits your users.

Q. *Are there easy ways to create structured data for storing in local storage?*

A. Many developers use JSON.stringify and JSON.parse to convert JavaScript string objects from JavaScript (stringify) and back (parse).

Q. *Can I use the same storage API to access different data stores?*

A. Data stores are protected in a similar fashion to cookies. If your script is on the same domain as the stores, then you can access it, even from different web pages, but you cannot access a data store set by another domain.

Workshop

The workshop contains quiz questions to help you process what you've learned in this chapter. Try to answer all the questions before you read the answers. See Appendix A, "Answers to Quizzes," for answers.

Quiz

1. What are three differences between web storage and cookies?

2. What is the difference between local storage and session storage?

3. What is the benefit to using Web SQL or IndexedDB instead of web storage?

4. How do you detect Web SQL or IndexedDB support?

Exercises

1. Add search functionality to the Birthday list application you built. Let your users search by name or month.

2. Add IndexedDB functionality to the Birthday list application. This will let the application work in Firefox. Add fallback support for browsers that don't support Web SQL or IndexedDB using basic web storage.

3. Convert the to-do list that you created in Hour 14, "Editing Content and User Interaction with HTML5," into a to-do list that saves the data to the local drive. The items should be stored in persistent storage and be retrieved when the user returns to the page.

Controlling the Browser History with the History API

What You'll Learn in This Hour:

▶ How to control the browser history

▶ How to add pages to the history to add forward and back navigation in dynamic sites

▶ Methods to navigate through the history

▶ How to use the History API to add and delete pages from the history

Anyone who has browsed the web is familiar with browser history, the sequence of pages that the user has visited, and everyone uses the back button (probably the most-used button on a web browser) to skip back to the previous page(s) in that history.

In the past, a web developer could use JavaScript to navigate the user through the history, but could not change the pages that were listed in the browser history (or the URL displaying in the browser window) without refreshing the browser and moving the user to the page.

In this hour you will learn how to create applications that have many dynamic parts such as applications built using Ajax and how to give them unique URLs by manipulating the history stack in the web browsers with the History API.

Why Control the Browser History?

The History API gives you the opportunity to change the history in your users' browsers. With the History API you can change the page titles and URLs that are already in the history as well as add and remove pages that are there.

While you can change the history to play games or mess around with the browsers, the most important reason for manipulating the browser history is to give your readers a way to navigate through your applications. Before the History API a scenario like this might happen:

1. The user comes to your Ajax photo gallery.

2. He navigates through 14 pages and then has to go.

3. He bookmarks the URL to come back later.

4. Later, when he returns to the bookmark, he isn't on page 14, he's on the first page, because the URL is to the first page.

This happens because Ajax updates only the photo and description and not the URI (Uniform Resource Indicator) of the page. When the user returns, the bookmark points to the main page, which is where he's taken.

Watch
Out!

> **The History API Does Not Create Pages**
>
> Just because you have created a URL in the history does not make that page suddenly exist on your website. If a user bookmarks one of your History API–generated URLs, you should have some fallback option that tells the browser what to display when that page is accessed directly. The easiest way is to create the page manually.

With the History API, you can give each picture in the photo gallery a unique URL that can be bookmarked and visited. When your user leaves and returns he will be on the fourteenth page, rather than the first, even though the HTML document is still the original document. In a normal web application, if the URL doesn't change, bookmarking it bookmarks the first page only.

The History API also helps your application load more quickly because you can use Ajax to refresh just the parts of the page that have changed, rather than having to do a page refresh to get a new URL. Fewer HTTP requests results in faster applications.

The History API is very effective when you have applications that have a series of events, such as pages in a document or a photo gallery. However, you can use the History API whenever you use Ajax to control the state of a page to give your users a new URL without a refresh of the page.

In many ways, the History API is very boring. It makes the browser do what users would expect the browser to do. When something about an application changes, users expect to be able to bookmark and share that new state. By using the History API to add URLs to the history, this type of bookmarking is now possible.

History API Methods

The three history methods you should already be familiar with are

- **history.back()**—This takes the user back one step in the history.

- **history.forward()**—This takes the user forward one step in the history.

- **history.go()**—This allows the user to move forward and back relative to the current page (index 0). To allow the user to move back one page such as in the back() method, you write history.go(-1). To move the user forward one page such as in the forward() method, you write history.go(1).

Internet Explorer Allows Strings in the go() Method

If your audience uses only Internet Explorer, you can put URL strings in the go() method and move through the history by URL. However, this method is not supported in other browsers—they use integers.

Did you Know?

The HTML5 History API adds two new methods to help you control the history, and not just navigate it:

- **pushState()**—This assigns a new URI to the current state in the browser window.

- **replaceState()**—This replaces the current entry in the history with a new one, again using the current state in the browser window.

You can also use three objects when working with the history:

- **history.length**—This displays the number of entries in the full history for this browser window.

- **history.state**—This returns the current state object.

- **window.onpopstate**—This is a new event on the window object that fires when the history changes.

Using the History API

The History API is currently supported by Android 2.2, Chrome 8+, Firefox 4+, iOS 4.2.1+, Opera 11.5+, and Safari 5+. However, support in Safari and iOS is buggy so you should test your application extensively on iOS and Safari before release. Also,

```
function getArticleList(page) {
    var length = articles.length;
    var counter = (parseInt(page)-1)*10 +10;
    var index = (parseInt(page) -1) * 10;
    var lastItem = index+10 > length ? length : index+10;

    // set page number
    $("#pageNum").html("Page number: "+page);

    if (page == "1") {
        $("#prev").attr('disabled', 'disabled');
    } else {
        $("#prev").removeAttr('disabled');
    }

    if (counter > length) {
        $("#next").attr('disabled', 'disabled');
    } else {
        $("#next").removeAttr('disabled');
    }

    // 10 articles per page
    $("#articles").empty();
    for (var i=index; i<lastItem; i++) {
        $("#articles").append('<li><a href="'+articles[i][0]+'">'+
➥articles[i][2]+'</a> Written: '+articles[i][1]);
    }
}

// this extension from jQuery Howto
//http://jquery-howto.blogspot.com/2009/09/
➥get-url-parameters-values-with-jquery.html
$.extend({
  getUrlVars: function(){
    var vars = [], hash;
    var hashes = window.location.href.slice(
➥window.location.href.indexOf('?') + 1).split('&');
    for(var i = 0; i < hashes.length; i++)
    {
      hash = hashes[i].split('=');
      vars.push(hash[0]);
      vars[hash[0]] = hash[1];
    }
    return vars;
  },
  getUrlVar: function(name){
    return $.getUrlVars()[name];
  }
});

</script>
</body>
</html>
```

You can see this page online at www.html5in24hours.com/examples/
history-api-example-no-history.html.

When you click the previous and next buttons in the application, the page updates,
but the URL stays the same. No matter what page you bookmark, you will always be
returned to the first page in the list.

Changing the URL with the History API

You could easily convert the example application to incorporate URLs for each page
because the URL functionality is already built in. If you visit
www.html5in24hours.com/examples/history-api-example-no-history.html?page=5
you will see the items from page 5 in the list. While you can get to page 5 by clicking on the next button, you won't see that URL, and if you try to bookmark page 5
you will end up on page 1 the next time you visit that bookmark.

In order to make this application work better, you need to update the URL in the history. To update the URL in the history, you would write:

```
window.history.pushState(state object, title, url)
```

The State Object Is Mostly Ignored

Most browsers currently ignore the first attribute, the `state object`. Firefox
stores state objects to the disk so that the pages can be restored after a restart.
There is a limit of 640KB in the state object, and you should write it as a JSON
representation.

By the Way

The data state isn't required for this application, so you can leave it blank, and the
title isn't used by most browsers, so you can leave that blank as well. This simple
function (called when the previous and next buttons are clicked on) will enhance the
application's usability:

```
function changeURL(page) {
    var baseUrl = "http://www.html5in24hours.com/examples/
➥history-api-examples.html";
    var newUrl = page != "1" ? baseUrl+ "?page="+page : baseUrl;
    if (hasHistoryApi()) {
        history.pushState(null, null, newUrl);
    }
}
```

To make this more functional in Firefox, you can set the data or state object to a
JSON notation, with whatever information you want. For instance, maybe you want
to include the page name and author information:

```
var stateObject = {
    title: 'History API Examples - Page '+page,
    createdOn: date,
    author: 'Jennifer Kyrnin'
};
```

You then include that variable in your `pushState` call:

```
history.pushState(stateObject, null, newUrl);
```

> ### The Title Is Universally Ignored
>
> The second parameter in the `pushState` and `replaceState()` methods is the title. However, this parameter is currently ignored by every browser. You can include a title for the page, or leave it as `null`. Including a title may make your scripts more future-proofed, as browsers begin to support it.

One thing about this application is that the previous and next buttons both set the URL, so the back button will continue to work. However, in most situations, telling the browser what it should do if the back button is clicked is a good idea. In other words, tell the browser that when the back button is clicked it should fake "moving backwards" to the previous URL, again without an HTTP request. You do this by adding a `popstate` listener on the `window` element:

```
window.addEventListener("popstate", action);
```

Here is how you would add the `popstate` listener to the articles application:

```
$(window).bind("popstate", function(e) {
    page = $.getUrlVar('page');
    if (!page) {
        page ="1";
    }
    getArticleList(page);
});
```

▼ **Try It Yourself**

Creating a Photo Gallery with the History API

In this Try It Yourself, you will create a photo gallery of images that works with or without JavaScript or the History API. You will create an index file for your photo gallery and hidden files for each of the photos.

1. Build your hidden data files. Put them in a directory called `photogallery` and build one file for each photo. These files will have just the HTML required to add the photo to your application:

```
<article id="photogallery">
    <h1>Shasta</h1>
    <figure>
        <img src="/images/pets/shasta1.jpg" alt="Shasta">
        <figcaption>
            <p>Couch potato
        </figcaption>
    </figure>
    <nav id="gallerynav">
        <p><a href="mckinley1.html" rel="next" id="next">Next</a>
        <a href="rambler1.html" rel="prev" id="prev">Previous</a>
    </nav>
</article>
```

Save them in the `photogallery` directory with the filename you used in the next and previous links.

2. Build an `index.html` page and preload it with your first photo:

```
<!DOCTYPE HTML>
<html>
<head>
<meta charset="UTF-8">
<title>Photogallery</title>
<meta name="viewport" content="width=device-width"/>
<script src="jquery.min.js"></script>
</head>

<body>
<div id="decimal"></div>
<article id="photogallery">
    <h1>Shasta</h1>
    <figure>
        <img src="/images/pets/shasta1.jpg" alt="Shasta">
        <figcaption>
            <p>Couch potato
        </figcaption>
    </figure>
    <nav id="gallerynav">
        <p><a href="mckinley1.html" rel="next" id="next">Next</a>
        <a href="rambler1.html" rel="prev" id="prev">Previous</a>
    </nav>
</article>
<script src="/photogallery/photogallery.js"></script>
</body>
</html>
```

3. Create the `photogallery.js` file and put it in the `photogallery` directory.

4. Add a function to switch the images, using Ajax and jQuery:

```
function switchPhoto(href) {
    var req;
    if (href.split("/").pop() == "index.html") {
```

```
        href = "/photogallery/shasta1.html";
    } else {
        href = "/photogallery/" + href.split("/").pop();
    }
    req = $.get(href, {},function() {
        $("#photogallery").html(req.responseText);
        buildLinks();
    return true;
    });
    return false;
}
```

This function checks whether the page is the index page, and if it is, changes the photo to switch to the first page (shasta1.html). If it's not an index page it passes the URL to the browser unchanged. It then switches the photo based on the href attribute of the next or previous link that was clicked.

5. Inside the switchPhoto() function is a buildLinks() function that you should add to the script file:

```
function buildLinks() {
    $("#prev,#next").click(function(e) {
        switchPhoto($(this).attr("href"))
        var newURL = "/photogallery/" + $(this).attr("href");
        history.pushState(null, null, newURL);
        e.preventDefault();
    });
}
```

This function ensures that the links are reset to the new URLs, and it also sets the browser URL bar with this line:

```
history.pushState(null, null, newURL);
```

If you want to set the state object or the title, you can change those here.

6. Check whether the History API is supported, and then run buildLinks() when the application is ready using the following:

```
$(document).ready(function(e) {
    if (!hasHistoryApi()) { return; }
    buildLinks();

});
function hasHistoryApi() {
    return !!(window.history && history.pushState);
}
```

7. Bind a popstate listener on the window object so that the back button works correctly:

```
$(window).bind("popstate", function(e) {
    switchPhoto(location.pathname);
});
```

You can see an example of this application at www.html5in24hours.com/
examples/history-api-examples-photogallery.html.

Dangers and Annoyances of the History API

The History API adds a lot of useful features to web applications, but it can cause
problems, too. If you stay aware of the potential problems, you can create web
applications that are more user friendly than ones that don't use the History API.

History API Works Only on the Same Domain

If you work on websites with multiple domains, the History API can be annoying
because it will only allow you to change URLs on the same domain as the page is on.

The History API has this security built in. When you try to change the history to a
new domain, nothing will happen. In other words, suppose your application is
located at http://www.html5in24hours.com/. Now suppose you attempt to change
the URL to a different domain; for example:

```
history.replaceState(null,null,"http://webdesign.about.com/");
```

If you do this nothing will happen. The browser will ignore that line as if no request
were made, and the URL in the browser window will stay the same.

Phishing Schemes with the History API

Some sites can be negatively affected by the History API—specifically sites with large
numbers of contributors.

For example, most universities have large websites that include areas of the site on
the same domain that students can use to put up their own pages and applications.

A malicious student could set up a phishing scheme to collect student usernames
and passwords by writing a page that looks like the standard login page and then
changing the URL with the replaceState() method to make users think they are
filling in the correct login page.

If you run a large website with untrusted contributors, you should consider moving
them to a separate domain for use of the History API, or disabling scripting alto-
gether for those users.

You can see a simple example of this issue at my About.com site. I don't conduct any phishing, but I can change the URL of the page: http://webdesign.about.com/library/bl-testing-history-api.htm. If you reload the page after the URL has changed, you will be taken to a completely different page on my site. If you then reload the page, you will go to that new page.

Annoying Animated URLs

Another, less dangerous but more annoying aspect of the History API is that it gives developers the ability to animate the URL. You can try it out here: www.html5in24hours.com/examples/history-api-examples-scroller.html.

The problem with animating the URL (beyond the fact that that type of animation is annoying) is that if you're using WebKit browsers on the Macintosh (Chrome and Safari) you can't get out of the page. Safari will let you navigate to a bookmark to leave, but Chrome will ignore even that request. The only way to leave the page in Chrome for Mac is to refresh the page, which usually results in a 404 error; close the browser window; or click on a link on the page.

If you must animate the URL bar, give your users a way to turn it off such as with a button or link on the page. Even if their browser doesn't prevent them from leaving the page, the animation feature is still very distracting.

Summary

The first thing you learned this hour is that the History API does not add a lot of flash to your applications. In fact, if you're using it right most people won't even realize anything fancy is going on. At most, they might think your pages are loading more quickly.

You learned how to use the History API to make an application work so that it is nearly invisible to the user, and that is what makes the History API so important. Using an application that can't be bookmarked is not a good experience for the user, so in this hour you learned how to fix a common problem in Ajax web pages where the current state cannot be bookmarked. Finally, you learned about some problems that the History API can cause and how to deal with them.

Q&A

Q. *One of the reasons I use Ajax to build web applications is so that I don't have to create all the pages on the site. But it seems like you are saying I need to create the pages that I add to the history so that if someone bookmarks them, they will be able to get to them. Do I really have to do that?*

A. Making sure that any URL you add to the history can be accessed from your website is a good idea. You can do this in many ways, so that you don't have to maintain dozens of extra pages. Some effective methods include:

> ▶ **htaccess**—Use `.htaccess` scripts to redirect pages you created in the history

> ▶ **JavaScript**—Use JavaScript and query strings as this hour did in the "Changing the URL with the History API" section to point to the same page, and update it with a script

> ▶ **PHP or other server language**—Use PHP, ASP, or another server-side scripting language to read query strings and update the page

Q. *Why are the state object and title in the* `pushState()` *method if they aren't used?*

A. These are included in the specification so that there is future functionality. The state object lets you pass along structured data with the changed URL. The title lets you define what the change is.

Q. *What about using the* `location.hash`*—do I still need to use it in my Ajax pages?*

A. Many Ajax authors got used to using `location.hash` to assign unique URLs to parts of their applications. This alternative is still viable and could be used as a fallback option for browsers that don't support the History API.

To use `location.hash`, you would change the URL by changing only the hash portion of the URL (everything after the # sign). You can change the hash without reloading the page, thus adding a unique URL for that new document:

```
window.location.hash = newHash;
```

You can find out more about this topic at the Ajax Patterns website (http://ajaxpatterns.org/Unique_URLs).

Workshop

The workshop contains quiz questions to help you process what you've learned in this chapter. Try to answer all the questions before you read the answers. See Appendix A, "Answers to Quizzes," for answers.

Quiz

1. What are the five History API methods? Which ones are new and how do they work?

2. True or False: Changing the URL with `pushState()` will create a new web page.

3. What does the `onpopstate` event do and why is it important?

4. True or False: Only one parameter exists for the `replaceState()` method.

5. True or False: You can include any data you want in the state object parameter.

6. True or False: You can change the browser history to any URL you want.

Exercises

1. Rewrite the photo gallery with a state object so that browsers such as Firefox can save the state in the event of a crash. You should change the state object to reflect the page name and the date.

2. Add in fallback functionality to the photo gallery so that browsers without History API support can still use it. The best way would be to change the URL to include a hash of the next filename.

3. Convert the photo gallery application into a one-page application, and change the URL as the user scrolls down to see the additional images. You will need to give each photo a unique ID, so that you can use it in the hash on the URL.

HOUR 23

Adding Location Detection with Geolocation

What You'll Learn in This Hour:

▶ How to detect location data with the Geolocation API

▶ How to handle privacy concerns with geolocation

▶ How to use APIs to work with location data

Geolocation allows web designers to solicit the physical location of their users and then provide information to them based on their location. The obvious use of this feature is in maps and directions, but you can also use it for games or promotions based on people's locations.

In this hour you will learn how to solicit the location data from your users and get some ideas for how to use that data after you have it. You will learn about how privacy concerns have been mitigated by the API itself. You will also learn how to build an application using two different mapping APIs.

What Is Geolocation?

The Geolocation API lets users share their location data with websites they trust. The browser gets this information from many different sources, including:

▶ The IP address

▶ The wireless network connection

▶ The cell towers a phone is using

▶ A dedicated global-positioning system (GPS) in the device

What's important to note is that the API doesn't care how that information is received. It doesn't require that users have GPS-enabled devices, just that the browsers they are using can figure out a location in some fashion.

The IP address provides the least-accurate form of geolocation. Generally, it is only accurate to the city level. Smartphone web browsers often use the wireless network to get locations accurate to 20 meters. Triangulation via cell towers is accurate to around 100 meters. Devices with an embedded GPS are typically accurate to around 10 meters in the United States, but this accuracy can change depending upon local laws defining the maximum accuracy. Some countries require GPS to be less accurate for national security.

Geolocation Accuracy Isn't Always Accurate

Keep in mind when you're building applications that the accuracy of geolocation can be hit or miss. In my tests at a desktop computer, I found that most of the browsers could pinpoint my location to around 61 meters from where I am. However, Internet Explorer 9 placed my location at least a mile west of where I am. The next day, on the same computer, Chrome placed my location as almost 5 miles north.

The Geolocation API is fairly well supported by browsers. It works in these browser versions and newer:

- ▶ Android 2.0
- ▶ Chrome 5.0
- ▶ Firefox 3.5
- ▶ Internet Explorer 9
- ▶ iOS 3.0
- ▶ Opera 10.6
- ▶ Safari 5.0

The API provides the latitude and longitude to JavaScript on the page, and the JavaScript can pass it to server scripts to do mapping or provide information about local businesses or other things.

Uses for Geolocation

It may not seem terribly useful at first, but you can use geolocation in many different ways to provide more information to your users. Some of the ways you can use geolocation include:

▶ **Mapping**—Maps and directions are the most common use. Geolocation lets you pinpoint where users are and guide them exactly where they want to go.

▶ **Photo locator**—Identifying photo locations is a useful feature. Many mobile devices and cameras include location data with the photos, which can be used in web applications as well.

▶ **Fraud detection**—Fraud detection using location data makes the internet safer. Online banking applications can use location data to help authenticate users.

▶ **Targeted advertising**—Targeted advertising can make the ads more relevant to the users by advertising local options, which are more likely to be clicked on.

▶ **Gaming**—Many online games already use location data to check in and gather points and prizes.

Many legitimate concerns surround the issue of the privacy and security implications of geolocation. However, more people are opting to allow websites to view and use location data. The more interesting applications there are that look fun or useful to use, the more users will opt in.

Using the Geolocation API

The Geolocation API provides a new global `navigator` object: `navigator.geolocation`. So, to detect support for geolocation, simply detect whether the browser has that object:

```
function supports_geolocation() {
    return !!navigator.geolocation;
}
```

You can use three methods with the Geolocation API:

▶ `getCurrentPosition()`—This method returns your current location. It takes two callback functions, `success` and `failure`, and options.

▶ `watchPosition()`—This method acts similarly to the preceding one, but continues to poll to determine whether your position has changed. It takes the same properties as `getCurrentPosition()` and returns an ID number that you can use to stop watching the location.

▶ `clearWatch()`—This is the method you use to stop watching a position. You pass it the number from the `watchPosition()` method.

Making a call to either getCurrentPosition() or watchPosition()creates a position object. Eight properties are on the position object:

▶ **coords.latitude**—The latitude of the position in decimal degrees. This will always be on the object

▶ **coords.longitude**—The longitude of the position in decimal degrees. This will always be on the object

▶ **coords.accuracy**—The accuracy of the position in meters. This will always be on the object

▶ **coords.altitude**—The distance above sea level of the position in meters

▶ **coords.altitudeAccuracy**—The accuracy of the position altitude in meters

▶ **coords.heading**—How the position has changed in degrees clockwise from true north compared to the last position

▶ **coords.speed**—How fast the position is changing in meters per second

▶ **timestamp**—The date and time of the position returned, such as a JavaScript Date() object

By the Way

> **Geolocation Distances Are Metric**
>
> When you receive location data from the Geolocation API, it will be delivered in meters and meters per second. If your application uses feet or miles, you will need to do conversions.

Other than the three properties that will always be returned (latitude, longitude, and accuracy), you may receive the other properties depending upon the capabilities of the device and the positioning server it talks to.

If something goes wrong in collecting geolocation data, there is also a positionError object that returns a numerical code that tells what happened. The codes are

▶ **PERMISSION_DENIED (1)**—When the user denies your application access to the data

▶ **POSITION_UNAVAILABLE (2)**—When the network is down or the satellites can't be contacted

▶ **TIMEOUT (3)**—When the network is up, but takes too long to calculate the position

▶ **UNKNOWN_ERROR (0)**—When anything else happens that prevents the position from being calculated and delivered

To use the getCurrentPosition() method, you call it in a function with a callback method for success and failure:

```
function getLocation() {
    navigator.geolocation.getCurrentPosition(mapIt, locationError);
}
```

Then the success method (mapIt() in the preceding line) uses the position object in some fashion:

```
function mapIt(position) {
    var lat = position.coords.latitude;
    var lon = position.coords.longitude;
    alert("You are at "+ lat +" latitude, and "+ lon +" longitude.");
}
```

while the error method (locationError() in the earlier snippet) provides feedback on any error received:

```
function locationError(error) {
    switch(error) {
        case 1:
            alert("Location services denied");
        break;
        case 2:
            alert("Could not contact location services network or
➥satellites");
        break;
        case 3:
            alert("Location services timed out");
        break;
        default:
            alert("Location could not be determined.");
    }
}
```

The watchPosition() method uses the same structure as the getCurrentPosition() method, but it returns a number. This number is what you use to stop watching the position with the clearWatch() method. So, to use the watchPosition() method, you call it with success and error callbacks:

```
var watch;
function getLocation() {
    watch = navigator.geolocation.watchPosition(mapIt, locationError);
}
```

If you then want to stop watching that user's location change, you would call clearWatch() with that number:

```
function clearLocation() {
    navigator.geolocation.clearWatch(watch);
}
```

Using Other Location Data Options

You can set three other options with the getCurrentPosition() and watchPosition() methods. These are placed in the third argument, the positionOptions object, for these methods. The options are

- ▶ **enableHighAccuracy**—A boolean property that determines how accurate the data needs to be. The default is false.

- ▶ **timeout**—A number in milliseconds to indicate when the method should stop trying to get location data.

- ▶ **maximumAge**—A number in milliseconds to indicate how current the current position data needs to be.

Both Android and iOS devices support two methods for determining location: triangulation with cellphone towers and using dedicated GPS hardware on the device. Triangulation is fast, but doesn't give very accurate data. GPS hardware is a lot more accurate, but it can be a lot slower than triangulation to provide location data. Plus, it won't work if the device is indoors or it can't access the satellites.

Not All Mobile Devices Have GPS or Cellphone Hardware

Most Android devices on the market have both a cellphone and a GPS in them, but the newer Android tablets are coming out with Wi-Fi only models that don't have cellphone hardware and may not have GPS hardware. iPods and some iPad models do not have either. These devices use IP address mapping from an Apple database of IP addresses for most of their location services.

If you don't need extremely high accuracy for geolocation, you can set the enableHighAccuracy property to false (or leave it as the default) so that your application loads more quickly. Remember that for things such as turn-by-turn directions, high accuracy is important, whereas showing the location of nearby pizza parlors doesn't need nearly as accurate a result.

To enable high accuracy, you write the following:

```
getCurrentPosition(mapIt, locationError, {enableHighAccuracy: true});
```

The timeout starts after the user has approved your application to get location data. After that timeout is reached, the position methods will return an error code 3. There is no default, so if you don't set a timeout, your application will keep trying until the user gives up or the user agent does. To set a timeout of a minute and a half (90,000 milliseconds), write:

```
getCurrentPosition(mapIt, locationError, {timeout: 90000});
```

The `maximumAge` property is useful for indicating how long location data will be valuable to the application. This property helps speed up the application by only requesting the information from the device when the maximum age limit is reached. So if you asked for data at 3 p.m. and the maximum age is two minutes, if you polled again at 3:01 p.m. the device doesn't recalculate the position, it simply returns the same data as before. To set the maximum age to two minutes (120,000 milliseconds), write:

```
getCurrentPosition(mapIt, locationError, {maximumAge: 120000});
```

You can also put all these options together into a variable, and deliver them that way:

```
var positionOptions = {
    enableHighAccuracy: true,
    timeout: 90000,
    maximumAge: 120000
};
getCurrentPosition(mapIt, locationError, positionOptions);
```

You can use these same options in the `watchPosition()` method.

Fallback Options for Older Browsers

Although geolocation has good support on modern mobile devices, Internet Explorer 8 and other older browsers don't support it.

Older Mobile Devices Have Device-Specific Geolocation

Although modern mobile devices support the Geolocation API well, older phones such as phones from Blackberry, Nokia, Palm, and OMTP BONDI built and supported their own Geolocation APIs. If you need to support these older devices, you need to provide fallback options for them as well.

Google and MIT provide a solution not just for Internet Explorer, but for older feature phones and smartphones that may have location support, but that don't support the Geolocation API. It's called geo.js (http://code.google.com/p/geo-location-javascript/) with Google Gears. Google Gears has geolocation built in and is used as one of the fallback options for geo.js. As of this writing, geo.js (with Gears) supports

▶ iOS

▶ Android

▶ Opera Mobile

- ▶ Blackberry

- ▶ Internet Explorer

- ▶ Nokia

- ▶ Opera Mobile

- ▶ webOS

- ▶ Windows Mobile

- ▶ And others

To use geo.js, you download geo.js and install both Google Gears and geo.js at the bottom of your document:

```
<script src="http://code.google.com/apis/gears/gears_init.js"></script>
<script src="geo.js"></script>
```

You then check for location services from any source with the `geo_position_js.init()` method. This returns `true` if the browser can provide location services, either through the Geolocation API or Gears.

```
if(geo_position_js.init()) {
    geo_position_js.getCurrentPosition(success_callback,error_callback);
}
```

As you can see in the preceding code, the `getCurrentPosition()` method is called in the same way it's called in the Geolocation API, with success and error callbacks.

In the success callback, you can then grab the position coordinates just like you would in the HTML5 API:

```
function success_callback(position) {
    var lat = position.coords.latitude;
    var lon = position.coords.longitude;
    alert('You are at:\nLat: '+lat+' Long: '+lon);
}
```

Keep in mind that geo.js does not support the `watchPosition()` method, so if you need to get continuous location data, you will need to poll `getCurrentPosition()` in your application manually.

Privacy and Geolocation

In regard to telling websites and applications where they are, people are very concerned about privacy, and the Geolocation API will not work without getting explicit permission from users to access their location.

You Can Get Location Data in Other Ways

If you've visited the web lately, you have probably seen ads that are related to where you live. These are not using geolocation to get your location, but rather your IP address. Many companies provide web developers access to databases that correlate IP addresses with physical locations. These may not be as accurate as true geolocation, but can be a way to bypass refused location services.

Web browsers will never force anyone to reveal their location to a remote server. The first time a user visits a page that wants to use the Geolocation API, the browser must prompt the user to find out whether that is okay. Figure 23.1 shows how Android, Chrome, Firefox, Internet Explorer, and iOS ask for permission to use the Geolocation API.

FIGURE 23.1
Android, Chrome, Internet Explorer, Firefox, and iOS (top to bottom) asking for permission to track a user's location.

This prompt has several interesting features that you should know about when building your location-aware applications:

▶ Users can switch away from the prompt to a new window by tabbing to or clicking on the "Learn More..." link to find out more information.

▶ The prompt is unconditional, and will appear every time the website attempts to use location services until the user chooses to share or not share.

▶ The prompt blocks the API until it has an answer, so you cannot get location data until the user has chosen to share it.

▶ Users can choose to never be asked again for your website or even turn off location services entirely

If a user chooses to deny you access to his location, your best response as an ethical web designer is to respect that choice and tell him that the application won't work for him. As mentioned earlier, you can get general location data from the IP address in other ways, but some people might consider that unethical, especially if the user denied access. The data is not always as accurate, but it can give you general data such as the city, state, and country an IP is originating from.

One site that provides free GeoTargeting by IP address is http://hostip.info/. For example, you can get the location of the server for this book's companion website by typing:

```
http://api.hostip.info/get_html.php?ip=69.164.199.170&position=true
```

> **Turning Off Location Services Is Easy**
>
> Both Android and iOS make turning location services on and off easy. On the Android, you use the Settings menu under Location & Security. On iOS, you use the Settings under Location Services. In iOS you can turn off all services, or choose the apps you want to allow and disallow. This will not turn off location data generated from IP addresses.

Geolocation by IP address is unreliable, as mentioned earlier. Plus, your users can deliberately block the information by using proxy servers and anonymizing systems.

Creating a Mobile Geolocation Application

The most common use of geolocation is to provide maps and directions to and from locations. But chances are you don't have your own mapping service that you can tie into. So instead, you need to use a maps API. You can choose from several map APIs, including:

▶ **Bing Maps API**—Bing Maps API is relatively new, but it offers many features for mobile and web applications (www.microsoft.com/maps/developers/web.aspx).

▶ **Google Maps JavaScript API**—Possibly the best-known maps API, the Google Maps JavaScript API lets you create solutions for both desktop and mobile devices (http://code.google.com/apis/maps/documentation/javascript/).

▶ **MapQuest Open API**—This service uses OpenStreetMap data to generate static maps, directions, elevation information, and more (http://open.mapquestapi.com/).

▶ **OviMaps API**—This is a maps API from Nokia, and it is the recommended alternative to the Yahoo! Maps API, which is shutting down in late 2011 (http://api.maps.ovi.com/).

Try It Yourself ▼

Building a Simple Mapping Application

This Try It Yourself shows you how to use the Bing Maps API to create an application that maps the user's current location.

1. Make sure you have a Bing Maps developer key. Sign in at www.bingmapsportal.com/ and go to Create or View Keys to create a new key.

2. Create a standard HTML5 page with jQuery:

```
<!DOCTYPE HTML>
<html>
<head>
    <meta charset="UTF-8">
    <title>Untitled Document</title>
    <meta name="viewport" content="width=device-width"/>
    <script src="jquery.min.js"></script>
</head>
<body>
</body>
</html>
```

3. Add the following in the <head> to link to the Bing Maps API:

```
<script charset="UTF-8" type="text/javascript"
src="http://ecn.dev.virtualearth.net/mapcontrol/mapcontrol.ashx?v=7.0">
```

4. For the HTML, create an area to indicate the support of geolocation:

```
<section>
<h2>Where Are You Now?</h2>
<p id="supports">Your browser does not support geolocation</p>
</section>
```

5. You should also include a section to display the map, the map options, and the trigger to get the map:

```
<section id="getMapInfo">
<h3>Map Options</h3>
<p>Zoom level:
Orbit (1)
<input id="zoomLvl" value="11" type="range" min="1" max="20">
Your yard (20)
<p><button id="getGeo">Get My Location</button></p>
<div id="map"></div>
</section>
```

6. In a <script> element at the bottom of the page, write the function to check for geolocation and add that to the document ready function:

```
$(document).ready(function(e) {
    if (supportsGeoLocation()) {
        $("#supports").html("Your browser supports GeoLocation. ");
    } else {
        $("#supports").html("Your browser does not support
➥GeoLocation. ");
        $("#getMapInfo").hide(); // hide the button and map section
    }
});

function supportsGeoLocation() {
    return !!navigator.geolocation;
}
```

7. Add a click function to the button to start the mapping process:

```
$("#getGeo").click(function(e) {
    getLocation();
    return false;
});
```

8. Add the getLocation() function:

```
function getLocation() {
    navigator.geolocation.getCurrentPosition(mapIt, locationError);
}
```

9. Add the error callback function locationError() to provide information on what error occurred:

```
function locationError(error) {
    switch(error) {
        case 1:
            alert("Location services denied");
        break;
        case 2:
            alert("Could not contact location services network or
➥satellites");
```

```
        break;
    case 3:
        alert("Location services timed out");
        break;
    default:
        alert("Location could not be determined.");
    }
    $("#getMapInfo").hide();
    $("#supports").append(" There was an problem mapping your
➥location, please try again later.");
}
```

10. Write the `mapIt()` function. This is where you use the Bing Maps API key or other mapping API of your choice:

```
function mapIt(position) {
    var lat = position.coords.latitude;
    var lon = position.coords.longitude;
    var zoom = parseInt($("#zoomLvl").val());
    var map, mapOptions, center, pin, pinOptions;

    // show a map from Bing
    mapOptions = {
        credentials: 'YOUR BING MAPS KEY',
        center: new Microsoft.Maps.Location(lat, lon),
        zoom: zoom
    };
    map = new Microsoft.Maps.Map(document.getElementById('map'),
➥mapOptions);
    $("#map").after('<h3 class="after">You are Here</h3>');
}
```

Be sure to change the credentials to your Bing Maps API key.

11. You might also want to add a custom pin to the map, so that you can easily see where the location is centered. Add these lines after the `map = new Microsoft.Maps...` line:

```
center = map.getCenter();
pinOptions = {
    icon: "/images/house.png",
    width: 16,
    height: 16,
    draggable: true
};
pin = new Microsoft.Maps.Pushpin(center, pinOptions);
map.entities.push(pin);
```

Figure 23.2 shows this application in Safari showing the browser's current location in Washington state. You can try this application yourself at http://www.html5in24hours.com/examples/geolocation-examples.html.

FIGURE 23.2
Safari getting a
location with the
Geolocation API.

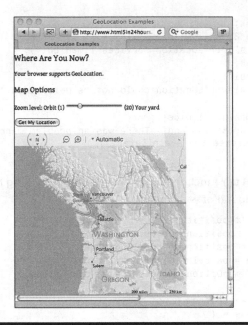

Another easy way to add static maps based on location data to your site is to use
the MapQuest Open API for static maps. This option just uses an image with URL
parameters.

To set up a static map, you create an image with the source pointing to
`http://open.mapquestapi.com/staticmap/v3/getmap?` with the following
parameters:

- **center**—The latitude and longitude of the center of the map
  (center=*latitude,longitude*)

- **zoom**—The zoom level from 1 to 16 (zoom=14)

- **size**—The width and height of the map (size=400,400)

For example:

```
<img src="http://open.mapquestapi.com/staticmap/v3/getmap?
center=40.0378,-76.305801&size=400,400&zoom=12">
```

All the map APIs also offer functionality to do things such as provide routes and
directions; add multiple pins to the maps you display; and display maps in views
such bird's eye view, aerial satellite map, or plain street maps. Find the API that you
like best and learn how to use it.

Summary

This hour taught you that location data can be collected by web browsers in many ways. Some, such as GPS tools inside smartphones, can be very accurate, whereas others, such as IP address data mapping, can be inexact, showing the location of the IP address provider rather than the true location of the device or computer. But as you learned this hour, browsers and devices that have access to the Geolocation API can provide that information to you for your web applications.

You learned about the navigator object `navigator.geolocation` and three methods (`getCurrentPosition()`, `watchPosition()`, and `clearWatch()`) to get the current location of the user agent. You also learned that when you get the position, you get the latitude and longitude of the device or computer and other information, such as the elevation or speed and heading, may be delivered as well.

This hour you also learned about some of the privacy concerns surrounding geolocation. Many people don't feel comfortable letting an unknown website view their location. The Geolocation API recognizes that and will not provide that information until the user has opted in to allow access to his location.

Finally, at the end of this hour you learned how to make a simple mapping application using two different map APIs. Although the Geolocation API will return location data in the form of latitude and longitude, using that data without some other program to turn it into something useful can be difficult. The map APIs convert location data into maps.

Q&A

Q. Why is the location data delivered so inaccurate? Why does it fluctuate even though I'm not moving?

A. The data is inaccurate because of how the data is gathered. When the location is determined by the IP address, location accuracy often depends upon how accurate the databases are that correlate IPs to locations. With internet service providers doling out IPs dynamically, keeping a database of locations accurate can be difficult. As soon as a new IP address is issued, any location data that was generated before the update is incorrect again.

Cell towers use triangulation to set the location. Although, this can be more accurate than IP addresses, if the towers are far apart or only two can be polled at a given time, the accuracy will decrease.

Wireless networks are getting more accurate with their location data because the network providers use tools from companies such as Skyhook (www.skyhookwireless.com/) that have ways of pinpointing locations. Several competing protocols are available for pinpointing user location.

Even GPS units can fluctuate in accuracy if the device is indoors, if it is an extremely cloudy day, if the device is under heavy tree cover, or if only two satellites are visible in orbit. Like cell towers, they use triangulation to determine location, and the more satellites that can see the device, the more accurate the location data will be (to the legally mandated maximum accuracy).

Q. *What does the* `navigator.geolocation` *object do?*

A. Simply referencing the `geolocation` object does not pull location data. This object is present in the browsers that support the Geolocation API and is what the geolocation methods are attached to. You must reference one of the two methods to request location data.

Q. *I don't want location data in latitude and longitude, I want it in an address form. Is there some way to get that information instead?*

A. The process of turning an address into a latitude and longitude is called geocoding. The opposite is called reverse geocoding. If you are interested in doing more with geocoding, Google offers a Geocoding API that has support for reverse geocoding (http://code.google.com/apis/maps/documentation/geocoding/).

Workshop

The workshop contains quiz questions to help you process what you've learned in this chapter. Try to answer all the questions before you read the answers. See Appendix A, "Answers to Quizzes," for answers.

Quiz

1. What should you look for to detect whether the browser supports geolocation?

2. What three properties will always be present on the `position` object?

3. What other properties may be present on the `position` object?

4. What can cause the error codes 1, 2, and 3?

5. When would you use the `enableHighAccuracy` property, and how do you use it?

Exercises

1. Convert the application you created in this hour to use geo.js as a fallback system.

2. Build an application that polls the location periodically and updates the map with the new location data.

3. Visit one of the other map API sites and rebuild the application using it instead.

Converting HTML5 Apps to Native Apps

What You'll Learn in This Hour:

▶ The difference between native and HTML5 applications

▶ Advantages of native and HTML5 apps

▶ How to convert HTML5 apps to native

▶ How to create icons for your mobile application

▶ How to test your applications on devices

▶ How to sell your apps in app stores

Creating mobile applications in HTML5 is great, but what if you want them to be sold in the various app stores for Android or in the iTunes Marketplace? For that you need to have a native application written in Objective C or Java.

Or do you?

This hour you will learn some of the ways native and HTML5 apps are different and how you can convert your HTML5 applications into native applications to sell in online marketplaces. You will also learn why you might or might not want to convert your HTML5 applications.

Comparing the Difference Between Native and HTML5 Apps

An HTML5 application is one that is run on a web server, usually in a web browser. A native application is one that runs directly on Android and iOS devices and is purchased or downloaded from the relevant app stores. The primary difference between HTML5 and native applications is that native applications use a programming language such as Objective C for iOS devices or Java for Android devices. With those languages you gain access to device-specific options such as the camera or push notifications.

As a web designer or web developer, you already know HTML, CSS, and JavaScript. However, you need to learn Objective C or Java or both to write native applications for iOS and Android.

In fact, this learning curve is often the reason that applications are only built for iOS or Android, rather than for both platforms. The more languages you have to write a program in, the more expensive that program becomes to build. Plus you must take into account not only build issues, but also maintenance.

> **Users Want All Platforms**
>
> If you go to nearly any software company's website, one of the most common questions you will see customers asking is, "When are you going to release a version on my platform?" Macintosh users want Windows games. Android users want iPhone apps, and so on. If you create a native app that only works on Android, if it gains any popularity at all you will start getting requests for it to be built on iOS (and then Blackberry and WebOS and so on).

Benefits of Native Applications

The biggest benefit of native applications over HTML5 applications is that they are generally faster. HTML5 applications have all the speed issues inherent in web pages, which primarily means that they work over HTTP and use a request/response mechanism. Every time an HTTP request is made, that adds more time to the application, waiting for the request to go out and return.

However, native applications offer some other benefits as well:

▶ **Push notifications**—These are notifications that are sent through an always-open IP connection to applications on iOS devices. Android has a similar feature called Cloud to Device Messaging.

▶ **Access to device hardware**—Most mobile devices have hardware such as a camera (or two), global positioning system (GPS), accelerometer, and so on. Although the GPS is accessed through the Geolocation API (discussed in Hour 23, "Adding Location Detection with Geolocation"), there are currently no APIs for cameras, accelerometers, or other device hardware for HTML5 applications.

▶ **File upload**—Native applications provide access to the file system in Android and to some files on iOS, but the HTML5 File API doesn't work on either operating system yet.

▶ **Access device files**—Native apps can interact with files on the devices such as photos and contacts, but these are hidden from HTML5 apps.

▶ **Better graphics than HTML5**—HTML5 has Canvas, but it is not going to create a full 3D experience (WebGL may change that as it gains in popularity).

▶ **In-app purchasing and advertising**—Arguably, it is possible to build in-app stores and advertising in HTML5 applications, but native apps have them pre-built by the app stores (such as iTunes). Plus, selling an app in an app store is easy, but HTML5 apps are just web pages that are more difficult to sell.

▶ **Offline access**—As you learned in Hour 20, "Offline Web Applications," HTML5 supports offline web applications. But a native application is already stored locally, so users don't need to access the web to start using the application.

Native applications have another benefit that is often overlooked: trust. Many users feel more comfortable using an application that they have downloaded from an app store than they do using a web page. Most users, if they are looking for a tool to do something, are more likely to go to an app store to find it than to a search engine.

Benefits of HTML5 Applications

Of course, using HTML5 applications has benefits as well. The biggest benefit to using HTML5 is that creating an application that runs on a wide variety of devices is relatively easy. This makes HTML5 application development much cheaper than native application development. You don't need to learn a new language and so development goes a lot more quickly as well. Many developers see HTML5 as a "write once, run anywhere" application language. Although HTML5 is not that functional yet, it's certainly closer to running anywhere with just one version of HTML than native app development is.

However, you shouldn't build an application in HTML5 just because doing so is easier than building a native app. If native applications run better than HTML5 applications, you owe it to your customers to build those types of applications instead. However, it's not precisely true that native applications work better. Several reasons exist why HTML5 applications work as well or better than native applications:

▶ **Users can't tell the difference**—In many cases, users can't tell that they are using an HTML5 application, a hybrid HTML5-native application, or a fully native application.

▶ **You can adjust the style for the device**—HTML5 apps can be viewed on any device that has a web browser, and with CSS3 media queries you can style the app to look however you want. HTML5 apps can look like a web page or an application, using the same code.

▶ **The functionality is coming**—HTML5 may not have support for every feature on a device, but it's coming. More and more APIs are being proposed every day to give web pages access to device hardware and software. Plus as you've learned in the previous hours, many APIs are already available for doing offline web pages, web storage, local databases, drag-and-drop, and so on. More functionality will keep coming.

▶ **HTML5 app performance is improving**—As more and more web developers learn techniques to speed up web pages, these techniques are applied to mobile HTML5 applications as well. Plus, many applications (such as news apps, mail, timers, and databases) don't necessarily need to be faster than they already are.

▶ **HTML5 is not device dependent**—As mentioned earlier, HTML5 works in desktop browsers as well as mobile devices, but this is important for more than just development purposes. Although mobile devices are popular, millions more desktop and laptop users exist than mobile, and if you want your application to be widely used, then you should design for the desktop market as well as mobile.

▶ **You're not locked into app stores**—Many different app stores exist for Android, and if you want to sell an app, you need to try to get your app in as many of them as you can. However, with an HTML5 app, you aren't locked into an app store. You create your application and then market it as you would any other web page.

HTML5 is an alternative to native applications, although in some situations (such as if you're building a huge graphical game) native applications are better to use. However, HTML5 makes creating applications for mobile devices possible for web developers without their having to learn new languages.

You can also create hybrid applications, which are a mix of HTML5 and native apps. Hybrid applications take a native feature, such as taking and using a photo, and embeds it in an HTML5 framework for the controls and user interface. Many native applications are just the website modified to be inside an application.

Converting to Native Apps

You can choose to build your application in HTML5 and then convert it into a native app. This option has most of the advantages of HTML5 apps and native apps.

You can use a few tools to convert HTML5 apps to native apps. Two of the best-known are

- PhoneGap (www.phonegap.com/)
- Appcelerator (www.appcelerator.com/)

Not All Devices Are Created Equal

When you build an HTML5 application, you have to worry about browsers, and the same is true when you convert your app to a native application. iOS and Android have different specifications, support different features, and can cause different headaches. Just keep that in mind while you're working on your conversion.

Note that Appcelerator is much more difficult to use to convert HTML5 applications to native applications than PhoneGap because that is not its primary function, which is to write native applications in Java. PhoneGap was built specifically to convert HTML5 apps to native apps.

What You Need to Start Converting

You need a few things to start converting your HTML5 application to a native application, whether you use PhoneGap or Appcelerator.

To build iOS applications you need:

- **Macintosh computer**—Apple requires that you build iOS apps on a Macintosh, and the software won't run on anything else.
- **Xcode**—This is the software you need to build and test your applications in an iPhone or iPad emulator.

You can get Xcode by joining the Apple iOS Developer Program (http://developer. apple.com/programs/ios/) for $99 per year. You should join the developer program if you are planning on putting your apps on the Apple App Store. The developer program also allows you to put your applications on your own iPhone and iPad devices to do additional testing.

You Can Buy Xcode Separately

Xcode is available from the Apple App Store (http://itunes.apple.com/us/app/ xcode/id422352214?mt=12) for $4.99. Buying it at the App Store lets you work on building your application and test it in an emulator before you commit to the $99 annual fee to join the Developer Program. However, you can't use it to put your application on your devices or upload it to the app store.

To build Android applications you need a few more things:

- ▶ **Eclipse Classic IDE**—This is a development environment that you'll use to manage your Android apps (www.eclipse.org/downloads/).

- ▶ **Android SDK**—The SDK is the development kit for building Android apps (http://developer.android.com/sdk/index.html).

- ▶ **ADT Plug-in**—This plug-in extends Eclipse to build Android applications. You install it from within Eclipse (http://developer.android.com/sdk/eclipse-adt.html#installing).

Note that you can build Android applications without using anything but the SDK from the command line, but Eclipse with the ADT plug-in makes the process much easier, and it's how Google recommends you build your applications.

Using PhoneGap to Convert to Native Apps

One of the great things about using PhoneGap to build native applications is that you just import your HTML right into the SDK, and PhoneGap does the rest. If you have built an application that works in Android and iOS, then using PhoneGap to convert it to a native app should work.

> **Another PhoneGap Option Coming Soon**
>
> PhoneGap, as of this writing, is beta testing an even easier way to turn your HTML5 into native applications. It's called PhoneGap:Build (https://build.phonegap.com/). With this tool, you create your HTML5 applications as you normally would, then upload them to PhoneGap:Build. PhoneGap:Build then converts your application into app store–ready apps for iOS, Android, and several other mobile devices.

▼ **Try It Yourself**

Building a Simple iOS Application in PhoneGap

Building an application in PhoneGap takes just a few steps. You don't need to know Objective C or even use JavaScript if you don't want to.

1. Download and install Xcode and the latest copy of PhoneGap.

2. In the PhoneGap iOS directory, run the installer package to install PhoneGap.

3. Open Xcode and create a new PhoneGap project.

4. Give your project a name and Company Identifier. You want your company ID to be in the format of a backwards URL: com.companyname. This will create a bundle identifier for you.

5. After your application is open in Xcode, right-click on the project name and choose Show in Finder.

6. Finder will show a folder called www. You need to drag that folder from Finder into Xcode onto your project.

7. Select Create Folder References for Any Added Folders, and click Finish.

8. Open the www folder and edit the `index.html` file. You can edit it with any HTML you want, but follow the comments if you want to add JavaScript.

9. Change the drop-down menu next to the Stop button to the version of simulator you want to test it on.

10. Click Run to see your app in an iPhone or iPad simulator.

As you can see, building an iOS application in PhoneGap is easy.

After you have the www folder inside your application, you can then edit the HTML in that folder to do whatever you want.

▲

PhoneGap Is Integrated in Dreamweaver

Dreamweaver CS5.5 has PhoneGap connectivity built in. So if you're already using Dreamweaver, converting your web applications to native apps right from within your familiar software is easy.

By the Way

Building an Android application is not quite as easy as building an app for iOS, because there is no package installer to build the application directories and files you need. However, building an Android app is still fairly easy.

Try It Yourself ▼

Building a Simple Android Application in PhoneGap

PhoneGap can help you build an Android application as well. It takes a few more steps than for building an iOS app, but all you need to know is HTML.

1. Download and install Eclipse Classic (www.eclipse.org/downloads/), the Android SDK (http://developer.android.com/sdk/index.html), and the latest version of PhoneGap.

2. After you have Eclipse installed and running, go to the Help menu and choose Install New Software. This will open the Available Software window.

3. Select the ADT Plug-in at this URL: https://dl-ssl.google.com/android/eclipse/ from the options.

4. After installing the plug-in, open a new Android project from the File menu. You may have to choose Other for the project type and search for Android.

5. Give your project a name and choose an Android version you want to target, and then click Finish.

6. Create two new directories in the root of your project:

```
/libs
/assets/www
```

7. From the PhoneGap installation, in the Android directory, copy the phonegap.js file into /assets/www and the phonegap.jar file into /libs.

8. In the /src directory, find the App.java file and make some changes:

   ▶ Change the public class line to read public Class *appName* extends DroidGap.

   ▶ Replace setContentView(); with super.loadUrl("file:/// android_asset/www/index.html");.

   ▶ Below import android.os.Bundle; add import com.phonegap.*;.

9. Right-click on the /libs folder and select Build Path, and choose Configure Build Path. Refresh the project (press F5).

10. Edit AndroidManifest.xml with a text editor and add the following after android:versionName="1.0">:

```
<supports-screens
android:largeScreens="true"
android:normalScreens="true"
android:smallScreens="true"
android:resizeable="true"
android:anyDensity="true"
/>
<uses-permission android:name="android.permission.CAMERA" />
<uses-permission android:name="android.permission.VIBRATE" />
<uses-permission
↪android:name="android.permission.ACCESS_COARSE_LOCATION" />
<uses-permission
↪android:name="android.permission.ACCESS_FINE_LOCATION" />
<uses-permission
↪android:name="android.permission.ACCESS_LOCATION_EXTRA_COMMANDS" />
<uses-permission android:name="android.permission.READ_PHONE_STATE" />
<uses-permission android:name="android.permission.INTERNET" />
<uses-permission android:name="android.permission.RECEIVE_SMS" />
<uses-permission android:name="android.permission.RECORD_AUDIO" />
```

```
<uses-permission
➥android:name="android.permission.MODIFY_AUDIO_SETTINGS" />
<uses-permission android:name="android.permission.READ_CONTACTS" />
<uses-permission android:name="android.permission.WRITE_CONTACTS" />
<uses-permission
➥android:name="android.permission.WRITE_EXTERNAL_STORAGE" />
<uses-permission
➥android:name="android.permission.ACCESS_NETWORK_STATE" />
```

11. In the `<activity>` element, add:

```
android:configChanges="orientation¦keyboardHidden"
```

12. Create a new file called `index.html` in the `/assets/www` folder and edit it to read:

```
<!DOCTYPE HTML>
<html>
<head>
<meta charset="utf-8">
<title>PhoneGap</title>
<script charset="utf-8" src="phonegap.js"></script>
</head>
<body>
<h1>Hello World</h1>
</body>
</html>
```

13. Right-click on the project, choose Run As, and click Android Application.

14. Select a virtual device, and if there isn't an appropriate one, you will need to create it. Your application will then run in an Android emulator.

Android Emulators Are Slow

Be patient when testing your applications in an emulator. The Android emulators, especially the tablet ones, can be painfully slow to load.

Watch
Out!

Android apps are a little trickier to build than iOS apps because of all the preparation you need to do. However, after you have the preparation set up, it's just a matter of building your web application.

▲

PhoneGap provides an API that helps you use native application features that are not available for standard HTML5 applications. With this API you can access the accelerometer, the camera, the contacts, the compass, events, and many other device-specific elements. Learn more at http://docs.phonegap.com/.

Creating Application Icons

One feature that sets apart native applications from HTML5 apps is the icons that are used to represent them. To get your HTML5 application ready for testing on a device and then deploying to an app store, you need to have icons that represent the application.

Apple has three different images and icons that are required for deploying to the app store and one that is recommended:

▶ **Application icon**—This represents the application on the device and in the App Store itself.

▶ **App Store icon**—This larger icon is used for display in the App Store. This icon must be recognizable as your application icon, but can be more detailed.

▶ **Launch image**—This image appears immediately after the application starts and stays loaded until the application is fully ready to use.

▶ **Spotlight search icon**—This is a small icon for search results and settings. This icon is not required, but creating it is a good idea so that your application renders more effectively in a search.

Android has only two required types of icons for deploying to the store:

▶ **Launcher icon**—This icon represents your application on the home screen and in the launcher window.

▶ **Console icon**—This high-resolution icon is used in various locations in the online marketplace.

When building your icons, keep the following in mind:

▶ The icons should be modern looking, and you should avoid clichés where possible.

▶ Icons are what people think of when they see your application, so they should be representative of your app.

▶ Use vector graphics where possible to create your icons, so that they can be scaled as needed.

1. Add your device to the provisioning portal by going to http://develope
   com/ios/manage/devices/index.action and clicking Add Devices.

2. Create a provisioning profile for your application by going to http://d
   apple.com/ios/manage/overview/index.action and clicking Launch A

3. Open your application in Xcode.

4. In the Info tab for your application, make sure that your app has the
   as the bundler identifier.

5. Make sure your iOS device is connected to your computer, and select i
   drop-down menu at the top.

6. Click Run, and the application will run on your device.

After you've moved your application to the iOS device, you can disconnect
just like any other application on your device. Figure 24.1 shows an applica
called Birthday List in testing on an iPad.

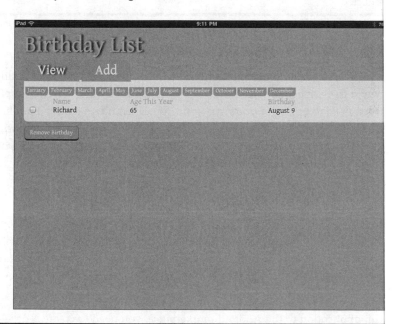

Android apps don't require an app ID or profile, but trying to test them on
Android device can still be confusing because everything in Eclipse and the
appears to be only for running in an emulator. The following Try It Yourself
explains how to use Eclipse to test your applications on an Android device.

When submitting your images and icons, you need to be aware of the exact file sizes. Table 24.1 details the file sizes for the different images and icons you need for your iOS application.

TABLE 24.1 Apple Icon and Image Sizes

Image	iPhone/iPod Touch (Pixels)	iPhone 4 High resolution (Pixels)	iPad (Pixels)
Application icons	57 × 57	114 × 114	72 × 72
App Store icon	512 × 512	512 × 512	512 × 512
Launch image	320 × 480	640 × 960	768 × 1004 (Portrait) 1024 × 748 (Landscape)
Search icon	29 × 29	58 × 58	50 × 50 (Spotlight search) 29 × 29 (Settings)

Apple also has some rules for creating your images:

▶ The icon must be saved in 24-bit PNG format.

▶ The icon must have 90° corners.

▶ There can be no shine or gloss to the icon.

▶ There can be no alpha transparency in the icon.

If you follow these rules, your application icons will automatically be given rounded corners, a drop shadow, and a reflective shine.

You Can Prevent the Apple Icon Customizations

You can add the `UIPrerenderedIcon` key to the `Info.plist` file to prevent Apple icon customizations of rounded corners, a drop shadow, and a reflective shine. For web applications you can name your icon file `apple-touch-icon-precomposed.png` to prevent the customizations.

Search the Apple iOS Developer Library (https://developer.apple.com/) for more help designing good iOS icons

You should create your Android icons in three versions for high-, medium-, and low-density screens. Table 24.2 details the file sizes for the required Android icons.

TABLE 24.2   Android Icon Sizes

Icon	High-Density (Pixels)	Medium-Density (Pixels)
Launcher icon	72 × 72	48 × 48
Console icon	512 × 512	512 × 512

Android has a couple of rules for launcher icons:

▶ The icon must be modern, minimal, matte, tactile, and te

▶ The icon must have a limited color palette and be forward

Visit the Android Developers site for more information about bu
icons (http://developer.android.com/guide/practices/ui_guidelin

Testing Your Applications

After you test your applications in an emulator, you should test
Testing on an emulator is easy; online emulators are even availe
Hour 8, "Converting Web Apps to Mobile," explains more about
on the devices themselves can be a little more difficult.

Before you even consider deploying an application to an app st
it on the devices you are going to support. Testing will show yo
responds, issues with clicking such as the size of your clickable
that are not included in the emulator such as GPS. You may ev
mountable bug when you get the application to the device and
at all.

As mentioned earlier, testing on an iOS device requires an Appl
account, which costs $99 per year. You also need an app ID tha
Apple provisioning portal.

▼ **Try It Yourself**

Putting Your Application on Your iOS Device

The steps in this Try It Yourself will help you get an app ID fror
sioning portal and get your application from your computer to
testing.

▼ **Try It Yourself**

Putting Your Application on Your Android Device

In this Try It Yourself you use Eclipse to connect with your device and test your
application there. This example shows a trick you can use to get the application to
run on the device.

1. Plug your Android device into your computer and then open your application
   in Eclipse.

2. In the Run menu, open Run configurations and change to the Target tab.

3. Change the target to Manual and click Run. The application will open on your
   device.

Unlike testing on an iOS, after you disconnect from the computer, your application
will be removed from your Android device. However, you can test how it runs while
▲ it's still connected.

Selling Your App in the App Stores

Deploying your application to an app store is the last step in the process of selling
(or give away a free application) a native application. To sell an app in the Apple
App Store, you need to apply for approval from Apple. Selling an Android application is a little easier, in that you don't need approval, but you have to choose which
stores you're going to sell your app on. Both platforms require that you sign legal
documents and pay fees to have your application listed.

To submit your application to the Apple App Store you need to prepare your application for submission, complete your financial information with Apple, gather
screenshots, set the parental controls rating and keywords, and then add the app to
iTunes Connect. If your application will include in-app purchases, you will also need
a contract with Apple. You can learn more about this process and how to get started
at the App Store Resource Center (http://developer.apple.com/appstore/resources/
submission/).

To deploy an application to the Android marketplace, you need to create a developer profile on the Android market. You will also need to pay a $25 registration fee,
and agree to the distribution agreement. Sign in at the Android market (https://mar-
ket.android.com/publish/signup) to learn more. Android apps must also be digitally
signed with a certificate where you hold the private key. This identifies you as the
author. You sign your application using the Eclipse export wizard. More information

is available on the Android Developers site (http://developer.android.com/guide/publishing/app-signing.html#releasemode).

A benefit of writing Android applications is more than one app store exists. Another popular marketplace is the Amazon Appstore. To join, go to the Appstore Developer Portal (https://developer.amazon.com/welcome.html) and create a developer account. There is a $99 annual program fee.

Options Other Than Converting to Native Apps

Although converting your HTML5 application may be tempting right now, it's not the only way you can get people to find and use your HTML5 application. Plus, the work (and cost) involved in creating a native application can be extensive.

You can make your application more appealing to your mobile users in some other ways, while not converting to a native app:

▶ Keep your app as HTML5 and use search engine optimization (SEO) and other marketing techniques to get exposure.

▶ Encourage your users to save your application to their desktop. If you have the application icons defined in your meta tags, the application will look and work just like a native app.

▶ Use application frameworks such as SenchaTouch or jQuery Mobile (as mentioned in Hour 5, "JavaScript and HTML5 Web Applications") to make your application look more familiar to mobile users.

▶ Open your HTML5 application with a wrapper app. A wrapper app is a native application that redirects to a web page. You can do that with something as simple as a meta refresh tag inside a PhoneGap application.

Summary

This hour talked about how to turn an HTML5 application into a native Android and iOS application. You also learned the benefits of both types of application so that you can make an informed decision about whether you want to make the change into native or not.

You learned that most native apps are faster, have access to technology such as push notifications, in-app purchases, and in-app ads, and can use the device's built-in hardware and software (camera, accelerometer, calendar, and contacts) more readily than HTML5 apps. However, you also learned that most users can't tell when they are using an HTML5 app or a native app (even with the speed differences) in most situations, and that HTML5 applications give you access to an even larger market than just mobile device users.

This hour also took you through the steps to convert an application from HTML5 to native using the PhoneGap and Appcelerator tools.

You learned about the images and icons you will need for your application to submit them to the Android and Apple App Stores. You also learned the steps needed to test applications on your personal devices as well as deploy them to the stores and sell your work.

Q&A

Q. *I have read many conflicting articles lately saying that native apps are the wave of the future and that HTML5 is going to kill all native applications. Which do you think is true?*

A. The truth is somewhere in the middle. There will always be some type of market for native applications, because people like the presumed security of applications going through a vetting process. However, as HTML5 becomes even more widely supported, these applications will become more and more widespread.

Q. *I've read that using applications such as PhoneGap is not allowed on the Apple App Store. Is that true?*

A. According to the PhoneGap FAQ (www.phonegap.com/faq), applications made with PhoneGap 0.8 and up do not violate the Terms and Conditions of the App Store. That isn't to say your app might not be rejected for some other reason, but it won't be because you used PhoneGap to build it.

Q. *You explained how to test the application on my personal devices, but is it possible to send my beta application out to other people to see how they like it and how it works on their devices?*

A. Yes, this is not only possible, but a very good idea, to make sure your app is as widely usable as possible.

With Apple, you need to add your beta testers' devices into your provisioning portal. You can have up to 100 devices added to your account. To do this, tell your testers to use an application called Ad Hoc Helper, available in the iTunes

App Store, to send you their UDID. You can add their device to your devices in the provisioning portal. Create a provisioning profile called Ad Hoc and add your app to it. Finally, build the application for distribution in Xcode and send it to your testers. They can use iTunes to install it. Go to the Apple Developer Center for more information. A company called TestFlight (https:// testflightapp.com/) can also help you set up beta testing for your iOS application.

Android doesn't have those restrictions. You can simply zip your project and have your testers install it the same way you did.

Hour 8 goes into more detail about beta testing your applications.

Workshop

The workshop contains quiz questions to help you process what you've learned in this chapter. Try to answer all the questions before you read the answers. See Appendix A, "Answers to Quizzes," for answers.

Quiz

1. What programming language are Android and iOS applications written in?

2. What are three benefits of native applications over HTML5 applications?

3. What do you need to build an iOS app or an Android app regardless of what tool you use to develop?

4. What two programs can you use to convert HTML5 applications to native applications?

5. What images and icons are required to deploy iOS and Android applications?

Exercises

1. Rewrite the Birthday List application from Hour 21, "Web Storage in HTML5," with an application design. Use a framework such as jQuery Mobile (Hour 5) to make it look like a mobile app or do your own design.

2. Convert the application in exercise 1 into an Android or iOS app using Phone-Gap. Be sure to test it in an emulator.

APPENDIX A

Answers to Quizzes

This appendix provides the answers to the quiz questions in each hour.

Hour 1, "Improving Mobile Web Application Development with HTML5"

1. HTML5 was started by a group of browser manufacturers and web designers and developers. They started defining a new version of HTML that took their needs into account for creating web applications, more hooks for styles, and more browser features. They struck out from the W3C because the W3C was determined to move HTML into an XML-based language—XHTML. The group that was formed was called the WHATWG (Web Hypertext Application Technology Working Group).

2. The first line in an HTML5 document is the doctype, and it reads: `<!doctype html>`.

3. The default web browsers on both iOS and Android devices are based on WebKit, which has strong support for HTML5. As more smartphones and tablets are purchased that use these browsers, more HTML5 will be used.

Hour 2, "New HTML5 Tags and Attributes with Mobile Development"

1. Many new tags can be used for layout in HTML5. They include `<article>`, `<aside>`, `<figcaption>`, `<figure>`, `<footer>`, `<header>`, `<hgroup>`, `<nav>`, and `<section>`.

2. The `<section>` tag is semantic. It is a tag that is used to indicate the meaning of the enclosed contents. A `<section>` tag encloses contents that are part of a unique section of the document.

3. There are both new event attributes and global attributes that assist in drag and drop operations. The new event attributes are ondrag, ondragend, ondragenter, ondragleave, ondragstart, and ondrop. The new global attributes are draggable and dropzone.

Hour 3, "Styling Mobile Pages with CSS3"

1. The three ways you can add styles to web pages are through inline styles right in the tags, embedded styles in the <head> of the document, and external style sheets attached in the <head> with the <link> tag. The best type to use is the external style sheet because it allows you to define styles in one place for your whole website, and because it is cached, the display of website pages speeds up.

2. A CSS selector is the part of a CSS style that chooses what elements to style in the HTML document. A typical style selector might be an element selector such as p to style all <p> tags in a document.

3. The border-radius property has two browser extensions: -moz-border-radius and -webkit-border-radius. Browser extensions are browser-specific versions of the style properties that must be used to ensure support of the properties in the respective browsers.

Hour 4, "Detecting Mobile Devices and HTML5 Support"

1. At the time this book was written, Google Chrome 10 and 11 both supported 84% of HTML5 and Opera Mobile supported 58%.

2. Adding an element to the DOM using scripts is easy, but if the browser doesn't support those elements, it will just give them the default attributes and nothing more. By checking for HTML5-specific attributes of an element, you can tell that the browser supports that element.

3. When you write an application that degrades gracefully, it will work, with diminishing functionality, in more browsers. This increases your audience. Plus, when users do upgrade their browsers, your application will seem to improve as well, with no extra work on your part.

Hour 5, "JavaScript and HTML5 Web Applications"

1. True. The `<script>` tag is valid in both the head and body of your HTML documents.

2. The `:link` and `:hover` pseudoclasses allow you to set a style on a text link and have that style change when the mouse hovers over it.

3. The `visibility: hidden;` property holds the space open that the element takes up. This is because the element is just made invisible. This feature is useful in situations where you want the text to be seen sometimes, but you don't want the layout to change. The `display: none;` property completely removes the element from the document (although it is still visible in the source document).

4. You need to link to jQuery in a script tag and then include the `document.ready` handler:

```
<script src="jquery.min.js"></script>
$(document).ready(function(){
});
```

Hour 6, "Building a Mobile Web Application"

1. A "SMART" goal is a goal that is Specific, Measurable, Achievable, Realistic, and Time-bound. Setting goals that meet these criteria make them more likely to be completed.

2. An em is equal to the current font size. On most computers, this is 16px.

3. The `apple-touch-startup-image` specifies an image to use as a startup screen for your web application. You indicate it with the link `<link rel="apple-touch-startup-image" href="startup.png">` tag in the head of your document.

4. You should follow many best practices, including:

  ▶ Offer a choice of viewing options and remember users' choices.

  ▶ Keep the data input pain free.

  ▶ Remember to keep things small.

▶ Use mobile-specific functions.

▶ Minimize perceived wait times.

▶ Optimize images and use good contrasting colors.

▶ Use ems or percentages for sizes.

▶ Keep your content clear.

▶ Beware of technology that may break.

▶ Avoid technology that does break.

Hour 7, "Upgrading a Site to HTML5"

1. Internet Explorer 5 and 6 had poor support for standards, and that lack of support was carried over into versions 7 and 8 with "compatibility mode."

2. Iterative design is a process where you make small changes to your website design and functionality and test to see how they affect your site goals. You should consider making iterative changes to your site so that your customers can get used to the changes gradually, rather than having to relearn how to use your website every few years. Iterative design also ensures that changes don't hurt your sales or page views.

3. The new `doctype`, the meta `charset` tag, simplified script and style tags, block-level links, new form input types, video and audio tags, and semantic HTML tags and attributes all work right now.

4. The `contenteditable` attribute and drag-and drop functions were both added to IE in version 5.5. IE 6 has also supported some Ruby annotations.

Hour 8, "Converting Web Apps to Mobile"

1. Testing existing pages in mobile devices gives you an idea of what you need to improve. Testing applications you've written specifically for mobile ensures that they work as you expect them to. The more you test before you launch, the happier your users will be.

2. If you are directing your site toward feature phones as well as smartphones and tablets, then you should aim for no more than 20KB for everything on

a page. Smartphones and computer browsers can handle larger pages, but the smaller they are the faster they load, so 30KB–50KB is still a good range to strive for.

3. The five elements of design are color, direction, lines, shapes, and texture.

4. Mobile design patterns make your designs more familiar to mobile users, so they are easier to use.

5. You can test a mobile application on devices by borrowing them from friends or family members, renting the devices, or using an emulator.

Hour 9, "Adding Meaning with HTML5 Sectioning and Semantic Elements"

1. The four new sectioning elements are <article>, <aside>, <nav>, and <section>.

2. C. Both an image and a block of text are valid within a <figure>.

3. True. You can use an <aside> element to mark up a site sidebar.

4. False. You should not use a <section> element just as a hook for styles. Use a <div> instead.

5. False. A sectioning root can have its own outline, but it does not contribute its contents to the outlines of its ancestors.

6. True. A <footer> is not a sectioning element. It defines the footer of the immediately preceding sectioning element.

7. The new, non-sectioning semantic elements in HTML5 are <mark>, <meter>, <progress>, and <time>.

Hour 10, "Drawing with the HTML5 Canvas Element"

1. When you write a <canvas> element in your HTML, nothing is displayed until you draw something on it with a script.

2. A. The clearRect() method creates an empty, transparent rectangle.

3. False. You can use RGBa alpha transparency with the strokeStyle property.

4. A. The default style for line endings is butt.

5. True. Circles are drawn on the <canvas> element using radians.

6. True. You cannot set box model styles such as margin and padding on text drawn on the <canvas> element.

7. To draw an image file onto a canvas, you need to reference that image file in either your HTML or your JavaScript, and then you draw it on the canvas with the drawImage() method.

8. B and C. Flash and SVG are vector based. Canvas is a bitmap-based drawing tool.

Hour 11, "Fonts and Typography in HTML5"

1. The six generic font families are serif, sans-serif, monospaced, fantasy, cursive, and script.

2. The six elements of spacing in typography are kerning, leading, tracking, measure, alignment, and ligatures.

3. False. You should not use shorthand text code for copyright notices when you can use the © symbol by typing in ©. Not using this entity makes your text look amateurish.

4. The five formats for web fonts are EOT, TTF, OTF, SVG, and WOFF.

5. You use the @font-face rule to embed fonts like this:
   ```
   @font-face {
       font-family: FontName;
       src: url(URL);
   }
   ```

Hour 12, "Audio and Video in HTML5"

1. The three commonly used audio codecs are MP3, Vorbis, and WAV.

2. Internet Explorer 9 supports MP4 and WebM (with an extension) video codecs. Android 3.0 supports all three—MP4, ogg/Theora, and WebM—but Android 2.3 does not support MP4.

3. You can add the source of a video with the src attribute on the <video> element or with a <source> element.

4. False. The loop attribute can be used on both <video> and <audio>.

5. The `type` attribute has the format `type='MIME type; codecs="video codec, audio codec"'`.

6. Any content inside the `<audio>` element other than `<source>` and `<track>` is assumed to be fallback content. Browsers that support HTML5 audio should ignore that content and browsers that don't will ignore the HTML5 tags they don't recognize. So, to add fallback content to an `<audio>` element, you add an `<object>` to embed a WAV file like you did in HTML 4.

Hour 13, "HTML5 Forms"

1. HTML5 adds the attributes `autofocus`, `placeholder`, and `autocomplete` along with the new `<datalist>` element to make your forms more usable.

2. The new date and time input types are `date`, `datetime`, `datetime-local`, `month`, `week`, and `time`.

3. The `<input type=search>` field has very specific styles set in WebKit that are difficult to override. They include padding, font size, font family, border, and background color.

4. The `<output>` element is used to display the results of calculations.

5. HTML5 provides three new attributes for working with form validation: `novalidate`, `required`, and `pattern`.

Hour 14, "Editing Content and User Interaction with HTML5"

1. The `contenteditable` attribute is supported by all the major browsers and versions, including IE 5.5, Firefox 3, Safari, Chrome, and Opera 9. The only browsers that don't support it are mobile browsers on iOS and Android.

2. The `contenteditable` attribute is a global attribute that is common to all the elements in HTML.

3. You need the `contenteditable` attribute and the `designmode` attribute to create a rich text editor.

4. When you are trying to detect `contenteditable`, Android and iOS report that they have this element on the DOM, but they do not support it. The only way to detect for it is by doing browser sniffing for iOS and Android devices.

Hour 15, "Microformats and Microdata"

1. You can mark up almost anything that has a standard format with microdata. Some examples mentioned in the book are events, contact information, recipes, reviews, resumes, and geography.

2. The itemprop attribute is used to name the property that the element represents. It has the same function as the class attribute in microformats.

3. RDFa stands for *Resource Description Framework in attributes*.

Hour 16, "Working with HTML5 Drag-and-Drop Functionality"

1. The two best elements for dragging and dropping are the <a href=""> and <img> elements. They are the most reliable because Internet Explorer recognizes them as draggable whether or not the draggable attribute is set. Using other elements can cause IE to behave strangely.

2. The preventDefault() method tells the user agent to not run the default action on the event. When dragging an image into a browser window, the default action is to open that image in a new window. The preventDefault() method stops that.

3. The six steps to create a drag-and-drop application are to define a draggable object, set events on that object, define a drop zone, set events on the drop zone, pass information between the dragged object and the drop zone, and define the effects for the drag-and-drop operation.

4. The drag-and-drop effects must match for the drag-and-drop operation to be successful. A dragged element that has an effect of only "copy" will not be able to drop onto a drop zone with the effect of "move."

Hour 17, "HTML5 Links"

1. The <a> element has one brand-new attribute—the media attribute. This attribute adds media queries to tell the user agent what media the link is intended for. The target attribute is not technically a new attribute, but it has been undeprecated since HTML 4, and is used to identify the window or frame that the link should open in.

2. To get a link inside an iframe to open in the container document, you should add the attribute target=_parent.

3. The image map element `<area>` now can use the attributes `rel`, `media`, and `hreflang` just like the `<a>` element.

4. Use the `rel=nofollow` attribute when you don't endorse the link's contents such as in comments or forum posts, on paid links, and when the search robot can't view or use the page.

Hour 18, "Web Application APIs and Datasets"

1. Web applications use scripts to interact, and that interaction is a critical part of the application itself. Web applications tend to stay all on the same page with only portions of the page changing without a reload.

2. A script can fire by processing a `<script>` element; running inline `javascript:` URLs; when an event handler is triggered; and inside technology such as SVG, which has its own scripting features.

3. Right now the `dataset` method is not widely supported by web browsers, so using the `getAttribute` method to view your dataset fields is safer. Eventually, the `dataset` method will be more widely supported, and it is much easier to use than `getAttribute`.

Hour 19, "WebSockets, Web Workers, and Files"

1. The WebSockets protocol has some security concerns that the Firefox and Opera browser manufacturers feel should be fixed before they will support this functionality. Specifically, a risk exists in some versions of the protocol that hackers can use for cache poisoning to attack users.

2. You add a new Worker to your script by writing a separate JavaScript file and then calling it in your main script:

```
new Worker("worker.js");
```

You communicate with it through messages:

```
worker.onmessage = function(e){
    e.data
};
worker.postmessage("message");
```

It sends messages back to the script:

```
onmessage = function(e){
    if ( e.data === "start" ) {
        done()
    }
};
function done(){
    postMessage("done");
}
```

3. The easiest way is to add two attributes to your `<input>` element—
   `multiple=true` and `accept="text/*"`. However, not all browsers support
   the `accept` attribute, so you should also check inside your script to verify
   that the file(s) uploaded are the type you want.

Hour 20, "Offline Web Applications"

1. The events that can fire when an application is being cached are
   `checking`, `noupdate`, `downloading`, `progress`, `cached`, `updateready`,
   `obsolete`, and `error`.

2. The keyword `CACHE:` indicates the explicit section, the `NETWORK:` keyword
   indicates the online whitelist, and the `FALLBACK:` keyword points to fallback information.

3. The first line of the cache manifest must read:

   `CACHE MANIFEST`

   Also, the cache manifest must be served as type `text/cache-manifest`.

4. The fallback section identifies what page should be delivered if a file has
   not been cached. The whitelist section tells the browser which pages on the
   site should always be served online.

Hour 21, "Web Storage in HTML5"

1. Web storage is different from cookies because:

   ▶ In web storage the data is stored and retrieved only when asked for,
      whereas cookies are sent with every HTTP request.

   ▶ Web storage can only be accessed by JavaScript, whereas cookies can
      also be accessed by server-side scripts.

▶ Web storage can be specific to a window as well as to the browser and domain.

2. Local storage is persistent and can be accessed even after the browser or computer has been shut down. Session storage is specific to the window that it's stored in. It is not persistent, and a new instance is created for every window—even on the same domain and web page.

3. Web SQL and IndexedDB provide structured data storage. Web storage is only a series of name=value pairs.

4. To detect for Web SQL, create a function that returns the value of openDatabase. To detect for IndexedDB, create a function that returns the value of window.indexedDB. For example:

```
function hasWebSql() {
    return !!window.openDatabase;
}

function hasIndexedDb() {
    return !!window.indexedDB;
}
```

Hour 22, "Controlling the Browser History with the History API"

1. The three old methods in the History API are history.back(), history.forward(), and history.go(). HTML5 adds two new methods: history.pushState() and history.replaceState(). The pushState() method adds a new entry to the history list, whereas the replaceState() method changes the current entry.

2. False. Neither of the two new methods will create new web pages; they will just change the URL in the browser bar and in the history listing.

3. The onpopstate event fires when the back or forward buttons are clicked. This event allows you to control what happens when these navigation buttons are clicked so that your pages load correctly.

4. False. The replaceState() method has the same three parameters as the pushState() method: state object, title, and URL.

5. True. As long as your data does not exceed the limit of 640KB, you can include anything you want to include there.

6. False. You can only change the URL to locations on the current domain.

Hour 23, "Adding Location Detection with Geolocation"

1. You detect whether the `navigator.geolocation` object is present.

2. The position object will always have `coords.latitude`, `coords.longitude`, and `coords.accuracy`.

3. The position object may also have these properties: `coords.altitude`, `coords.altitudeAccuracy`, `coords.heading`, `coords.speed`, and `timestamp`.

4. The `positionError` object throws error code 1 when the user denies access to location data, 2 when the location data can't be retrieved because the network is down or satellites are unavailable, and 3 when it takes longer than the set timeout.

5. The `enableHighAccuracy` property is one of the position options that can be set on the `getCurrentPosition()` and `watchPosition()` methods. You set it to `true` when you need the position data to be as accurate as possible, such as for turn-by-turn driving directions. To use it, you write:

```
getCurrentPosition(success_callback, error_callback,
{enableHighAccuracy: true});
```

or:

```
watchPosition(success_callback, error_callback, {enableHighAccuracy:
true});
```

Hour 24, "Converting HTML5 Apps to Native Apps"

1. Android applications are written in Java, and iOS applications are written in Objective C.

2. Native applications have push notifications, access to device hardware, file upload, access to device files, better graphics than HTML5, and in-app purchases and advertising. They work even when offline, and people tend to trust native apps more than web pages.

3. For developing iOS applications, you need a Macintosh computer and Xcode. For developing Android applications, you need Eclipse Classic, Android SDK, and the ADT plug-in for Eclipse. You can build Android apps with just the SDK, but doing so is a lot harder.

4. PhoneGap and Appcelerator Titanium are two programs that you can use to convert your HTML5 applications to native applications.

5. iOS applications have two icons and one image that are required: the application icon, the App Store icon, and the launch image. Android applications have two required icons: the launcher icon and the console icon.

APPENDIX B

HTML Elements and Attributes

HTML elements and attributes are the building blocks of a web application. This appendix will give you a brief explanation of them and indicate which ones are new in HTML5. You should be aware that the HTML5 specification is still in development at the time of this writing, and if you have any questions you should refer to the W3C HTML5 specification for the most up-to-date information (http://dev.w3.org/html5/markup/elements.html).

HTML5 Elements

HTML5 elements are, for the most part, the same elements as in HTML 4.01. There are a few new elements as well. The following list shows you the HTML5 elements and what they are used for.

Tag	Explanation
<!-- -->	Comment tag
<!doctype html>	Document type definition for HTML5
A	Anchor tag, used to link to other areas of the web
ABBR	Abbreviation
ADDRESS	Contact information for the page
AREA	Clickable area of an image map
ARTICLE	Article or syndicatable content (new)
ASIDE	Content of tangential relationship to the page or site (new)
AUDIO	Audio stream (new)
B	Text normally styled in bold
BASE	Base URL for the page
BDI	Text separate from the surroundings for the purpose of bidirectional formatting (new)

Tag	Explanation
BDO	Override control of the direction of text
BLOCKQUOTE	Long quotation
BODY	Body of the page
BR	Line break
BUTTON	Form button
BUTTON TYPE=BUTTON	Form button with no semantic meaning
BUTTON TYPE=RESET	Reset button
BUTTON TYPE=SUBMIT	Submit button
CANVAS	Canvas for dynamic graphics (new)
CAPTION	Table title
CITE	Citation
CODE	Code fragment
COL	Table column
COLGROUP	Table column grouping
COMMAND	Command or action on the page (new)
COMMAND TYPE=CHECKBOX	Option that can be toggled (new)
COMMAND TYPE=COMMAND	Command with associated action (new)
COMMAND TYPE=RADIO	Selection of one item from a list (new)
DATALIST	Predefined options for other controls (new)
DD	Definition list description
DEL	Deleted text
DETAILS	Additional on-demand information (new)
DFN	Definition
DIV	Generic flow container
DL	Description or definition list
DT	Definition list term
EM	Emphasis
EMBED	Embedded element for plug-ins (new)

Tag	Explanation
FIELDSET	Group of related form controls
FIGCAPTION	Figure caption (new)
FIGURE	Figure with optional caption (new)
FOOTER	Footer (new)
FORM	Form
H1	First-level heading
H2	Second-level heading
H3	Third-level heading
H4	Fourth-level heading
H5	Fifth-level heading
H6	Sixth-level heading
HEAD	Head of the document and metadata container
HEADER	Header (new)
HGROUP	Heading group (new)
HR	Thematic break
HTML	Root element of a web page
I	Text normally styled in italics
IFRAME	Inline frame
IMG	Image
INPUT	Input form control
INPUT TYPE=BUTTON	Button
INPUT TYPE=CHECKBOX	Checkbox
INPUT TYPE=COLOR	Color input control (new)
INPUT TYPE=DATE	Date input control (new)
INPUT TYPE=DATETIME	Global date and time input control (new)
INPUT TYPE=DATETIME-LOCAL	Local date and time input control (new)
INPUT TYPE=EMAIL	Email address input control (new)
INPUT TYPE=FILE	File upload control

Tag	Explanation
`INPUT TYPE=HIDDEN`	Hidden form field
`INPUT TYPE=IMAGE`	Image input control
`INPUT TYPE=MONTH`	Year and month input control (new)
`INPUT TYPE=NUMBER`	Number input control (new)
`INPUT TYPE=PASSWORD`	Password input control
`INPUT TYPE=RADIO`	Radio button
`INPUT TYPE=RANGE`	Imprecise number input control (new)
`INPUT TYPE=RESET`	Reset button
`INPUT TYPE=SEARCH`	Search input control (new)
`INPUT TYPE=SUBMIT`	Submit button
`INPUT TYPE=TEL`	Telephone number input control (new)
`INPUT TYPE=TEXT`	Text input control
`INPUT TYPE=TIME`	Time input control (new)
`INPUT TYPE=URL`	URL input control (new)
`INPUT TYPE=WEEK`	Year and week input control (new)
`INS`	Inserted text
`KBD`	User input
`KEYGEN`	Key-pair generator input control (new)
`LABEL`	Caption for a form control
`LEGEND`	Title or explanatory caption
`LI`	List item
`LINK`	Interdocument relationship metadata
`MAP`	Client-side image map
`MARK`	Marked or highlighted text (new)
`MENU`	List of commands
`META`	Meta information about the document
`METER`	Scalar gauge (new)
`NOSCRIPT`	Content when scripts aren't available

Tag	Explanation
OBJECT	Generic external content
OL	Ordered or numbered list
OPTGROUP	Group of options in a select list
OPTION	Option in a select list
OUTPUT	Result of a form calculation (new)
P	Paragraph
PARAM	Initialization parameters of an OBJECT
PRE	Pre-formatted text
PROGRESS	Progress indicator (new)
Q	Short inline quotation
RP	Ruby parenthesis (new)
RT	Ruby text (new)
RUBY	Ruby annotation (new)
S	Text that has been removed from the document
SAMP	Sample output
SCRIPT	Embedded script
SECTION	Section of the document (new)
SELECT	Select or drop-down menu lists
SMALL	Small print
SOURCE	Media source (new)
SPAN	Generic inline container
STRONG	Strong emphasis
STYLE	Style and presentation information
SUB	Subscript
SUMMARY	Summary, caption, or legend for a details control (new)
SUP	Superscript
TABLE	Table

Tag	Explanation
TBODY	Table body rows
TD	Table cell
TEXTAREA	Multi-line text input control
TFOOT	Table footer rows
TH	Table header cell
THEAD	Table heading rows
TIME	Date and/or time (new)
TITLE	Title
TR	Table row
TRACK	Supplementary media track (new)
U	Text normally styled underlined
UL	Unordered or bulleted list
VAR	Variable or user-defined text
VIDEO	Embedded video or movie (new)
WBR	Line break opportunity (new)

HTML5 Attributes

HTML5 attributes are items that further define the HTML5 elements listed in the preceding table. They are added to the elements following a space in the opening tag. For example: <div accesskey=a>.

Global Attributes

The global attributes are attributes that can be applied to any HTML5 element.

Attribute	Explanation
Accesskey	A key label or list of labels to associate with the element as a shortcut key to activate or give focus to that element.
Class	Style classifications for the element.
Contenteditable	Indicates whether the contents are editable (true) or not (false). (new)

Attribute	Explanation
Contextmenu	The ID to associate with this element as a context menu. (new)
Dir	The direction of the text (ltr or rtl or auto).
Draggable	Indicates whether the element is draggable (true) or not (false). (new)
dropzone	Indicates the types of content that can be dropped on the element. (new)
hidden	Indicates that the element is not yet or is no longer relevant.
id	A unique identifier for the element.
lang	The primary language for the contents of the element.
spellcheck	Indicates whether the contents are subject to spelling and grammar checking (true) or not (false). (new)
style	The CSS styles that apply to the element.
tabindex	A number that indicates the order in which this element should be tabbed to.
title	Additional information about the element.

Event-Handler Attributes

Event-handler attributes are used to define actions that should occur when an event occurs in the browser.

Attribute	Explanation
onabort	Loading the element was aborted by the user. (new)
onblur	The element lost focus.
oncanplay	Video or audio can resume playing. (new)
oncanplaythrough	Video or audio can resume playing without rebuffering. (new)
onchange	The value of the element changed by the user.
onclick	The user clicked on or over the element.
oncontextmenu	User requested the context menu for the element. (new)

Attribute	Explanation
ondblclick	User clicked twice on or over the element.
ondrag	User is continuing to drag the element. (new)
ondragend	The user stopped dragging. (new)
ondragenter	The drag operation entered the element. (new)
ondragleave	The drag operation left the element. (new)
ondragover	User is continuing to drag over the element. (new)
ondragstart	The user started dragging. (new)
ondrop	User dropped over the element. (new)
ondurationchnage	The duration of the media element changed. (new)
onemptied	The media element returned to the uninitialized state. (new)
onended	The end of the media has been reached. (new)
onerror	Element failed to load properly. (new)
onfocus	Element received focus.
oninput	User changed the value of the element.
oninvalid	User put in invalid contents in a form element. (new)
onkeydown	Key was pressed down.
onkeypress	Key was pressed.
onkeyup	Key was released.
onload	Element finished loading.
onloadeddata	Media can be rendered for the first time. (new)
onloadedmetadata	Duration and dimensions of media established. (new)
onloadstart	Browser has started looking for media data. (new)
onmousedown	User clicked down on element.
onmousemove	User moved mouse.
onmouseout	User moved the mouse off the element.
onmouseover	User moved the mouse over the element.
onmouseup	User released the click on element.

Attribute	Explanation
onmousewheel	User rotated the mouse wheel.
onpause	User paused playback. (new)
onplay	User started playback. (new)
onplaying	Playback has started. (new)
onprogress	Browser is fetching media data. (new)
onratechange	Playback rate changed. (new)
onreadystatechange	Element and all subresources have loaded. (new)
onreset	Form element was reset.
onscroll	Element or document was scrolled.
onseeked	Seeking in a media element has ended. (new)
onseeking	Seeking is happening in a media element. (new)
onselect	User selected text.
onshow	User requested the element be shown as a context menu. (new)
onstalled	Media data is stalled. (new)
onsubmit	Form element was submitted.
onsuspend	Media not being downloaded. (new)
ontimeupdate	Current playback position changed. (new)
onvolumechange	Volume of the media has changed. (new)
onwaiting	Playback has stopped because next frame is not yet available. (new)

APPENDIX C

HTML5 and Mobile Application Resources

How to use HTML5 and the related APIs is a lot to learn. Many books and websites are available that you can use to learn more.

Books

The following books can teach you a lot about HTML in general, and about some of the related HTML5 APIs.

- ▶ *Sams Teach Yourself HTML and CSS in 24 Hours* by Julie C. Meloni and Michael Morrison. Sams, 2010. ISBN 978-0672330971.

- ▶ *Introducing HTML5* by Bruce Lawson and Remy Sharp. New Riders, 2010. ISBN 978-0321687296.

- ▶ *HTML5: Up and Running* by Mark Pilgrim. O'Reilly, 2010. ISBN 978-0596806026.

- ▶ *HTML5 for Web Designers* by Jeremy Keith. A Book Apart, 2010. ISBN 978-0984442508.

- ▶ *HTML5 & CSS3 For The Real World* by Estelle Weyl, Louis Lazaris, and Alexis Goldstein. SitePoint, 2011. ISBN 978-0980846904.

- ▶ *Sams Teach Yourself CSS 3 in 24 Hours* by Kynn Bartlett and Chris Montoya. Sams, 2010. ISBN 978-0672331022.

- ▶ *Designing with Web Standards* by Jeffrey Zeldman. New Riders, 2009. ISBN 978-0321616951.

- ▶ *HTML5 Canvas* by Steve Fulton. O'Reilly, 2011. ISBN 978-1449393908.

- ▶ *The Definitive Guide to HTML5 Video* by Silvia Pfeiffer. Apress, 2010. ISBN 978-1430230908.

- ▶ *HTML5 Geolocation* by Anthony T. Holdener. O'Reilly, 2011. ISBN 978-1449304720.

▶ *Programming the Mobile Web* by Maximiliano Firtman. O'Reilly, 2010. ISBN 978-0596807788.

Websites

The following websites will help you learn more about HTML5 and related APIs:

▶ **W3C (www.w3.org/)**—The W3C is where the HTML5 specification is updated. It has the most up-to-date information about the specifications. It is where you should go first when you have a question about web standards. The W3C also has a validator that you can use to check your HTML5 applications and make sure they are written correctly. Also see www.w3.org/TR/html5/ and http://validator.w3.org/.

▶ **HTML5 Rocks (www.html5rocks.com/)**—HTML5 Rocks provides places to play with the new standards, as well as updated tutorials and information and a selection of examples to show you how to use HTML5 in your own websites.

▶ **HTML5 Doctor (http://html5doctor.com/)**—HTML5 Doctor will help you get started with HTML5. This site has a regular article about different elements in HTML5 as well as an index of all the elements so that you can learn more about specific parts of the specification.

▶ **The HTML5 Gallery (http://html5gallery.com/)**—The HTML5 Gallery shows off sites that are using HTML5. It is a great place to get inspiration and get advice on how to use HTML5.

▶ **Web Design and HTML at About.com (http://webdesign.about.com/)**—Web Design and HTML at About.com is a site I maintain where I write about HTML5, web design, CSS, and web standards. You can learn the basics of HTML or dive into more advanced topics. Also see http://webdesign.about.com/od/html5/qt/html-5-information.htm.

This Book's Website

At this book's website you can find all the examples and sample code listed in the book, as well as updates to the book and where to get more information about HTML5:

www.html5in24hours.com/

Index

X-Y-Z

Sams **Teach Yourself**

When you only have time
for the answers™

Whatever your need and whatever your time frame, there's a Sams **Teach Yourself** book for you. With a Sams **Teach Yourself** book as your guide, you can quickly get up to speed on just about any new product or technology—in the absolute shortest period of time possible. Guaranteed.

Learning how to do new things with your computer shouldn't be tedious or time-consuming. Sams **Teach Yourself** makes learning anything quick, easy, and even a little bit fun.

HTML, CSS, and JavaScript All in One

Julie C. Meloni

ISBN-13: 978-0-672-33332-3

PHP, MySQL and Apache All in One

Julie C. Meloni

ISBN-13: 978-0-672-33543-3

Drupal in 24 Hours

Jesse Feiler

ISBN-13: 978-0-672-33126-8

Android Application Development in 24 Hours, Second Edition

Lauren Darcey
Shane Conder

ISBN-13: 978-0-672-33569-3

iOS Application Development in 24 Hours, Third Edition

John Ray

ISBN-13: 978-0-672-33576-1

Sams Teach Yourself books are available at most retail and online bookstores. For more information or to order direct, visit our online bookstore at **informit.com/sams**.

Online editions of all Sams Teach Yourself titles are available by subscription from Safari Books Online at **safari.informit.com**.

FREE Online Edition

Your purchase of **Sams Teach Yourself HTML5 Mobile Application Development in 24 Hours** includes access to a free online edition for 45 days through the Safari Books Online subscription service. Nearly every Sams book is available online through Safari Books Online, along with more than 5,000 other technical books and videos from publishers such as Addison-Wesley Professional, Cisco Press, Exam Cram, IBM Press, O'Reilly, Prentice Hall, and Que.

SAFARI BOOKS ONLINE allows you to search for a specific answer, cut and paste code, download chapters, and stay current with emerging technologies.

Activate your FREE Online Edition at www.informit.com/safarifree

> **STEP 1:** Enter the coupon code: JIOQYYG.

> **STEP 2:** New Safari users, complete the brief registration form.
> Safari subscribers, just log in.

If you have difficulty registering on Safari or accessing the online edition, please e-mail customer-service@safaribooksonline.com